CIRCUS QUEEN
&
TINKER BELL

CIRCUS QUEEN
&
TINKER
BELL

THE MEMOIR OF TINY KLINE

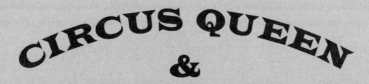

TINY KLINE

EDITED BY JANET M. DAVIS

8/26/08

To Joy,
Thank you so much for your
help with this project!
With deepest
admiration
and gratitude,
Janet M Davis

UNIVERSITY OF ILLINOIS PRESS
URBANA AND CHICAGO

Published with the aid of a University Cooperative Society
Subvention Grant awarded by the University of Texas at Austin

Library of Congress Cataloging-in-Publication Data
Kline, Tiny, 1890–1964.
Circus queen and Tinker Bell : the memoir of Tiny Kline /
Tiny Kline ; edited by Janet M. Davis.
p.   cm.
Includes bibliographical references and index.
ISBN 978-0-252-03312-4 (cloth : alk. paper)
ISBN 978-0-252-07510-0 (pbk. : alk. paper)
1. Kline, Tiny, 1890–1964.
2. Women circus performers—United States—Biography.
3. Circus—United States.
I. Davis, Janet M. II. Title.
GV1811.K56A3   2008
791.3092—dc22 [B]   2007052552

To Jeff, Andrea, and Zack,
for giving my life great joy,
and to Fred Dahlinger,
for making this project possible.

CONTENTS

ACKNOWLEDGMENTS

After many, many years, I am delighted and relieved to arrive at the stage of this project when I can thank all of the amazing people who have made it possible. First of all, I owe an enormous debt to Fred Dahlinger. Years ago, Fred told me about Tiny Kline and generously provided me copies of her unpublished memoir. I was immediately hooked by Kline's story. Along the way, Fred also provided invaluable suggestions and access to additional source materials. I will always be grateful for his remarkable generosity of spirit and intellectual camaraderie. I also owe a huge thanks to Ellsworth Brown and Rick Pifer of the Wisconsin Historical Society for graciously granting me permission to publish Kline's memoir with the University of Illinois Press. Both have provided unstinting support for this project. Rick Pifer, along with Greg Parkinson, kindly tracked down illustrations at Circus World Museum in Baraboo, Wisconsin, for inclusion in this work. Thanks also to Erin Foley and Meg Allen at Circus World Museum's Robert L. Parkinson Research Library. Their efforts in finding arcane materials have enriched the annotations. I am indebted to Debbie Walk and Liz Gray at the John and Mable Ringling Museum of Art in Sarasota, Florida, for their tremendous generosity on all fronts. I'd like to offer a special note of thanks to Steve Gossard at Illinois State University's Milner Library for his help in checking several key references. Thanks also to Rebecca Cline at the Disney Archives for kindly sending me materials concerning Kline's work at Disneyland. Librarians and archivists at the New York Public Library for the Performing Arts, the Buffalo Bill Historical Center in Cody, Wyoming, and the Harry Ransom Center for the Humanities in Austin, Texas, have provided additional help. A huge thank-you to John McConnell, who provided key photo reference information at the eleventh hour. I'm deeply grateful to all.

Relatives and neighbors of Tiny Kline and Otto Kline were incredibly generous with their time and insights. It is a great pleasure to thank Sheila McKay Courington, Julie Kreinbrink, and Olivia Grieco LaBouff. Donna Haddad, who lives in Otto Kline's hometown of Naperville, Illinois, also provided me with wonderful source materials.

Dialogue and scholarly feedback at professional meetings have broadened my understanding of Tiny Kline's life and career. Thanks to the following people for their insights: Susan Porter Benson, Fred Dahlinger, Fred Pfening Jr., Stuart Thayer, Steve Gossard, Jan Todd, Desley Deacon, Kathy Peiss, Riv-Ellen Prell, David Roediger, Bill Slout, Fred Pfening III, and Richard Reynolds. A special thanks to Eleanor Zelliot, Bob Bonner, Linda Gordon, Paul Boyer, and Tom McCormick for their mentoring and intellectual fellowship over the years.

Fred Pfening Jr. has kindly granted me permission to reprint revised portions of an article that was published in *Bandwagon: The Journal of the Circus Historical Society* (2001), which appear in my introduction. Fred has also given me permission to use photographs from the article here.

The University of Texas at Austin has provided substantial financial support for this project in the form of a Dean's Fellowship, a Faculty Research Grant, and a Summer Research Assignment. A generous University Cooperative Society Subvention Grant helped defray the costs of the illustrations and production. Moreover, the university has given me invaluable support in the form of research assistantships during my tenure as department chair. A big thanks to Erin McClelland, Phil Tiemeyer, Audrey Russek, and Rebecca Onion for their excellent work. Moreover, I thank my wonderful colleagues in the Department of American Studies for creating such a pleasurable work environment. A special thanks to Cynthia Frese for all of her help and collegiality.

Liz Dulany has been an ideal editor—enthusiastic, accessible, astute, and kind. Liz has believed in this project over the long haul; it has been a genuine pleasure to work with her, in addition to Rebecca Crist, Cope Cumptson, and Matthew Mitchell at the University of Illinois Press. Joy Kasson and Don Wilmeth were likewise ideal readers for the press. I am deeply indebted to them for their rigorous and brilliant critique of the manuscript. Every author should be so lucky to have such terrific outside readers.

In October 2001, I spent ten memorable days with my beloved mother, Jean B. Davis, in Madison, Wisconsin, which served as my base for my research trips to Baraboo each day. My stay was punctuated with long evening walks, good conversation, and delicious dinners. Little did I know that my mom would die of cancer six months later. I will always treasure her steadfast love and compassionate view of the world. Thanks to my siblings, Steve Davis, Betsy Moran, and Kathy Messerich; my father, Hugh Davis, and my stepmother, Heidi Harkins; my mother-in-law, Karen Osborne; and my father-in-law, Jim Osborne, and his wife, Karen Osborne, for all of their love and continued support. My kids, Andrea and Zack, have kept me centered with their unconditional love and good humor. Finally, my deepest thanks to Jeff, my best critic and best friend, for his unwavering kindness, patience, and love.

JANET M. DAVIS

Tiny Kline in her dressing room at Disneyland, Anaheim, California, 1963. Used with permission from Thomas Nebbia.

nists such as Benjamin Franklin, Booker T. Washington, P. T. Barnum, or the fictional Ragged Dick succeed through hard work, thrift, sobriety, and single-minded drive. When Kline worked in the circus, for example, she labored tirelessly to move up in an intensely hierarchical work culture where one's occupation determined where one ate, slept, and dressed. Throughout her life, the immigrant Kline was ready to display her patriotic American credentials, from knitting socks for U.S. servicemen during World War I with her colleagues on the Barnum & Bailey Circus to her work as a censor and translator during World War II: "Yes, there was a war to be won, and why wasn't I out there pitching in? I suddenly felt conscience-stricken. Why not, indeed? What did I have to offer—two or three foreign languages?" During World War II, Kline also played a representative of the "Fighting French" for Irving J. Polack's Shrine Circus, which boasted an all-Allies cast of performers.[1] Despite Kline's pluck and industry, her entrée into American culture was primarily through the disreputable realm of bodily display, which provided her a route to financial security and finally—ironically enough— respectability. Consequently, Kline's story, particularly in her last incarnation as Tinker Bell at Disneyland, also illuminates the curious synergy between propriety and titillation in American popular culture.

Tiny Kline wrote the memoir that follows this introduction. It goes without saying that her narrative provides the foundation and mortar for cobbling a broader life history of this amazing—if little-known—woman. However, Kline's account primarily focuses on her years with the circus. She likely arrived in the United States on January 31, 1905, on the ship *Ultonia* from Fiume (current-day Rijeka, Croatia). Listed under her birth name, Helen Deutsch, Kline's prior home was Hungary, a homeland that was also confirmed by her probate records and conversations with one of her last surviving blood relatives.[2] (I have found no trace of her birth records.)[3]

Helen Deutsch was part of a flood of immigrants from Southern and Eastern Europe seeking prosperity in America's booming industrial economy. Of the twenty-three million people who immigrated to the United States between 1890 and 1924, seventeen million began their new lives at the port of New York.[4] Deutsch, too, entered the country at Ellis Island. Traveling under dank and congested conditions in steerage along with the other poorest passengers aboard the *Ultonia,* Deutsch was a young teenager and a member of a Hungarian dance troupe. According to the ship manifest, she was a domestic servant and could read and write.[5] She had no guardian.[6] Her precise reasons for staying in the United States are unknown, but like hundreds of other young Jewish immigrant women between the ages of fourteen and thirty, Deutsch soon found refuge at a boarding house and industrial school, the Clara de Hirsch Home for Working Girls. As an elderly woman, she remembered the institution with deep affection and left the majority of her estate to the home, according to her will: "in gratitude for taking custody of me when I came to America as a minor in 1905, having no guardian."[7]

Incorporated in 1897, the Clara de Hirsch Home was part of the landscape of Progressive-era reform. The German baroness Clara de Hirsch was its cofounder and benefactor. Elite German Jewish immigrants comprised the other founders and officers in an organization imbued with the cosmopolitan worldview of Reform Judaism, a modern, liberal denomination that did away with traditional practices like wearing the *yarmulke* and *tallis* (prayer shawl), adhering to the kosher dietary laws of *kashruth,* the *ketubah* (marriage contract), and the breaking of the glass during the marriage ceremony.[8] With its wealthy German–Jewish American leadership and its cast of predominantly Eastern European Jewish immigrant pupils (Ostjuden), the Clara de Hirsch Home embodied the problematic relationships between "respectable," assimilated, reform-minded women of privilege and the working-class Eastern European Jewish women whose values and comportment the reformers hoped to fashion along proper, middle-class lines. The historian Nancy Sinkoff has written that the founders consciously chose to locate the Clara de Hirsch Home on Sixty-third Street between Second and Third Avenues, a "safe distance from the 'solid block of Europe' that was the Lower East Side."[9]

Like other philanthropic organizations targeted at young, working-class immigrant women, the home's board of directors and its professional staff trained their charges to become economically self-sufficient and morally resilient, but in class-specific ways.[10] Its certificate of incorporation included the following objectives: "to improve [residents'] mental, moral, and physical condition, and train them for self-support; to instruct them to become domestic servants; to provide industrial training . . . to provide them with opportunities for industrial, social, and moral improvement."[11] The Polish-born Jewish American writer Anzia Yezierska lived at the home around the turn of the century. Her benefactors awarded her a four-year scholarship to Columbia Teachers' College—but with the stipulation that she would become a teacher of "domestic science" to uplift other young Eastern European immigrant women (which she did briefly after graduation).[12] In Yezierska's autobiographical novel, *Bread Givers* (1925), the narrator, Sara Smolinsky, also attends an industrial school. Upon enrollment, she is met with derision when she informs a teacher that she wants a broad, liberal education: "'What do you want to learn?' asked the teacher at the desk. 'I want to learn everything in the school from the beginning to the end.' She raised the lids of her cold eyes and stared at me. 'Perhaps you had better take one thing at a time,' she said, indifferently. 'There's a commercial course, manual training. . . .' 'I want a quick education for a teacher,' I cried. A hard laugh was my answer."[13]

In its early years, the professional staff and the board of directors at the Clara de Hirsch Home emphasized the needle trades and domestic service as the most moral and most effective means of achieving self-sufficiency before marriage. Yet the home scrapped its training program in domestic service in 1902. According to an informational pamphlet published in 1906, "Immigrant girls were not willing to spend six months in training when there were many housewives willing to accept them as they were, at wages from $10.00 to $14.00 per month, the demand for girls being so much greater than the supply. Second—Other girls whom we attracted were too young and physically unable to do the work required of them in the ordinary household."[14]

Still, as Sinkoff demonstrates, the home's board members and professional staff stressed a domestic education—in conjunction with a vigorous promotion of moral uplift through marriage—as the best means to inculcate middle-class values. They firmly believed that well-supervised young women would not succumb to the popular temptations of the streets. Clara de Hirsch students were constantly policed with a steady whirlwind of classes, planned leisure activities, and set curfew times (10:30 PM on weekdays and 12:00 AM on weekends). Home directors actively discouraged their charges from seeking well-paying factory jobs for precisely these reasons: unsupervised, working among men, with wages in their pockets, female factory workers were symbols of independent, sexually emboldened public womanhood, which subverted Victorian American notions of separate spheres.[15]

These gendered representations had special resonance for specific ethnic groups. The historian Riv-Ellen Prell argues that the American stereotype of the working-class Jewish "Ghetto Girl"—loud, brassy, flirtatious, and wearing flashy, fancy clothing that she purchased with her factory wages—encapsulated an array of cultural anxieties that reflected the problematic position of American Jews after the 1880s. At this time, American anti-Jewish sentiment no longer differentiated between assimilated German American Jews and the new, "alien" Russian and Eastern European immigrants.[16] According to Prell, "Americanization required men and women to distance themselves from undesirable former selves. Immigrants tried, sometimes desperately, to Americanize by changing their language and their appearance. The process seemed to require them to differentiate themselves from some other group or gender of Jews. To distance oneself from a vulgar, noisy Jewish woman was another way to assert one's status as an American."[17]

In reality, Jewish working daughters contributed, on average, nearly 40 percent of the family's total yearly earnings—despite the demonizing stereotypes of the Ghetto Girl callously blowing her precious wages to buy garish clothes and cheap entertainment.[18] To avoid this anxiety-ridden intersection of labor, sexuality, female power, and ethnic identity, the staff at Helen Deutsch's first home in the United States did their best to keep their charges away from the factory. If factory work represented higher wages and female independence in a mixed-sex setting, it also placed vulnerable young women in the dangerous world of the streets, away from the watchful eyes of parents and guardians.

Yet Deutsch flatly rejected the home's promise of domestic refinement by seeking a career in the "leg business," or burlesque. Her successful entry into burlesque and vaudeville represented the antithesis of the home's goals. According to her grandniece, Sheila McKay Courington, Deutsch's occupational roving also led to a virtual estrangement from her sister Fanny. For this reason, Courington's grandmother rarely spoke of Tiny. Kline left three thousand dollars of her estate to Fanny, or $2,664.24 after taxes (in contrast to $21,142.32 to the Clara de Hirsch Home and $3,536.90 to Naomi Arnell, her neighbor, friend, and executor).[19] Kline mentions Fanny only once in the memoir, referring to her on the dedication page as one of four people to whom she dedicates the book.[20]

Deutsch entered an occupation that her benefactors and family found distasteful, but she remained faithful to the cosmopolitan, tolerant worldview of Reform Judaism, even though she did not identify herself specifically as Jewish in her memoirs: "I confess being deeply religious—mind you, not the bigoted fanatic type of any one specific denomination but rather of one based on universal principles, applicable as an auxiliary to all faiths." Moreover, she remained resolutely affectionate toward the Clara de Hirsch Home, as her probate records indicate. Her ecumenical, tolerant Weltanschauung nurtured by Reform Judaism (in addition to her experiences in the countercultural, itinerant milieu of fin-de-siècle popular amusements) is particularly apparent when she describes the flourishing gay and lesbian culture that existed in the early twentieth-century amusement business. She simply chronicles and remains nonjudgmental. For instance, while part of a chorus line, Deutsch worked with a lesbian couple. After one of the women was dismissed from the show, her partner yearned for her when she fell ill while on the road:

> Occupying the adjoining room, I remained with her at night during the crisis to give her the medicine as the doctor ordered and otherwise looking after her, bringing the mail left for her at the theater. When she confided those intimacies, I believed she was raving as a result of the fever or that she was being melodramatic, as choristers are prone to self-glorification and sometimes resort to exhibitionism in their effort to stir the others' imaginations with their exploits. Seeing I was unimpressed, she knew I

doubted her story; bent on convincing me, she let me read some of the letters from Miriam, which left me dumbfounded with confusion and amazement, containing tender love messages such as only a poet could compose, expressing vehement desire to see her, urging she leave the show to join her at once.

By becoming a burlesque dancer, Deutsch had entered an urban amusement world that progressive reformers deemed dangerous. As the historian Kathy Peiss has written, cheap nickel dumps (movie theaters), dance halls, dime museums, skating rinks, and amusement parks like Coney Island were all places where working-class teenagers freely mingled without adult supervision. Even the seemingly respectable physical culture movement was vulnerable to regulation: the impresario Bernarr Macfadden was arrested under the Comstock purity laws shortly before his 1905 Physical Culture Show in New York City for displaying "lewd" pictures of reclining athletic women dressed in union suits and a man wearing a leopard-skin breech cloth.[21]

Helen Deutsch became an integral part of this rollicking, titillating world of public amusement within six years of her arrival in the United States. In the summer of 1911, at the age of twenty, she was a burlesque dancer in Altoona, Pennsylvania. Thereafter, she played vaudeville, performed as a sideshow cooch dancer, and worked as an ice skater with men in drag. But burlesque, in her words, was her "forte," specifically ethnic impersonation through an "Oriental dance specialty." The media scholar Robert Allen argues that burlesque had been a mass entertainment that appealed to a broad range of social classes when it arrived from London in the late 1860s. Burlesquers spoke loudly and made fun of contemporary politics and Victorian gender norms. However, the initial mass appeal of burlesque hastened its downfall because middle-class reformers worried about its widespread corrupting influence. Quickly banned from "legitimate" theaters, burlesque moved to the rough male audiences of the concert saloon and the Wild West and circus cooch shows. Its female performers were now largely mute, simply serving as objects of sexual display.[22]

In her early career, Helen Deutsch performed primarily in these male-only audience settings. Her memoir vividly recounts her marginal position in the seamy world of burlesque and the cooch show. Performing her "Oriental" dance number at the crowded sideshow "annex" at Arlington and Beckman's Oklahoma Ranch Wild West Show in 1913, she recalls the volatile, dangerous scene, as men made catcalls, jostled each other to get a better view of her, and tried to grope her:

W. A. (as we called Mr. Shannon [the spieler]) would start his "spiel" by saying: "Gather 'round me a little closer, men, don't want the ladies to hear this, but you are about to get a little treat inside this curtain," et cetera . . . and that was when we'd give them the flash to help the sale. . . . The place filled up in no time. We could hear the wisecracks and otherwise smart remarks from behind still another curtain—our dressing-room—as they gathered in anticipation of seeing "those muscles shake and shiver like a bowl of jelly in a gale of wind; the dance that John the Baptist lost his head over" (Shannon's sales line). On a short, shrill note of the flageolet—the signal—I came out first. Climbing up to the platform, which was roped off all around for protection against the impudence of the standing audience, who might make a grab at our limbs (which they sometimes tried anyway), I went into my dance, a short routine of about two minutes' duration, doing high kicks and the split, which was then considered naughty. There wasn't anything in that music to inspire dance spirit within me. I could never feel the mood nor figure out the timing.

Dressed in a long "bead-fringe" over green or red tights, Deutsch's bold, sexually explicit (for the times) dances burlesqued contemporary stereotypes of the Ghetto Girl. Deutsch's labor provides a performative counterpart to what the literary scholar Laura Browder has termed the genre of the "ethnic impersonator autobiography," or narratives written under the disguise of a specific—yet false—ethnic identity, such as the African American janitor Sylvester Long, who recast himself as a fictional Native American, Chief Buffalo Child Long Lance. According to Browder, "These narratives stand as monuments to the tradition of American self-invention as well as testaments to the porousness of ethnic identity."[23] Kline engaged in a similar process of self-reinvention and Americanization through ethnic camouflage in her performances. Throughout her early career, this "Oriental" disguise was a common part of her acts. As late as 1919, when Kline had become a circus trapeze artist, she performed, in the words of the Ringling Bros. and Barnum & Bailey Circus program, "an Oriental revolving trapeze novelty performed at dizzy heights."[24] In her memoir, she notes that she shocked her audiences with her bare midriff.

Like thousands of other new immigrants, Helen Deutsch sought to hasten her assimilation into American society with a new name. Undoubtedly, she sought to remove all traces of her Hungarian Jewish identity in a society that was often hostile to immigrants, particularly those from Italy and Eastern Europe, whom native-born European Americans frequently viewed as racially inferior. Capitalizing on the eroticized mystique of European womanhood,

Tiny Kline in ethnic disguise as a Native American. Unidentified and undated newspaper clipping. Used with permission from Julie Kreinbrink.

Deutsch renamed herself Tina Helen Duchee. In her memoir, she states that she made the name change to appear more "glamorous," but the decision quickly backfired:

> [S]how people they never pass up an opportunity of wisecracking, especially at the expense of—or to annoy—the other fellow, making him (or her, as the case may be) a target for ridicule. As soon as I joined a unit, a production, or vaudeville act, and the members heard my name Duchee (pronounced Doo-shay) for the first time, they immediately began to poke fun at it, and from that very day, everybody with the company called me "Douchebag." I abhorred it, but there was nothing I could do about it. Once it got started, I couldn't stop it—my very closest associates would call me thus—anywhere I happened to be, and the more I'd protest, the funnier the situation became. So after a while I'd just ignore it till I joined another company, and the cycle started all over anew.

After the "douchebag" debacle, Deutsch was thrilled to take the name of her new husband, the world-champion Wild West rider Otto Kline, in 1915. After dating from afar for nearly two years, Deutsch and Kline married after a shared show date in Pittsburgh on March 17, 1915. Kline's real name was Otto Kreinbrink, and he was a German immigrant whose family had settled in Naperville, Illinois. I tracked down Deutsch and Kline's marriage certificate from the Pittsburgh City County Building, hoping to find additional information about their families; however, what I found was more revealing. Both lied about their backgrounds. Kline claimed to be a second-generation American, born and raised in Livingston, Montana, while Deutsch, listed as Duchee, wrote that she was born and raised in Denver, Colorado. In reality, both were born in nations that would soon be at war with the United States: Germany and Austria-Hungary. In the context of heightened anti-Semitism and anti-German hostility during World War I, Deutsch and Kline's decision to conceal their real identities might have been a matter of avoiding trouble. Or they simply might have enjoyed fooling the justice of the peace with a fictitious identity. However, their decision to lie remains a mystery.[25] Sometime thereafter, Helen assumed the name "Tiny," owing to her diminutive size but also as a playful, redundant pun in homage to her ethnic background: Kline (i.e. "klein") means tiny in Yiddish and German.

Kline worked hard to leave the "low" world of "for-gentlemen-only" amusements, where ethnic impersonation and titillation had been a vehicle for her entry into show business. She joined the Barnum & Bailey Circus in 1916 and labored vigorously to move up in the show's occupational hierarchy. She worked first as a lowly statue girl (posing motionless in classical attitudes clad in little else but messy white or bronze greasepaint), then as a more respectable standing Roman rider for the next two years. Starting in 1919, she moved up even further as a trapeze flyer and (briefly) working on the rings; concurrently she developed her signature act, an iron-jaw, breakaway "slide for life" in which she would break what would appear to be the only rope suspending her and slide from the top of the canvas tent to the bottom, dangling by her teeth. Like many other female players, Kline got her start in the circus through a familial connection: Otto had been a Wild West rider for Barnum & Bailey.

The couple first met in the lunch (dining) car while they worked for the Arlington and Beckman Wild West Show in 1913. Otto Kline worked as a trick rider, while Helen Deutsch (as Tina Helen Duchee) danced provocatively in the cooch show. When they finally married in Pittsburgh, Otto was performing with the circus, and Tiny danced for the Cracker Jack Burlesque Company. Kline was blissful in the immediate five weeks after her marriage. She and Otto planned for her to quit burlesque and join the circus. Her colleagues on the chorus line teased her and crocheted baby booties for her as she counted the days until Barnum & Bailey began their season on the road.

Tragically, Kline's euphoria ended quickly. After the finale at Baltimore on April 21, 1915, her stone-faced manager handed her a telegram: "Otto Kline died today. For disposal of remains, advise immediately. Frank A. Cook,

Care of Barnum & Bailey Circus." Her husband had been killed in a riding accident during a performance. Tiny was grief stricken, and she never remarried. Instead, she kept working. Within a year of Otto's death, Tiny was playing the state of Rhode Island (owing to her diminutive size) in a giant ice-skating revue, "The Ballad of the States," as part of a colossal stage show, *Hip-Hip-Hooray,* at the Hippodrome in New York City. In the spring of 1916, she was hired at the circus.

In joining the circus, Kline became a part of an entertainment that had self-consciously defined itself as respectable and moral since the postbellum era. Other live, mass amusements, like vaudeville, made similar claims as they sought to broaden their audience base to include middle-class families with increased leisure time in the maturing industrial economy.[26] The three-ring railroad circus had marketed itself explicitly to families since the 1870s, when P. T. Barnum reentered the circus business as a show owner. (Barnum argued that marketing to families was good business: for every child he admitted at half-price there was a full-paying adult in tow.) Impresarios emphasized with a nudge and a wink that the display of muscular—albeit scantily clad—athletes and trained exotic animals was educational and morally uplifting family fare. On one level, these claims about wholesome, safe fun were dubious because the crowded showgrounds were potentially dangerous places, particularly at night, where drunken male spectators gambled, picked fights, and leered blatantly at seminude circus women. Yet, on another level, impresarios' ostensible mission to "instruct the minds of all classes" (in the words of a Barnum & Bailey program) succeeded because the circus, unlike other mass forms, was not a target of purity reform during the Progressive era, despite its titillating bodily performances.

The circus was also a staging ground for ethnic identities in the late nineteenth and early twentieth centuries. Its cast of clowns, in particular, played a range of ethnic characters—Hebrew, Irish, German, and Yankee farmer, among others, most commonly displaying these types through grotesque drag representations of the female body—in addition to a constellation of racialized characters (most commonly the "missing link" and the "savage"). Such displays perhaps solidified the circus's diverse white ethnic audiences, who laughed collectively at what they—ostensibly—were not.[27]

Kline's memoir provides an intimate glimpse at circus life: its caste system, itinerant character, sexual mores, and structural development during the twentieth century. At the circus, Kline was excruciatingly self-conscious about her "low" past. She keenly felt every slight, every snub from other performers who occupied a higher position on the circus's social hierarchy.

Kline remembered that the size of one's trunk and the position one occupied in the congested dressing tent reflected one's position in the caste system: "Indeed, the place of your trunk determined who you were." Kline and her fellow statue girls—covered in greasy white paint—were isolated from the other performers in a small, faraway corner of the women's dressing tent, while elite bareback riders and aerialists positioned their trunks along the first row against the tent's partition wall. At her first Fourth of July celebration with Barnum & Bailey—a day on which social equality was briefly the norm at the circus—Kline was drafted to dance for the women because "word had gotten around that I could shake a wicked hip." Even after Kline had "moved up" in the hierarchy in 1919, when she began performing a revolving trapeze act, she felt that others treated her as an "interloper." Fred Bradna, the equestrian director with the Ringling Bros. and Barnum & Bailey Circus (comparable to, but not the same as, today's ringmaster), told Kline not to stand on the ring-curb to take her bow because the superstar bareback rider May Wirth already used that "styling." After performing on the rings in 1919, Kline incurred the wrath of her sometimes friend Lillian Leitzel, who was outraged to find Kline's rings already set up (off to the side) before Leitzel's act. Leitzel fumed and scolded, telling her potential competitor that she was actually better built for iron-jaw work. Consequently, prompted by Leitzel, Kline had an epiphany: she decided to leave the rings to Leitzel and develop her skills with the iron-jaw and trapeze.

For the next four decades, Kline crafted her trademark, iron-jaw breakaway act, the "slide for life," and she was billed as the "world's most sensational aerial daredevil." Hanging by one's teeth was popular with trapeze performers looking to make themselves more salable with more breadth and range. Best of all, the iron-jaw required no rigging equipment other than a rope and pulley. Yet the learning process was excruciating: "[O]nce the extreme agony of the first two weeks' practice was lived through, the next two weeks would see a gradual tapering off of the pain in the eyes, nose, and jaw, and the temples would also cease that hammering sensation. The vertebrae that made that cracking sound in the back of the neck every time the mouth took the weight of the body would be quite silent by the third week. The obnoxious smell of the strap and the flavor of tannic acid would be the only lingering elements."

Kline's long career demonstrated her flexible movement across various cultural hierarchies, oscillating continuously between work in "low" and "respectable" entertainment venues. Always infused with a touch of bewilderment regarding her next move or her next employer, she chronicles her peripatetic and varied employments from the 1910s until the late 1930s, when she bought a house and decided to settle permanently in balmy Southern California because of the region's predictably warm and sunny weather.

In 1917, she wintered in Cuba, first performing with an elephant act and then as an aerialist. She fell in love with a Cuban pharmacist; he jilted her in 1919, poisoned by rumors spread by one of Kline's jealous male colleagues in the circus. However, Kline possibly fabricated this entire romance. In her Author's Note, she indicates that she took "liberties" regarding her romantic adventures, "thus giving the story added color . . . to satisfy readers with a taste for sensational literature." In an interview in 1961, Kline claimed to have participated in a mock wedding (which was reported in the *Billboard*) in order to dissolve her contract with a circus where marrying during the show season was forbidden.[28] She subsequently lived periodically in Cuba for eleven years, working as a dance instructor in Havana. She performed sometimes for American circuses, an occasional "frolic" or burlesque date (including a week at a house on skid row in November 1927—"which wasn't as bad as I expected"), on Broadway in Billy Rose's 1935 production, *Jumbo* (on the golden anniversary of the death of P. T. Barnum's celebrity elephant), in movie roles, and in multiple outdoor thrill shows.

Public spectacles became Kline's trademark. From August 1 through 8, 1931, she slid one thousand feet from a 125-foot music tower at Westchester County's Playland in Rye, New York.[29] With disappointment, Kline wrote to the *Billboard* on January 2, 1932, that Parisian gendarmes denied her permission to perform a "slide for life" from the Eiffel Tower.[30] But in October 1932, she made international headlines after thousands of astonished passersby watched her slide 1,134 feet dangling by her teeth several hundred feet above Times Square, gliding from a sign atop the Edison Hotel to the Palace Theater roof. Kline was hired to perform this harrowing stunt as a way to drum up publicity for a touring R. K. O. Circus vaudeville production in which she starred. (The *New York Times* reported that Kline was arrested for disorderly conduct, but a judge dismissed the charge.)[31] In the summer of 1933 she appeared as the Zep Girl, performing aerial acrobatics on the trapeze and rings at an altitude of 1,500 feet suspended from a blimp hovering over George Hamid's Steel Pier at Atlantic City. Kline later quipped: "'I worried at first about falling in the water because I couldn't swim. But then I decided I wouldn't have to be concerned about drowning after I'd fallen 1,500 feet.'"[32] These thrilling exhibitions of Kline seemingly conquering modern technology, like countless contemporary aerial circuses (containing female acrobats dangling from airplanes), were highly popular in a modern society enthralled with speed and flight.

Kline remained a perceptive witness to the social and economic forces that were changing the circus in her lifetime. She saw the circus participate in the trend toward monopoly formation in the twentieth-century entertainment industry: vaudeville, movie theaters in conjunction with production companies, and radio limited the playing field by creating monopolies. About working for Barnum & Bailey when the show merged operations with the Ringling Bros. Circus in 1919, Kline observes: "Not a day passed by without some excitement, arguments over trivialities. We, the Barnum people, felt that the other gang was there by the grace of kindness from us, whereas the Ringling bunch was under the illusion that we were the poor orphans who needed adoption, letting us know it in no uncertain terms. It was confusing. During the first week, the Garden was like an arsenal of explosives, where everyone trod lightly. Then, gradually, each got bolder and stood his ground, maintaining that his side was in power." This 1919 merger was part of a larger trajectory in the circus industry. At the turn of the twentieth century, nearly a hundred different circuses roamed America; by 1956, that number had dwindled to thirteen, the majority of which were owned by the Ringling Bros. and Barnum & Bailey Circus.[33]

Kline also saw changes in the ways that the masses of casual labor dealt with low wages and exhausting working conditions. The commonest form of protest in the old days was simply to quit. But in the context of the industrial union movement in the 1930s, circus laborers (a.k.a. "roustabouts" or "workingmen") began to organize collectively and, consequently, in 1937 signed a contract with the American Federation of Actors (AFA) to create a new union. When John Ringling North decided to cut wages the following year (arguing that the show would otherwise go into bankruptcy), circus laborers voted to strike. On June 22, 1938, workers walked off the job in the union-friendly, working-class town of Scranton, Pennsylvania—a location that the AFA thought would be sympathetic to the strikers. But faced with complaints of "wild animal aroma" and unwanted media publicity, the mayor of Scranton levied multiple fines on the show, finally forcing it to pack up, close for the season, and travel back to its winter quarters at Sarasota, Florida.

Kline personally felt the impact of the circus strike. Filling in part-time as a waitress at the cook tent, Kline and other performers labored in other areas of the show to compensate for the absence of striking workers with the Al G. Barnes Circus's final tour in 1938. There, Kline faced a humiliating layoff with pay (but no dismissal). Her furlough was prompted by John Ringling North's decision to merge parts of the now-idle Ringling Bros. and Barnum & Bailey Circus with the Al G. Barnes show, leaving significant numbers of performers (like Kline) without work. Despite charges of intractability from a few of her coworkers on the show, Kline refused to appear in the parade or the spectacle in lieu of her regular act because her contract stipulated that she was a feature act. She remained adamant about controlling her own labor and thus staying with the show: "I owned an apparatus. I was boss of my own act and was classified as a private contractor."

Kline also had a familial connection to the industrial labor movement in addition to her employment experiences with the Al G. Barnes show. Kline's sister Fanny was married to Oscar Tabory (Americanized from his Austrian surname Tabor, meaning "drum"), who worked as an attorney for the United Mine Workers in the West Virginia coal country. According to his granddaughter, Sheila McKay Courington, Oscar Tabory was likely a political refugee who was smuggled out of his native Austria-Hungary at the turn of the century, narrowly escaping execution. An Austrian Jew, Tabory was deeply committed to the radical politics of his youth. He met Fanny Deutsch in New York City; they married and had children, and he thereafter lived the dangerous life of a union attorney, settling finally in Logan, West Virginia.[34]

Kline observed the impact of the changing postwar landscape upon the circus. When she visited the Ringling Bros. and Barnum & Bailey Circus during its stint in Los Angeles in 1948, she noted that the Greatest Show on Earth had become more compact. No longer did the show spread out magnificently over nine acres; the big top was smaller. Given the explosion of postwar suburbs, highway networks, and the Baby Boom, open areas relatively near the urban core had become rare. Costuming and music had also become standardized at this new circus, which, in Kline's mind, was more polished, like Broadway rather than the idiosyncratic costuming and comportment of old. Ultimately, she viewed this new circus to be a "production rather than a circus," assembled and torn down with hydraulic stake drivers and trucks (no longer solely with humans, horses, and elephants!). She was doubly shocked to see that titillation played an even bigger role that it had in her day with the Big Show; she sat stunned as voluptuous "showgirls" performed a raunchy dance number with male dwarfs and half-naked women rode in a rocking, undulating motion with legs spread atop elephants. Tiny waxes nostalgic for the more "wholesome" days of the early twentieth century: "It is my opinion that it was a lamentable state of affairs—almost a sacrilege to the noble institution, so typically American and so dear to the heart of every child and grownup who remembers the circus as the first big thrill of his life." Yet movies, radio, automobiles, airplanes, electricity, and television made consumers considerably more sophisticated than the turn-of-the-century audiences who had thrilled to see a live elephant. Gone were the days when "Miss Electra" could sit in a mildly electrified chair at the sideshow and shock and mystify her gullible audience of rubes who flocked to her show.

Television, in particular, complemented the increasingly privatized "homeward bound" lifestyle of suburban Americans during the cold war, an ethos that was increasingly antithetical to older public amusements like the circus, baseball, and grand urban movie palaces.[35] Triggered by low-interest mortgages through the 1944 GI Bill and inexpensive, mass-produced housing stock, millions of white families packed up their belongings and headed to the suburbs, while minority families moved into the urban housing stock recently vacated by the new suburbanites. Racial fear was an important reason for white suburbanites' reluctance to return to the urban environment for leisure time. Deindustrialization and capital flight concurrently hastened the "decline" of the city and its once-vibrant popular forms.

Tiny Kline's home in Inglewood, California, mirrored the broader transformation of the nation's racial landscape in the postwar period. When she moved to Inglewood in 1939, the city, which bordered Los Angeles, was perhaps best known for a powerful earthquake on June 21, 1920, its booming chinchilla farms, agricultural economy, nearby airport, and elaborate cemetery (which contained a fancy monument to the circus-star couple Alfredo Codona and Lillian Leitzel). During World War II, the town quickly became a thriving industrial center with the explosive growth of wartime and postwar defense industries.[36] The majority of Inglewood's housing stock was built after World War II.[37] Until the early 1960s, the city's population was largely Anglo-American. However, the migration of people of color seeking work in the city's flourishing industrial economy and the racist practice of blockbusting led to massive white flight.[38] During the last years of Tiny Kline's life, her neighborhood became largely African American.[39] This demographic transformation remains evident today: Inglewood has a black majority, followed closely by a large Latino population.[40]

From 1939 until her death, Kline lived alone in her small, tidy, wood-frame home at 2617 West Seventy-seventh Street. She performed in road shows until 1943 and worked periodic thrill acts thereafter, including televised slides for life across the Los Angeles Coliseum in 1948 and 1958, in addition to show dates at the Shrine Auditorium, the Million Dollar Theater, and the Rose Bowl during halftime performances, among other venues. But primarily she worked in her garden and rode her bicycle around town on errands. According to Kline, "I preferred to devote my time and energy to improving my home." As a child, Olivia Grieco LaBouff lived a few doors down from Kline at 2607 West Seventy-seventh Street, and she remembers the semiretired iron-jaw lady vividly: "Tiny Kline always fascinated us. She was always part of our childhood lore."[41] On a block of solidly middle-class Anglo families, there were few people who were, in LaBouff's words, "different." She recalls that, aside from her own family ("the Italians, as we were known"), there was a Mexican American family living across the street from Kline and then Kline herself, whom the neighborhood children fearfully regarded as an eccentric: the mysterious, muscular, heavily accented, blunt, solitary, older woman who had rings dangling inside her garage instead of a car. "What did she do on those rings?!? We wanted to know!!"[42] Born in 1942, LaBouff recalled the first time she met Kline. LaBouff was riding her bicycle, and Kline admonished her to watch out for the buckled cracks on the sidewalk in front of her house (the product of shifting soils that also cracked Kline's foundation):

> She had a gardener's tan, a rich, reddish color. She used to wear wonderful fifties blouses that buttoned down, and she tied them in a knot at her waist . . . [and] she wore baggy, cotton shorts. . . . It was unusual to see a woman dressed like that. We had brief exchanges on sunny Los Angeles afternoons. Some kids feared that she'd bark out some order to stay out of her garden. She was blunt, tough, and no-nonsense. Her hair was always white in my memory, and it was flyaway. She wore it in a knot in the back. She wore no makeup. And she had hands that were like workers' hands. She looked strong; she had muscular legs and arms. She was a very physical woman. She had a nice shape, and she loved being outdoors. . . . Her bicycle was her only transportation. Of course, not a lot of women were driving in those days. But Tiny Kline was very much her own person. Very physical. She leaned forward on her bicycle. No wobbles. She was a woman who knows how to ride a bike. And she did it strictly to get around. Not to exercise.[43]

Kline mentioned her bicycle riding in newspaper interviews, emphatically stating that she would never drive. When she worked at Disneyland, she took the bus, even though her neighbors offered to drive her to Anaheim: "'I just feel safer in a bus. This traffic is awful.'"[44]

In addition to Kline's striking muscular physicality, the neighborhood children noticed her reserved demeanor. LaBouff never saw the inside of

Kline's home, and she never saw visitors out front. Although the neighborhood children knew that Kline hung by her teeth for pay, few people knew much else about her. One neighbor who did become Kline's good friend was Naomi Arnell, who served as Kline's executrix. Arnell's backyard on Seventy-sixth Street (along the border between Inglewood and the City of Los Angeles) abutted Kline's, and the two women struck up a friendship across the privacy of their shared fence. According to Kline, "I like to parley especially with my good neighbor, Naomi, over the back fence." Kline's dedication page notes that Arnell urged her to write her memoirs—"But for her suggestion, this book might never have been written"—a statement that hardly surprises LaBouff, who remembers Arnell as a captivating, avant-garde woman whose Tudor-style home enthralled the neighborhood children with its Native American artifacts and animal-skin rug: "Naomi was extraordinary; she would have had an appreciation for an unusual story."[45]

Indeed, Arnell had a remarkable background that likely made her sympathetic and welcoming to an outsider like Tiny Kline. Arnell and her brother, the famed southwestern author Frank Waters, were born in Colorado Springs at the turn of the twentieth century, shortly after the boomtown years of the Colorado gold rush. Their mother, Onie Dozier Waters, came from a large Southern Methodist family who disapproved of their part-Cheyenne father, Frank Jonathan Waters. According to Frank Waters: "My father, with his dark skin and straight black hair, was of a different breed than the Dozier clan. . . . One of his best friends was a vegetable huckster named Joe, a Cheyenne. Father often rode with him on his rounds. Sight of my father neatly dressed in a suit and polished boots as he sat on the plank seat of a rickety wagon beside an Indian huddled in a tattered blanket with moccasins on his bare feet always disconcerted Mother. She was even more upset by Father's frequent visits to the Ute encampment on the mesa."[46]

Naomi and Frank were well acquainted with their father's American Indian friends and his religious beliefs. Both were deeply shaken by his death from pneumonia while they were still children. After an itinerant young adulthood as an oil worker and engineer, Frank became a writer in the 1920s and a significant part of the literary and artistic community of Taos, New Mexico, which served as a cultural meeting ground for Native American and Euroamerican artists, writers, and intellectuals. Along with other seminal figures like Tony Luhan, Mabel Dodge Luhan, Georgia O'Keefe, and Elsie Clews Parsons, Waters helped sustain a vibrant bohemian enclave in this stark and arresting desert mountain landscape of pueblos and yellow aspen. Naomi was an important part of this creative world and was intimately familiar with Frank's work because she typed his manuscripts: "When a chapter was finished, I sent the handwritten manuscript to Naomi, who was married and living in Los Angeles. She typed it and held it until the book was completed and ready to be sent to a publisher."[47] Naomi Arnell's life experiences coupled with her own ethnic background undoubtedly made her sensitive and welcoming to a countercultural figure like the Hungarian-born Jewish iron-jaw lady, Tiny Kline.

Despite the fact that Kline's memoir treats her neighbors with affection, she conveys a perpetual awareness of herself as an outsider, whether performing in a burlesque show or digging with solitary determination in the rock-hard clay soil of her garden. Living in Inglewood, Kline had given up her nomadic lifestyle for one of relative stasis. She had traded a way of life that was "showground bound" (the original title of her memoir) for one in which gardening and home repair became her primary focus. As an immigrant Hungarian American Jewish widow who labored in a seemingly incomprehensible line of work—serenaded by her signature song, "Can You Tame Wild Women?" during her iron-jaw act at the circus—Kline remained an unconventional person in an era when marriage, motherhood, and domesticity were the norm. Her probate records indicate that she built a small addition proportioned to her diminutive size attached to her garage, where she reportedly lived in violation of city ordinances zoning the area "for single-family residences only."[48] The reserved, tough, muscular circus lady whose garage contained dangling rings and a separate residence remained an enigma to Olivia Grieco LaBouff, who likened Kline to the mysterious and elusive Boo Radley in Harper Lee's *To Kill a Mockingbird*.[49]

Although Kline's body remained strong and capable into her seventies, she noticed that her opportunities in the increasingly youth-crazed entertainment industry were shrinking as she aged. Leroy Prince, the dance director for the 1940 film *Road to Singapore,* which starred Bing Crosby, Dorothy Lamour, and Bob Hope, flatly refused to consider Kline for an iron-jaw number because of her age. "When I explained the effect while in the air, he still wouldn't buy. I couldn't understand it. I wondered if I should remind him of the American Legion show he directed in Havana, Cuba, in the early spring of 1927, in which I also participated."

Ironically, Kline's last big act came playing the ageless, Anglo-Saxon cartoon character Tinker Bell at Disneyland from 1961 to 1964. Kline first performed for Disney at the Hollywood Bowl in Los Angeles at a special show, "Disney Night at the Hollywood Bowl," on August 1, 1958—where

Walt Disney saw her work her iron-jaw slide-for-life routine. (However, there is little extant information concerning Kline's eventual hire as Tinker Bell.)[50] Ascending to the top of the Matterhorn, Kline put on her harness, attached her rigging, quietly stepped out onto a ledge, and waited, wand in hand, for the spotlights to shine on her. Suddenly illuminated, Kline waved to the crowd and slid into space toward Sleeping Beauty's castle. According to Kline, "I can actually feel the thousands staring at me from the sea of faces below."[51] She clearly enjoyed this last act of her life: "'Every night when the searchlights come up to pick out Tinker Bell, then, up there on the mountain, I'm young again.'"[52] The feeling of youthful transcendence must have been acutely powerful for Kline as she battled cancer (and kept performing) during the last two years of her life.

Although Kline lived a relatively solitary existence outside of the Magic Kingdom, her role high in the air as the blond, flittering, elfin Tinker Bell placed her publicly in the assimilated mainstream of American popular culture. In Disney's 1953 feature film *Peter Pan,* Tinker Bell is a mute, buxom, platinum-blonde, butterfly-sized character (reportedly modeled after Marilyn Monroe) that communicates with a tinkling sprinkle of magical pixie dust. The film was based on the eponymous play and novel written by the Scottish novelist and playwright James M. Barrie (1860–1937). *Peter Pan* first appeared on the London stage in 1904, as a novel, *Peter and Wendy,* in 1911, and in multiple stage and film adaptations thereafter.[53]

On stage, a single spotlight beam commonly represented Tinker Bell instead of a live actress. In one of the play's most powerful scenes, recently re-created in the film *Finding Neverland* (2004), Tinker Bell is dying but can be saved if enough people believe in fairies. The distraught characters appeal to the audience, urging the crowd to demonstrate their faith in fairies by clapping; immediately, thunderous applause signals Tinker Bell's recovery. Only the audience's applause can (and does) bring her back to life. The Disney film version is considerably sunnier. Tinker Bell is petulant but heroic: despite her jealousy of Peter Pan's friendship with the adolescent Wendy Darling (who wishes to remain a child), Tinker Bell alerts Peter when the evil Captain Hook holds the Darling children hostage in Neverland. Peter comes to the rescue, and the story ends happily.[54] *Newsweek* magazine emphasized Tinker Bell's curvaceous physical attributes, stating that she represented "'a particularly enduring little vixen compounded of blond hair, feminine curves, and a pout, and just a little too bosomy to fit through an oversized keyhole.'"[55]

Tinker Bell remains a part of Disney's corporate iconography as an abstract, zooming ball of light arcing over a silhouette of Sleeping Beauty's

Tiny Kline dressing as Tinker Bell, assisted by unidentified woman, 1963. Used with permission from Thomas Nebbia.

castle on the company's film division logo (much like the stage representations of old). As a synonym for the diminutive, Tinker Bell also lives on in
the popular imagination. The heiress celebrity Paris Hilton owns a pampered,
well-televised Chihuahua named Tinker Bell. But Tinker Bell's sexuality as
a mute, winged woman-in-miniature in a movie and multiple stage shows
whose characters do not want to grow up offers potentially liminal meanings
as a metonym for ambiguous sexuality or a slang term for male homosexuality. And by association, Neverland, the 2,538-acre ranch belonging to the pop
singer Michael Jackson (who was acquitted of sexual abuse charges against
children), captures the character's ambivalent cultural meanings.[56]

Preceded by Walt Disney's new television show, "Disneyland," in 1954,
the theme park of the same name opened in Anaheim in 1955 and was an
essential feature of the suburbanizing, postwar sunbelt landscape—the same
landscape that helped displace the gargantuan tented railroad circus of old.
Citing labor conflicts, rising costs, logistical difficulties, and declining audiences, John Ringling North decided to tear down the canvas tents once
and for all in 1956 and moved his show to air-conditioned indoor arenas.
Disneyland's carefully regulated and spotless grounds catered to suburban,
middle-class consumers who could afford the park's expensive ticket prices.
Yet Disneyland also provided a startling contrast to the world of cheap,
public amusements in which Tiny Kline came of age as a burlesque dancer
at the turn of the century. The historian David Nasaw notes that Disneyland
and other new suburban and exurban amusement parks were isolated from
former urban ethnic enclaves, located in a demographically homogenized
suburban setting of single-family homes, off major highways, or, in the case
of Disneyland, surrounded by "a twenty-foot earthen wall . . . almost deliberately obscured from public view as if announcing that the space within
did not wish to be a part of the city."[57] In this social environment, grand
old movie palaces, theaters, baseball parks, and amusement parks across the
nation crumbled, were condemned, and were torn down.

Tiny Kline died of cancer on July 5, 1964, at the age of seventy-three at
a local hospital. There was a brief obituary in *Variety* and a short notice regarding Kline's funeral arrangements in the *Los Angeles Times,* but otherwise,
the passing of this Hungarian Jewish immigrant whose life experiences were
interconnected with key cultural transformations in the United States went
virtually unnoticed.[58] Given the absence of close family or friends with young
children, Kline stipulated in her will that her costumes and beloved iron-jaw
apparatus should go to a children's charity (perhaps like the Clara de Hirsch
Home). These items ended up at Goodwill Industries of California, where

an official assured Kline's executrix that they could "utilize the costumes for dressing dolls for underprivileged children."[59] One wonders if the worn leather straps, rings, and chains that suspended Kline fearlessly from blimps and carried her across coliseums and rooftops had any broader meaning to the kids who played dress-up with these key physical vestiges of Kline's life. The dynamic world of Kline's old haunts along Times Square had also died by 1964. Peep shows and prostitutes now dominated this once-vibrant (albeit always seedy) urban landscape where Kline had danced, ice-skated, and triumphantly slid through the air by her teeth.

Yet, in the 1990s, an ironic thing happened. Tinker Bell's parent company, the Walt Disney Corporation (among other corporate apostles of the New Urbanism) turned its sights away from the suburbs toward Times Square as a way to capitalize on growing public nostalgia for exciting, pedestrian-friendly urban spaces. In 1995, Disney bought and renovated the old New Amsterdam Theater to show its own productions like *The Lion King* and also purchased new retail space to house its Disney Store. Long gone are the ethnic ma-and-pa businesses of the turn of the century. Now giant superstores dot the urban landscape, while NASDAQ, ABC-TV, Disney-TV, and Morgan Stanley have located their corporate headquarters there.[60] Consequently, in 2005 rental space was nearly five hundred dollars per square foot, the third highest in Manhattan.[61] A night at Times Square (including Broadway tickets and lodging) can easily run over six hundred dollars. The city's regulation of gender and sexuality has been of critical importance in reordering this urban landscape. A city zoning law mandates that no more than 40 percent of adult stores' materials can be pornographic.[62] Proponents like the historian Kenneth T. Jackson argue, "'[P]ersonally, I think the neighborhood's character has improved significantly. A grandmother should be able to take her granddaughter to a play in Times Square and not be assaulted by signs that say "Nude Girls!"'"[63]

At the turn of the twenty-first century, the transformation of Tiny Kline's world has come full circle, touching the site of her earliest beginnings in America. A volatile staging ground for Kline's early career, the so-called Great White-Washed Way of corporate conglomerates has been emptied of its original diversity. Although the area has become safer for the thousands of pedestrians who walk through Kline's old haunts every hour (crime has dropped 69 percent since 1993, and neighborhood activists now complain about too much foot traffic in the area), its diverse "cheap amusements," small businesses, and shared public spaces are gone.[64] In a fitting coda to the destruction of Tiny Kline's early amusement culture in New York City, the television show "Ripley's Believe It or Not!" recognized the seventieth anniversary of Kline's slide across Times Square—not in New York City but in Las Vegas. On October 9, 2002, the aerialist Tavana Luvas reenacted this event, sliding by her teeth across the sunbelt city's facsimile "New York, New York" skyline of casinos and hotels, which represents the modern incarnation of Tiny Kline's cheap amusements of old curiously mixed with the titillating, glitzy, corporate flash of what that culture has become today.[65]

The Contours of the Memoir and the Editorial Process

For many years, Tiny Kline's unpublished memoir languished among the vast archives at Circus World Museum in Baraboo, Wisconsin. Library staff members were at a loss as to how to proceed because there was no statement of gift on record, nor any trace of the memoir's arrival in Baraboo. Consequently, the librarians were forced to classify the memoir as an abandoned manuscript. Without a clear establishment of the library's copyright, the manuscript potentially fell under the paralyzing jurisdiction of the Copyright Term Extension Act of 1998, S.505, which automatically extends an author's copyright to seventy years after his or her death, unless otherwise stipulated by the author. (This law is better known as the Mickey Mouse Protection Act because of Disney's extensive lobbying efforts on its behalf and is even more famously known as the Sonny Bono Law, since the late congressman and former pop star initiated the bill shortly before his death.) Without clear evidence of the library's copyright ownership, Tiny Kline's manuscript would remain virtually frozen, unusable and outside the public domain until 2034, or seventy years after her death.

The extraordinary librarian Fred Dahlinger encouraged me to investigate the manuscript's legal status further. Fortunately, Kline's probate records provided the clichéd "smoking gun." Her will revealed that she bequeathed all of her unpublished writings—"some unfinished"—to her friend, Sam Abbott, of the Billboard Publishing Company, "to dispose of as he sees fit."[66] Abbott in turn gave the manuscript to Circus World Museum, thereby establishing the museum's legal ownership of the memoir, and the mystery was solved. With the museum's blessing, I was free to proceed. Kline's work was now legally publishable and would at last reach the broader audience she so desired.

Tiny Kline's memoir is a remarkable document. It provides an intimate, virtually microscopic view of the rich, salty world of American public amusements in the early to mid-twentieth century. Few performers of the period recorded their impressions of show life, but here one senses vividly the sweaty eyes and reaching hands of the cooch show, the grit and hustle of trying to improve one's occupational standing in the hierarchical world of the circus, or the unnerving dangers of hanging by one's teeth at bone-tingling heights. Kline wrote two drafts of her memoir—collectively nearly one thousand pages of text. Both focus primarily upon Kline's career in the circus. The first version, "Showground-Bound: Stranger than Fiction, Exposing Trade-Secrets and Little-Known Facts about Circus and Its Affiliated Branches in Show Business," is a meandering, unguarded, often meditative work. It is approximately one hundred pages longer than the second version and is occasionally earnest and didactic in tone, with extended musings on the history of the circus. While she mentions no specific works, Kline makes it clear that she is attempting to set the record straight in correcting some of the more outrageous accounts of circus life:

> It is high time to blast these tall tales to kingdom come, but since no one came forth with the idea, it occurred to me to undertake the gigantic assignment to expose the imposters by writing this book, which I have been planning and laboring on for some time: A book debunking falsehood, exploding like a bombshell that would rock the rafters of old Madison Square Garden—yes, even rock the swivel-chairs right from under the bottoms of the scribes writing those phony yarns—and defying any contradiction on facts as stated herein (and I certainly cover a large margin, just about every phase of the big top and the kid top, from train to showground and back).

Moreover, Kline seems to long for posterity—someone who was not nationally famous in her lifetime taking a crack at forging some sort of legacy for herself. While amazingly upbeat chronicling a difficult life, Kline also wishes to settle some scores and is unsparing in her criticism of those who acted unethically or pompously. The first version is also fresh and open in its attention to gender and sexual politics, while the second omits much of this material.

The second version of her memoir, "This Way—The Big Show," is more compact than the first. Perhaps on the advice of an editor or friend, Kline deleted most of her rambling rehash of circus history; her prose is considerably tighter; the manuscript has removed many of the more personal insights into other performers. Owing to the second version's relatively spare syntax and grammar (in conjunction with the demands of my editor to economize length), I have opted to keep this entire version virtually intact. I have also taken the liberty of removing the majority of Kline's retelling of American circus history that does not pertain directly to her own story.

Still, I have had a difficult time deciding what to delete and what to keep simply because this is Kline's story and I do not want my editorial decisions to alter her unique voice and experiences. Nor do I wish to jeopardize Kline's desire to speak as an authority on the circus apart from her own life with the show. Consequently, this is a hybrid memoir. In addition to keeping the relatively compact prose of the second version, I have preserved the first version's freewheeling anecdotes that Kline deleted from the second. In addition, I have removed the omnipresent scare quotes from both versions. Perhaps Kline viewed scare quotes as an effective way to engage humorously and sarcastically with her reader, or maybe as a non-native English speaker, she felt compelled to place scare quotes around every word and turn of phrase that was novel or unfamiliar to her. Yet they are distracting and add little to Kline's story, so I deleted them here. Kline's writing style verges on the conversational and fragmentary, which makes for difficult reading when one is constantly navigating a chatty, meandering stream of ellipses and dashes. I have transformed fragments and run-ons into complete sentences with semicolons and periods to improve the syntactical flow.

Although Kline's memoir moves chronologically, roughly from 1911 (when she was working exclusively in burlesque) to her retirement from road travel in the spring of 1943 (and after, when she primarily worked local thrill acts), the narrative often drifts from the distant to the recent past. Trancelike, Kline zooms into alleyways, crowded big tops, stuffy dressing tents, smoky hoodoos, and more. However, she tells us nothing about her Hungarian childhood, her motives for immigrating to the United States, or her family background. Frustratingly, she provides no information that accurately dates either draft. She describes her reunion visit to the Ringling Bros. and Barnum & Bailey Circus when the show appeared in Los Angeles in 1948, in addition to mentioning her occasional iron-jaw gigs in her current state of semiretirement. These clues date the manuscript to the 1950s, especially in light of the fact that there is no mention of her work as Tinker Bell—a job she began in 1961 and enjoyed deeply, according to the photographer Thomas Nebbia, who met and photographed Kline in 1963 while on assignment with *National Geographic*.[67] Both versions of the memoir end with the same incident, leading me to believe that they cover the same time span. Thus, despite its disarming intimacy and immediacy, this is still a memoir clouded by mystery. Other primary materials—press releases, marriage and death certificates, interviews, newspaper articles, and photographs—have helped me round out Kline's life as fully as possible.

Throughout the edited version, I have made numerous endnote annotations to provide the reader with a broader feel for Kline's enormous web of associates and the volatile businesses in which she worked. I have included birth and death dates for the people she mentions whenever I have been able to access this information. My endnotes also include a fuller description of various acts Kline performed, in addition to some clarification of the often murky, insider language of the circus. Based on information culled from obituaries, feature articles, other memoirs, show programs, and business records, the annotations give the reader an intimate sense of the colorful cast of characters populating the early to mid-twentieth-century amusement business—folks such as the luminous singing wire-walker Bird Millman, the child acrobat turned real-estate and entertainment mogul Sam Gumpertz, or Adgie, the fleetingly famous lion tamer who later died obscure, senile, and broke. These vivid people emerge from an itinerant world of public entertainment that has since virtually vanished.

CIRCUS QUEEN
&
TINKER BELL

**IN DEDICATING THIS BOOK,
I FEEL IMPARTIALLY GRATEFUL TO:**

My sister Fanny,
Whose patience, tolerating my shortcomings during those struggling days,
was transcendent, and whose home served me as a base—a privilege I too
often abused and only later learned to appreciate.

Mrs. Mary Sumner,
Under whose gentle tutelage I learned the key to extract the essentials from
reading and inject them into writing—guided by the principle of the five W's.

Naomi,
The first to recognize I have a story that should be told. But for her
suggestion, this book might never have been written.

Charles Pusey,
My friend and instructor, without whose guidance and encouragement this
book would indeed never have been published.

—TINY KLINE

AUTHOR'S NOTE

That truth can be as strange as the most fantastic fiction is proven in a number of circumstances and occurrences herein related. The veracity of events as told may be accepted as facts to the letter, as I have perceived them and lived them with other participants mentioned. Nothing I have said of persons, individually or collectively, has been exaggerated; with data entrusted to my memory, I can positively substantiate every statement. Although I am aware that a number of my contemporaries, having passed on, may no longer contest my impressions and opinions of them, I have not willfully abused or contorted the truth with malicious intention but faithfully adhered to the facts. I have taken liberties in the treatment of character with but one person, myself, in relation to the later amorous entanglements in the concluding chapters, which I did pointedly, thus giving the story added color in order to satisfy a certain group of readers with a taste for sensational literature. In view of the fact that in so doing I sacrificed my chastity in the eyes of the reader following the narrative in chronological order, it is my sincere hope that this paragraph shall redeem me—straighten matters out. While I have strived throughout the book to capture the interest of readers of all ages—young and old alike—the resulting achievement seemed like all work and no play. I felt it was lacking in something vital—that my life was void of that normal human emotion: romance. Those who know me will understand; my vindication is directed to the others, who don't.

In conclusion, it may be fitting that I confess being deeply religious—mind you, not the bigoted fanatic type of any one specific denomination but rather of one based on universal principles, applicable as an auxiliary to all faiths. For I believe in the divine law of retribution: that agony, pleasure, sorrow, and joy are, in extreme proportions and in due course, balanced—each against its antonym—as in a clearinghouse, as sure as I live. As I go along recounting and reliving those days of great moments—be they of grief or of happiness—I also come across those of reckoning, liquidating the debt whether in compensation or punity. The reader will find at least two good examples of the Great Equalizer balancing the scales, proving my implicit theory. And when checking on the multiple accounts of the lives of others recorded on these pages, it will perhaps serve to further substantiate in the minds of my readers the existence of this *phenomenon,* the faith I shall adhere to unto my last day.

PROLOGUE

This book came into being in response to questions the public has been asking for many years: How circus performers come to be; something regarding their living facilities; and their moral code and social behavior while trouping under canvas—that fairyland of a child's dreams.

Best qualified for the task would unquestionably be a circus press agent who, although lacking thorough knowledge of behind-scene activities, wields the pen with greater skill than one whose specialty is climbing ropes and riding horses—just as he couldn't substitute for an acrobat, each an expert in his own line. Yet all my search for such a book—one that is authentic in all respects—has been futile. In all the years of circus history, not one writer has produced a complete work with true facts on the subject which the public, as well as the circus members themselves, would like to read. Can it be that the press agent can't get out of that rut—his accustomed routine of gilding the lily—to sell the front- rather than the backdoor life with the show, or that writing something true and sincere would be against ethics or conflict with his style? Surely there is nothing shady about circus life in general; the moral behavior of everyone connected with a show of this type is of the highest standard. The personal hygiene and sanitary conditions in all departments are truly commendable. The training and treatment of animals is exemplary of human kindness. And taken as a whole, in the march of time through the progress of changes from the early to the modern, this institution is perhaps the only branch of show business that never clashed with censors. The clean, wholesome entertainment of mirth and merit: the keynote in that magic word *circus*.

I have read some articles, short stories, and books on the circus that were so absurd in their description of background and characters that I was seething with rage while reading them. It is obnoxious to one thoroughly versed in the subject to read such grossly distorted tales written by persons who, as evidence points, never have seen the back end of a show. I am referring especially to one book that is positively outrageous in its depravity in treatment of the subject referring to the private lives of the circus people. His imagination running amuck, the writer paints a behind-the-scenes picture so abominable that it is an affront not only to the show folks but also to the intelligence of the average circus fan and reader.[1]

Among some of the impossible situations and deeds therein described are the following boners: that the stars of the show hobnob with the sideshow freaks; that they wear their dressing-robes on the street, leaving their tights on all day and even wearing them home at night; that they eat a full-course dinner just before going on for their act (an aerial act, incidentally); and that the feature acts enjoy the luxury of pianos in their dressing rooms. The owner-manager of the show in this abortion of a brainstorm is characterized as a racketeer and criminal. The terms applied to the workmen and to their specific duties are ridiculous—quite annoying to one accustomed to our own jargon.

But the writer actually insults the intelligence of the public in describing the proportions of the arena, fixing the distance between rings at 150 yards, which is an absurdity—first, because in the circus we measure by terms of feet, and second, because of the exorbitant misjudgment of distance. There are usually three rings in a circus, with a stage (platform) between them, taking up a space of thirty feet, hence, the difference—but what matters! The entire account is so preposterous that it doesn't merit debate; I mention it only as an example to prove my point regarding the gross miscarriage of facts in reporting pertinent matters.

This is the sort of material one finds in the general run of circus stories, leaving the reader up a tree, since the author doesn't specify that it is fiction. The public, eager to grasp the information the book contains, will naturally accept it as factual, whether it be true or false.

It is high time to blast these tall tales to kingdom come, but since no one came forth with the idea, it occurred to me to undertake the gigantic assignment to expose the imposters by writing this book, which I have been planning and laboring on for some time: A book debunking falsehood, exploding like a bombshell that would rock the rafters of old Madison Square Garden—yes, even rock the swivel-chairs right from under the bottoms of the scribes writing those phony yarns—and defying any contradiction on facts as stated herein (and I certainly cover a large margin, just about every phase of the big top and the kid top, from train to showground and back).

There is a void in the heart of every ex–circus trouper after one has outlived the span of active life with the show yet in spirit is still trailing along the road: the nostalgia for the smell of sawdust, stables, cages, the sweet fresh grass; for the sight of the white tops with the banners waving from the poles, the stream of smoke curling upward from the cookhouse; to hear the calliope tooting the current song hit, the band, and the announcer; to mingle with the folks in the dressing room. You feel an intense emotion hearing the applause on the conclusion of an act well timed, and all your senses are stirred by the very thoughts while reflecting on those *yesterdays*.

Reminiscing alone is like talking to yourself; you long to exchange views with others, to debate and even contradict their arguments. They may recall some incident you have long forgotten. This is the book I had in mind—written in my own style, without declamatory essays, yea, even unorthodox in its grammar and sentence construction; but I promise to bring out something revolutionary in the form of a circus memoir without resorting to unholy methods of prevaricating or stretching an issue, as writers often do, in order to create far-fetched situations. Reforming everything previously attempted in this category is my purpose.

But seen from the writer's angle, no one could possibly, just by watching a show from the seats, cover the multiple particulars it entails. Occasionally a writer will join the show in some capacity, just for the experience and to gather atmosphere for his endeavor. As usher or candy butcher[2] he could only hope to get a perspective of the front, while as a groom or propertyman[3] he would still be under handicap in pursuit of his aim, since he wouldn't be privileged to mingle with the performers, not even to eat in the same section of the cookhouse, which, divided by a partition, comprises two distinct compartments—one for the performers and staff, the other for the workmen. And once he joined up as a work-hand, he could never hope to be promoted to the performers' class no matter how good an idea for an act he may conceive in the interim. In order for him to crash the ranks, he would have to get a new start on another show. Therefore, if he wants to write about circus people in general, unless he started as a performer, where he could be in their dressing room and in their section of the train, he made the wrong approach from the beginning.

Of recent times, some self-styled biographers have made use of a nomen, "gillie"—a term supposedly meaning an outsider, one not connected with show business. This word is unknown in the circus. Eager to exhibit authority on his subject, a scribe will avail himself of any tool he believes will clinch his objective as a means to an end; in seeking words to authenticate his theme, he quite often snatches up a colloquial expression as employed by a character, knocking about with some cheap little mud-show or carnival, aggregations rated low by standards of a first-class show traveling by rail. In all the years of trouping, I never heard the noun "gillie," though on one occasion, while visiting some performers at a fair, I heard a barker refer to the general public as "ump-chays," using the unsubtle code of pig Latin. Of course, he was a pitchman, using shills (stooges) planted among the crowd, who start off the sale after his opening (sales talk), buying his wares with money with which he reimburses them; it is therefore expedient he distinguish the two classes.

I have taken great care in compiling this book to take the reader into the realms of backdoor—or back-stage—life, as if he or she were one of us. The action throughout the narrative is described in the idiom employed by the circus people in general, with definitions of unusual terms of the jargon given as they occur, as well as a reasonable excuse for their origin. For example, "kinker," the workman's term referring to a performer, derived from contortion and acrobatics (twisting, turning, tying themselves in a knot, hence: kinkers). The term applies to all performers, from riders to clowns.

With this prologue I wish to bring out the points of the subject treated— the cause and the effect thereof. I should also wish, in my humble way, to recommend this book to my readers as one I would have my mother and children (if I had any) read. The language employed throughout is as innocuous and clean as the subject matter and its characters.

Respectfully,
THE AUTHOR

CHAPTER

1

THE BEND
IN THE ROAD

It was way back during the winter season of 1917–18 when I first met Minnie Fisher.[1] She was doing an iron-jaw act.[2] But frankly, I wasn't interested in her act. It was just seeing her that wholly filled me with pity. "Poor old soul!" I thought. "She must have lived the wrong way to arrive at this age, at least forty-five—surely forty-five, if a day—and still have to work!" That was when I made a resolution: Nobody's going to feel sorry for me when I get old, no siree! And I am if forced by circumstances to earn a living, it will not be in show business.

Many seasons had gone by since. So many things had happened: promotions, accidents, publicity. All these things I accepted as my fate, in the order in which they came and without keeping account of the time, trudging along, season after season, with no thought for the year. Then one morning, while tinting my hair to cover up those telltale gray ones—rushing, always rushing lest I be late for the show—it suddenly struck me that the time had already arrived. That pledge I made years ago—that time is now! Oh, but the show! Past noon. I'll be late for the matinee! I'd better hurry—no time to eat. The show—I'll be late for the show!

The show in question was the Polack Bros. Shrine Circus, a unit of circus acts playing Shrine-sponsored dates, at that moment playing the Auditorium in Oakland, California.[3] It was a circus adapted for indoors, which has become a vogue of recent years; the idea was probably copied from the Cirque d'Hiver in Paris, which could be viewed from a comfortable *fauteuil*. That week was

Tiny Kline working at Polack Bros. Circus, 1941. Used with permission from Fred Pfening Jr., Pfening Archives.

to terminate the official indoor season, which now suited me perfectly. It jibed with my sudden decision and eliminated the obligation of my having to give two weeks' notice.

"Why," I thought, "I can leave the show tomorrow after the last performance. Yes, that's what I'll do. Let me see now. Only four more times to go through that tenseness—not the act itself, I'm all right once I'm on. It is that preliminary—that anticipation just preceding the act when I'm completely possessed by . . . stage fright, what else? Even after all these years, my nerves turn raw, my heart starts to pound, as if driven by a demon who cries, 'There's the overture! Hurry up, you'll be late! Run—there's the curtain-music!'" This ever-haunting nightmare would no longer drive after tomorrow night. Gleefully, I twisted my hair up after the last rinse, hoping it would curl in time for the performance.

All in all, it had been a hard grind week after week—it seemed like an endless chain. At last it would be broken.

Mr. Stern, the treasurer and junior partner of the management, always paid us after the last show at each stand. Ever since the notion hit me, it was difficult to keep it on my chest. I wanted to get it over with. So while he was filing away my signature after handing me the pay-envelope, I told myself, "This is the time! But what? How shall I say it?" And, as if aided by fate, came the opening. Turning, Mr. Stern reminded me that the next stand, as well as others to follow, would be set up outdoors—ballparks or fairgrounds—and, since the space under those conditions would be unlimited, the acts that can cover a wider scope of height and distance will be expected to cooperate. He added that the management knew of my eagerness to give my best and was counting on the long slide. Here was my cue.

"That's just what I wanted to talk to you about," I said. "My entire equipment will have to be changed for the outdoor paraphernalia, which is stored in a warehouse in Los Angeles." I explained that it would require my personal attention to sort out what was needed and that I couldn't possibly make the next stand at Reno, Nevada. Besides, I wanted a vacation.

"Best that we call off the summer dates!" I said coolly. "I'll be back for the regular tour in the fall!" I lied. To Mr. I. J. Polack, the senior partner of the firm (the big boss, as we all called him, sometimes), I said nothing.

Dragging my steps, I walked out of the office. Only then did I realize how tired I was, how much this work sapped my energy, how jittery and ill-tempered I had been growing daily. Besides the *artistic* endeavor seen by the paying customers, the real work I actually did was behind the scene. Setting up and taking down the apparatus at each stand—that was no small task.

Then the daily readjustment: that breakaway wire had to be fixed so it would "break" again in the next performance; the rings which I removed during the act so that I could go into my swivel also had to be hung back in place on the crane-bar; guylines loosened from backets and struck to clear the space for the other acts that followed had to be reset, checked for correct line of crane-bars and proper tautness. All this going-over on act number one.

Act number two, the slide for life, was usually lower down on the program, and I always had to strike myself after the show was over by removing the jack at the low end and carefully tucking it under the seats, where it would be safe and out of the way, then releasing the block and tackle and coiling up the 250-foot cable (the usual length required to reach from one end of the average-sized auditorium to the other). This had to be neat— rolled one turn over, one under, so it would pull out true, without any twists or kinks, when the propertymen pulled it across and set it up during the brief time of the intermission. Even then I would stand by and watch the procedure; it must be right. With a plain robe over me to attract the least possible attention of the audience, many times I would lend a hand at tugging the wire and setting up the jack under it. Time was limited to a few precious minutes, and I had to make sure it was all set for the act before I rushed back to the dressing room to change into my costume, according to the time I went on, allowing myself long enough to finish dressing just five minutes before the act. Spangles and metallic fabrics tarnish with the body heat, and once you have your tights on, you must remain standing or they get baggy at the knees and look like long underwear.

Both acts required utmost precision and calculation. On arrival at each place, I would look the building over and go to work setting up act number two first. No two places are alike: each offers different conditions with so many obstacles to cope with. The main object is to make the best of things in order to give a thrilling moment for the spectators. The angle must be considered—so much height to so much distance. The declivity determines the speed on the descent; therefore, any great variation from my established standard would result in disaster.

I never carried insurance. As a matter of fact, I usually signed a release with the management, waiving all claims for injury I may have received during the engagement the contract covered. In case of accident—be it due to faulty rigging or my own or any other person's carelessness—the responsibility was mine alone. No indemnity for disability or medical attention. This was, perhaps, the point in my precaution: always to tie that cable to a solid anchorage.

After completely finishing the erection of the slide to the last detail, I would mark everything with chalk and friction-tape before striking it, making it simple to set it up in a hurry. Nothing must interfere with the other fellow's act; lest some of my rope or wire dangle loosely after my act was finished and bother someone, it had to be cleared. This was done with the aid of a tripline, a light rope and pulley rigged up overhead, which could be used to remove the offending object—pull the tripline, tie it off to something: "Presto!" The performing area was cleared. Everything had to work with minimum time required.

This done, I would rig up act number one. This was indeed an intricate affair, and since it was my very own brainchild, no one else could figure out how it was assembled to go up; the secret was that it must coincide *exactly* or fail, and when I say coincide, I mean horizontally as well as vertically. Here's why: what the spectator sees is that I take hold and bite on a mouthpiece while up in the air, letting go my hold on the rope—my weight on the teeth. Something breaks: Zoom! And down I come. "An accident!" is the impression it creates. But just before I reach the floor, I am really hanging by my teeth from a thin wire the mouthpiece is attached to, which is trimmed so that I clear the floor by an inch or two. It affords a tense moment for the public—the worst I get out of it is a terrific jerk on the neck as the wire reaches the low point, taking my weight—that is, if all goes off as planned. There was that time—about a year and a half ago—at the Shrine Mosque in Peoria, Illinois.

The unit showed there the week of Thanksgiving. Everything was put up in a hurry. We had made the jump from Wichita, Kansas. Some jump! The icy roads slowed down the motorized caravan of trucks; they were late getting in—the elephants never made it till the next day of the opening. We blew the matinee; trucks arrived about 4:00 PM. Everybody went to work unloading the material, which three hours later was a circus.

This was my first appearance in the Mosque, and I had to get my bearings. Measuring, calculating, I found it rather low for the distance, to get a good pitch for the slide. The ceiling was beautifully decorated; no way of breaking through the plaster to find a beam. The only thing to do was to build a jack, tie the cable to a four-by-six, and jack it up against the ceiling through an open door in the gallery. Obstacles, always! There were fire department laws to observe—can't block an exit. One had to be a genius to invent contraptions to meet all situations. And you couldn't scratch or leave any marks on some of those fancy places.

Well, I got the slide up and thought it was quite a feat accomplished in the short time. "Tomorrow I shall rig up number one," I planned. It was 7:00

PM, and I heard that assistant manager call: "Doors open!" which meant, "Everybody clear out; the public is arriving!" "Doors open!" echoed through the auditorium again, this time—I knew—for my benefit. I was just gathering up odds and ends—some pieces of rope, a drop line, clamps, wrench. I picked up everything and hurried out. I hadn't even found out where the dressing rooms were located. Waiting tensely since my arrival that morning for the trucks to get in, I dared not leave the building, not even to get a cup of coffee—anyway, I felt no hunger. At times like these, nature's functions cease; the rigging is the paramount thing, nothing else matters—"The show must go on!"

Rushing out toward the back end, dodging clown props and whatnot, I tripped over a heavy cable stretched across the corridor, which I hadn't seen in the semidarkness. Just as I was about to explode with a few choice remarks on the carelessness of whoever left such a dangerous obstacle in the way without a warning sign, I saw Billeti, the owner of the cable, groping in the darkness with turnbuckles and beams, anchoring his high wire in the hallway. He was late with his rigging, too.

Billeti and I felt a comradeship for one another, if only for the one thing we had in common: rigging problems. (By the way, how did he manage to get permission for drilling through the walls to pull his wire through?)

In order to get to my rigging box, I had to go around the string of horses Carlos had already brought in and roped off. One of my bags containing hanging wire and ropes was almost under the horses' hoofs. This, too, ruffled me. My rigging—any part of it—was sacred to me. But space was scant— besides, I was fond of Carlos. (Could it be that I even harbored a secret love for him because he resembled Rudolfo Valentino so much when in the ring, putting those beautiful black stallions through their paces?) Cautiously, I pulled the bag away and stacked all the pieces of equipment on top of each other—this way, they were less likely to be trampled or sat upon by the performers and others standing around or waiting to go on.

I looked around for the callboard to see the dressing-room list, wondering whom I was laid out with—it always irked me to share the room with anyone who smoked. I can't stand the smell of stale smoky odor in hair or clothes. Whenever it happened to be my misfortune to be dressing in one large room with all the other women, I kept my costumes in my trunk all week, pulling out one at a time, just before putting it on. Such was the case this time. The list read:

Ladies:	Right side, downstairs
Men:	Left side, downstairs

| Clowns: | #1, Stage floor |
| Castang's chimpanzees: | #2, Stage floor |

The chimps always get a private dressing room. Not that they'd object dressing with anyone, but they occupy the room, day and night, an attendant constantly with them. He prepares their meals—they are really vegetarians, but they also get meat substance in the broth he cooks for them. They are especially fond of rice pudding and custard.

To further clear up confusion in the dressing room list: yes, clowns are *men* also, and hard-working men.[4] They have many quick changes; hence, the dressing room close by. Some of their gags are so bulky—those shoes simulating large bare feet, for instance—they couldn't run up or down stairs with them. It is done with a purpose for the good of the show. Clowns are the backbone of a circus; underrated, they're the unsung heroes. If an act is dull, there's always a Joey around somewhere to amuse you. (The name Joey originates from Joe Grimaldi, who in the middle 1850s created the character we know as the clown today.)[5] Who covers up those gaps while striking the big cage or setting up the net for the flying act? And when someone gets hurt, who keeps the show going, ad-libbing? Right, these zanies, of course. It requires ingenuity to be a clown, and though there are a number of old gags and entries used repeatedly, such as the Wedding, the Fire Department, Boxing-bout, and others, there's never a new fad or current event that escapes his burlesque. Watch that Walk Around! It will bring you up-to-date with what's happening in the world today. You will appreciate his quick wit and creative ability. Hurrah! And a big hand for the clown.

When I got in the dressing room, all the places were taken. No reserved seats here. First comers grabbed the choice spots: where the light was brightest, where there was a mirror (we all carried mirrors in the makeup box, but it was nice to have an extra one), and near a clothes rack, if it happened to be the only one there. Mark off the space desired with your name, spread a towel across the table or shelf, lay out the glamorizing gadgets, and it meant, "Keep off, I staked this out. Find your own place!"

In these large dressing rooms, there usually are long tables with benches such as seen at picnic grounds. Sometimes there are no seats at all, and you have to scout around to find one—maybe in the next room. You take it; it's okay as long as it isn't tipped downward against the table, which is already covered and reserved by someone else. As a last resort, you open the lid of your trunk and sit on part of it, using the other part to spread out your makeup; you can't expect luxuries and comfort when trouping—even in these modern times.

There may be a washbasin right in the room. And I have seen instances where the hot water faucet worked too. Oh, boy! Was that cozy! But you can always wash up outside in the lavatory.

I pulled up my trunk close to the edge of the long table, opened it, took out my makeup box, and pushed it ever so gently against the other girl's spread. After all, I've got a right to some space, even if I did come in late. I was the only one in there putting up my own rigging; the others were either married, their husbands attending to it, or they worked in a troupe with the male members or a private propertyman doing that work. They had no worry outside the dressing room. It was very unusual for a woman to do rigging—seldom seen. The show management carried a gang of regular riggers and propertymen to do, or assist in, the setting up.

The first day in a new place, everybody is cross, acting like total strangers, though it was only yesterday in the last town that we were one happy family. Anyway, on opening day there's no time for sociability. Everybody is tense, going about with a chip on the shoulder. Tomorrow comes, and we are all congenial again.

"My, here we are," I thought, "established feature acts, every one of us, yet we behave no differently from the fresh, young chorister in our selfishness and lack of consideration for the other." In the chorus, however, one gets a break, for there is the wardrobe woman; she presides over the girls' dressing room. Everyone gets impartial treatment—no preference to first arrivals under her ruling.

I spoke not a word, and no one seemed even to notice me. My face and hands were black with the muck and grime I collected from my own rigging and in the junk-room while picking out some lumber for the jack in the gallery. At this moment, I heard my name called from the stairway. It was Mr. I. J. himself, and from the tone of his voice he meant business—serious business. I reached for my robe, slipping it on as I crossed the dressing room on my way out, fairly flying up the stairs.

"Where is your rigging?" he demanded, referring to act number one. "There was no time to set it up," I replied quite earnestly. This enraged him all the more, possibly because he realized I was within my rights.

"I won't let any of my performers run my show!" he stormed. "That rigging goes up right now! I pay men here to do it. They put up the others' riggings—why can't they set up yours?" he fairly shouted at me. And he knew well enough why *not* mine. Still, I patiently explained the tricky angle of it.

I should explain that in most places, we worked in the center of the building with the seats all around us, but some auditoriums follow the theater plan and have a stage large enough for the presentation. The Mosque was one of these—a very modern stage, I may add, with counterweight system for the battens (those long rods or pipes on which scenery, drapes, and border lights are hung; in many cases, they serve for holding props in the air). In a pinch, even a trapeze can be hung on a batten, provided it is just for a simple, posing routine with no swinging action. These battens hang from the grid floor up above by thin cables which run through sheaves, counterweighted to balance the batten and its load for lowering and ascending. Any aerial act with some punch in it, however, has to be hung directly from the girders on the grid floor above the stage. The height of these vary from sixty to a hundred feet, so that an asbestos curtain, film-screen, or anything not in use at any time is completely out of sight when pulled up in the loft. A crane-bar is hung from the grid by two wires and is made stationary by four guylines (probably a derivative from "guidelines"), which are fastened to the stage floor. From this crane-bar then is hung the trapeze-bar, rings, or such equipment as the artist uses in his or her particular specialty.

"What's the matter with your rings, then?" he went on. "Why can't you hang them from a batten?" He was calmer now. "Just do the ring routine and finish with the swivel. I'll have them hold the curtain till you get it set." He looked at his watch as he said, "It shouldn't take long."

The last phrase sounded more like a request than a command. Mr. I. J. knew every technicality of the business out front as well as backstage. I had great respect for his shrewdness and showmanship. It was opening night, and he wanted to give 'em everything he had—the success of the week's business hung by the criticism of this audience as well as the press. It's got to have that sock!

So without further ado, I rushed to my rigging pile, tore down the pyramid of bags and things I had stacked up minutes before, and took from each what I needed. Out came the rings and swivel-mouthpiece from the rigging box, three shackles from the tool kit in a smaller box, an ascension rope from one bag, and four pieces of sash cord from another. I signaled to the man on the fly-floor, a regular stage employee of the Mosque—his job was flying the battens. I pointed to the one I wanted him to let down on the stage.

With the sash cord, I lashed the ascension rope and three shackles to the batten, taking several wraps so they wouldn't slide out of place, hooked the rings in the two outer shackles, the swivel in the center shackle, and signaled the fly-man to take it away.

"Hold it!" I yelled as it reached the borders. Just a slight lift on the reverse rope, and it stopped. He put the safety brake on, and there it was. How simple! Since this act was the first on the program, it could be left right there in place—all set for the show. The whole rigging took about ten minutes.

As I stacked up the pieces again, I could hear Carsey's band playing the overture, and knew I had less than twenty minutes to be all dressed and ready.

Three aerial acts worked at one and the same time. All of us started and (since I wasn't doing the breakaway) finished together at this show. No fanfare, no announcement. "Gosh, it was flat—wonder if the audience felt that way about it, too?" I pondered.

As we all left the stage together I felt so inferior I didn't even look at the others. My pride was crushed at the thought that *I* should do a hokum, mediocre turn—a "chambermaid's frolic," as they used to call it. "Well, I did it in a spirit of cooperation, for the good of the show," I consoled myself.

The slide in the second part of the show went off without a hitch. Still annoyed over the incident of the first act, I could hardly wait for tomorrow to come to set things right and redeem myself with that punch finish.

On the job bright and early the next morning, I soon came to the conclusion that there was no place to put up the two crane-bars I used. Bobbie's flying act took up all the room up-stage; Teresita's trap was in mid-center; down front were a double trapeze, a cloud-swing, and a couple of web acts, interspersed with several borders—some holding lights, others, the fringe trim that is part of the scenery; they form the ceiling effect from out front.[6]

There was no use attempting to squeeze in; it would get all fouled up when they go to strike it. Besides, I'd have to kill that cloud-swing—I wondered if Carolyn's husband would mind moving it downstage a few feet. No, that's out, I answered my own question. No space to guy out properly—and she's too crabby to work on a loose rigging, especially for my benefit. I finally decided to use the same batten as the night before and put the break on it, using guylines to keep it steady. I'd used this solution in vaudeville, and it had worked. I promptly got out all the things necessary and waited for the stagehands to arrive, since no one else can touch the switchboard or battens. It was going to be so easy.

The men came, and the batten was lowered. I measured out the distance from the rings to where the breakaway should go and adjusted the length of the wire to suit the space between. The upper end was lashed to the batten, and guylines were attached. The only way I could get the vertical trim was to have the flyman take it up for the test, with the wire hanging down. I measured the height from the mouthpiece down, allowing the tape measure to touch the floor on sixty-eight inches: my feet pointing downward add five inches to my height, leaving a two-inch clearance to the floor. I wasn't concerned over the strength of the cable holding the batten—any drape outweighs my 105 pounds.

"Okay! Mark it and let 'er in again!" I shouted. This time I fixed the wire with the mouthpiece by the rings. Now he took it up for the last time. "Watch for that mark!" I warned him. "It must be tied off exactly on the mark, and be *sure it is tied off good!*"[7] I concluded my direction with marked emphasis on the last six words, confident he'd understand the importance of the detail.

"Yeah—*sure it is tied off good!*" He repeated this last line after me in a tone as if mocking me, which I ignored. I was quite accustomed to this occasional lack of respect from a workman who sees me for the first time—in overalls, like any rigger—and my pocketsize doesn't add much to my importance, either. But at this time, what mattered? It was the show and the first performance at each stand. After that first show, things would adjust themselves automatically.

I finished the groundwork, finding places to secure the guylines and checking that they all pulled even. That was that.

Then came the matinee. I was all set to do a good act. There were some old-timers visiting backstage. "They'll see how I can strut my stuff," I thought. I climbed up very smugly and went into my routine with a half somersault back, dropping into a hand and foot, when I felt the whole works shake and quiver as though being rocked in a boat by huge waves. I had expected it to wobble—it is impossible for four little guylines to keep a seventy-five-foot bar steady—but not like this.

"Oh, well, what the heck? So it wobbles now with the ring act—what will it do in the breakaway, especially at the end of the drop? But I shall be close to 'terra firma' by then!" This was going through my mind as I almost mechanically continued my routine without a pause.

After the iron-jaw spin, I took a leg-wrap on the ascension rope and paused for a bow, while the master of ceremonies announced: "Watch her!"

Always there's a hush as the music stops—"Well, here goes: the climax!" With sly glee, that mischievous joy of anticipation of the awe and surprise in store for those people out there that I always felt just before this last trick, I reached out for the mouthpiece on the end of the wire, clamped my teeth on, and let go of the rope.

"What in heaven's name?" I thought, when instead of the break there came a violent quake accompanied by sound effects like thunder—the world coming to an end. And instead of plunging downward, I remained suspended in the air.

When hanging by one's teeth, the head is tilted back, giving only an upward view. I couldn't see what was going on below or about me. All I saw were the border lights suddenly fused in one long streak of lightning—with everything in the loft in motion—a wild rhapsody of counter-tempo. Every hanging object—from cyc [cyclorama] to proscenium arch—was swinging haywire, giving me the effect of dizziness.

In this tense moment I did a mental check-back to the rigging. "Where did I slip up?" The gimmick hadn't parted as it should have—that is, not immediately. Then it broke! I could feel that sickening little snap in the back of my neck—the sting in my eyes, nose, and ears; just like always—when it breaks away from above.

"Okay, now," flashed through my brain as I braced myself for the big jolt on the drop (like an uppercut in boxing) to the jaw and neck—yes! It broke loose at last, and so did the tie-off on the batten, which the flyman had assured me was good. I dropped through space.

My feet didn't clear the floor that time.

I was down on my knees when I regained my presence of mind, still hanging on to the mouthpiece on a slack wire. The batten must have slipped down about three feet from the mark, I judged. Then I remembered I was still before my audience. I tried to recuperate my poise quickly—to cover up this undignified display of clumsiness, this most awkward situation for an aerialist—to descend other than on tiptoe. Taking hold of the wire with my hand and releasing my bite on the mouthpiece at the same time, I pulled myself to my feet. The stage was still mine, so I took a feeble bow, meekly— mortified and in humiliation I started to leave the scene. It just couldn't be soon enough; this was one time when I wished there had been a trapdoor under me so I could have fallen through the floor. But alas! Letting go my hold on the wire, I collapsed. My feet—what happened to my feet?

The clowns, standing by as always, rushed on with their happy capers and falsetto voices ringing out. I knew I was covered. Billeti picked me up and carried me downstairs to the dressing room. I could hear the master of ceremonies announcing the next act, and the show went on.

I tried to stand on my feet, but they were powerless; they didn't pain much but caused me nausea. There was quite a commotion. Everybody wanted to help—each had a different formula: "Walk, keep walking!" said one, as she was holding me up under my arms. "Keep her off her feet," said another.

Mrs. I. J., who was out front and saw the incident, rushed for her first-aid kit and took over—hot water, cold water, liniment, massage. Somehow I had always felt a great affection for her—the big boss's wife; she was so sweet, so attentive with everybody.

My feet were puffing up like balloons by now—the left one, with abrasion of the skin, was turning dark. "Put her shoes on!" said Gwen, who worked the elephants. "When Mona stepped on my foot, I kept my shoe on all week, till it didn't swell any more." The Olvera girls started to put my makeup away. "Hold it!" I said. "Not so fast—I've got to make the slide yet." I pulled out another change of costume from my trunk—I couldn't get any pumps over my feet.

It was intermission now. Mrs. I. J. got a doctor who happened to be out front watching the show. He just took a look at my feet and recommended I go to his office for x-rays, which revealed a compound fracture of the first and second metatarsals of the left foot, and a simple fracture of the second metatarsal of the right. He gave me the name of the hospital where I was to go to have a cast put on. A *cast?* Oh, no! This came as quite a shock to me. Then I wondered what kind of a doctor he was that he, himself, couldn't put it on. Heaven only knows the effort it is to get around so handicapped. I called a cab and got to the hospital.

In the emergency room, after reading the contents of the envelope, the young intern examined my injured feet. Even as he did so, I couldn't help noticing the sportive glint in his eyes and the mischievous smile on his lips.

"High or low heel?" he quipped as he set about to encase my left foot in a plaster cast.

"What a morbid sense of humor!" I thought, to be making a joke of a situation that to me was a tragedy. But after reflecting on the general public's concept of people in my profession, I understood and wasn't vexed. My case history stated not only my name and injury sustained in the accident but my occupation as well: circus performer. The word "circus" is at once associated with clowns and merriment, which instinctively brought out the little boy in this future eminence of surgery.

When he finished the pasting, I had a nice knee-high boot with the fashionable open toe, a metal brace forming the heel. The right foot bandaged up tightly with adhesive tape matched up well with the left. The price: five dollars for cast, one dollar for bandage. "Not bad," I thought, as he helped me off the table, but I found that I was completely helpless. A cab drove me back to the hotel where I was taken upstairs by the clerk.

The next day I could hobble along with the aid of a crutch. I knew it was a six-week vacation forced upon me by fate.

It was a sorry sight I presented there in the Mosque on Thanksgiving Day, packing away my belongings. The men had taken everything down the day following the mishap. There it lay in a heap, offstage. I coiled up the wires and ropes and tied up loose ends, checking everything off by memory as I packed. All this was done in a sitting position, with the cast-foot extended. I had no definite plans, but for the time being I'd have to remain in Peoria. The show was scheduled for Oklahoma City next. The time was getting close to the matinee; although I had started early in the morning, there was still a lot to be done—a slow and painful procedure, to be sure, having to rest my arms ever so often. That stationary position tired me so, cramping my legs and my back.

The performers started straggling in, singly and in groups. They all came over to talk to me, lamenting my plight. Then they hurried down to the dressing rooms, chitchatting, discussing the usual topics on the way. Mrs. I. J., hearing I was there, came backstage. She spoke softly, so optimistically—up until then my morale held up pretty well, but now I began to break and to feel sorry for myself. The bubble exploded when she asked me to be her guest for dinner that night.

Mr. I. J. had gone on to Oklahoma City to look over the promotion (advance business). "We'll dine at the Pere Marquette, just the two of us, and forget the show," she comforted me. Giving me a gentle pat on the shoulder, she added: "You be dressed and wait back here. My chauffeur will pick you up at six."

I looked down to my crippled feet, the tears welling in my eyes.

As the week passed—on Friday, to be exact—the doctor made inquiries as to my financial status. When told at the box office that *I* would be the one to know that best, he sent for me. Without interest as to my condition, he asked me if I had any insurance or compensation. On hearing me say no on both counts, he seemed quite concerned as to who would pay his fee. When I asked him how much it was—that I would pay it—he replied, "fifty-five dollars." Fifty-five dollars for reading x-rays? Outrageous! He hadn't laid a hand to my anatomy. I promptly paid the amount and demanded a receipt. In my eyes, this man of exalted profession suddenly assumed a character of a grifter in a gyp-joint. I didn't trust him.

But the episode didn't end here! A year later, playing a return engagement there (this time with better luck; I did my own tie-off), when Mr. Stern paid my salary for the week, he deducted twenty dollars, handing me a receipt which read: "Received: $20.00 for x-rays" (signed by the same medico). I was furious and amused at the same time; he outsmarted me after all, even if it took a year to do it: in the fifty-five-dollar receipt of the previous year no mention of x-ray had been made.

The preceding is but one of a score or more of harrowing experiences—mishaps—that have occurred to me from time to time, despite all the precaution taken to prevent them; always at my own risk, they have been costly to me, both physically and financially.

Taking the optimistic viewpoint of the whole, I consoled myself that it could have been worse, as, for instance, that other accident occurring to me some years previous, in Hartford, Connecticut, in which I broke my jaw. That was truly a catastrophe to me, who earns my livelihood by my jaw. That I shall cover with other events that come under the untoward sign of the Jinx.

On his return, Mr. I. J. insisted on taking me along with the show. "I'll only be excess baggage," I pleaded. Taking his offer as a gesture of kindness, I couldn't accept. But he spoke business this time; his faith in the performers being supermen and superwomen couldn't be daunted. "The doctor said I can't work for six weeks," I argued. "Poppycock!" he exclaimed. "What does he know about it?"

Somehow he assumed that we aerialists, defying the laws of gravity, just couldn't remain grounded any length of time. He was right. The following week, in Springfield, Missouri, I did the slide while dressed as a comique character in an old-fashioned costume with long, lacy pantaloons. The cynical old bromide "funny as a crutch" was just that, as I hobbled out on stage and stepped into the sling which carried me across the auditorium over the heads of the spectators. Halfway in my ascent, I turned upside down and hung from a foot-loop. The people laughed, believing the cast was part of the makeup, little suspecting that under that plaster shell, broken bones were in the process of knitting.

So went the rush-rush-rush of my existence—the cycle of incidents—that has been my life since. And just as every road must come to a turning, there had to be a break to this grind sometime soon; and the more I thought of it, the firmer my decision became that it had to be be now—while I could beat fate to it and make my own. So this was it! The turning point in my career, you may say.

Earlier that night, I casually told a few people in the dressing room that I was leaving, but none took me seriously—show people are forever talking of quitting when dispirited. Not even I could believe that that night was to be my last show.

How strange it all seemed as I sat there, outside the back entrance to the auditorium, first on the rigging box, then on the toolbox, jumping up at the sound of every passing vehicle, waiting for the expressman to come and pick up my gear. The show trucks with everything loaded immediately after the last night's performance were all gone, and all the private trailers and cars of the performers were likewise gone—on their way to the next spot. How deserted and dead the terrain appeared. I felt so alone—like an orphan, stranded with no place to go. Yet I was impatient, in a hurry to go—somewhere, anywhere—but get going. It must have been the heat of the midday sun beating down on me that gave me those heebie-jeebies. I had closed with shows before and didn't need a compass to get my bearings. The man came at last and filled out the bill of lading in triplicate forms, giving me a copy:

1 Trunk
2 Boxes
1 Reel Wire Rope
1 Bundle of Pipes
2 Bags Manila Rope
     Destination: Los Angeles

Later, as I examined the itemized slip, the reference to my uprights as pipes instead of bars irritated me. It shouldn't have mattered, but it did.

AS MRS. PRIVATE CITIZEN, VIEWING THE PARADE

I entered an entirely new phase in life—that of settling down and living like those people I used to envy when going through a residential section of a town. Only those who have gone through the extreme emotions of anxiety—buildup and let-down—of house hunting could, more or less, understand; getting all enthused over a prospect today, then finding great obstacles tomorrow. It is odd, when you have never owned any property—you look for something that only exists in your imagination, a picture that you have been dreaming of and building up for years, sort of a castle in the air.

You pass up something solid and practical and get all worked up over a flimsy shell because it offers possibilities of remodeling. All my life I had been dreaming of owning some ground, working in the soil, growing trees, shrubs, flowers—yes, even vegetables. A little house with sunken bathtub all my own. It was an illusion—the great incentive that carried me through all the struggles, over those rough roads I traveled for so long. "How wonderful to plant seed and watch it grow!" I mused while in one of those trances, gazing into the future.

I finally acquired that piece of land which fate willed. (It must have been fate, because it was far from what I originally had my mind set on.)

But the housing shortage was acute, and real estate was soaring by leaps and bounds—within a few weeks the value doubled. I grabbed at the first likely opportunity, because the house looked nice on the surface.

How gullible I was only dawned on me too late—what did I know about cracks along the foundation or in the walls, especially when covered with a new coat of Bondex? And what about termites? Who would suspect that those poplar trees out front—so graceful with those whispering leaves—could be such a menace and were even now undermining the plumbing and cracking the cement driveway with their powerful roots? Who anticipated the mess those leaves would make when they began falling? The lawn looked so fresh—greener than all the others. The boxwood hedge around the house was so lush. The dainty white fence, separating the garden from the backyard; a peach tree just loaded with fruit; and a boysenberry bush. "This is it!" I whispered to the agent as I got him off to one side from the owner, who couldn't help smiling at my enthusiasm—and we closed the deal.

It wasn't long before I found out that I was shortchanged on more than one item in the transaction—not only in the improvement end but the soil, alas! The one thing I hoped would bring me joy turned out to be the biggest flop—heavy, black clay; adobe, they call it. What a disappointment! It requires all the physical strength I had built up through the years of gymnastic work to dig into and turn over. When moist, it adheres to the tools; when dry, it takes a pickaxe to break it up.

But I tried to console myself by counting the redeeming features to offset the bad points. It is, after all, situated in a quiet, single-family residential zone. Nice neighbors are on either side of me—people who love their home. Sooner or later, you get to know everybody on the block—biding the time of day when passing by or exchanging pleasantries while tending the lawn. There are the Cornings, the Boones, and the Ramseys; what fine people! Indeed, it was Mrs. Ramsey who came to my house on that first Christmas Eve, fours years ago, bringing a gift package of homemade cookies and a jar of apricot preserves. From then on I knew they accepted me as a worthy member of the community. Seeing me working about the place—repairing, painting, landscaping (chores essential to upkeep)—they asked no further questions. To them I am just another resident. Now, come to think of it, there isn't any difference between show people and folks in private life—when you subtract the show.

I like to parley especially with my good neighbor, Naomi, over the back fence. She lives in Los Angeles; I live in Inglewood—the dividing line of city limits runs between us. Inglewood is the continuation of Los Angeles, a suburb popular with sport fans for its beautiful country club, its vast golf course, and the race track, of course—but why they call it Hollywood Race Track I shall never guess, unless to give it glamor. Hollywood is northwest, while Inglewood is definitely southwest of the Los Angeles business and civic center. Worthy of mention is the airport terminal built in Inglewood just recently, the helpful and courteous attendants in the Morningside branch library, and genial Mr. Leftwich in City Hall, whose counsel shoos one's troubles away.

Inglewood's fame, however, is due largely to its cemetery. "Inglewood Park Cemetery, Largest Cemetery in California," the sign reads. I have gone past this cemetery any number of times by bus along Manchester Boulevard and by electric car on Florence Avenue while in transit to the township of Inglewood, but not till the other day did I make a special trip directly to the cemetery to look up a certain grave, marked by a memorial as famous today as the two principal characters whose names are headlined thereon were headlined in life, yesterday. This I learned when, on arriving at the beautiful fountain-flanked gate at the Redondo Boulevard entrance, I inquired of one of the gardeners working nearby if he knew the location of this tomb. Indeed, on the mere mention of the name, he at once directed me to the spot. This original design, conceived by the surviving mate who was to join her in death about six years later by taking his own life while still in his prime, is oddly enough titled "Reunited."

As I gaze in awe at the beauty of lines of the figures in the statue, I am overpowered; they actually live on that pedestal before me. Having known them both so intimately, I can see them alive. How adequate, befitting, this monument—how dignified, yet there it is. Suddenly I see that human frailty—call it conceit, call it vanity—so characteristic in show people, irrespective of sex, asserting itself even at this time of deep sorrow and bereavement. I can see it all too clearly. Professional jealousy: it has no bounds, knows no chivalry. Only producers know the headache of having two stars of equal category in the same show of either or both sexes, each clamoring for his or her name to appear in primary order, topping the list on the program and billing. No gallantry is shown here; that strife for glory is consuming. Glory supersedes family ties, even romance—most powerful of all human emotions, with show people at any rate.

I know a number of fellow artists who have taken a cut in salary in preference to second-rate billing (agents sometimes talk). In this profession, at least, the ambition for fame eclipses that for riches, and here it is, even unto death: depicting himself as the male angel with huge wings extended, his arms about her waist, holding her to him; her arms are twined around his neck—their lips almost in a kiss, she without wings. Thus embraced, both seem to be floating in midair under his wing power. This bigger-than-life-sized statuary of the two is mounted atop an eight-foot-high monument serving as base, which bears the inscription engraved in the marble: "In Everlasting Memory of My Beloved, Leitzel Codona, Copenhagen, Denmark, February 15, 1931. Erected by her devoted husband Alfredo Codona."

And here again the ego—that competition for top billing. She was never known by any other name but Leitzel, which served as first as well as surname. In fact, the announcer, when presenting her to the public—to make it sound impressive—would add the name Lillian thus: Lillian Leitzel. The surname Codona, inscribed on the same line with Leitzel, seems out of place here somehow. There would have been far more tenderness and sincerity of devotion expressed had the name been left just Leitzel, as she was known to the world. This is especially apparent since the text clearly indicates their relationship with his full name.

On either side of the monument, a bench is attached, almost as if carved out of the same block of marble; then at the foot in front of the monument, a two-by-seven-foot slab covers the actual grave of Alfredo, whose mortal remains rest there. Leitzel's body was cremated abroad; her ashes are guarded in a niche inside the monument. At the head of the marble slab on the ground, the design engraved depicts a flying trapeze. Directly below this, inserted in the stone, is an oval-shaped bronze frame in the form of a king-sized locket, the face of which may be opened, showing a picture of Alfredo in watercolors. This memorial is so distinctive, in fact, as I found out later, in the office, that it is highlighted among the attractions of the cemetery in the exploitation or publicity department. I reflected then that these two get feature billing postmortem.

I also noticed a discrepancy in the spelling of the name: Leitzel, with the "i" preceding the "e." However, this could be the engraver's error. The name Leitzel is a derivative from Lillie. Her mother called her Liezel in German—pronounced "Leetsel" (hence, the name Leitzel), a sort of pet or nickname. Her mother coached her. She worked on rings and, owing to a peculiar physical phenomenon (top-heavy, one might say), she could perform feats of strength excelling any ever having been attempted by other aerial gymnasts, barring none. She had an extra-large head and shoulders, out of proportion with the rest of her body, which from there tapered down to almost child's size. Her shoes, smaller than size one, had to be made to order. Her height was four-foot, eight-inches, in her working pumps, but over these she always wore extra high-heeled mules, going in and out of the arena. With the advantage of head and shoulders overbalancing the rest of her anatomy, she developed a trick of hanging by one hand—her wrist locked in a rope-loop, taking all the punishment. She would throw her head back, thrust her feet in continuous aerial back-somersaults, doing dislocations of the supporting arm at each turnover; she did about fifty revolutions at every performance. They were perfect—just like a windmill, over and over without any seeming effort.[1]

Lifting my gaze upward again to the monument just above the cornice, I could see—chiseled in the marble—a half-circus simulating a proscenium arch, under which the design shows a pair of rings such as she used in her incomparable work, with one of the rings broken, symbolizing her tragic end. The accident occurred on a Friday, February 13, while she was filling an engagement in Copenhagen, Denmark. Alfredo, with his troupe, was in the Winter Garten, Berlin, at the time. On receiving the news, he flew to her side on the next day. He found her still alive, but the spinal injury suffered in the forty-foot fall paralyzed her almost from the neck down. She told him not to worry—to go back and fill his engagement—she'd be all right. He left. She died the following day—on February 15, 1931.[2]

Just below the trapeze theme, I noticed several bronze plaques around the monument, four on each side, five across the front, which, from left to right, are from Aunt Tina, using the colorful salesman's line, "To the One and Only Leitzel." Next in order as the plaques are arranged: from Bill and Victoria; from Leitzel's mother, "To my beloved and only daughter"; then one reads, "To our beloved Muñequita, Dad and Mother Codona" (Muñequita is Spanish for little doll). The fifth one: "Loving memory darling Leitzel, Mabel." Mabel, Mabel, I kept repeating the name as I turned to leave.

A FLIGHT ON
GOSSAMER WINGS

The year was 1916, about mid-March; the show was *Hip-Hip-Hurray* at the New York Hippodrome.[1] A thinning down in the cast for the extension of the season was in progress. All the members in the last scene—"A Frolic at St. Moritz," starring Charlotte—were held for rehearsal after the night performance.[2] Because the ice was still uncovered, it saved time and work for the crew in charge of the refrigeration; replacing and lifting up again those boxlike sections of double flooring—covering an area of about sixty by one hundred feet—involved quite a lot of labor. Besides, the mornings were given to rehearsing the other scenes in the show. In addition to the specialty skaters, there were ski jumpers and the German Ice Ballet—imported especially for this production. I was one of the forty-eight girls of the regular corps de ballet of the Hippodrome cast, used in this last scene as filler or atmosphere. When Mr. Burnside, while producing the show, first called for this selected "forty-eight" who could skate, few were enthused, since it meant forty-five minutes longer in the show at each performance; most girls were anxious to rush out to meet their dates, others to get home to their families—husband and children—maybe.

The Hippodrome show was the first I have known where youth was of no consequence in the chorus—three generations danced side by side if they matched up in size. The building could change owners, new management—Dillingham taking over from the Shuberts—but these gals went on forever. They were part of the deal, a fixture. As long as R. H. Burnside was the director of the production, they were sure of their jobs.[3] Having rehearsed so many shows under his direction, they almost anticipated his next move, were never surprised, and were ready for every new trick he may pull out of his sleeve. He could be sarcastic at times, but they loved him as a father—more, they idolized him.

To newcomers like myself, the *Hip* was not just a show—not like any I have ever been with. It was an institution. It was like working in a shop with two shows, six days a week, and Sundays off. I thought it would become monotonous—no travel, change of theater, dressing room, or hotel—just stay put. Outsiders in line-ranks called it "The Old Chorus Girls' Home."[4] Getting beyond that certain youth, when managers turn you down, "Go to the Hippodrome!" was their slogan. Of course, I don't know what happened once they got there; the channel through which I came to be a member was a letter of introduction from Fred Stone to Charles B. Dillingham.[5] Stone and his late partner, Dave Montgomery, had starred in 1915 at the Globe Theater in Dillingham's production, *Chin-Chin*.[6]

I was quite surprised that Mr. Dillingham should see me himself, but a letter from his pet star must have been the trick. My, but he was a handsome man, the type that models clothes for *Esquire,* his prematurely gray hair and mustache adding dignity to his appearance—truly the man of distinction personified (minus the glass in hand).

On being interviewed regarding experience, I recounted to him briefly my former activities, stating my dancing ability. I had polished up on toe work during that spring, under the coaching of Mademoiselle Maria Bonfanti, the dean of ballet. Each lesson had augmented my ambition and hope that someday my name would be on that marquee over the Palace Theater, which I passed just before climbing the stoop to Mademoiselle's studio, right next to the Palace. As my forte, however, I stressed on the Oriental dance specialty I had done with burlesque shows and in a sideshow of an outdoor outfit, a Wild West show. While he listened politely, he didn't seem much impressed; evidently there was nothing about me indicating star material—not even a minor principal element, as I soon found out when he referred me to his casting department and I signed up for . . . but that you already know.

And even for this lousy job in the merry-merry I was required to fill out a questionnaire, listing qualifications such as: Drive a car; swim; ride a bicycle;

dive; ice or roller skate; ride horseback, plus the usual requirement of quality and range of voice. Dancing—the basic one—was accepted for granted.

On reading the contract, I could see it was for the coming attraction in the Hip, which was going in rehearsal within a few days.

We rehearsed for about five weeks in the Thirty-third Street Armory, during which time the Hippodrome stage was being prepared for the show. In place of the large tank under the floor, mechanics were now installing the refrigeration for the ice skating, which was to be the new feature under the Dillingham management, replacing the water-scene of season after season of the Shuberts' reign. Scenic artists and carpenters also had to finish their work before we could come in, then two more weeks of rehearsal in the Hip with props, costumes, and scenery, a couple of full-dress rehearsals with lights and orchestra (instead of the lone piano we'd been given as musical accompaniment during the building of the show), and *Hip-Hip-Hurray* opened, a blazing, glorious success!

The salary in the chorus ranks: eighteen dollars per week, minimum. However, each number requiring extra effort besides singing and dancing paid an extra premium, from two to five dollars. For example, in the "Ladder of Roses" number, for climbing up the ladder, two dollars per week. It was a cinch to pull down a fairly good weekly wage. Sixteen ladders suspended from a batten comprised the huge drop, which was decorated with screens supporting garlands of roses in between the ladders, thus creating the effect of a mammoth trellis with flowers in bloom. Six girls were assigned to each ladder; on the music cue they started climbing on all sixteen in tempo until they stood five-high on the rungs. The sixth girl on the bottom completed the picture. My place was on the bottom rung, while the other five climbed up. No climbing, no money. I realized then what seniority signified. I was new, not one of the regular gang. Somebody had to stand at the bottom; anyway, there were fifteen others. Of some of the paying numbers I was left out altogether. Mr. Burnside said I was too small, yet he put in Jean Hoppe, who was smaller than I. What about Sylvia Diamond, whom I suspected to be a midget, but she worked in all the lucrative numbers? It wasn't fair, I thought, that he'd give the old girls the preference always. Some of them had worked there since the very first presentation rehearsal in the building even before Frederick Thompson had it completed. The girls often spoke of that rehearsal without a roof over their heads, how Thompson almost lost his bet had he not finished it in time for the scheduled debut.

A colorful figure, a wizard in designing and building novelties, Frederick Thompson contributed much to the amusement world. He married one of the famous Taliaferro sisters. He was the pioneer builder of the roller coasters. A brilliant architect, engineer, and artist, he was responsible for "Toyland" at the World's Fair held in San Francisco in 1915. An artistic success, it ruined him financially. And his health and money vanished together so that a benefit show had to be staged in order to raise funds to cover hospital and other personal debts. Show folks from all branches paid him high tribute at his death.[7]

But to return to the forty-eight girls who wished to work in the ice scene, I was among the first to concur. "Why not?" I asked myself. "I have no outside interest!" Besides, I liked to skate, and the five dollars extra it paid was an inducement I could hardly pass up. Still, these rehearsals in midseason were getting me down. After all, I knew my part—all forty-eight of us did, for that matter. Our contribution to the scene was ad-libbing in the background till the finale, when we formed circles as in "Ring-around-Rosie," going round and round, lending action to the curtain, which, on closing, ascended from below.

Waiting around with nothing to do was tiresome and boring, but worse yet was having to get up early in the morning for a week, a standing call daily for 9:30 "in practice-clothes on stage," according to the call board. "Sure be glad when we are set once again with no more rehearsals," I meditated, watching the endless session of the specialty skaters going over the routines, which likewise became boring with the show's run, as did the entire show. The musical numbers were left practically intact; the trimming down affected only some of the principals. Nevertheless, we had to be there to see if, by cutting on the lines and specialties, we could still make the changes of costumes. Those wardrobe women and dressers certainly had their hands full, though we all helped by forming a line hooking each other's dresses. With the system used in a big production—every girl with the same time allotted—there is no excuse for missing or being late: if some can make it, they all can. It is regimentation. There were ninety-six of us in a dressing room, one dresser to twenty-four girls. But if the changes were intricate, the wardrobe women in charge of mending, cleaning, and general upkeep of the apparel would jump in and give a helping hand.

The management owned all the costumes and accessories used. As each change was made, the dressers would hang up the clothes on long racks in the center of the dressing room; the wardrobe women would then look them over to see if a button or hook needed be replaced or otherwise repaired. Then the costumes would be covered with a sheet and ready for the next performance. Principals or minor principals had private dressing

rooms, devoid of dresser's service. Stars usually had their own maid or valet. There were call boys who went through the passageway leading to all
the dressing rooms, which sometimes were quite a distance from the stage,
three or four flights upstairs, calling out the warning of the next number.
No one was allowed to stand in the wings (side of stage) unless waiting
for an approaching cue to go on. Time between appearances was spent in
the dressing rooms till such warning was given by the call boy. Just before
the show, he calls, "half-hour," "fifteen minutes," then "five minutes"; on
the latter, you'd better run if you are in the opening scene because almost
simultaneously the stage manager calls out, "On stage everybody!" then,
"Places!" Any absentee from a scene is fined—usually five dollars, better to
have stayed home, but what excuse for that? There is no other business as
exacting in attendance—to my knowledge—as show business. No alibi is
accepted. One must be on the border of death to miss a show. You don't
belong in show business till you learn that the show must go on, and you
are the show. It isn't hammy; it is a ritual.

Absentees in the Hippodrome (as with any other show) were soon eliminated and substitutes promoted to permanent positions in their place. Principals have understudies for their roles. Among the lower ranks in the cast
and for the element in the lines there are about eight extras, or substitutes,
of all sizes who check in daily and just stand by. They must know the routine
of dances of all three groups: ponies, mediums, and showgirls; the latter
group—comprising those tall, shapely creatures—does very little dancing.
However, unison in the picture created by this group, used mostly to dress
the scenes, is equally important.

The Hip was the first place I had seen the card system in use—check in
on entering and check out on leaving the building, punching the time by
the clock at each move. Immediately following his half-hour call before
each performance, the call boy lists the name and number on any card that
is still on the out rack, turning it in to the stage manager. One of his three
assistants then calls on the substitutes—small, medium, or large, according
to absentees. They must be ready to jump in and fill the places where needed.
Much the same system is employed still today in any large production.

Not to be overlooked for mention is the group of chorus boys—one
hundred of them—of which ninety-six were set permanently, while four of
them were substitutes.[8] Ah, the chorus boys, those beautiful men! Yes, the
majority of them could even wear a gown gracefully. They sing and dance
and—like the showgirls—add color and charm to the show. They (with few
exceptions) use makeup on the street, knit and crochet in their spare time

between numbers, and give the girls a run in competition in conquest of the male—even to the point of rivalry, inciting jealousy.[9]

Extremely fraternal (or the feminine facsimile thereof) toward their kind, they call each other by feminine names. Very interesting indeed are some of the monikers they use: from the classics such as Venus to the elements such as Spring Breeze, Dawn, et cetera. In great favor among them also are the names of candy bars, of all things.

There's something strangely fascinating about these sex-confused individuals; they are, as a general rule, charming in their demeanor. They usually possess greater physical strength than they care to display; a vocation in the chorus is ideally suited to their complex. For what they lack in masculinity they compensate for in ingenuity and talent for the finer arts. The spark of genius is clearly reflected in their contribution to the artistic field in all branches.

Their creative ability for beautiful things is unique. Some of the most brilliant theatrical producers, dance directors, and scenery and costume designers that I have known belong to this species. Endowed with originality and keen wit in their conversation, they have an appeal to both sexes.

They are reputed as being highly strung, with frequent outbursts of what we in show business call artistic temperament, but these individuals like to refer to it as their violent temper. As a matter of fact, I have never seen one that was violent or engaged in physical combat such as a fist fight; even at the heat of temper they behave like prima donnas—foot stamping and tongue lashing are their vent of tempest. Occasionally one of them will enter a field where intrepidity is essential. I know at least one famous wild-animal trainer and a couple of others (not so famous) training elephants and horses, while there are a host of aerialists doing exceptionally well in the latter line, their natural grace and poise enhanced in the air. (According to hearsay, the wild-animal trainer had been a normal man until one day while grappling with the beasts; one of them attacked and emasculated him, effecting a change toward effeminacy.)

Tracing their origin, most any region contributes its share of these odd men more or less, though in France, where foppish males abound, one finds comparatively few of these effeminates. Like midgets that with but rare exception are regional products of Austria and Hungary, the greatest number of foreign-born neutrals I have encountered came from Germany— an abnormal sight to see a Herculean body with the softness of mien more befitting a fairy princess.

But where I least expected to find one of these fairies or homosexuals was among the race referred to as braves, who pride themselves on the superiority of males, the American Indians. He was a member of the Aztecs, one of many tribes represented at the San Diego Exposition in 1935. Moctezuma, by name, was really an artist in dancing as well as painting, although the latter accomplishment he limited to his own person, the first time I have seen that particular art, for art it was—a weird and monsterlike character when he finished his makeup.[10] He had some movie-studio experience and was quite polished. Besides his own tribal lingo, he spoke English and Spanish. The point of his conversation was shop. Invariably, he would boast of making his own wardrobe, which in itself was nothing unusual but for the fact that instead of the beaded Indian togs typical of his tribe, this odd fellow used spangles on long, flowing robes of satins and laces. I often wondered whether the other three hundred or more of the various tribes housed in the Indian Village resented him, since his behavior was strictly on the queer side.

While their preferences in *affaire romantique* is directed definitely toward the male sex, some do get hitched up with women and even marry them, in most cases for convenience or political reasons. Strangely enough, it is not unusual that children are born as a result of such a union—proving the inconsistency of nature, the conflict between mind and matter.

The feminine counterpart—lesbians—is quite rare, at least in comparison with the number of males. During all my years of trouping, I have come across but two of these Amazons, who, to outward appearances, seemed completely normal, with nothing about their mannerism to betray their natural inclination for erotic relations with one of their own sex. But once they find the object or ideal, they make their point known in bold advances much as a male suitor would, asserting their ardent desires to possess the affection and undivided attention of the adored one. They are extremely jealous of the chosen mate, guarding her against flirtation or association with men with the shrewdness of which only another woman would be capable.

One such team traveled with the same musical show with me one season. Since girls frequently double up in order to save on hotel expenses, no one suspected anything strange about Ethel and Miriam sharing the same room. Not until Miriam was dismissed and Ethel (the one in the feminine role) fell ill did I come upon this strange discovery. Occupying the adjoining room, I remained with her at night during the crisis to give her the medicine as the doctor ordered and otherwise looking after her, bringing the mail left for her at the theater. When she confided those intimacies, I believed she was raving as a result of the fever or that she was being melodramatic, as choristers are prone to self-glorification and sometimes resort to exhibitionism in their effort to stir the others' imaginations with their exploits. Seeing I was unimpressed, she knew I doubted her story; bent on convincing me, she let me read some of the letters from Miriam, which left me dumbfounded with confusion and amazement, containing tender love messages such as only a poet could compose, expressing vehement desire to see her, urging she leave the show to join her at once.

When I asked her whether she reciprocated this strange affection, inasmuch as according to her own admission, she was a perfectly normal girl, she replied that a love such as Miriam's couldn't be compared with any other—it was something so sweet and gentle that it would be hard to take the rough handling of a male wooer after being spoiled by Miriam. It remained a mystery to me. I believed it to be a unique case until not long after, with another unit, in vaudeville, playing on the same bill with a musical girl sextet, the harpist seemed to show a sudden deep interest in me. I remembered the case of Ethel and demurred from close association with her, glad when the week was over and our paths led in different directions.

In conclusion of this subject, I wish to clarify my statement regarding the chorus men: while these odd, mysterious offspring of Mother Nature comprise the largest percentage of a line, they are not to be confused with the others who are real he-men, albeit they work in the chorus. Lined up in a mixed group, there is no mistaking them for the others whose every move—walk, use of hand, and affected speech suggesting femininity—distinguishes them as night from day.

The scenes in the Hippodrome were changed in blackout of lights, in time reckoned in seconds. No revolving stage, as many people supposed; no Houdini's or Thurston's magic acts; just plain efficiency. After scenes with over four hundred performers taking part, the lights went out; everyone knew where to exit blindfolded, figuratively speaking. Stagehands manned each piece of setting; they had to work quietly, almost like ghosts, one group carrying off, another bringing on sets and props without colliding. With us girls it was a mad scramble, following a certain red or blue light offstage, then up the stairs to the dressing room where the dressers were ready for us with sheets spread on the floor. We stepped out of our bulky costumes (they are usually bulky); they took our hats or whatever needed to be handled with care. The next change was already laid out on our chairs, unless it happened to be a trick costume such as we wore in the "Cat Cabaret," the opening scene of *Hip-Hip-Hurray.*

In that scene, over three hundred cats were onstage with some of the best animal impersonators in the business participating. The set showed a New York roof at midnight with thousands of housetops in the distance, looking as far east as Brooklyn and showing the bridges spanning the East River with boats passing under them in motion. Millions of tiny lights glimmered through windows of skyscrapers and on signs, dark blue flood lighting the scene throughout. The music was a masterpiece composition that even cats could understand and appreciate. Cats started congregating on rooftops—there was a bit of pantomime, some business of leaping over parapets, acrobatics, wire walking, perch climbing, and some mighty fancy dancing, all of this and some more antics, executed wearing heavy fur skins like teddy bears with enormous heads, made of papier-mâché (or plaster), covered with the same fur as the body and having movable eyes, which we worked with strings to give lifelike expression. This head alone weighed about eight pounds. We could see only through the opening of the mouth, getting very little view—and that, directly in front. The heat of these suits was terrific. To dance in them with our feet inside the pelt I never believed possible till we did it. The large tail, reinforced with spring-coil so it would protrude and yet be flexible to follow our movements, certainly got in the way of the others; yet it was accomplished and was the hit of the show, a fantastic curtain raiser (pardon, *dropper* in the Hip).

When the scene was ended we made our exit in the dark—oh, brother!—but once we got as far as the wings, there were helpers to remove those heads which they handled with great care. Each head was made to the measurements of the one wearing it, with the name on a tag sewed right in. We had to be ready and downstairs at least ten minutes before curtain time to pick out our own heads out of twenty-four, as they were all lined up on long tables with numerals indicating the group thus: first 48, #1—I knew that my head would be one of the twenty-four on that table.

The scene that followed ours had its own group of performers who entered as we were making our exit. The immensity of the stage made it possible to alternate from half to full depth without any seeming perception by the audience. When a full-stage scene is over, the participants turn half around and run upstage (toward the back) as the drop is being lowered from the loft; we come running on from both sides while the others exit backstage, and the light finds us doing our stuff.

This mystery baffled Hippodrome attendance for many years. Of course, it required a large cast to work it in two shifts like that. As I remember, the number, including personnel, staff, and ushers, exceeded eight hundred.

That many dimes were contributed toward the humidor we all planned to present to Mr. Sousa as a gift on his seventieth birthday. Ah! That was something to remember. That little party literally broke up the routine of acts that followed "The Ballet of the States," the number in which he was featured.[11]

The set portrayed the national capitol. Mr. Sousa and his band of one hundred men spotted the steps in front of the capitol, and as each state—represented by six girls—filed by, the band played a chorus of a popular tune synonymous with the state, accompanying the girls' dance. There was no need for signs or banners to identify them—the music and costumes were symbolic enough. This subtle way of working the imagination of the audience met with instantaneous success, if judged by the spontaneous applause that greeted the entry of each group. In fact, it was just one continuous acclaim during the entire scene, one thunderous hand after another as the states kept coming on in geographical order, from Maine to California.[12] It didn't require much stretching of the imagination when seeing six stately showgirls dressed in shimmering, gold-lamé gowns, file in and do a graceful routine to the chorus of "I Love You California," or those six mediums prancing in, wearing fringed buckskin skirts, boots, and ten-gallon hats, stepping out a lively buck-and-wing to the accompaniment of "Cheyenne, Cheyenne," and others like "Maryland, Maryland," and of course, "Louisiana Lou," all easy to associate.[13]

I considered it a privilege to dance by in front of this greatest of bandleaders. Six of us stepping on it when his band segued into "Yankee Doodle," the tune he chose for Rhode Island, the state we small-fry represented. It is only now that I can fully appreciate the cleverness in the casting and characterization of that stupendous production. At the time, I was too dizzy and too vexed by petty annoyances to see the fine points; for example, I resented wearing that blonde curly wig with my brunette features, but all six had to look identical, and that was that!

On finishing their dance, the girls took their appointed place on either side of the stage, leaving the center open for the state that followed. When all forty-eight were on, the formation depicted a living map of the Union.

The chorus boys were also in the scene. Rhode Island was one of the early states to go on. As we took our place, I found myself standing right by these gorgeous hunks of men. The number ran a good half-hour, and when the states following ours took their places in front of us according to positions assigned them, we were practically blocked out from view, wedged in between the tall ones—and the fun began. With all the vigilance of the stage manager and his three deputies always standing in the wings watching for shirkers, we seldom slacked. In this number, however, we, buried in the crowd, carried on a regular social (are you listening, Mr. Stewart?). Here I really had a chance to get acquainted with the queer clique. With the music drowning out vocal sounds, we told funny stories, laughed, exchanged views—all while the show was going on. One of the assistants snooping around did catch me an inch out of my place one day, reprimanding me severely. That same young man, named Fleming, was to cross my path some years later during a stunt I was negotiating. He was with the RKO publicity department, which sponsored me, and we had a good laugh recalling the old days. He probably never guessed how innocent and harmless our carryings on had been—just like talking with a group of girls, but sex was never brought up. And so it went on all season. Of course, I've seen them behave differently in the company of men, sometimes very shy and submissive, other times quite coquettish. And, I understand, they prefer the aggressive, brutish type almost to the extent of sadism, though this side of them they never divulged to me. From conversation among themselves I caught many of their little slips now and again.

In this particular scene, the chorus boys wore a uniform of some sort, possibly the National or Home Guards. It couldn't have been the armed forces; we were still too happily at peace with the rest of the world to even suggest anything pertaining to war. The conflict in Europe was raging in its second year but thus far hadn't reached out to affect us. We were so sure we could remain neutral, feeling quite secure with the vast ocean between continents—at least at the time the show went in production there was no inkling of getting involved later. All had been serene here: didn't the manager import all those ice skaters, including Charlotte, from Germany?

On this eventful day, just as the display reached its climax, the band striking up the "Stars and Stripes Forever," the entire ensemble singing it with the specially written lyrics, the audience in a frenzy with enthusiasm, suddenly the impromptu party swung into session; a solemn hush, a short eulogy delivered by one of the principals, the presentation of the gift by the stage manager, then pandemonium broke loose! Everybody (not belonging in the scene) rushed on, including stagehands, janitors, even to the scrubwomen of the building. The audience must have gotten a kick out of the informal show we put on as we all crowded around this grand maestro singing, "Happy birthday, Mr. Sousa, happy birthday to you!" He was sweet, and we just adored him, this king of marches.

It was Charlotte in her famous "Arabesque" pose—leg straight up in back, outlined in lights—that graced the electric sign in front of the building and, like a rubber stamp, was used on all publicity material. She became the trademark of *Hip-Hip-Hurray*. I visited frequently in her dressing room during the intermission. We got quite chummy, since I spoke German, the only language she knew, and I taught her a few sentences in English. She was always chaperoned by her parents, Mama and Papa Oelschlager. So very young, about sixteen, she was amply endowed by Mother Nature—a beautiful body to match that face of strong, perfect features. With her long, blonde hair falling in ripples below her waist, costumed in a frosty-white ensemble from head to her silvery skates, she looked like a graceful bird on the ice. Her pivots were prodigious. It can be said it was Charlotte who made the American public skating-conscious.[14] And this show started the trend for one-hundred-percent ice revues. She had been signed up with the show independently, as a feature act, apart from the ice ballet unit. Always so natural, so unpretentious, never realizing the height to which this enormous publicity had skyrocketed her in importance—that was Charlotte.

There were a number of celebrities from every branch of the business with this mammoth crazy-quilt production, including Orville Harold and Belle Story of opera fame and Toto the clown, a new importation. Toto was exceptionally clever in comedy pantomime; as a natural-born clown, he needed no makeup. Very slight of build, his neck was the biggest part of him; a marvelous contortionist, he could fold himself up into a tiny box. He always made his entrance inside a toy wagon, propelling it by unperceivable power. Seeing him stepping out of it always created astonishment, like an optical illusion, fantastic, he appeared rather voluminous in an oversized frock coat and trousers of which one leg alone would have been sufficient to enshroud him. His appearance was really grotesque. Toto clowned through most every scene, burlesquing the outstanding features. He stalked through the ice scene, dressed as a Tyrolese and on the points of skis as if on stilts. Though typically European in his style of work, he never talked while on. The only sound he emitted was a cackling laugh, a sound similar to running up or down the scale on an instrument. With a surname like Novello, it was hard to tell his origin.[15]

And how could I forget that weird, creepy music this same Mr. Hubbell, the orchestra director, played in accompaniment (improvising it as he went along) for my Oriental dance at the party we celebrated after the regular show was over on Christmas Eve?[16] What a program! A list of specialties the paying patrons never saw. That was when the principals sat out front watching the latent talent wasted in the line come bursting out like a spring. On that night we showed them—like sweet revenge—what we could do if given a break. Of course, it was all in the spirit of the holiday; a sort of amateur show, really. We had a nice tree, all decorated, buffet luncheon, and refreshments, the management footing all expenses. Since we had to give the usual two performances the next day—on Christmas—we appreciated this small share of the joyous Yuletide backstage. Checking out that night, all the girls were given a box of candy, the men, a carton of cigarettes as they passed through the vestibule.

Another time we were treated to a performance given especially to the entire Hippodrome force, cast and personnel, by Mr. Dillingham's new show, *Stop, Look, and Listen,* which was the current hit at the Globe Theater, *Chin-Chin* having gone on tour. The show was presented in the morning, as we had a matinee daily, while they, only twice a week. The star was Gaby Deslys, the girl with the pearls for whom Manuel of Portugal was thrown off the throne.

True, she was beautiful, blonde—and that was all, unless a French accent may also be counted as an asset. A former music hall entertainer, her dancing and singing were mediocre, but the public—even then—craved sensationalism, and that publicity connecting her with a king paid off nobly at the box office. Her voice was too coarse, husky for such a dainty damsel. (An operation on her throat later, in her native France, caused her death.)[17] But the show, as a whole, was refreshing, a change from the Hip. It gets weary—the same music, the same scenes, day in, day out, ceasing to be anything but work; no glamor, no nothing—just routine. So I rather enjoyed the change this show offered to my eyes and ears, even if served up for breakfast.

And what an ensemble was gathered the day it occurred to Mr. Dillingham to have a panoramic picture taken of both companies under his direction, combined. This event also had to be scheduled for morning—too early for getting in the mood for smiling at the birdie. Most of the folks were pretty grouchy. Adding to the already ruffled dispositions, Charlotte was late in arriving, holding up the shot. Gaby, quite annoyed, remarked derisively, "Why we wait? Maybe she go back to Germany!" It was then that I realized how wrong one can be in judging people by facial characteristics. Gaby wasn't the exotic, sophisticated type; on the contrary, her innocent, childlike physiognomy seemed to be in contradiction with the publicity— the adventuress hidden there. Hearing this sardonic expression coming from her, naturally, surprised me.

Only the Hip stage could hold two such large casts with everyone in the picture distinguishable; any member could obtain a print for seventy-five cents. My copy? Well, it would be difficult to remember in which storage warehouse the trunk containing it had been left the way many other trunks were left—unclaimed.

IN PURSUIT
OF A MIRAGE
TO YESTERDAY

Unusually cold for March, it was punishment to go outdoors. As we filed out after rehearsal that night, punching my card I looked at the clock: 2:00 AM. "Not many winks of sleep before it's time to get up again!" I thought, and rather than go, I wished I could have curled up in some corner to pass there the few remaining hours left before the next session without having to leave the building. But that was against the rules. Opening the door to the street, the cold blast almost took my breath away. Once outside, we scattered—some going east, most of them, however, crossing Sixth Avenue to Jack's for a late snack. I had a housekeeping room on Forty-fifth Street, between Eighth and Ninth Avenues. There I prepared all my meals, so I kept right on going along Forty-third Street.

At this time of night, the streets are pretty well deserted, even on Times Square, and the neighborhood got tougher with each block west of Broadway. Prohibition was not even dreamed of at that time; there was a saloon on every corner. In these wee hours, a number of inebriates could be seen staggering here and there. I always had a terror of these irresponsible creatures, almost to the point of phobia, and would zigzag my way home, dodging them, crossing the street several times. The distance didn't warrant taking a car, and a taxicab would have been beyond my means. While several members of the cast lived scattered about in the vicinity—one couple in the next house to me—none of them were in the last scene. After passing the Forty-third Street subway entrance, I was left alone.

Saying goodnight to the bunch subway-bound, I looked across the wide gap where Broadway and Seventh Avenue run parallel. Parting them to the south is the Flatiron or Times Building. Standing alone there, this immense structure marks the boundary line of the famous center stretched out over five blocks—from Forty-second to Forty-seventh Streets—known as the "Crossroads of the World," alias "The Great White Way," alias Times Square. I have great respect for this tall, triangular edifice and always take in its full view on passing, surveying it as if it were a privilege, feeling I am part of the scheme of things which make up Broadway.

On this night as I looked upwards, straight ahead to the southwest corner of Seventh Avenue, something in motion caught my attention. Atop the building, some men were at work putting up a poster there on a billboard. As I paused a few seconds before crossing, watching the men pasting on the bright-colored lithograph, I was spellbound to read: "Barnum & Bailey Circus."

Instantly I was transferred to another sphere; not even the bitter cold and the fury of the wind that blows at this intersection as in no other place could touch me. I was now immune to sensations and removed from material environment. All I could see and feel was the text on that poster. Everything that happened during the past year was, all of a sudden, completely obliterated. I just gazed, fascinated, at the sign.

Oh, I was living again! It was wonderful to feel that thrill of anticipation, of something too heavenly to describe, which the magic of that poster held for me. And for the first time in a whole year I was happy again, because, while under the spell, I was carried off the earth on wings of imagination; to me that signboard really spelled the name of Otto Kline.

It was just a year ago, the Seventeenth of March, to be exact, when he—en route from Naperville, Illinois (his hometown) to New York, to open with the show in the Garden—stopped off in Pittsburgh, Pennsylvania, where the Cracker Jacks show I was with played that week, that we were married after a courtship of nearly two years. The courtship during the greatest part of the time was carried on by remote control. It all seemed so vivid, just like yesterday. Leaving Alderman Kirby's office after the ceremony, we went to see Theda Bara in *A Fool There Was,* then to the theater where I had my two shows daily to do. He sat in a box out front where all the girls focused their attention on him, as he was also the target for the comedian's jokes. I was so proud of him, it was hard to realize how happy I was. The week went by too soon; he went on to New York, where I, after a week of one-night stands, was to join him for the two-week run my show had been booked there.

Arriving on the Jersey side, I saw the posters (as now) of the Barnum & Bailey Circus, and, almost as if he had stepped out of one of them—he came to meet me. There he was! And the next instant, I was in heaven—his arms. Deliriously happy, we ferried over to New York. It was Sunday, no show. He had found an apartment right close to the Garden on Twenty-sixth Street, and after we got my bag unpacked, it took on a homey aspect. I prepared lunch. Everything seemed so natural. We knew that we just belonged together. Later in the afternoon, he had to be at the Garden for the general assembly, when all the people under contract with the circus have to report, a sort of roll call. He took me along and introduced me to friends and companions. It was the first time I had ever been inside Madison Square Garden. The place looked huge, and so many people, so much chitchat, these friends and rivals saying "hello" after a five-month separation during the winter—a glad feeling, at this reunion, to be back trouping again. There was the roster: from the brightest star to the insignificant statue girl, the lowest rank among circus performers. But in this motley crowd it would have been impossible to distinguish one from the other; everyone was dressed in Sunday-best street clothes.

The stock had arrived from Bridgeport, Connecticut (the show's winter quarters), during the previous night. There was the smell of horses and wild animals perceptible in the air. I sat in one of the sections of seats with others not directly connected with the circus, while Mr. Bradna, the equestrian director, checked off the list of acts. The circus was to open April 1. The next three days were devoted to whipping the show into shape—timing and grouping the acts in their corresponding spots on the program.

Having to report early the next day at the Academy of Music, where I had two shows daily, we saw little of each other through the day. I didn't get to see the circus at all when, at the end of two weeks, the Cracker Jacks took to the road again. Ours was a much-interrupted honeymoon, as if dished out to us on the installment plan. I remember now, we overslept—no time for breakfast. He came as far as the train with me. I just made it. I know he kissed me, but I can't recall what his last words were—those precious last words! I was so concerned over getting aboard that train, never looking back to catch another glimpse of him after parting.

A split week was followed by a week in Baltimore, which was to have been my closing week. While still in New York, Otto had made arrangements to take me along with the circus, a privilege married performers are given for their mates in exchange for any small service these render to benefit the show; in my case, most likely, to go in parade and maybe pose in the statues. I was to join the circus in Philadelphia, the first date under canvas after leaving the Garden. It was going to be grand—to be together always. I had been counting the days, the hours—would Sunday ever come? I was to meet him on the lot.

It was Wednesday, "Our anniversary—married five weeks today!" I wrote to him earlier that day in reply to his daily letter, which, on this particular day, contained a check—my first allowance. But more, he had sent me all the surplus cash left after paying his expenses, telling me I was to be the banker. So thrilled by this new development of conjugal life, I just had to show the check to everybody in the company.

The girls were forever playing tricks on me, ribbing me incessantly—crocheting baby booties and other ridiculous things that pleased their fancy, leaving them on my makeup shelf. Glad for another day to discount, I put extra pep in that finale of the night show, and not because I noticed our manager, Mr. Falke, in the wings even then eyeing me with a somber expression on his face; I just felt exceptionally gay. The curtain came down. The others in the scene, also seeing Mr. Falke, remained on the stage instead of breaking up and rushing to the dressing rooms; his presence backstage was significant. "Wonder what the old man's got up his sleeve?" I remarked to Bernice, next to me in the line. "He seems to have a grudge, from the looks he is casting in my direction!"

"Maybe he's going to fire you!" she replied, intending it to be a joke; they all knew I had given my notice.

He came directly over to me. "Have you heard from your husband lately? Has he been ill?" he asked.

Believing this to be another gag, I just laughed it off, saying, "You, too!" And then he gave me the telegram received out front during the performance, which he intercepted and opened; he already knew the contents. I read, flabbergasted: "Otto Kline died today. For disposal of remains, advise immediately. Frank A. Cook, Care of Barnum & Bailey Circus."[1]

I couldn't grasp the meaning those words contained. Only after reading it over for the second time did the message begin to register. Then panic seized me. I began screaming hysterically, though not a tear came to my eyes. "It can't be true, it can't!" I kept repeating. "There must be some mistake!" was my one consolation. The girls packed my makeup, helped me all they could; at the hotel too, packing my trunk with personal belongings—clothes I had bought that week, practical for trouping: a dark blue serge suit and some conservative wash dresses. I looked vacantly at the little brass burner I had bought and taken apart for study on the previous day, to see how it functioned with kerosene fuel. This little stove would have served us to make coffee in the cars at night and on Sunday mornings. "What good is it now? I shall never have any use for it!" I burst out bitterly.

They called a cab and escorted me to the station. The train didn't leave till 2:00 AM, but I could get aboard the Pullman. No sooner did I get in the compartment than a woman passenger came in, "to help you in distress," she said. She had overheard those faithful companions telling the conductor of the tragedy so he might look after me during the journey. A minister's wife, she was a pious woman, and I welcomed her company. Neither of us made use of the berth; we just sat and talked—of life, of the mysteries of fate, of superstitions and omens. I wanted to tell her of Otto Kline, of his virtues, his prowess in his line of work. That was the topic I wanted to talk about foremost.

The night passed somehow. And then I remembered that he loved my hair because it was soft and shiny, so, excusing myself, I started to shampoo. "I must be spick-and-span for him when we meet."

Daylight showed the trees in bud. It was the Twenty-second of April—spring had arrived. All along the route, the fields looked so fresh and green.

Arriving in New York, I took a taxi to the Preston Hotel where he had been staying, having given up the apartment after I left (too lonesome there without me, he wrote in one of his letters). At the hotel, I rushed to the desk, greatly agitated but still unbelieving as I asked the clerk: "My husband—Otto Kline—how is he?"

The man looked at me pitifully, saying: "He's pretty badly hurt!"

This reply lifted me out of the chaos; almost relieved, I asked: "He is only hurt, he's not . . . ?"

By way of answering my unfinished question, he simply pushed the two morning editions he was reading before me. On the front pages of both papers, the bold headlines: "Cowboy Rider Killed before Circus Crowd," and "Circus Rider Killed in Ring before 5,000," told the sinister news that I must accept as the truth.[2]

My hopes now shattered, I inquired where I might find him—his body—when just at this moment, three of his comrades, Cy Compton, Sam Garrett, and Tex McLeod appeared in the lobby.[3] They told me briefly how the accident had occurred during the matinee. Otto had been doing the vaulting (during which he grips the pommel, swings out of the saddle, letting his feet touch the ground, then swings his body clear over the horse and touches the ground on the other side. This continued all around the arena without

RIDER FALLS TO DEATH.

Otto Kline, who was featured in a "rough riding" act with the Barnum & Bailey Circus, called "Fifteen Minutes of the Wildest Wild West," fell from his horse during his exhibition, at the matinee performance in Madison Garden, this city, April 21, and suffered a fracture at the base of the brain, from which he died that evening, in Bellevue Hospital.

He was twenty-eight years of age, and leaves his widow, who is a member of the Cracker Jack Burlesque company.

OTTO KLINE.

"Rider Falls to Death," *New York Clipper,* May 1, 1915. Image no. WHi-41681, used with permission from the Wisconsin Historical Society.

his once touching the seat of his saddle while the horse ran at full speed). According to their deduction, his hands must have slipped, and as he fell, his skull was crushed beneath the horse's hoof. They suggested I join their women folks, while they would attend to having the body transferred from Bellevue Hospital to the mortuary where I could see him later.

Cy's wife, Lill, took me to a little dress shop, where I bought a black dress and veil. As she was pinning the veil onto my hat, I suddenly became conscious of the fact that, married such few days—barely having time to remove my bridal togs—and already I was wearing a widow's veil. And so came the first tears that mercifully relieved that pressure, the torment that gnawed and tore my heart out, being deprived of everything I had worth living for.

Accompanied by Lill Compton and Ruby Garrett, I arrived early at the funeral parlor to get a view of him. Too early, I was told: it would be another hour before the embalming and general preparation would be finished. On hearing this, I agreed with my companions to go to a nearby coffee shop to pass the time, but food was repellent to me; I watched the hands of the clock which seemed to stand still. We returned to the undertaking establishment, where funeral services were to be held right after the matinee, so his friends and comrades might pay their last tribute. It all seemed like a nightmare, a bad dream from which I would awaken soon.

As we entered the chapel, there lay the still form of one so active, so full of life only yesterday. I walked over to the casket—dazed, not believing what my own eyes saw. There he was before me, yet—still skeptical—I looked for a mark I knew so well, that scar he had near his chin where, during his early Wild West days, he had been gored by a steer while bulldogging. Yes, the scar was there. Then, I took his hand in mine and looked for the signet ring; that too, was there on his small finger with the initials O.K. engraved on its facet. I held his hand to my cheek, as if by warming it I could bring life back, and then I noticed a cut on the palm of his hand—a deep gash. I could understand now how he had lost his grip and fallen.

Otto's comrades brought newspaper clippings to me, believing that the wide publicity his popularity rated, the articles eulogizing his achievements and pictures of him spread all over the pages, would be of some consolation to me. To some extent it served that purpose, especially those articles in which I was referred to as Mrs. Kline, for beside the honor this great hero bestowed upon me by leaving me his name, he forevermore lifted me out of the mortification I have been exposed to ever since I took a notion to change my name from Deutsch to Duchee.

In my innocence I thought it sounded more glamorous, unaware that I was laying myself open for the derision that was to follow me from show to show. For show people never pass up an opportunity of wisecracking, especially at the expense of—or to annoy—the other fellow, making him (or her, as the case may be) a target for ridicule. As soon as I joined a unit, a production, or vaudeville act, and the members heard my name Duchee (pronounced Doo-shay) for the first time, they immediately began to poke fun at it, and from that very day, everybody with the company called me "Douchebag." I abhorred it, but there was nothing I could do about it. Once it got started, I couldn't stop it—my very closest associates would call me thus—anywhere I happened to be, and the more I'd protest, the funnier the situation became. So after awhile I'd just ignore it till I joined another company, and the cycle started all over anew.

How it comforted me to be called Mrs. Kline, a name I shall ever cherish, a glorious name. And—who knows?—I may even perpetuate it in the public's memory. I looked at the black velvet sombrero and the purple muffler which I had made him with the letters O.K. embroidered in one corner. I remembered how he quipped while watching me in our little apartment sewing away on the initials, he said: "You'll never get another fellow whose 'brand' is O.K. like mine." These objects, which Lill Compton picked up when the show's doctor was examining him before the ambulance took him away, she handed me when I went to her room. I shall keep them as mementos—these items so close to him, his person. Seeing the hat, I almost felt his presence about.

Need I describe the agony of that trip—to be on the same train with him, yet eternities apart? The meeting of his grief-stricken family—the funeral, each nail securing the lid to his casket was driven straight through my heart. The hometown paper went all-out in following up the story—the obituary in memoriam for the local boy who was a credit to the town and the entire community.

Then on Monday, the day after the funeral, I received a letter from him—it seemed supernatural, like a dream—yet it was very real and very material, a moment's flashback to happiness. He had written the letter on the fatal day; it had been returned to New York and thence forwarded to me in Naperville. In his last letter, he mentioned having cut his hand on a loose tack in the trunk when putting his saddle away—the precious, tooled and silver-decorated saddle, one of the trophies he won at contests, adding optimistically, "It is nothing to be concerned about."

In addition to firefighting equipment and other safety measures against unforeseen catastrophes, the circus carries a very capable doctor on the staff who serves in all emergency cases as well as conducts a private practice for individuals on the show. It was the show's doctor who, examining Otto, on finding he was bleeding through the ear, ratified his condition as grave, before calling the ambulance.

When I returned to New York, the circus was already on the road; I wandered about like a lost soul. Only one more place to explore to get some more facts concerning him; I went to Bellevue Hospital to talk with the doctors who attended him. They had operated on his skull in back of the right ear, but with no success to revive him. I asked the nurse in Ward 13 to show me the bed where he expired, but seeing me dressed in mourning, she told me the bed was occupied and might have an unpleasant effect on the patient. She took a parcel out of a locker and handed it to me. It contained Otto's personal effects: the shirt stained with blood was a yellow-colored one.

Among the messages of condolence, there was one from Fred Stone, offering to help me in any way he could. I didn't know Fred Stone personally, only from reputation as a big star on Broadway, but he knew Otto very well. In fact, they played polo together at Stone's estate in Freeport, Long

Island, the Sunday prior to his death in the Garden. It was his offer of help I took advantage of when I went to see him in the Globe Theater, and he gave me the letter of introduction to Dillingham, which ultimately led to my engagement in the Hippodrome.

The *Billboard,* a trade publication referred to as the showman's Bible or "Bill-boy," carried the following poem in its October 2, 1915, issue:

"Otto Kline, In Memoriam,"
　　by Paul Case.

A brave boy from our midst has gone,
His place can ne'er be filled;
His soul is boldly marching on
Although his voice is stilled.
No more he'll rubes and guys amaze
Nor hardship's ranges ride;
He's climbed the pass in deep'ning haze
And crossed the Great Divide.

A daring cowboy to the last,
Whose heart beat ever true,
A champion—adroit and fast—
Trick rider through and through,
As countless thousands oft acclaimed
Who watched his daring ride.
How many know his grave's unnamed—
He—crossed the Great Divide.

Let's see his grave is marked, boys,
And keep it trim and green,
For grief is often salved with joys
And sore hearts turned serene
By duty; so let's write his name
On granite deep and wide,
And thus preserve one cowboy's fame
Who's crossed the Great Divide.

But even before that date—in the August 14 issue, to be exact—the editors suggested starting a movement to erect a monument over his grave by popular subscription, which was seized upon at once by Guy Weadick, a leader of rodeo promotions and contests, whose name headed the long list of contributors published weekly in the *Billboard,* among which were names such as Will Rogers, Fred Stone, Colonel Cody (Buffalo Bill), and others.[4] The subscription's popularity was so spontaneous that in almost no time at all there was the fund raised for the mighty dignified memorial—a testimonial of over five hundred friends and associates of the circus and theatrical world the country over for a fellow artist with so vibrant a personality.[5]

I was elated when I read the announcement of the erection of the monu-

Otto Kreinbrink's original gravestone. Used with permission from Julie Kreinbrink.

Monument to Otto Kline, funded by contributions to the *Billboard*. Used with permission from Julie Kreinbrink.

ment toward which—having saved up fifty dollars from my meager earnings—I was so happy to have added my share to the tribute paid by those who loved him.[6]

The monument, of crudely carved granite, is of imposing proportions. The design, symbolic of his calling, depicts a sombrero over one corner at the top, a lasso looped over the other corner, and a spur lower down near the base. The center shows a floral design expressing a tribute from friends; over this is the polished tablet, lettered "Otto Kline." Nothing more, yet it tells so much!

A TOUR BEHIND THE PLATFORMS OF THOSE STRANGE PEOPLE

I met Otto Kline the summer I danced in the sideshow. Walter A. Shannon was the spieler[1] and manager, as well as doubling in a mind-reading act with Leona, a dancer like myself in need of a summer job. Shannon had taught her the key to the act: a series of cues and clues arranged in numerical order, from one to ten, the answers being concealed in the words employed in compiling the questions asked. At least that is the basic component of the mystifying art. Shannon, on a previous meeting, had tried to get me interested in the idea by giving me a rough outline of its principle. However, at the time the partnership didn't appeal to me because I was under the impression that anything you can't lay a finger on is illegitimate, and moreover, it would confine me too closely to a man with great difference in our ages. I was young and romantic—besides, I couldn't visualize the future it held. I turned down his offer.

The team formed by Shannon and Leona later became a headline act on the big-time vaudeville circuit, under the billing: "The Girl with the Thousand Eyes."

Ah, yes! This was the annex of the Oklahoma Ranch Wild West Show, owned by Eddie Arlington and Fred (Pop) Beckman, a branch of the Miller Bros. & Arlington's 101 Ranch.[2] The sideshow (pardon, annex) with the usual freak acts, which today would be billed "Ripley's Believe It or Not!" was an exhibition for a mixed crowd: men, women, and children. The annex was composed of about twelve different attractions and was livened up with a twenty-people (colored) plantation or minstrel show. The price of admission was ten cents.

Curtained off toward the rear was another compartment with a high platform; that was where we—another girl and I—danced. After the crowd had seen every act in the tent, the spieler would call in to us the password— "ballyhoo"—which meant that we were to come out in front of the curtain in our costumes, composed mostly of beads—lots of beads—hanging down in fringes from the chest and hips, the purpose of the beads to accentuate the movements of those parts. We were to come out, give 'em a flash, then scuttle back inside.

Two years before, when I worked in a summer-stock burlesque in Altoona, Pennsylvania, Millie DeLeon, "The Girl in Blue," was the feature attraction for a week. The house was packed for every performance. I was just a young-ster doing my first show out of New York, but I was curious to see what she had that everyone wanted to see. Well, I never missed a show, watching from the wings everything she did. To this day—in my estimation—she remains in a class by herself. She didn't use beads; instead, her full dress was covered with iridescent spangles, the bodice with oval-shaped bangles, which were sewed on from one end and dangled from the garment. Covered from head to foot, figuratively speaking, with not even a midriff exposed, she sold her stuff like the great artist she was. Hat, parasol, shoes, and stockings all matched the color of her sky-blue ensemble.

She first tossed out some garters to the audience, with a button bear-ing her picture attached to each. Then came her routine, which included a shimmie-shaking of shoulders and breasts from side to side, all the while her hips and abdomen did a rotary motion—truly a difficult feat to coordinate these movements of upper and lower parts of the body in contrasting direc-tions. It required complete control of the muscles, like trying to mark a circle with the hand clockwise and foot counterclockwise at the same time.

That gal—a mature woman, then—had everything plus personality that a stag audience clamored for, and without exposing her skin.

I tried to imitate or copy her style but, like many others who tried before me, failed. However, I did master the shimmie (which later became a fad). With this shimmie I combined a little routine all my own, and from then on I had a snappy little specialty, presenting it in other shows and then with the Oklahoma Ranch Wild West sideshow.

The long bead fringe over green or red tights made a flashy attire to attract the customers. The other girl, who was the feature dancer, leaned heavily toward ruffles. On the stout side and using red costumes consistently with all the ruffles, she looked like a red powder puff. But she could do the real Oriental dance. Her husband, an Arab, played the flageolet, an instrument that resembles a flute and sounds like a bagpipe; another Arab beating out the rhythm on a drum completed our musical accompaniment.

W. A. (as we called Mr. Shannon) would start his spiel by saying: "Gather round me a little closer, men, don't want the ladies to hear this, but you are about to get a little treat inside this curtain," et cetera, ending up with the price of admission: "Only one quarter—twenty-five cents!" and that was when we'd give them the flash to help the sale. Of course, he knew his line, having been a pitchman for many years; to sell fountain pens, watches, or shaving soap required the same art as selling a dancing show, and he was a past-master with words, not the "tell ye what I'm gonna do!" type but an elocutionist. The place filled up in no time. We could hear the wisecracks and otherwise smart remarks from behind still another curtain—our dressing room—as they gathered in anticipation of seeing "those muscles shake and shiver like a bowl of jelly in a gale of wind; the dance that John the Baptist lost his head over!" (Shannon's sales line). On a short, shrill note of the flageolet—the signal—I came out first. Climbing up to the platform, which was roped off all around for protection against the impudence of the standing audience, who might make a grab at our limbs (which they sometimes tried anyway), I went into my dance, a short routine of about two minutes' duration, doing high kicks and the split, which was then considered naughty. There wasn't anything in that music to inspire dance spirit within me. I could never feel the mood nor figure out the timing; always against tempo, I finished with a fast fouetter, a twist-kick spin, and climbed down. Then came Helen, the other girl.

She did what in Algiers might be considered a sedate parlor dance but here in America they called Hootchy-kootchy. The most outstanding feature of it was the way she could make her head slide from side to side while looking straight at you, just like a serpent—done by the neck muscles—on the order of pecking, but stretching the neck from right to left instead of forward.

And while the men were thus amused, Leona would go to work on the women. In addition to the mind-reading act, she also told fortunes. That is, she sold cards with the fortune already printed on them, as in a slot machine. And for fifty cents, any female could buy a picture of her future husband. After buying obsolete plates of old photos of men with beards—negatives that studios are glad to dispose of—Leona would take prints of them out

Although there is no substantive evidence that Kline performed topless, other circus burlesque dancers sometimes wore little costuming. Unidentified burlesque "coochee" dancer (no date). Frederick Glasier Collection, neg. no. 1005; black-and-white photograph, copy from glass plate negative, museum purchase, Collection of the John and Mable Ringling Museum of Art Archives, Sarasota, Florida.

of the solution still undeveloped and place them on the purchaser's palm. In a little while the seemingly blank paper exposed to light would begin to take form. Of course, her humorous answer for any beefs was simply to tell them the features may not be seen clearly, being concealed beneath the beard; this was usually good for a big laugh from others standing by.

Some time ago, before the general public became mechanical-minded, there was a Miss Electra act. A chair was wired with electricity. The girl seated on the chair with the current passing through her would naturally cause a slight shock or sting to anyone invited from the audience to come up to touch her. The act—a tremendous novelty back in 1912 or 1913—would be ridiculous today, however.

Now let me mention some of the many legitimate novelty acts one may see in the annex, sideshow, or kid-top (some of the titles used in circus jargon in reference to these exhibits). Some acts were natural phenomena, others self-developed, like the rubber-skinned man, who stretched the skin under his chin to a point where he could cover his entire face with it, pulling it over like a mask. And pinching his cheeks between his fingers, he could stretch the width of his face to an unbelievable twenty-four inches across.

It seems incredible that a man, vain by nature, always striving to put his best front forward to impress his fellow man, would sacrifice the most outstanding feature—his face—even for art's sake, as does this rubber-man who deliberately disfigures himself, developing those ugly nipples under his chin and cheeks, resembling more a turkey gobbler than man.

Yet more fantastic is the business of the human ostrich, that transgressor of dietary regime—the man who devours glass, tacks, and other indigestible material—whose performance is so repulsive to the spectator of delicate constitution that, amazing though it may be, definitely does not belong under the heading of entertainment; still, they are quite common. That's not rock candy he crushes between his teeth but drinking glass and electric bulbs (thin glass is preferred), cutting his mouth quite frequently. It might be interesting from a medical point of view to look into these individuals' lifespan, which is practically retarded suicide. I shall cite here one example (coming from sources I can vouch for).

The subject of the following narrative, doing a comedy mule act with an outdoor show at the time—given to epileptic fits—died during the performance following one of these attacks. In view of his sudden demise, his wife of a brief marital period insisted on an autopsy, and so it came to light: the tumorous growth attached to his stomach, when dissected, revealed bits of glass, nuts and bolts, and other small hardware embedded in that semblance of a gizzard, as if Mother Nature, when seeing this human trying to imitate the fowl, went right along with him in his unhealthy pursuit, aiding him. The man had previously been working in the role of the human ostrich, which he had to abandon when those convulsions developed.

Though more spectacular as a show, I don't attach as much merit to the fire eaters as to those who walk over red-hot coals; the latter really astound me, just as the sword swallowers do. I marvel at them every time I see them perform because of their tenacity to accustom themselves to their work. The public is usually skeptical about those knives and daggers, believing that they fold up like a telescope instead of going down the throat of the performer. I assure you this is a fallacy. The lady (whom I have known personally) doing this act confided the secret in these words: "As soon as you overcome that gagging sensation when the object comes in contact with the back of your tongue, you've got it licked. But never try it before an audience until you are quite calloused, or you will produce an unfortunate situation of vomiting."

The bear-woman trouped with the same show I was with for one season. She was an internationally famous oddity, yet to me she seemed quite normal in every respect except that she lacked the lower half of her extremities— below the elbows and knees—her hands and feet being attached to these first joints. Some clever Englishman had discovered her in Calcutta, India, taking her to the mother country as a great novelty, especially with the appealing billing "bear-woman." To live up in part to the billing, he compelled her to walk on all fours when on public exhibition. Her being a member of the colored race added to the attraction, since at that time Negroes were a rare sight in many parts of Europe. Later she was brought over to America by Sam Gumpertz, the successor to Barnum in specializing in the handling and putting over of freaks, or sideshow attractions (as one prefers), in the United States.[3] However, she didn't go over quite so big.

To see her dressed in ordinary street clothes, she looked no different from another dwarf with oversized body and short extremities. Her show value was perceivable only when she got in character wearing a brown fur leotard (a body-fitting garment covering the torso) and walking like a quadruped back and forth on the elevated platform where she was exhibited.

Each act is a separate unit represented by a business manager who looks after the interest of his act year round. He signs the contracts and is generally responsible for things concerning the presentation. He signs up for the current season at a stipulated sum, of which he rakes off his percentage or pays the act a flat salary, keeping the balance as his share. According to the contract, meals in the cookhouse and accommodation in the coaches are included. The small exhibits along the midway—or, as we say, out front; for instance, the snake pit or anything under separate top—is a private enterprise, worked on a percentage basis with the show. The candy butchers, balloon vendors, and juice-stand owners—inside and out front—are independent contractors or concessionaires; they pay a flat rate to the show for the exclusive, or rights of trouping, which also includes meals and sleeping accommodations, the same as everybody with the show.

The Oklahoma Ranch Wild West Show was conducted on the same plan as her older sister, the 101 Ranch, but on a smaller scale, of course. The train comprised about six sleeping cars for the performers and personnel, about twelve stock cars for the horses, and approximately seven flats for wagons and other paraphernalia. Roughly, it was a twenty-five-car show. The trains were also show property, bought by the railroad company after they become obsolete to the railroad. The sleeping cars, for instance, were old coaches from which the seats had been removed and berths built in. These berths were simple wooden frames without springs, two-high for the performers and three-high for the personnel. A thin mattress, linen, and blanket were added. The grooms slept in the stock cars wherever they found room, while the roustabouts and razorbacks just boarded the flats after loading the train. I often wondered where they bathed or changed their clothes, since there was no place of privacy for them on train or lot. Occasionally, while walking across the lot alongside the canopy they put up for the horses, one could see some shirts or underwear hanging on a line, or large tin containers propped up over a log fire with clothes boiling away in a concoction which was referred to as crum-stew, and on grounds well founded.

It must have been wanderlust that kept these men on the show, with a two-dollar weekly wage and their food nothing to write home about. The cookhouse on a small show is never any good, as I was to learn later by comparison: boiled spuds in jackets, three times a day, is the only staple I can recall clearly. The performers (who got the choice food) had to buy their own groceries if they wanted something decent to eat. So pity those poor workmen!

Fred Beckman, the joint owner, was manager of the show. Pop (as we all called him) and his wife, Ollie Swan, occupied two-thirds of a car, the other end of which—office and stateroom—was reserved for Eddie Arlington, co-owner, who came on occasionally to check on the business, then went back to the 101, of which he was business manager and partner of the Miller Brothers, Joe and Zack, both of whom took active part in the performance of that show, requiring Arlington's constant presence in the office.[4]

Oh! And there were Indians with the show, real Indians! Over fifty in number, they occupied a car all to themselves. One night, while the train was rolling, I heard the beating of tom-toms and their weird chants loud enough to be heard above the clickety-clackety sound of the rumbling wheels; a papoose was born that night, and they were having a powwow in honor of the event. Interesting people they are, to be sure; I was enchanted by their dances, watching them at every chance, and on the day following the birth, I saw the papoose on the mother's back as she joined the dancers.

Fittingly, every car was named after some Indian chief of the Cherokee tribe. The car in which Helen and I shared a lower berth was the Woponooka. The upper berth over was occupied by the two Arabs, one of whom was Helen's husband. Since there was no other single girl in the car, this arrangement was the nearest way to save on space. Everybody had to double up; otherwise, married couples were always laid out together. Across the aisle from us in the lower was Pop Gilletti, who routed the show and arranged for moving the train by contracting for the locomotive from the line on which we happened to be—every day in a new spot, traveling by night. The show covered hundreds of towns from coast to coast and Canada as well. The cost of moving a show like this is based on mileage—I know they never counted heads.

Pop Gilletti shared his berth with a likeable young chap named Jimmie Orr, who was in the publicity department—better said, *he* was the publicity department. Press agents such as he, who troupe with circuses, have the prearranged write-up on the show, including the exact number of tomorrow's attendance, make contact with the local newspapers, and try to get the editors to print it as a news item rather than pay for it as an advertisement, leaving in reciprocation a whole block of Annie Oakleys (as passes are called).[5]

Over their berth were the two ticket sellers of the sideshow, two jolly lads, Chris and Red (the nickname of the latter denoting his bright red hair) Vollman. Getting in the cars at night, everybody went right to bed, too tired for visiting, but on long runs we had quite a social. Chris and Red were young and full of fun; they'd sit there with heads stooped forward owing to the low ceiling, their feet dangling down, which annoyed Pop. They were so much fun; we told jokes, discussed shop, laughed, and sang. Pop was furious, sticking his head out through the curtain and shoving their feet aside yelling: "Shut up, you roughnecks!" That was the worst term he knew to apply to avenge his anger; he wanted to sleep through the tedious journey—about the best way to spend the time while being confined to such reduced and uncomfortable quarters.

During the first week, it was agony to pass a night in those berths, like lying on the floor—no give to them. I felt like every bone in my body was coming through my skin. But once I got accustomed to these hard bunks, it felt equally uncomfortable to rehabilitate myself to a soft bed: no solid spot to rest on.

Only half of the Woponooka was fitted out with berths; the other half served as the lunch car—"privilege car" is the circus term for it, and some refer to it as the "pie car." Privilege cars, though owned by the show, are run on a percentage basis between owners and car managers. The purpose of these diners, besides a nifty profit, was to accommodate the show people while on the train by serving light lunches, sandwiches, and coffee, soft drinks, and such. Sometimes they were licensed to dispense beer, but never anything stronger. Hard liquor was taboo on any outdoor show, at any time, anywhere.

The general plan resembles a club or lunch car: a long counter with a few tables on the side for those who wish to sit down while taking their snack, then, later on, for those with insomnia, it serves as a propitious place for little card games and, yes, gambling, in a small way.

The privilege car is for members of the show exclusively—no outsider may enter.

The manager of this particular car—that is to say, the part that was the privilege car—was one Eddie Brown, scarcely more than a punk as he appeared. I wondered how he could hold down a position with so much responsibility. As restaurateur or steward, he had to know about buying supplies, planning the meals, and the business in general. Evidently he did.

This tall, dark, and handsome lad had an adorable disposition, a face you love without knowing why. This affable J. Ed. Brown some years later was to be synonymous with every World's Fair, from Century of Progress in 1933 to one held on the West Coast the year 1939–40. To each he contributed something as public-relations executive. His official title: Mayor of the Gay-Way. His thousands of friends in the show world agree that the warmth of his personality just radiated like the sun. In all the years I have known him, he has remained just himself. Good-humored, poised, truly a noble ambassador of outdoor showmen.

All Woponooks occupants had to leave and enter by way of the pie car, since the other end (including the toilet department) was partitioned off for Mr. Arlington's private use as office and stateroom on occasions when he'd visit our show. It was pleasant to come to the coaches at night just to say hello to Eddie Brown, passing through the car on the way to my bunk. The tables were always occupied, and I was too self-conscious to stand at the counter; anyway, having had three meals on the lot, I figured a night-lunch may not be advisable. Extra weight was a thing to dread. Besides (and this is it), you have to pay for what you get in the privilege car.

About three weeks after I joined this fabulous outfit, I made a steady diet of sneaking under the sidewall to watch the Big Show. The sideshow stops its grinding after the Big Show starts, the public all inside. Helen would come along with me occasionally. She knew all the cowboys and cowgirls from the 101 Ranch show, where she had worked a number of years. In fact, she was a very good friend of Mr. Arlington's. There were rumors of . . . but I never bothered about petty gossip.

One by one, she would point out the feature performers with the show: the Mulhall family—old Colonel Zack and son, Charlie, but the daughter, Lucille Mulhall . . . well, there was a star! The way she could handle a lariat, rope steers—throw and tie them—a man would have to take a back seat with her in the class. I really had to be educated into appreciating the dexterity of this branch of amusement. This woman Lucille, her blond hair in two long braids swinging in back from beneath her sombrero with beaded band, a black-and-white unborn calf bolero over an orange-colored silk blouse, a buckskin divided skirt touching her boots just above the ankles, became the prototype of my ideal cowgirl, one I would wish to emulate. Her freckled face didn't need the aid of makeup to bring out the personality she possessed. The man with the fine features and rich baritone voice who sang with the band—Martin Van Bergen—was her husband, but they were never seen on the lot together. Instead, tall, shaggy-type Homer Wilson, chief of the cowboys, often walked along to the cookhouse with her, and a couple of times, I've seen them in town, between shows, together.[6]

With sidewall all around, a canopy over the grandstand only, the bleachers, or "blues" as they are called (after the color they are painted), as well as the large square arena were under open sky, which may be the reason why these performers keep those cumbersome hats on throughout the performance for protection against sun and rain.

Everybody in the Big Show had to go in the street parade, an obligation from which sideshow people have always been exempt. However, one day Helen wanted to go to town shopping but lacked transportation, since no trolley line was near the lot. Seeing that the parade was just lining up, she happened to spot the stagecoach emerging with its passengers who would rather have remained on the lot to do the washing or other chores of private interest. It was a cinch. We took their places in the parade, and during one of the halts downtown, Helen got out with no one the wiser. But thereafter we were obliged to ride the coach every day.

Tex Cooper was the driver of the coach; he was married to Dollie the midget (twenty-three inches high) in the sideshow. Texas was the typical pioneer character—over six feet tall, slim, with long hair, mustache, and goatee—who years later was featured in a Western movie in the role of Buffalo Bill.[7]

At first, I could hardly tell these cowboys apart because of the similarity of their wardrobe: all looked alike. They always wore their outfits to and from the lot to the coaches. Only on Sundays did the Wild West performers wear regular street clothes. Gradually I grew accustomed to their boots and spurs, the gaudy colored shirts and mufflers. The brims of their hats, all having the same rolled angle with a point on the front, became only part of their makeup, beneath which I could distinguish their physical characteristics.

One day as I watched an event called the Pony Express, a very slick looking cowboy with a mail pouch over his shoulder rode dashing in with speed

Texas Cooper, steer riding at the Miller Brothers Real Wild West Show, 1909. Frederick Glasier Collection, neg. no. 0167; black-and-white photograph, copy from glass plate negative, museum purchase, Collection of the John and Mable Ringling Museum of Art Archives, Sarasota, Florida.

like the wind; he got halfway around the arena, leaped off his mount, and almost flying through space mounted another horse already in full gallop. "Gosh, that was neat!" I thought. By then he repeated this changing of horses about four times without a pause. "Who is that one?" I asked Helen. "He is marvelous!" I cried out. It was then I heard the name Otto Kline for the first time. For, although the arena director announced the names of the feature acts, out in the open air—without the aid of the present-day public-address system—it just sounded like a jumbled mumbling; I never even paid attention to the announcer. But I was so enthralled with the grace and speed of this young hero, I had to ask Helen if by chance she had a speaking acquaintance with him. "Oh, I know him slightly," she replied tauntingly. "But you haven't seen anything yet. Wait till you see his trick riding. He is the world's champion, I'll have you know!"

For his trick-riding act later, he had removed his boots and wore white tennis shoes. He came charging in so fast it took my breath away and started whirling round and round in the saddle using no stirrups; around the horse's neck, under the mount's belly, climbing back from the opposite side. Sitting now on the horse's rump, he let himself slide down the tail and without losing momentum, as his feet touched the ground in the rear, he made a flying leap forward, landing in the saddle; then up he went into a shoulder stand, followed by the vaults for which he was famous.

Thrilled to my fingertips, I said to Helen, "I'm going to meet this champion!"

It was Eddie Brown who introduced us one night in the privilege car. Otto was there when I came in. The sideshow always worked after the Big Show let out. I had already raved about him to everyone who'd listen to me, and Eddie, seeing how hopelessly I was smitten, intervened as Dan Cupid on this occasion.

So afraid I might say the wrong thing and leave a bad impression, with odds already against me (the role I played in the sideshow), how could I convince him that I was really a modest maiden? My apprehension and fear were soon allayed when I found how easy it was to talk to him on topics common to us both. He was a performer and had worked in vaudeville. We spoke the same language.

I don't remember if he ever came into the sideshow, except that one day when a heavy downpour almost washed the show away. He brought me a pair of his boots and, spreading his slicker over both of us, led me to a high place out of the water—and I loved rain ever after.

Life was more beautiful with each new day; the privilege car was our rendezvous, where he always saved a place for me. Sundays we'd always go to a movie or an amusement park—we both liked roller skating. If there was a swimming pool in any town, the whole show was there, but we saw only each other. He was a natty dresser; seeing him in street clothes, one couldn't imagine how he could wear the Wild West togs equally as well. Then came August and his obligation with the rodeo contests. After all, he had to defend his title—there were prizes to take into consideration, and yes, there was glory attached to it.

Competition was very keen in the field, yet for three consecutive years he came out on top with the championship. Guy Weadick, the energetic promoter of the biggest contests, was one of Otto's ardent admirers, and a very strong friendship existed between these two. He counted on Otto to appear at contests such as the Round Up at Pendleton, Oregon, the Stampede at Winnipeg, Frontier Days at Cheyenne, and other important ones. Besides his skill and diversity in tricks, Otto was a showman and an artist.

Having finished his commitments, he rejoined the Oklahoma Ranch show at Pawnee, Oklahoma, after an absence of almost six weeks—an eternity to me. Going to the cookhouse that day, I flashed the diamond ring he brought me. I'm sure everyone must have envied me.

The show closed soon after. He returned to vaudeville with Gus Hornbrook's Cheyenne Days act. I picked up the Blanche Baird Company burlesque show; touring, we met once through the winter season. The following spring, he signed up with the Barnum & Bailey Circus Wild West unit, a new feature. I went abroad. Returning in the fall, I joined the Cracker Jacks, while his option with the circus was picked up for the 1915 season, and that's where we started on that eventful tour that day of the Seventeenth of March, so blissfully happy.

DESTINY SMILES, BUT NOT ON SHMOONTSIE

Under the impact of Otto Kline's death, I lapsed into a kind of subconsciousness; whatever I did was through force of habit until the night after I saw the poster on the billboard above Times Square. Partially released, I lived over again the precious moments. Then, when the spell had worn off and I began to think of my own life again, it was bright daylight. It was almost time to get started for rehearsal.

While sipping my coffee, it occurred to me to stop by Mabel's house on the way to tell her about the circus billing. When I rang the bell of her apartment on Forty-fourth Street, it was Harry, her husband, who opened the door leading to a small vestibule.

"Where's Mabel?" I asked. "It's time to get going to the Hip; the call is for 9:30 AM, or did she forget?"

"Mabel is still in bed; she ain't going to no rehearsal!" he said with both pride and contempt in his tone. Recognizing my voice, Mabel asked me in; all three of us sat on the bed of the small room as we talked. What I thought would be exciting news was old stuff to them, for Harry showed me the call in the *Billboard* announcing the date for reporting at the Garden. Mabel had already handed in her notice at the Hippodrome.

How I envied her! She was going with the circus—she'd be with her husband, just as I would have been.

By an odd coincidence, of all the girls in my own group—and the other groups, for that matter—Mabel was the one I struck up a close friendship with, maybe because she had a certain sympathetic aspect about her. We soon exchanged confidences, but what made it a coincidence was that Mabel and her husband, Harry Clemings, were both connected with the Barnum & Bailey Circus. Harry, as a clown, had been with the outfit for a number of seasons, while Mabel got her start in 1911, when the circus went classical—presenting a ballet as an added feature. This was repeated for three consecutive seasons, and many a famous lady circus performer can date her career back to the ballet rank comprised of about sixty girls. Mabel was of the first season's crop, and she and Harry married after the closing of the 1911 season. During the winter, there isn't very much a clown can do except odd job occasionally with an indoor circus or as Santa Claus around Christmas time, so Mabel usually picked up a show in New York, and the Hip was favorable, since they could be together the winter through.

It was during a pause at rehearsal that I was struck by the idea of trying for the circus. It seemed preposterous—I knew it—yet there was that miracle I hoped might happen. Wishful dreaming perhaps, but already I was snapping out of my listlessness. The very thought of it worked like a tonic: "I'm going with the circus!"

"But what can you do here, Mrs. Kline?" asked Mr. Bradna, the debonair equestrian director, when a few weeks later I went over to the Garden, between matinee and night show, to apply for that much-coveted privilege.

"Since we have no ballet, your dancing ability is of no use to us," he continued. "I'm sorry." Completely dejected, in my despair I asked for permission to see the horse that played such an important role in my drama. This was granted; in fact, he walked down the ramp with me to the pad room. There was the black mare. She was beautifully groomed—her coat so shiny, like satin. I threw my arms around her neck and hugged her so tightly. Mr. Bradna was moved at the sight of this picture and told me to wait while he sent word to the publicity department. That did it. The camera caught it. Seeing me there with the horse while I was being interviewed for a story and remembering Otto Kline, he somehow associated me with riding.

"Well, okay, if you are satisfied with what little we pay you—ten dollars per week—I will make a place for you with the show!"

"Oh, Mr. Bradna, I am most grateful to you!" I cried, as I jubilantly clasped his hand. "And when do I start?" I asked eagerly, forgetting the ethics of giving notice at the Hip.

Ballet girls (and ballet boys in drag) (no date). Frederick Glasier Collection, neg. no. 0485; black-and-white photograph, copy from glass plate negative, museum purchase, Collection of the John and Mable Ringling Museum of Art Archives, Sarasota, Florida.

"Well, now, let us say you can join us in ten days when we go on the road. Meanwhile, you may come down here in the morning hours to practice on any of the show's horses you like."

This was all I wanted to hear. Now I was beside myself with excitement, walking on air. The prospects of being with the circus was a thrill hard to describe. Even before I got back to do the night show, I was already planning on the big things I was going to do—or die in the attempt, yes, die like he did. It would be glorious!

When I read the article next morning in the *New York Tribune,* under the headline, "Dancer Finds Solace at Scene of Cowboy Husband's Death," I was in for a shock when I noticed the date—the great joy came exactly on the anniversary of my deepest sorrow, April 21, 1916. Somehow I knew it was his spirit that was guiding my future.

Mabel was the first person to hear the news of my impending venture.

"Of course, you know the size of the trunk is a regulation twenty-six-inch Taylor for anybody of your rating; just for personal effects—no worry about any wardrobe!" she said. "But be sure it is a *circus* trunk; they have the zinc-reinforced bottom to keep the water out."

"Oh, that's all right—I'll get one. What concerns me now is the kind of accommodation I'll get for my cat; Shmoontsie is rather spoiled and may not like trouping," I joked lightly in discussing the triviality, as it seemed.

"I'm afraid you'll have to forget the idea of taking Shmoontsie. You see, the rules are: No children, no pets. But maybe the janitress here would be happy to take care of her, or even adopt her," she went on as she saw the joy fade from my face.

Indeed, this presented quite a problem. Shmoontsie had been my sole companion for almost a year. I got her during the time when I was so upset emotionally that I was afraid of being alone day or night. She was just a tiny kitten then, though not much bigger now—I had tried stunting her growth by adding alcohol to her milk so she would remain a kitten always. I was very sad over this ruling. "No children, no pets," kept ringing in my ears. For the next few days I meditated but couldn't arrive at a solution. What to do about her? The janitress in Mabel's house had a little girl, so that was an obstacle. I was aware that children sometimes abused animals, and knowing Shmoontsie's independent nature, I knew they'd clash. I lay awake nights holding her close to me, realizing how unwittingly I'd grown so attached to a cat that my heart actually ached at the thought of how she would grieve for me when we parted, as I knew from experience. On times I had been detained at night rehearsals, opening the front door, I could hear her mournful "meow" from two flights above. Then, when I got upstairs, that happy little "prrrt" sound—like a short chirp of a bird—as she heard me turning the key to my room. Nobody else could understand her language. At the sight of me she'd do several rollovers on the floor, then race up the lace curtains and leap to my shoulder, sometimes landing on my head. I knew nobody else would understand these efforts of expressions of her appreciation of my companionship, nor the times she would dig her claws into my shin and run, which was her say of getting even with me for ignoring her when she was in the mood for playing hide and seek.

She shied of any living creature; whenever anyone came to see me she would remain in hiding all during the time of the visit. She hated baths, and although she knew she'd lose the argument, she'd hide when she heard me draw the water in the bathtub, and these made up her character.

Only those who have at some time or other been in a like situation can appreciate the dilemma that was confronting me now. It was not like parting with a loved one—another fellow creature—the loss of whom we bemoan, yet, if reasoned out, in the analysis we find that our grief is actually motivated by selfishness: we have lost someone who was a source of our pleasure; we feel sorry for ourselves. No! This was genuine compassion, purely concern for this little defenseless creature whose future looked so bleak. Would that I had the foresight to have a veterinarian end it in sleep eternal. But no, I respected the *law of divinity,* the right to life for every humble creature, and so I came to the conclusion to take Shmoontsie to the Bide-a-Wee Home for Friendless Animals.

I bought a whole pound of liver, which I fried just the way she relished it. She sat up on her hind legs—her way of saying, "I want some of that," when she perceived the aroma. It was like wringing my heart when I packed it neatly in a glass container to be served to her by another's hands. She always slept in my bed, and in the morning when I removed my nightgown, throwing it over the foot of the bed, she loved to jump on it while it was still warm; she'd trample it down with her forelegs, kneading it, then lastly wrap herself in it; and that's how she spent the day.

"I will take one of these nightgowns along to comfort her in her new home!" I thought as I was getting dressed.

At the Bide-a-Wee, I found the attendant to be a sympathetic, spinsterly type woman who understood my tears while checking in the new guest in the register. While she entered the name, feature characteristics, habits, et cetera, in the book, I asked if I might see how they house these protégés, cats and dogs.

"You will find them quite contented. We give them the best of care," she said as she led the way out into a huge loft, which was sheltered against rain and wind but bitterly cold. There were the individual cages, one occupant in each, piled up one on top of another, resembling shelves or pigeonholes. Some of the cats, with streams of mucus oozing from nose and mouth, presented a pitiful sight behind the wire-screen barrier, not in the least stirred at the sight of people. The dogs—various sizes and species, probably more harmonious socially than cats—were grouped in pens, howling and barking in every tone imaginable. I was still hanging on to Shmoontsie inside my coat, remembering how she loved heat, how many times I had come home from the Hip to find the room was ice-cold because she had sprawled herself over the hot-air grill. She was now all tense with her claws hooked in my dress, clutching to me for dear life, as though she sensed what was to come, and she defied it.

"And what is the ultimate fate of these animals?" I asked with concern for all.

"They eventually find homes with people who come here seeking pets," she replied soothingly, then adding that Shmoontsie stood a fair chance of getting a home within a few days, not only because of her diminutive size, but her coloring was also out of the ordinary—most uncannily marked: a white foundation with a black coat over her back involving the tail; a perfect frock coat. The tips of her paws were black, as if she had shoes on, and the top of her head, including both ears, was also black—just as if she were wearing a beret, jauntily pulled over one eye. Incidentally, the eye on the side of the black fur was blue, while the right eye having white fur on that side was brown of color.

Seeing what was to be Shmoontsie's cell, a box about the size of an ordinary birdcage with newspaper on the flooring, I asked the woman to be sure to place the garment I had brought inside the cage for bedding. The acrid odor of creoline and chloride of lime was nauseating, and I was glad when we returned to the little office in front. She shook down the ashes in the potbellied stove, putting some egg-shaped coal (coke) in the fire.

I opened the package and put some of the liver in Shmoontsie's dish, which I had also brought along, hoping that these familiar objects—material reminders of what had been her world yesterday—would help to overcome the strangeness of her new surroundings and serve to cushion the abrupt change. But she refused to eat; her eyes bulged as if looking for a way to escape, while her body was shivering with terror.

I had not the heart to see her placed in that torture chamber, and with my last plea—"Please take care of my Shmoontsie, please!"—I left without looking back at her there on the floor.

A NEW LEAF,
A NEW LIFE

I had made two trips to the Garden to practice my riding preparatory to my adventure. Dick Shannon, the boss of the ring stock, knew just by looking at me that I had never mounted a horse. He walked over to a certain string of creams, ordering their groom to saddle up Star. I watched as he pulled on the girth with all his might; the horse never even budged. Sidesaddles have to be cinched tightly because the rider, especially an inexpert one, will pull it over off-balance, riding the horns rather than the horse.

We went into the arena. Placing my left foot in the stirrup, the groom boosted me up by cupping both his hands to serve as a springboard under my right foot in mounting. Taking the lines, he led the horse once around the track on a walk. There were guylines dangling from aerial riggings above, which he swung out of the way as we passed.

Bears were practicing their skating and cycling on one stage, an acrobatic troupe was just breaking the four-high pyramid in the ring next to it, liberty horses were going through their drills in another ring, and yes, the boss trainer, Mooney, was putting through a herd of his charges in the new act: baseball, played by elephants in the third ring.

With all these goings on in the center, Star just kept his even pace walking, never shying at any sudden movement of the others. He seemed assured that his role in this great show is as important as any of those mentioned. Star was a model of stability; he had given many beginners their first riding lesson. He also served for Cy Compton to stand on while spinning out the hundred-foot rope loop called the Wedding Ring during the Wild West exhibition. I don't know what else he was used for in the show. Always easy to handle, he would stand transfixed till given the cue: "tsk," a clucking of the tongue.

When the riding lesson was over, I walked back to watch the other acts practice. The bears were just about the most delightful things. As I stood fascinated at seeing one of them ride a kiddy-car, the lady assisting the trainer stepped off the stage and came over to warn me not to get too close because that big Siberian gray who looked so tame and gentle was really a vicious fellow, especially when he was practicing the tightrope walking.

She was a nice person who didn't mind telling me that her name was Pallenberg. Even as she spoke, I noticed she had been crying. I asked if the bear had turned on her.

"No, he would never harm me as long as my husband has hold of his leash and he knows me, but he doesn't like strangers to see him practice. He likes to perform the act when it is 'finished' and running smooth."[1]

Then she explained the reason for her tears. Only that morning she had left their infant son on a farm in Connecticut, and this had just about taken the spirit out of them. Emil Jr. was the light of their life. But as important as their act was to the show, they were given the choice to take it or leave it—no children were allowed on the show. "I don't know why I keep talking about it—you wouldn't understand." I recalled Shmoontsie and thought I understood a little.

Time was flying on wings the last two days between preparation and doing my usual two shows at the Hip, where I worked up to the last moment before embarking on the circus train on Saturday night.

To pick out the most essential items to pack in that little trunk took some time, deliberating what I needed most. There just wasn't any space for anything with so many trays. True, I was allowed a suitcase as well. So after I had separated the preferred effects, having placed the large wardrobe trunk in storage, I was all set Saturday morning to move out of the room, which had been my home for ever so long. I took the little trunk down to the Garden in a cab; the boss propertyman, Mickey Graves, was to take charge of it.[2] Seeing it unlettered, he asked what my capacity was with the show; of course, I didn't know. He then looked over a long list of names arranged alphabetically. Yes, finding the name Kline, he knew the category. Calling one of his boys, who did a little painting business on the side, I watched him lettering the top: "Tiny Kline" in the center, "Statues" directly under. I took it for granted that this was done for their convenience, quite ignorant of the fact that it was a service which called for a tip just as did *every* little act, whether part of the scheme of the show or an extra service; the tipping on a circus is without limit. This long-established custom dates back to the era when workmen with the show used to travel for their health or the adventure, and the sooner one learned to be generous the more pleasant the firsthand impression of the environment was likely to be.[3]

And if I had thought my last days had been a series of hustle-bustle, it was before I saw the activity that was going on there in the back end, with newly painted red wagons being lined up ready to receive their corresponding load of performers' trunks. These wagons (really, vans), sturdily built of wood with metal reinforcement, besides bearing lettering of the show's name were also numbered to enable the contents to be identified after the wagons were loaded. The same wagon was used for the same load throughout the entire season. When the show was late getting in at some spots, Mickey and his gang knew exactly which wagon to unload first by the number painted on all four sides. In loading them, the men were trained to use up every inch of space. The old superstition about the camelback trunks being a Jonah was quickly debunked when I saw that they didn't stack up solid in the wagons. The ill omen was pinned on to discourage performers from bringing them on the show.

Mickey Graves told me to leave the suitcase in the wardrobe department, where Rose Wallace was the boss, assisted by two other women, one of whom was old Mother Talbot, now in her eighties, only kept on the show as a relic. A male assistant was stationed around the men's dressing room in case of an emergency of a fastener or button needing to be sewed on. On these four persons depended the responsibility of handling the enormous pile of costumes for man and beast, not forgetting the uniforms worn by the personnel of the various departments, each of which had its own special design and color scheme, making it possible to identify its members anywhere on the lot.

The performers own and care for the costumes they wear in their own particular acts. In most cases, they design and make them up themselves, which accounts for the many colors and styles. Usually they are conceived to be practical and flattering, to suit the special sort of work the wearer will use them in, and this goes for footgear as well. However, the show furnishes and the wardrobe department maintains the care of all costumes worn by the performers in the street parade and that colorful gala spectacle which precedes each performance, sometimes referred to as "tournament" or "spec." This extravagant pageant depicts some great moment, mythical, biblical, or historical. The display of pomp and splendor is rampant in the glorious glitter of costumes beyond the wildest fancy of the imagination. The show owns all this wardrobe, the gorgeous bedecking of the elephants and horses, even to the jockey suits worn by the monkeys in the races, which had to be replaced almost daily. These simians are jealous and poor sportsmen, and though each monkey is chained to his mount, they'd break loose somehow, leap over to the other pony passing theirs, and a fight would ensue right in the middle of the race. Sometimes at the end there would be three monkeys on one pony, and the beautiful satin jockey suit would be torn to tatters; regardless of who won the race, it was the fight that mattered.

In the Garden (the original Madison Square Garden), the dressing rooms were arranged so the ladies dressed on the Twenty-sixth Street, the men on the Twenty-seventh Street side. There were no private rooms for privileged characters, except Prince, the educated chimpanzee who had a room on the top floor all by himself and his owners, Mr. and Mrs. Heller. Having watched Prince work out that morning, I believed I had seen everything, and not only did I agree with Darwin, I thought this ape was underrated.

The act was so perfect that I followed them upstairs to see how this artist behaved offstage. Mrs. Heller was preparing an eggnog, which she poured into a glass and placed on the table before him with a straw. He sat on a high stool, drawing the drink through the straw much the same as a child would, delighting in the bubbles he blew through it. Then he unlaced and removed his high shoes, as well as his practice clothes, and started to jump. Up and down he bounced; then, forgetting his manners, he made a grab for me. I was stricken with fear at this sudden move; however, the Hellers assured me no harm was meant; he just liked to show his affection by a tight hug.

Prince was the first and last ape I have seen correctly housebroken to the use of a chair with a pot, the same as is used in nurseries. The Hellers told me that what I had seen that morning represented three years of patient training. The first year they just lived with him, treating him as though he were another human being. He slept in pajamas, and in the morning he would be dressed completely with underwear, shirt, overalls, socks, and shoes, which he learned to put on himself. The Hellers ate at the same table with him, which accounted for his easy manipulation of knife and fork. He was part of every function in the household. The Hellers owned a nice country estate.

Prince would go along rowing with them in their boat and even liked fishing. He did everything but talk, and thus he was taught that marvelous act which took another two years to perfect. Mr. John Ringling went to see him perform in the Hellers' home before signing the contract, since it involved an important sum of money—money he thought was well spent.

The Hellers owned the first house-trailer I had ever seen, which was housing on the road. It was loaded on the flats the same as the cages and wagons, setting thereby a precedent in transporting this mobile home; it solved the problem of the tedious trips between lot and train, but more important, it made it possible for them to be always together and protected against weather changes—these apes were greatly susceptible to colds and consumption (tuberculosis). Ironically, the act did not last a season. Mrs. Heller was taken ill and died in a hospital as a result of a surgical operation. Mr. Heller couldn't leave the show to be at her bedside; an ape is a bigger problem than a child—they will not stand for a sitter or substitute caretaker as a baby would. And lo, scarcely a few weeks after Mrs. Heller's death and notwithstanding the tender care Mr. Heller gave him, Prince died of pneumonia.

Fate works in a strange and mysterious way. Three years later, while arranging for transporting my equipment to the Garden, I thought the name of the Theatrical Transfer and Express firm had a familiar ring—yes, it was Heller's. Odd, how I met him and his family on the day I first joined the show. The Hellers were big shots, yet not too snooty to treat me with politeness—a quality very rare among feature or even lesser-grade performers, as I soon found out. People such as the Hellers one long remembers. Meeting with him now was a heartwarmer.

We exchanged notes. He was interested when I told him that presently I was bickering with Charlie Ringling, holding to my claim that the contract, or the option thereon, wasn't worth the paper it was written on unless my aerial act were given consideration. The contract he tried to hold me to was for a minor turn of the previous seasons, with a clause reading, "and make herself generally useful." I didn't like that line. I felt that I had outgrown that stage, having an act of my own, complete with apparatus. Anyway, Mr. John would have something to say about that—he was the only boss I recognized on that show.[4] The main thing was to get him to see the act, so I had Mr. Heller haul my rigging down.

He hadn't remarried nor broken in another ape. I shall never forget that great act as I had seen it that time, long ago; too bad it had such a short run. But *what* an act it was while it lasted!

The stage was set with a clothes-tree, a table, and a chair. Prince, attired in formal dress-suit, cape, and high silk hat, was twirling a cane as he stepped up on the stage, accompanied by his valet, Heller; he neatly hooked his cane on the tree, removed his cape, which he handed to Heller, and with a wide sweep of his arm removed his hat as he took a bow to the audience. Then, sitting down at the table, he picked up the menu. Heller served him whatever the fare, which this Prince ate with the proper manners befitting his noble name; he drank what looked to be wine; then, crossing his legs, he lit and smoked a cigar amid great applause. By this time the propertymen had set up a wire across the stage. Prince, removing his full dress-suit, dropping his trousers, got a howl of laughter from all over the house. By the way, I might mention the fact that Prince worked holding the arena to himself; every other space was blacked out. Wearing only trunks now, he not only walked on the wire but swung from it while doing gymnastic tricks no human could accomplish— giant-swings, cutaways, now by his arms, now by his feet, his toes gripping like fingers—it was breathtaking and humorous at the same time.

Having checked my belongings for the season's tour, I went to the Hip for my last day's work; that night I would sleep on the circus train. Returning to the Garden after the show, I simply tagged along with Mabel and Harry, who knew just where the coaches were located in the freight yards over on the Jersey side.

This was a big event—the first night the circus people got aboard. During the four or five weeks while at the Garden in New York, every member lived much like any actor or workman while footing his own expenses. But from this night on, it was all on the show. No more worry of housing and meals for the next six or seven months. (It was considered a long season when Thanksgiving dinner was served on the lot.) This was when the real season started; from this day forward, the show would be given under canvas.

All the performers, with suitcases and bags in hand, left the Garden as soon as their act was over, most of them getting back the same berths they occupied the previous season. Feature acts, eligible for staterooms, knew exactly which car to get on. The newcomers had to see the boss porter, Mr. Shaeffer, who had the list of the entire show's people. Harry and Mabel were in one of the married people's cars, number 96. (On this show the cars were numbered, most likely because they were too numerous for names.) I was assigned to number 91, the single ladies' car, or "virgin's car," as most folks referred to it. I had an upper all to myself, which was a privilege, since most of them were shared by two persons. In this car a woman porter was in charge, which made it possible for us to run up and down the aisle in our nighties, but then, with the open washroom (no division between aisle and toilet room), there just couldn't be a man present even in the role of a porter.

I noticed that most of the ladies wore pajamas and soon found out the reason. All those in upper berths have to get up and down without the aid of a ladder by stepping up at the foot-end of the lower berth, grabbing hold of the horizontal curtain-bar above, and doing a pull-up in tempo till your knees reach the upper. From then on you are all set on your shelf. Descending, one does the same act in reverse. Care must be taken to be far enough toward the foot-end not to step on the occupants of the lower. A nightgown is an awkward habiliment for this gymnastic feat, especially on the descent. It usually gets pinched against the side of the berth as you slide downward so that the only part that remains covered is your head. The sight of nudeness was shocking to all concerned, and I soon learned to wear pajamas.

Under the lower berth, there was space for suitcases of both upper and lower occupants, but the difficulty of getting at them in the narrow aisle space made it expedient to remove the toilet articles and items of daily necessity and keep them in pockets (on the order of shoe bags) tacked against the wall of the berth. Shoes were left on the floor in front of the berth before retiring, and the porter (in our case, porteress) would shine everybody's shoes each night. There was also a locker in every car where the porter kept a hanger with our Sunday clothes and coat all through the season. The open lavatories were necessary to keep some selfish persons from monopolizing the place by converting it into their private beauty salon. With everybody in line looking on, especially with the porteress (whose upper berth faced the washroom) watching that no one washed below their neck and arms and that hair was put up in curlers in individuals' own berths and makeup in their own mirrors—with such vigilance no one would dare take her good time about her toiletry.

The porters worked only in the cars and got their meals in the privilege car free. They keep the cars immaculately clean. The sleeping cars of the Barnum & Bailey Circus were regular Pullmans; the beds were always left down—ready for use. Linen was changed every Monday and the soiled linen sent by express to a laundry in a town a week in advance of the show's route, where it was redeemed on arrival. Fifty cents for porterage was deducted from each performer's weekly salary, plus the customary tip of another fifty cents given to the porter by each individual every payday. Each porter would kick back to the boss porter a portion of the tips received. That one, being responsible for the entire section of the train, didn't come into personal contact with the occupants—no berth to make up, no shoes to shine. His job was to see that the cars were watered and the sanitary conditions taken care of day after day.

The uppers having no window, I was quite surprised on awakening and drawing the green drapes aside to see the bright sunshine from the window of the lower across the aisle. It was Sunday morning, and with no show obligation, most of the ladies leisurely remained in the car, sitting in their berths all along the line and sewing on bright-colored cretonne pockets over matching drapes which they tacked against the sides, covering the entire interior of the berth including the ceiling like a miniature boudoir, with lace curtains over the windows—each berth was a masterpiece of interior decoration, the artistic expression of its occupants. Combs, brushes, lotions, and other articles of toiletry half protruded from this wall-dresser with elastic-bound pockets so jolting of the train wouldn't shake them loose; so neatly arranged, there seemed ample room for the accessories of both occupants. Everything seemed to have its proper place: towels hung on a small rack, slippers in a buckram pocket at the end of each berth, night garments and robes stuffed inside a cretonne slip simulating a cushion—nothing left on the berth or the floor which might deter the cleaning. Yes, I liked the idea and planned to follow suit. Light-colored cretonne covering all the woodwork might even lend to that dingy upper a cheerful and bright reflection.

I swung down from that horizontal bar like a female Tarzan, feeling for that little arm piece under my feet. Going to the washroom, I found several girls there squatted on the floor (wherever space permitted), each with a little Primus stove in front of her making coffee. The aroma was so inviting, but not so the operators; no one offered me a cup, and this was quite understandable. Usually the two who bunk together pool the expenses on these little breakfast parties. The pot was quite small and held just the amount to satisfy their own needs. Besides, the milk, sugar, and cups were in the berth where the table was being spread by the other partner. So this too I noted and tucked away as part of my education. I didn't linger; dodging the squatters with their little roaring apparatuses—like so many blow torches—battling the temptation of the appetite-teasing smells of bacon and coffee, I made a hurried dash for the door of the little room at the end where, at this time, I didn't have to stand in line for a turn.

This car, though occupied almost to capacity, had only one washroom; the other end of the car was partitioned off by a wall. One-fourth of the car connected with the service room had been cut off and converted into a comfortable stateroom, which was occupied by Mr. and Mrs. Bradna. All the other cars were accessible from both ends—one for the ladies, the other for the men. In the cars of mixed sexes, man and wife entered from different ends because washrooms were exposed from the aisle. The small compartment with the water closet was the only complete privacy the men and women had at either end aboard the coaches. With a passage terminating in a dead end, as had been the case in the virgin's car, and the wide-open lavatories at each end of the other cars, it would have been impossible to pass through the section from car to car while the train was in motion except in extreme emergency, and then I doubt any of us could have crashed through that division.

There were staterooms, of course; one whole car of these private rooms. Only acts of extraordinary merit were given staterooms—one to each troupe—and in most cases they were more crowded than the regular sleeping cars, but it was the prestige that counted, and the privacy. If crowded, at least only their own immediate family was involved, and when a troupe comprised more than a family, the other members had to sleep in the other coaches. Staterooms were reckoned as a twenty-five-dollar weekly privilege. That amount was set against the stipulated salary according to agreement.

I had neither felt nor heard the train moving during the night, but gazing through the washroom window, I could see the lettering on the station a short distance away: North Philadelphia. Looking through across from the opposite side, all I could see was an endless number of stock cars and flats, painted a bright yellow color with blue and red lettering on the side of each: "Barnum & Bailey Circus—Greatest Show on Earth," as far as my vision could behold. They were unloaded and set on sidetracks in double and treble lines. It was awe-inspiring, and I was swelled with pride to be part of this colossal enterprise even in a small capacity. In a moment I was all buoyant with animation, dressed before I realized. As I stepped off the platform, I wondered if Mabel was still in the car, or had she gone out to the showgrounds. If she had, all I had to do was trail several of the folks passing and I'd get there, but I decided to walk ahead to number 96 and inquire. "Have you seen the Clemingses?" I asked of the tall, pleasant-faced young man who at that moment appeared on the end of the car. In jumping off the platform without using the steps (not having seen me approach from the side of the train) he almost landed on top of me.

"Oh, sorry! I didn't see you there. Clemings, did you say?" he reflected for a moment. "Too bad, you just missed them, they left a little while ago—must have gone to the lot."

"How do I get there?" I asked.

Midway, menagerie, and big top, Adam Forepaugh and Sells Brothers Circus (no date). Although Kline worked for Barnum & Bailey, this photograph of Forepaugh and Sells provides a sense of the enormity of the circus showgrounds. Frederick Glasier Collection, neg. no. 1406; black-and-white photograph, copy from glass plate negative, museum purchase, Collection of the John and Mable Ringling Museum of Art Archives, Sarasota, Florida.

"If you don't mind walking, I'll show you the way—about a mile from here." And having walked during this chitchat, we were already off the railroad property by then, headed toward the street leading to the lot.

"You live here?" he asked. "I haven't seen you with the show!"

"But I am with the show," I said proudly. "I start working tomorrow."

We talked as we walked along. I found out he was Paul Jerome, a clown.[5] He and Harry were in the same category; he was single and slept in the berth over the Clemingses (married couples were always given the preference of the lowers). In a few minutes, we were approaching the tents, which looked like huge white mountains from a distance—a nine-acre city, sprung up overnight with multifarious banners and flags waving briskly with the early May breeze from every pole.

"By gosh, look! The flag is still up!" Then, looking at his wristwatch, he continued, "Almost nine o'clock. If we cut across the big top, we can still make it. You want breakfast don't you? We've got five minutes before they close."

We just got through the roped entrance when the doorman started to pull down one of the four flags flying from the poles, the blue field with the silver stars. Simultaneously, he drew a cord which closed the flap across the entrance, but we were inside. Stepping over a plank seat, we sat down before a long table, covered with a red-and-white-checkered cloth. Cups and plates were turned downward to keep the dust out of the business side of them, and as the white-coated waiter came, asking if we wanted the cereal and hotcakes, he picked up the setups (as knife, fork, and spoon are referred to), wiping them with the cloth he carried over his arm.

"Bring us a full-house!" Paul replied, which meant everything on the bill of fare. By now, a stocky little redheaded man, carrying two gigantic coffee pots—each one containing at least two gallons—stopped by and asked: "Tea or coffee?"

"Mine is java!" Paul said, then turning to me, "Is that okay for you?"

Something about this Paul disarmed me completely; I felt quite at home with him. The little man set one of the pots on the ground and, turning the cups upward with the free hand, he poured coffee for both. Milk had already been added out in the kitchen. It didn't look very good—no aroma perceptible—and tasted as it looked. After I added the sugar, it was just something warm, moist, and sweet. However, I drank it because it was called coffee. The cereal was oatmeal, and almost simultaneously, bacon and eggs were set before us—my, but that *did* look good. Meantime, the tea and coffee man had made another round in the aisle, filling the cups without asking— he just keeps them filled all the time.

I couldn't eat the stack of hotcakes, not knowing they were a side dish to the bacon and eggs when I—rather, Paul—had ordered them. The cups were likewise filled when we left the table. I felt sort of guilty for the waste of food. However, I learned later that the food left untouched was distributed among some poor, hungry folks who habitually came around to glean at the back of the cookhouse. The coffee, however, was a waste; I wondered why they didn't stress quality rather than quantity.

There had been a few performers scattered here and there when we came in. On their way out, they nodded a greeting to Paul. We were the last to leave as we started for the dressing room. I was sure of seeing Mabel there. Yes, I recognized her at some distance away talking to some girls. By this time Paul had disappeared behind the flap to the left. The ladies' side of the dressing room was to the right. The flap drawn across the entrance was plainly lettered with black paint over both sides: Men and Ladies.

"I just ordered a bucket for you," Mabel said after we exchanged greetings.

A propertyman, one of Mickey's gang, emerged from seemingly nowhere with a load of brand new zinc pails stacked inside of one another. He took orders for them from those standing by. The price was thirty-five cents, but if one lacked the cash, credit was good. He'd put the name down in a little book he carried. Harry had come out of the men's side with a can of red paint, marking both of theirs on the inside near the rim. Then asking me how I wanted mine marked so I could pick it out from among about two hundred others, I told him "T.K.X."—adding the "X" to further the distinction. Afterward, I noticed it was a favorite letter of a score of others.

In a little while, another of these agents came along, this time with campstools and easy chairs of a collapsible type, but Mabel advised me to buy a metal-framed stool in town, one I could pack in my trunk, thereby saving carrying charges. Clothes racks were also sold by the boys on the lot. Probably the invention of some ingenious brain in the show's own blacksmith shop, they were made of small diameter gas-pipe in the shape of a T, the cross-section studded with multiple metal hooks. This rack, about five or six feet high, may be taken apart in small sections with threaded ends, the bottom piece ending in a spear so it could be driven into the ground with very little effort. This was a practical and necessary item, since there was no place to put one's street clothes while working.

So I began to become established in my new life.

WHERE CASTE IS OBSERVED, ACCORDING TO RANK AND RATING

Presently, Mabel led me through the flap to the right—that sanctuary, called the dressing room, the only place the circus performer can call home during the tour. It is where he or she spends all the spare time through the day—from the early hours in the morning, after leaving the coaches, until getting back to them after the night show. Once your trunk is spotted, that three-by-three-foot space is your private property, as rightfully yours as if you held a deed to it, and that right is respected by the others; during the activities requiring your presence outside, nobody would infringe by sitting on your chair or even take a peek in your mirror in your absence. That space before each one's trunk: One's Domain.

The dressing room was a three-pole top, oblong in shape and quite large in proportion. This tent was made of terra-cotta colored canvas, no doubt to eliminate a free shadow-show of the people dressing or undressing. Contrary to the arrangement of the entrance to the cookhouse at the broad side, the dressing room entrance was at the end side (the one nearest to the back door of the big top). A high partition wall of the same colored canvas, which was tied up to the poles, ran through the center lengthwise—from one end to the other—dividing the room, men to the left, ladies to the right side. On entering the ladies' side, there were large tables jacked up on saw horses and a few immense trunks to the sidewall. Sewing machines to the center wall comprised the wardrobe department, where the costumes for parade and spec were distributed.

Following the wardrobe department, the actual dressing room began. Looking toward the rear, the performers' trunks were arranged end to end in four straight rows running to the far end. The first row was backed against the partition wall; the next row ranged directly opposite with a seven-foot distance between, forming an aisle. Both rows of trunks, when opened, faced toward the center of this aisle, and it was here that one could appreciate the class distinction of the performers, for it was between these two rows—this first aisle—where the aristocrats, those top-notch ladies with the circus, dressed. Their trunks were placed significantly according to their rating, starting with the bareback riders to the left, backed against the partition, and the aerial performers on the right-hand side; when the lids of their trunks were up, it placed them in a simulated private dressing room, shut off from the second aisle. Of course, the farther down this queens' row led, so did the rank of the performers, decreasing in importance still more when their trunks started with the third row, which were placed back against the second row with just sufficient space between so the lids may be opened against each other. The fourth row was set against the outer sidewall, and the space between this and the third row formed a second aisle, or main thoroughfare, for it was through this aisle where all the traffic passed and through which we, the statue girls, reached our little sanctum—a small wedge at the extreme far end of the tent, completely isolated from the others by another partition. By the time the fourth-row group was classified, it was reduced to the riff-raff caste. The statue girls, still lower, were looked upon as interlopers.

The performers in the second aisle, especially those whose trunks were placed against the outer wall, were at a terrific disadvantage. They suffered greatly from lack of privacy, with everyone who passed bumping against their chairs, but particularly from the weather, being exposed to the elements of wind and rain from over and under the sidewall.

As if that weren't punishment enough, there was a space left vacant here for *all* the ladies to duck out under the sidewall, to hang out their washing on a line they'd string between a guyline and a wagon, and also to make their way to that little comfort station erected almost directly against the facing sidewall. This little project, commonly referred to as "donniker" (in circus parlance)—accommodating six persons—would have stumped even

Ladies' dressing tent (no date). Frederick Glasier Collection, neg. no. 0400; black-and-white photograph, copy from glass plate negative, museum purchase, Collection of the John and Mable Ringling Museum of Art Archives, Sarasota, Florida.

the famous Chick Sale for ingenuity and speedy construction, yet it met all the requirements of the sanitation laws then existing. It was here, in the intimacy owing to the nature of this department, where queen and low-brow sat side by side within touching distance, where everybody was reduced to equal standing (or sitting?).

Indeed, the place of your trunk determined who you were. And while I only describe the side of the ladies' layout, the same applied to the men on the other side of the partition, with the same class distinction (excepting the statue girls' rating, nonexistent there). The lowest rank of the male performer is held by the clown, unless he happens to have something to elevate him above the average: someone with international fame, like Marcelino, who retired while still a feature attraction and opened a restaurant with equal success.

These may seem trifling details to the general reader, but they are the very vibration of life to these men and women who make circus performing their lifelong career. The only social life they know lies behind that curtain, through which they enter in the big top to do their work; social codes and etiquette which they enact and abide by demonstrate the possibility of living proximate and at the same time dignified and aloof—above those they consider their inferiors, whose lineage or merit of performance doesn't match their own (although the latter comes second in order).

Having reached the far end of this corridor-shaped room and making our way through the loose end of the partition which was to shut us off from view of the other ladies, Mabel said, "Now this is our dressing room."

I looked about. There seemed hardly room for all those trunks scattered about in disorder. They were left standing on ends for each to pick out her place, whom she wants to be next to or between. Mabel, arriving early, had already placed hers against the partition nearest the exit. The only other trunk arranged in place, with clothes rack already set up alongside it—even to a small board-platform in front of the trunk, so precise, it caught my eyes— sat across the inner corner like a sentinel, its thirty-inch imposing size quite in contrast with the others, a privilege given only to performers who own and carry their wardrobe. Mabel explained that the large trunk belonged to the head statue lady and that the entire number—all three groups—were under her direction. She arranged the various poses which were replicas from famous statuary. "So she's going to be my boss," I thought, as I read the lettering on her trunk: "Ena Claren, Statues." Evidently someone looking after her interest had already been on the job to spot her place. I picked out my trunk and dragged it over next to Mabel's. Now I already felt at home.

The show was to remain a whole week in Philadelphia. This first stand under canvas fixed the permanent place one was to have in the cookhouse; grouping was according to rank, class, and department. Sideshow people had their own table; the ushers and ticket sellers, the band men (musicians), the Wild West performers, et cetera, all were placed at tables corresponding to their particular group, and each individual was assigned to one specific seat. One waiter to serve about twenty-four persons was about average.

This was also to be the only time I had to juggle my own trunk in place; for after everybody was settled, Mickey Graves and his painter assistant went over every trunk, putting a number on each in consecutive order as they were spotted in the dressing rooms. Each dressing room had its own series. *LDR* (Ladies' Dressing Room) took care of where to leave the trunks when unloading them; *MDR* stood for men's. The number on each determined the spot it was to be placed in throughout the season. Mine was labeled Statues number 21, Mabel's number 22, side by side. They are always facing in the proper direction to get at. The number system was so efficient. The propertymen handled things with such accuracy that on the second stand, there was no apparent change inside the dressing room. It was hard to believe the show was in a different town—that things had been moved at all.

Private dressing rooms under canvas were nonexistent on the Barnum show (as the Barnum & Bailey Circus was called among its people). Privileged persons, such as Mr. Bradna, famous animal trainers (because of their need for relaxation between shows), and heads of departments were given wagons to dress in after trunks had been unloaded.

Bandmen had a top of their own for changing into uniforms; likewise ushers and others who had to make a change of clothing for their assigned duties. Other dressing rooms for performers were located in a separate top assigned to the Wild West people, whose performance while on the road was sold to the public as an aftershow in front of the grandstand. This was a means of cashing in on the time during which the workmen were taking down the other seats and aerial rigging with other equipment, preparatory to moving. The reason for the separate tent arrangement was chiefly to save time in getting off the lot; by the time the aftershow (referred to as "the concert") was over, the big dressing room was no longer there; trunks were all loaded in their wagons; canvas and poles were taken down and gone; only the puddles of water from the wash buckets, as the propertymen emptied and stacked them into each other before loading them, marked the place that had been the scene of a combination community hall, private home, and glamorizing parlor only moments earlier.

This small square top, referred to as "hooligan" (for the obvious reason that there was no class distinction among its occupants) had a three-way division, as a letter *T*. Each compartment had a separate entrance—formed by overlapping sidewall at the corners—which needed no lettering. The one nearest to the show center's backyard was invariably the cowgirl's side. The cowboys were directly opposite, with the partition between. The third compartment was occupied by the Chinese troupes, all males.

The system of placing trunks with mark and number, as in the big dressing room, was applied here as well—*WWM* indicating Wild West Men, *WWW* for women; the Chinese characters for names put on by their owners sufficed for mark; the trunks were numbered, however, for places.

Although as performers they rated to be in the big dressing room, these Chinamen were happier dressing out here in the hooligan all by themselves, since hardly any of them spoke English. Besides, here they could brew their pungent aromatic herbs and cook their favorite dishes when the cookhouse didn't suit their taste or sate their appetite. Here too, no one kicked about the stench of the fish they strung out on a clothesline to ripen and dry in the sun. And yes, here they could give vent to their grievances fighting among themselves—knifing each other to death—had it not been for the timely intervention of the cowboys. Whenever they would stop that singsong chatter and all was quiet, the cowboys on the other side of the partition knew there was something rotten besides the fish. Rushing in on them—West meeting East—they'd put an end to that sanguinary saber-dance by quelling the feud, taking the injured one to the doctor's tent, by force if necessary, to get his wounds dressed. A peculiar custom of theirs: all talking at one and the same time and most all of the time. A sudden dead silence was ominous. There was a thousand-dollar bond put up by the show with the immigration authorities for each one of them, and while they seldom caused any trouble, they had to be watched for their own protection.

Their interpreter as well as manager was a Chinaman called Pat Murphy. He was one of the most lovable characters I have ever known. Himself an ex-performer of magic, he was a natural comique—Americanized as he could ever be, he still retained his queue which he, like his compatriots, wore draped around his cranium. Even the jagged, brown stumps—left of what once were teeth—along the gum line seemed to have been a contributing part to the individuality that made up this unforgettable personality. He spoke in pidgin English, as was affected by impersonators of his race; many times I wondered if this was just another expression of the jester within him. His attire: half Oriental, half Occidental. The shellacked silk coat and black felt shoes with soft platform soles he always wore were typical of his native land. He was a simple man who seemed to reflect the spirit of Confucius. Beneath that self-effacement could there have been a great philosopher?

Pat was slue-footed or some impediment dating back perhaps to those vaudeville days when, as a magician, he would produce a huge goldfish bowl—seemingly out of thin air—filled with water and fish. The trick contributed to breaking down his feet in this manner. That bowl he carried strapped to his waist and hanging down between his legs, where it was concealed under the traditional mandarin coat, put terrific strain on his arches, especially if he retarded this trick as a closing feature. His feet became permanently infirm as a result, yet he would walk from train to lot and vice versa at night, even with transportation facilities available, a distance of over three miles sometimes. There he'd be trudging along, both feet turned outwards, as if each wanted to go its separate way.

He was best known for his blaspheming, but coming from him it sounded cute. The most familiar of his exclamations were, "Col' like hellie" or, "Hoc' like hellie!" "No damn good!" and "Damn too lon' walk!" One could associate him only with these expressions—the limit of his conversation. Everybody on the show knew and loved Pat Murphy the Chinaman—a fine example of those sons of the East.

Of the others, there must have been over forty of them (the entire arena—three rings and four stages—seemed filled with them during their number). Only three had wives, Caucasian women who spoke only Russian; all three participated in their husbands' troupes. Every time I passed their places in the second aisle against the outer wall, I stopped to admire their kaleidoscopic costumes; especially attractive were those glittering tiaras—the headdresses they wore—like beautiful fans, with gaudy tassels at the sides. The whole ensemble created a gorgeous picture, dressing the scene just standing there in the background, while the men would go through their intricate tumbling and tortuous poses. I simply marveled at one of them in particular, who performed atop a high pedestal with only a square foot surface and would actually roll himself up like a snail, seemingly having hinges even to his leg bones. All of them stressed contortion work. And that's not all. While going through those impossible flexures of body, their minds concentrated on juggling plates over the points of sticks of straw thinness. These fellows just kept them spinning, two or three in each hand. It seemed unbelievable, for either trick was an outstanding feat in itself. Their secret: practice, practice from morn till night. Every spare minute is given to plate juggling and body bending.

The routine finished, they all got set for the climax, the trick in which the wives took part, one woman in each of the three rings taking the cue from the center one, all working in perfect unison. Removing their headdresses, each woman stepped in the foreground joined by her husband; each couple sat down to a small table to which the chairs were attached at the base, facing each other with a tea service before them. Two ropes were lowered from a crane bar overhead as the assistant passed the hook attached to the rope through the tightly braided and twisted knob of hair of each, while man and wife interlocked their legs under the table. At the signal of the equestrian director's whistle, all three couples were hoisted into the air; joined by their legs, they appeared to be sitting relaxed on the chairs, though actually being suspended by their hair, supporting the weight of the table as well.

With the pulling of the scalp affecting the facial expression, it took on a look of fright, as if they had suddenly seen a ghost. Sitting there in the air, they poured and sipped their tea as though they enjoyed the party, thus holding the attention of the audience. Meanwhile, four of their comrades were being hoisted up at various points along the track to the ropes, stretched from the top of quarter poles at far ends of the big top, down toward the center, and as the tea party was lowered to the ground, down came these four flying Chinamen in a slide for life suspended by their queues, each one carrying the American flag in one hand, the Chinese flag in the other, thus assuring themselves of applause, which I am sure they would have earned even without presenting colors. A spectacular number, theirs, always. Next! The equestrian director's whistle was heard.

Mabel opened her trunk and unfastened and pulled down the split tray, from which she took out some clean undies and a towel, placing them on her chair and turning the tray up into the lid again. Lifting another tray up, which also catches against the top, she removed a kit containing her clothes rack; this she assembled and set up at the end of her trunk, close to mine. I watched her as she went about things in a businesslike way, noticing when she opened the cover of the utility tray how neatly it was arranged, along the same line as the berths. Here also, a wide band of colored elastic was tacked against the cover in proper spaces to hold articles like a comb, scissors, whisk-broom, and nail file—essentials to have on the lot right at hand. Seeing her tear the wrapper from a cake of soap, all at once it dawned on me that I was not a visiting guest here, that I was with an outdoor show—and promptly got busy in front of my own trunk.

"A water-wagon must be around somewhere close by," Mabel observed. "Chances are the gang won't bother filling the few buckets out there today," she said as she nudged me. "Let's go find it!"

"Oh, I meant to ask you," I piped up as I was arranging my own things. "Do they have a 'commissary wagon' here?" I asked this more than anything to show off my former trouping experience. Then to follow it up I added, "I forgot to pack soap for the lot. What I have is down at the cars."

"Commissary? Why, certainly!" she replied, as if resenting my question.

"What I mean . . . is it open today? This being Sunday and no show. . . ." I hurried to make amends for my stupidity.

"Oh my, yes; it is open from the time it hits the lot; you'll always find it in front of the cookhouse!" she said in a voice more agreeable now as we both made for the exit.

On our way out, I noticed quite a number of women in the big dressing room by now—each with her own set or troupe—getting established in front of her trunk. Outside, we picked up our buckets. Mabel knew there was always a water wagon by the pad room, so we headed in that direction. As she turned the wheel opening the flow, I held the pails under the stream. Close by was an open bale of straw for the horses' bedding. We each picked an armful. It was a nice grass-covered lot, all except our end, which must have been part of a trail that cut across with hard, bare ground. The straw would keep the dust down in front of our trunks.

We met others coming along toward the water wagon, a regular bucket brigade. A woman at the dressing-room entrance sent a message to her husband by the first man who happened to come along entering the men's side; though only a canvas partition between, no one called a spouse across that wall. The men and their wives came out to the entrance after they had been summoned, and there they imparted whatever their wish. At this time it was water, more than likely, the women wanted their husbands to get for them. The wives customarily did their husbands' laundry, took charge of the upkeep of costumes, and washed the tights for all the members of their troupe, so that in tinting them they will be of uniform color and shade. However, single men seemed to do well enough on their own.

I set my bucket before my trunk and on leaving the dressing room, followed the route over which Paul Jerome led me earlier and found the commissary, a typical country dry-goods store on wheels. Anything from a postage stamp up, the commissary has it. It can outfit the workmen from hat to shoes. Of course, ladies' apparel is limited to raincoats and rubber boots, with perhaps one or two grades of staple underwear and stockings if milady is caught short. But milord can always find his favorite shirts, collars, socks—even a pair of trousers in a pinch.

I got the soap and some route cards; these cards revealed the itinerary of the show's movements. Usually four weeks of advance dates were printed on them so the families and friends of the show people would always know where to reach them from day to day. These cards were very informative; they were divided into five columns, indicating everything of essential interest in connection with each stand: date, town, state, railroad line, and mileage to each succeeding stand. They cost five cents each, and hardly anybody bothered copying them. They were bought and mailed to as many as one cared to correspond with; one card was always tacked to the inner lid of one's trunk for reference. A route card was the source of a common slogan with a circus, a satirical insinuation to one slow in grasping a situation, late in arriving for some event, or not well-informed: the person was told to get a route card. Used in the wide margin of gags, the card also served as a guide for the show folks who hailed from all points, looking forward with anticipation to each new issue, whereon they might see their hometown scheduled, thrilling with thoughts of a reunion with their families and loved ones. The first day they went on sale, the route cards formed the topic for conversation all over the lot, from pad room to the stake-and-chain wagon. The workmen were keenly interested in news and gossip concerning the show and in these route cards; they made plans according to them—dropping off at a certain spot that had been their original goal at the time they joined out. Thus transportation problems were solved. And for every one that dropped out, there were two to take the place left vacant.

Each town had its applicants of workhands—usually young punks with romance and adventure in mind. They soon realized that neither was to be found with the circus; not romance, at any rate, since there were no females of equal class by circus standard. Any gesture toward socializing, even in the form of a friendly greeting between a performer or statue girl and a groom or a cookhouse flunky, was frowned upon and cause for dismissal of one or both. However, there *was* adventure in the freedom for any youngster breaking away from his family to mingle with the adults. He became a man overnight.

Workmen in all departments were habitually named after the town or state of their origin. No one knew their given or family name except the boss of their department and the cashier in the red-ticket wagon—the office of the show, where all the pay envelopes were made up. Every Wednesday these were distributed to them in their side of the cookhouse, the only time they were called by their proper names. To all others, they were simply known as "Boston" or "Kansas," or perhaps a nickname after their nationality or unusual characteristic, such as "Frenchie," "Dutch," "Freckles," "Blackie," "Shorty," Limpy," or even "Iodine," for one whose proper name was Ioni. Some were named also for famous men, including "George Washington," "Abe Lincoln," and "Daniel Boone." These were hung on roustabouts and propertymen on the big show because of some semblance to the original.

It seems I'm taking mighty long with that cake of soap back to the dressing room to take that bath; but then, anybody would hesitate to strip off and stand before that icy cold water freshly drawn from the wagon and start washing from the face down, a genuine sponge bath which left you as clean and refreshed as lettuce. After finishing the bath, one usually gathered up all the soiled linens and things to wash them right there and then in the same bucket, returning to the wagon for more water to rinse them. The clothesline, which everyone had tucked in a compartment of his trunk, was strung outside the sidewall. The washing was hung up with clothespins, also the property of each individual with one's initials penciled on—just in case they got confused somehow with the neighbor's, whose line was stretched parallel within a few inches.

I soon learned that the reason for the partition between the main dressing room and this little corner for the statue girls' use was not so much that we were rated as untouchables but was chiefly due to the nature of our makeup. That messy white ointment required complete freedom of any covering while bathing in order get it off without smearing it all over. This nude bathing was taboo in the big dressing room. According to the rules of those aristocratic ladies who dictated the laws, no self-respecting female would disrobe completely, unshielded by a kimono or bathrobe, which was kept over her constantly during her bath. The trick was to remove outer garments and immediately get under the robe which then hung from her shoulders and served as a private bathhouse while removing undergarments. Then fastening it under the arms, a lady would proceed with her bath, starting with her face, neck, and arms, which were washed and dried, then the protective covering was raised and fastened at the neck so the rest of the anatomy could be washed and dried in small sections under the robe until reaching the feet, which could be finished sitting down immersing them in the pail.

I have never found a satisfactory answer to this exaggerated modesty, which was forced on all, including those who would otherwise not have gone to such extremes. I thought of the possibility of a sudden storm, a blow down catching them with their clothes off; but no, that was too remote. It was just an old custom handed down from grandma and adhered to through the generations like other antiquated laws in their moral and social codes which would soon undergo a change.

Smoking among the fair sex had not yet become widely popular, and the few who had acquired the habit were certainly not with the circus. Of the large number of women with the show, the only one who had been addicted to smoking was Muzzie. As the mother of Bird Millman, the greatest wire artist of the time, she enjoyed the privilege of traveling along with her famous daughter without taking part in the show herself.[1] The time on her hands may have accounted for her irrepressible desire for a cigarette, though smoking was banned in the ladies' dressing room. However, Muzzie, being resourceful, proceeded to cultivate the friendship of the cowgirls, whom she'd visit in the hooligan, just so she could smoke. Here the women—while they themselves were not given to smoking—were liberal-minded on the subject and didn't consider it vulgar for a woman to light up and puff away on a Fatima, or whatever the favorite brand of each was back in 1916.

Gradually, the performers arrived on the lot, and everywhere one could see and hear small groups happily commenting on the nice warm sunshine, ending the conversation with, "Have you seen the mailman?" Acts with animals took a look at their charges to see if their pens were clean and well bedded down and the cages serviced. Usually this was done by private grooms or caretakers for dogs and other trained stock privately owned. Aerial acts turned to the big top to inspect how their apparatus appeared set up under canvas hung from the bail-rings by falls, which their private riggers together with Mickey Graves's gang had already pulled up in the air.

I just wandered around. To me, it all seemed miraculous, like having been transferred to another sphere. Suddenly I saw everybody congregate in one large group. Yes, the mailman had arrived. There he was by one of the wagons, unloading large bundles of letters from his pouch. They were neatly stacked with rubber bands around each bunch, which he laid on the floor of the wagon till he finally came to the stack he was looking for. He must have known just about everybody because as each one approached him, without mentioning any name, he'd shuffle through the stack of letters he was holding and hand each one his or hers, or say, "Not today!" if there was none.

I wonder how many people realize what a big job it was to serve as mailman on a show with so many people. Yet it was only a sideline with him. Actually, he was one of the musicians in the band. I really don't know how they'd come to be appointed to this extra—but important—assignment, which did require certain qualifications such as reliability and honesty. He must have rated high of character to merit the utmost confidence of the management, which, by the way, was an honorary appointment. The only salary he drew at the wagon was the regular musician's pay for his work in the band; yet he put in many extra hours, making two trips daily, including Sundays and holidays, to the local post office in each town, picking up the great volume of the show's mail, sorting it out—each department in a separate bundle. He knew the names of all the performers, staff, sideshow people, concessionaires, and most names in the workingmen's departments, leaving each bundle with the corresponding boss of the crew for distribution, and when in doubt as to a name, he would ask the head of each department until found. He laid out his own money for transportation, requiring a cab in most places to reach the lot with the heavy load of correspondence, magazines, and *Billboards*—the weekly trade publication to which 75 percent of the circus people subscribed.

He would leave a route card in each post office for forwarding mail that may arrive after the show had gone. However, he was compensated for the greater part of his work, and his expenditures were chalked up as a good investment, for at the end of the season, each performer would give him two dollars (the statue girls would give him one dollar), and if all departments contributed something (which most did), he must have collected a pretty nice little nest egg to take home with him so he wouldn't have to eat snowballs through the winter.

Harry and Mabel had gone downtown to visit some friends of theirs, and I was left on my own. I skipped lunch but kept watching for that flag to go up announcing dinner. This time, I was one of the first to arrive. At the entrance to the right—the performers' side—I noticed a man stationed with a clicking gadget in hand checking the number of the performers going through. On the left-hand side, the doorman sat behind a large box, which had a slot at the top for each workman from the various departments to drop a ticket in—the same as on entering a theater. These tickets were issued by their bosses. No free meals to gate crashers or any man playing hooky or lying down on the job. There were always local men and boys, put on as helpers in the big top, to carry chairs and planks, who also got meal tickets plus passes to see the show.

As I got through the entrance, I was met by the boss of the cookhouse, Mr. Henry, who asked what troupe I was with. This time, I knew what to say, and he showed me to the table that corresponded to the statues; there, the waiter assigned me to a seat. At a long table as that was, it would have been difficult to memorize one's place (especially if close to the center) for the next time, unless by noticing who sits next or opposite. I took notice of the slim dark girl already seated on my right. Here I felt free to ask the name of someone I would be so close to for the entire season. Her first name escaped me; all I remembered was White when she emphasized this last name, adding, "My husband is Cap White, Zip's manager, but he'll sit with the sideshow bunch." Then she went on smilingly, "I'd rather be here—I'm so used to eating with the girls."

I became curious about Zip, and one day, visiting the sideshow, I satisfied that curiosity.

Here's a profile of that so-called Nature's Phenomenon.

William Henry Johnson, otherwise known as Zip, sitting in sideshow pit with Johanna the Gorilla Girl, Ringling Bros. Circus (no date). Frederick Glasier Collection, neg. no. 0699; black-and-white photograph, copy from glass plate negative, museum purchase, Collection of the John and Mable Ringling Museum of Art Archives, Sarasota, Florida.

Zip was one of P. T. Barnum's original sideshow attractions when Ringling Bros. bought the Greatest Show on Earth, and he was kept on in that capacity during his remaining years. Actually, Zip was a normal colored man, born in the South and not *South Africa*. The only freak value about him was his makeup. He was presented in tights to his neckline, with long, wooly nap simulating fur, which blended in color with his dark-brown skin and outlined his slight, pliant form. What furthered his oddity was created unwittingly by his parents, who, thanks to an ancient superstitious custom to slash and bleed the head of a squalling infant that might be obsessed by the demon, caused his skull to be a mass of scars, excepting a small area at the top where the hair tissue hadn't been destroyed. The long tuft of hair at this point accentuated grotesquely the oblong appearance of his head. Billed as the "Missing Link" and the "Original Barnum's What-Is-It," he played up the role.

Zip was never to utter a word before the spectators, yet he played the violin and did whimsical poses commanded by the announcer during the exhibition. He played his role well. But after the show he could be found down on his knees in the circle with the other freaks, before a blanket spread out on the ground, shooting crap (their favorite pastime) and with typical southern accent, repeating the magic words used in the game: "Come, seven! Come, 'leven! Baby needs new shoes! Bet I'll make it! Here I come!"

Going to the coaches at night, on passing the sideshow car, I often heard Zip not only playing the violin but singing as well—a treat withheld from the paying public.[2]

Since their livelihood was exhibiting themselves, freaks had to have managers to transact their business and support them between engagements. Zip had been Cap White's protégé for many years, White earning his own livelihood through Zip.

(Although we sat side by side at the table and were in the same dressing room all during that season, somehow I can't recall this White girl's first name even at this time, but Louise is close enough.) She went on to explain that married people had the privilege of sitting with their mates at the same table regardless of the group each belonged to individually.

Louise's romance—like Mabel's—had its start during the ballet epoch about two years back; evidently, she was quite proud of her conquest, although Cap was up in years. But some years later, I was shocked at the account of their divorce as I read it in the news. She charged cruelty, alleging that Cap pinched the pennies to the extent of making her life with him unbearable. Through the winter months he would insist on living in one room with her and Zip, the three even sharing the same bed when there was no extra accommodation, though this latter accusation seemed somewhat exaggerated. The most serious of the charges, from her point of view, was Zip's continual playing of the violin, the same tunes day after day, without variation; this, she charged, caused her to suffer a nervous breakdown. This provided the public with a juicy bit of scandal when aired in the court, aside from the human-interest story it contained, which was promptly picked up by the syndicate and printed in the papers throughout the country.

Two other girls came along directly. "Guess this is it," said one, as she nodded to Cap's wife and ignored me. Her companion spoke with a decidedly British accent. Both were commenting on the Sunday blue laws of the town of brotherly love, leaving no place of amusement, not even a movie theater or an ice-cream parlor, open. I studied them indirectly. Something about their regular features, their sharp, cold profiles, and their height—yes. It didn't require much stretching of the imagination to see two living statues there before me. These two could have served as models from head to toe for any sculptor or painter; and one, Millie Hall, proved to be a professional model touring with the circus during the summer season. Millie could go about nude the greater part of the time in our dressing room, yet would appear perfectly decent—perfectly dressed, somehow.

The two continued to lament not being able to attend Gibson's All-Colored Revue downtown, which gave a midnight performance (legally Monday) because the show let out about 3:30 AM, and the parade was to leave the lot at 8:00 AM sharp, which wouldn't allow them sufficient sleep to be in fit condition for that first and longest parade of the season—over the main part of Philadelphia proper, about sixteen miles round-trip. These horses would be frisky after their long vacation in winter quarters, difficult to hold in place. I gathered from this that, like myself, they were also in a mounted section—and suddenly I lost my appetite. Though the chicken dinner appeared tempting a minute ago, who could eat when there was so much to worry about? Their conversation was strictly between themselves, yet it affected me as though it was directed straight at me. I knew my night would be a sleepless one even as I made my way toward the cars.

I was awakened by half-dozen alarm clocks here and there in the various berths; it seemed everybody had set hers for 6:00 AM—just one continuous ringing. I opened my drapes and peeped down. The girls below, already out of their berth, were probably in the washroom to get ahead of the rush. I dressed, putting on most of my clothes before I swung down, and, taking soap and towel with toilet kit tied to me like an apron, headed for the end of the car where the activity was reaching a peak, and a line had already formed before the door of the little end room. All three washbowls were busy. Fortunately, the girls didn't linger long. All were anxious to get out as quickly as possible.

The last section near the washroom was occupied by the three wardrobe women; the boss, Rose Wallace, shared the lower with Mother Talbot, while Mrs. Dawson (wife of one of the publicity men whose car was strictly stag and attached to another section of trains) slept in the upper. All three women were gone before the others got up. I am sure they would have protested had they known that their lower berth served as the depot for the ones waiting. With room for four girls to sit down, it was always filled to capacity during the rush. Marie, the light-colored porteress in the upper directly opposite, watched from her perch. Though no one touched anything, she constantly kept one eye on the washroom, the other on this berth.

Things ran on schedule—everybody strove to be on time, everything punctual. "Time and parade wait for no man!" is the way we heard the slogan. I was on my way to the dressing room after a good breakfast in the cookhouse when I heard a bugle call—the same as in army barracks calling assembly—and every mortal on the lot was suddenly alerted to action, rushing hither and thither, each to his respective post, at the same time saying, "There goes the first bugle!" which in circus is equivalent to the half-hour call in the theater. Everyone who made parade rushed to the tables in the big dressing room, where the wardrobe women had the list of the different sections with the name of each performer thereon. Every costume was wrapped in an unbleached muslin covering; the sizes varied, and each was given one according to his or her measurements, more or less: medium, large, and small. Hat and footgear were tried on for size and marked for future use. After this first parade of the season, each performer—man or woman—wrapped up the costume worn (including footgear) in the same piece of muslin, fastened the bundle with a safety pin, and marked it with his or her name in large letters (to make it easy to pick out) before turning it in to the wardrobe department. The large trunks holding these were packed and loaded immediately after parade—the first step in moving to the next stand. The same costumes were worn throughout the season. For rainy days there was another set of wardrobe—the gala set of one season was used on rainy days for the next.

The costume I drew was a royal-blue plush riding habit, trimmed with silver braid and metal concaves—fit for a princess or some titled lady. It had puffed sleeves and poplin on the jacket with a fluffy white jabot at the front. The hat was also a fantasy, but the skirt was even more intriguing. The train extension was at the left side—volumes of material on that side lavishly studded with concaves to catch the sunlight and glitter like miniature mirrors.

Our makeup for the street parade was quite light—everything in moderation befitting the times. Conspicuously applied paint would have been in extremely bad taste with the public in those days when lipsticks and compacts had not yet become part of the equipment in milady's handbag. Women of disreputable character were the only ones who used paint; it is therefore obvious why we had to use it with discretion. However, youth needs no camouflage. Since the object of makeup, tactfully applied, is principally to enhance the attraction of one's features rather than mask them, these women bearing the stamp of perfection could stand close inspection by daylight without the aid of artifice.

Here is where one can appreciate the value of judgment of that outstanding colorful figure, Mr. Bradna, equestrian director supreme—indeed, the greatest casting director of all times, who, with an imagination of a genius, could pick a type at a glance. His choice could always be relied upon as being correct. Thanks to his extraordinarily sensitive and fine taste, that grand procession, the street parade, was in reality what the motive behind it intended it to be—a sample of color and beauty, a part of the show that served its purpose of whetting the appetite of the public, from banker to farmer, to see the talent of these supermen and gorgeous women.

Only the younger women were chosen for mounted sections in the parade; troupes with young and attractive women members were always given the preference; they were considered an asset for the value they represented in the street parade and the spec, which was also an important feature of the show because it displayed the huge cast. However, the latter event, under artificial light, allowed a more liberal margin to bring on the older matrons, who, with their well-preserved and still-beautiful bodies, could touch up their faces with makeup and look simply glamorous. Circus performers seldom aged from the neck down, proving that physical exercise is a preservative. Nevertheless, the lines of their faces told tales at close range. These older women were not eligible for street parade, where natural bloom of youth was as essential as good looks by the circus standard.

An overflow of privileged performers' wives traveling with husbands, unless they came up to that standard, always caused consternation to that wizard of artistic taste, Mr. Bradna. One look at the subject would bring a frown to his face. His small black moustache would be drawn in a crooked line as he turned sideways, exclaiming, with his famous outcry, "Cheesescroise! Where will I put her?" But he found a place for these too, or created one. The high float, depicting the Oriental splendor of a sultan and his harem, called for females lavishly decked out with beautiful costumes and veils over their faces. This was usually the solution to the problem of age or nature's shortcomings. Even excess weight could be concealed under the veils and robes, seated there above eye level.

This float is not to be confused with another one, also of Oriental design but having occupants in direct contrast with the first mentioned. It bore the cream of womanhood, for it was the Beauty float. And if the statue girls didn't rate with the seasoned lady performers, they certainly did with Mr. Bradna. It was on this group that he would draw for dressing up a choice spot. He appreciated the value of their freshness in youth and beauty since they were chosen from the large number of girls who apply at the Garden each year. Just by looking over these twenty or more girls, one would have to admit that Mr. Bradna was a connoisseur of feminine pulchritude.

The Beauty float—one of the highlights of the mile-long procession—was painted a delicate shade of ivory in harmony with the enormous elephant tusks which projected from its base along the lower ledge. Adorned with gold leaf to set off its sumptuous design, it was truly a thing of exceptional art and grace. Like columns, the tusks separated the seats of these beauties—handpicked, every one of them. The sides of the float, simulating steps, culminated in a throne where sat her majesty, the queen—ah, she was just that, and she would have retained that title in a beauty contest anywhere.

Oddly enough, she was not from the statue group. Not only beautiful, as a performer she was equally peerless. This queen was one of the four Melillo girls—contortionists of great merit. This one (I never memorized their first names) was exceptionally gorgeous. A French type, with honey-colored hair and a creamy complexion with very fine chiseled features, she had incredibly big blue eyes. Delicately built, she was exquisite from head to foot—truly worthy of occupying that place of honor on top of the float.

The Oriental theme was further carried out in the richly adorned costumes the girls—the queen and her court—wore. The dresses simulated bare midriffs, and jeweled cups marked the breasts; rhinestones, pearls, and other imitation precious gems made up the tiaras, with ornamental pendants over the ears. All carried spangled parasols to protect themselves against the burning of the sun. These parasols were almost too bright and dazzling to the eyes for the spectators to properly appreciate the beauty and charm under them. One thing was certain: no king ever boasted of an array of beauties such as these.

The most enviable place, however, from a spectator's point of view is in the houdah atop the elephant. Every town celebrity, wishing to go in the parade for publicity or popularity (usually arranged by the local authorities or the press), asks to ride in this coveted spot, only to become disillusioned before riding two blocks. It is the roughest seat in the entire parade, jogging the entrails out of one.

I carried my costume to the end dressing room, where all the trunks were in the places they would be found for the balance of the season. Now there seemed to be room for all. Miss Claren, in charge of the statuary, was classed as a privileged performer—she didn't have to make parade; she was not there at this early hour. Star performers were exempt from this obligation, an agreement usually arrived at when signing the contract. While it seemed to be a glorious function to the First of Mays (as beginners were called), the parade becomes a monotonous chore carried out in rain or shine, heat or cold. Of the feature acts comprising several members in the troupe, only one—perhaps two—would be released from parade, as were also acts owning trained animals or intricate riggings, which required their personal attention.

Everybody was busy getting ready; I didn't get to look over my new colleagues, who were old associates among themselves by now. Those who had joined out this season were already veterans of four weeks' experience in the Garden. Nor was the parade a novelty to them after riding around the arena in spec; Mabel was my only standby. Her costume—like several others in there—was identical with mine; we corresponded to the number 2 mounted section. The only difference between this and the number 1 was the lack of plumes on our hats. There were sixteen girls to each section.

When the next bugle call sounded, that meant, "Mount!" Everybody filed out of the dressing rooms, some looking around for their floats, others going to the menagerie for elephants and camels, but most of them making for the pad room, which seemed to be buzzing with activity. There the horses with their trappings—some with beautiful coverings of plumes and fringes of gay colors—were ready for the riders.

Everyone was so excited—it seemed to be in the air. Some were disappointed at not getting the same mount back. Like people, horses too get past the age for trouping and are sold during the winter. The boss, Dick Shannon, pointed in the direction Mabel and I were to find the two sorrels he had assigned to us. Of the four the groom had on his string, Mabel recognized Beckie immediately. She had been riding the same mare for two previous seasons. Mabel stroked Beckie's head and talked to her while the groom gave my foot a boost as I mounted the bobbed-tail horse standing next to Beckie.

"You'll like Johnnie. He's a might rough-gaited, but gentle," he said as he adjusted the voluminous train of my skirt over the horse's rump. The train covered the better part of him and was long enough to hang down below my shoes on the side I was sitting. Mabel led the way as we ducked through the door. Once outside, I had no trouble keeping Johnnie close to Beckie; they were used to being side by side. Forming a group with the others in the same costume, we followed our marshal, John Fuller, out to a side street. There we lined up, two abreast, ready to fall in behind the red bandwagon carrying the colored band from the sideshow. Marshals were picked for horsemanship, most of them from the hooligan. Others were drafted from the ranks of bareback riders—men like Poodles Hanneford, from the great Hanneford family;[3] Orrin Davenport; Fred Derrick, riding partner of Mrs. Ella Bradna; and several others.[4] The shiny black boots were the only bright touch to their dark gray uniforms, yet they looked as snappy as any army generals.

These marshals galloped up and down the line, not only to show off but to relay communication between front and rear of the procession, reporting any mishap or traffic congestion causing a halt along the line between any of the sections. The show paid high license fees in some communities for the street-parade permit yet had to give the right of way not only to fire department, ambulance, and other emergency vehicles but also to ordinary intersection traffic by regulation. Sometimes the parade paralleled a funeral cortege, and we were always glad to come to the turning in the road, parting these two extremes of life and death.

Mr. Bradna, dressed in white flannel sport suit, drove a beautiful pair of blacks hitched to his classy little carriage, which cut a handsome figure at the head of the parade. The marshals kept him posted on its progress during the entire march. The picturesque steam calliope brought up the rear of the over-a-mile-long procession.

Nothing can throw you into a greater panic than to arrive on the lot about the time of the second bugle call, just as the parade is getting lined up. You will try to make an effort getting into the costume and mounting the horse, which is all trapped up waiting for you in the pad room—not only because of the five-dollar fine, which will be deducted from your salary for missing it, plus the ribbing you takes from companions ("Get with it!" "Get a route card!"), but it is not tolerated by the management; if it happens twice in a row, you are subject to be dismissed. There is no use trying to catch up on a gallop once the formation has moved off the lot. The diligent marshal will chase you back; your name has already been turned in as being absent. No excuses will exonerate you. The parade was always scheduled for 10:00, which meant 10:00 in front of City Hall; time for leaving the lot depended on the distance to the center of town. That fear of missing the parade became a phobia with me, and after all these years, it still haunts my dreams. I just can't get it out of my system.

It may have been due to a slight favoritism on the part of John Fuller, remembering me as the weeping widow of a comrade just a year ago, or that he knew Johnnie to be a lead-horse, one that you can't hold in back of another horse, but in either case, Mabel and I were placed at the head of the section, following the bandwagon. Since this was considered somewhat of an honor, and I was just a newcomer, it didn't make me too popular to start off with.

It was a long, long march from 8:00 AM to almost 1:00 PM. Back at last on the lot, the girls to the rear broke out of the line and tried to beat us to the pad room. Johnnie, who had behaved like a gentleman all through the parade, resented the other horses catching up and even passing him. He suddenly laid his ears back, stopped short, and kicked up both hind heels at the horse in back and an instant later stretched his neck forward to bite the one trying to come in first. Unprepared for this amusing display of horse honor, I burst out laughing, but my mirth was dispelled when Mr. Shannon, who watched us come in, told me reprovingly that the rider is responsible for any damage the horse might cause, and I must keep him under control at all times while on his back.

I found I was so stiff from the cramped position of riding sidesaddle through the long journey that the groom had to lift me off. Picking up my long skirt, going toward the dressing room, I saw the sea of buckets outside— filled with water—and some of the people picking theirs out and taking them inside. I recognized mine close to the entrance, so I too picked it up, but just as I got through the door, Rose Wallace called me down for doing such a thing while I had the costume on. It was more than I could stand without breaking down in tears. I wondered what my next offense would be and if it were possible to go through life here without constant friction of some kind.

Dropping the bundle containing the parade costume into one of the large trunks in the wardrobe department, I proceeded to the cookhouse for lunch. The choice was beef stew or cold cuts. Because time was limited before matinee, I decided on making a sandwich of the assortment of cold cuts already on the table; this would eliminate waiting for service, I figured, and I could eat it at my leisure in the dressing room after the bath. Going through the door, however, the checker stopped me.

"What have we there?" he asked, seeing the sandwich with paper napkin wrapped around it.

"Why, it's my lunch. I have no time to sit down!" I answered.

"Sorry, you'll have to eat that here—against rules to take anything out!" he said in a polite but firm manner, while blocking my way at the exit.

"Well, I wasn't hungry in the first place," I thought as I left the sandwich on one of the tables nearby, knowing it would be wasted anyway.

After being exposed to the sun all morning, the water was lukewarm, I noticed on starting my bath. There were several others busily engaged in the same way, but I confined my attention to my own little space. When

Mabel came in, she introduced me to those present—only first names were used. Presently, a very tall and stately woman came through the flap, almost touching me for lack of aisle space as she passed by. She was very fashionably dressed with a long cape over her smartly tailored suit and a neat toque over her classic hairdo. Even before Mabel presented me as, "This is a new girl—Tiny Kline!" I knew she was Miss Claren. She removed her street clothes and put on a smock; from her triangular corner she could look over the entire little camp. Sizing me up, she asked Millie Hall how many she had in her group; then turning to Margaret Mayes (of the British accent), who, like Millie, was a top figure, Miss Claren discussed the grouping with her and made some changes in the positions. It was decided I go in Margaret's group in ring number 3.

"You show her the poses, Miss Rogers!" she said to one of the girls (whom Mabel had introduced as Madeline). Miss Claren always addressed everyone by her last name, adding the prefix "Miss" or "Mrs.," as the case required. The switch affected Madeline—she was to show me her poses while she got instruction for new ones.

In statues, the top figure on the pedestal was the principal representative of the theme of each group; the figures at the base comprised the atmosphere—a bit of detail. For example, in the America pose, the principal on top holding a torch represented the Goddess of Liberty, while the ones grouped around the three tiers at the base—each in a pose with props pertinent to the story—completed the picture. In this particular pose, I was stooped over a wheel symbolizing Industry, while Madeline stood next to me with a blindfold over her eyes holding a spade in one hand and a balance in the other, as Justice. There were about seven subs at the base of each pedestal, each one a part of the subject. Miss Claren, herself a famous model imported from some other art center in Europe, posed in number 2 (the center ring), while Millie Hall was top in ring number 1. There were four changes of poses, which took place inside that circular curtain resembling a king-sized shower ring, pulled up overhead during the exhibition of each pose and lowered again for changing poses and switching props for the ones to be used in the next picture. Because I was to go in without a rehearsal, all my positions were either sitting down or otherwise well supported. This was important, since I was not accustomed to standing on a narrow ledge, and when the table on which the whole structure was mounted started rotating, it was worse than keeping poised on a merry-go-round. Only then did I fully appreciate the dexterity needed for the top job. Especially difficult was that pose in the center ring, for which Leo, the understander in the Picchiani troupe of acrobats, stepped up on top of a less-than-two-foot square surface while holding Miss Claren over his shoulder—a towering height. The subs at the base depicting the story—some in dance pose, expressing joy, others down on a knee with face buried in cupped hands for grief or sorrow. The title: "The Abduction." I could look over from ring number 3 when the table,

Unidentified living statue (no date). Frederick Glasier Collection, neg. no. 0646; black-and-white photograph, copy from glass plate negative, museum purchase, Collection of the John and Mable Ringling Museum of Art Archives, Sarasota, Florida.

turning, was right for that angle—it was very exciting! My own group's subject during that pose was Spring, wherein I sat quite comfortably with legs extended, holding a garland of flowers over my head.

Leo Picchiani (though not one of the family, it was customary for members to assume the name of the troupe with which they worked) might well have posed for Apollo. With whitening all over him and clad only in what appeared to be a fig leaf (statuary is always nude—must be that true art is naked truth), he was the perfection of the masculine physique. He was the only masculine statue and took part in that one pose only. When Broadway went in for nudism in the early twenties, this same Leo, having left the Picchiani's, did well as a male strip in the Ziegfeld Follies at the Winter Garden in New York.

The bugle call was heard all over the lot in the most remote corner of the dressing rooms, announcing the half-hour before the show. Suddenly the entire aggregation was astir. It was the time of the greatest activity—animals were roused to prepare them with their trappings; performers, grooms, and helpers all worked feverishly to enact that great moment: the show.

Now there was another rush on the wardrobe department for the spec costumes. The theme of the spec during the 1916 season was the Queen of Shebah in a procession through Delhi. Whatever the pantomime, I missed it; the costume I was issued marked me as one of the numerous slave girls, yet it was richly adorned with spangles over the heavy satin and velvet material; a wig with two long black braids of hair and red sandals completed the outfit. I noticed that Madeline Rogers, the girl who prompted me on the statue poses, didn't wear a wig; her natural hair was exactly as long and as black. She was small otherwise—about my size—and like the majority of the girls, she was from the ballet of previous years. After the second bugle, still fifteen minutes before the show started, the people in the dressing rooms got on their way. Some—the ones who were mounted—left for the pad room, while the others would just go outside. It was the only chance men and women could visit and carry on a flirtation without being conspicuous. There they stood, by the back door, crowded tightly against each other. No one knew who was interested in whom, except the two—any two in that crowd, for that matter. Next show, they would pick a little different spot to stand so their fellow performers wouldn't get ideas about them. Those minutes of waiting outside the back door have been the start of many a romance and broken heart. The swain mounted on his horse with the regalia of a prince, a slave girl standing right close, petting his horse or playing with the gear—anything to demonstrate her affection. Of course, this was understood by the other party, since this was as close as they could ever get.

Romances on the show were taboo; no man and maid dared sit side by side in the big top between shows, or anywhere on the lot, for that matter. Sometimes they would try to pull the wool over the eyes of others by going in to practice a new trick—but that was soon discouraged when suspicions were aroused. Measures were taken against maneuvering a date in town. Everybody knew George Black, the Edgar Hoover of the circus, but no one knew who were his confederates—those working as private detectives for him. It was their business to track down any crooks or imposters who might try to infringe on the integrity of the show and also to watch out for the Romeos and Juliets who might wish to evade the rigid rules of moral behavior imposed by checking in as Mr. and Mrs. John Smith, downtown.

EQUESTRIAN DIRECTOR PAR EXCELLENCE

When I saw the others leaving the dressing room, I followed suit. This being my first day, I had to be shown my place in the procession of the spec. The band finished the overture and filed out through the curtain, going to their top, where they changed into some Oriental robes and fezzes in less than three minutes' time and were back by the door.

Then, with great pomp and ceremony, Mr. Bradna, in full dress suit, high silk hat, black patent leather shoes, and immaculate, white gloves, appeared at the door. Everybody's attention was focused on him. He presented the picture of a foreign diplomat: class and dignity. Around his neck he wore a fine black cord, holding not a monocle but a whistle. This instrument controlled the entire performance—that whistle packed a greater wallop than the loudest cracking whip, emphasizing the strong points of an act or halting whatever was going on. Once that whistle was blown, the act was over, whether the performers had succeeded in doing all their tricks or still had some left up their sleeve. The ring was no longer theirs. This whistle stopped the music when concentration of attention to a feature was requested. Too much importance cannot be attached to that shiny little whistle of this fabulous Fred Bradna, who for half a century graced the arena of the Greatest Show on Earth. He was the spirit of the show.[1]

Mr. Bradna blew the whistle, a shrill, penetrating sound, yet easy on the nerves. The doorman pulled the cord opening the curtain—the back door—and the trumpeters on horseback, at the head of the band, sounded off with a fanfare heralding the procession. The band struck up the "Triumphal March" (specially written music for the production), following the trumpeters through the door and along the hippodrome track. The show was on!

The band was followed by sheiks on gorgeously bedecked horses with plumes and streamers setting off the trappings. "Ohs" and "ahs" could be heard from excited spectators as they saw one eye-opening wonder after another. The array of coloring and glitter was dazzling.

There came elephants with jeweled tusks and shiny ornament-covered blankets carrying on their heads beautiful girls with gigantic fans or dowagers seated in houdahs strapped to the elephants' backs; twenty-four Shetland ponies drawing the Oriental facsimile of a Cinderella coach of the *enfant noble* in the procession; some oddly dressed characters on camels; and still another mounted section, wearing hoods and masks, beating kettledrums rigged to the flanks of their mounts, giving out with weird sounds.

But the center of attraction was the queen seated on a golden throne, impersonated by Mrs. Silbon of the Siegrist-Silbon troupe (a flying act). A brunette with jet-black hair, she made a regal queen. There was something about this woman that commanded the respect of everyone. Try as I would, I failed to put a finger on what made her so attractive. She was neither young nor beautiful of face, but there was strength and majesty of carriage about her beautifully formed body, a true Queen of Shebah.

From a social viewpoint, she was snobbish to extremes; a sample of it is shown in the order in which she had the trunks of the girl members of the troupe arranged. Her trunk was the first to the right in the first aisle; next to hers she had Marian's (one of the two Bordner sisters, working in the act and now known as Silbon), whom she was very fond of. Then followed the trunk of her niece, Emily, with Helen Bordner's in succession, Clara's, and then Bella's last. Clara, a happy-go-lucky girl, though having been with the troupe longer than the Bordner girls, was next to last because of her carefree disposition, which was erroneously taken for lack of dignity—besides the rumors rampant that she and Alfredo, one of the two Codona brothers (also members of the Siegrist-Silbon troupe at the time), were that way about each other, which didn't please that mistress of pride and propriety one whit. However, Clara was still preferred to Bella, whose former connection with the ballet had not yet been lived down. Bella was blonde and beautiful (on the Mae West type) and popular with the boys, shockingly so—hence the reason for being placed furthest, the last in line of her troupe.

Following the queen, King Solomon entered with the pompous ceremony behooving his wealth and high station, reclining on what appeared to resemble a grandly ornamented chaise lounge, carried on shoulders of black slaves. Evidently, having a prearranged date to meet the queen on one of the stages near the center ring, the king arrived first and was settled on the carpet-covered platform with his statesmen and guards surrounding him so that only the grandstand spectators had a vantage point from which to view this ceremonious spectacle. Having arrived, the queen, likewise, was carried seated on her throne and deposited on the opposite stage by the center ring, which was also covered with rugs and tiger skins plus a few live tigers about, held on leashes by attendants. The queen, too, had a large following, which shut her off from the view of all but the grandstand side.

Some silent acting on the stages was accentuated by music and gestures; pages chasing to and fro across the ring between the stages relayed messages between the king and queen. All this part I never did get a good view of as I looked through a small opening in the curtain while waiting outside with other slave girls and subjects. I don't, to this day, know to which sovereign I belonged or served. Our cue was the band's segue to the intermezzo, a monotonous dirge to which some of the men added their own lyrics—"Oh, my! The kidney stew is hard!"—to fit in with the repetitious strain which they sang all over the lot. That was our cue to line up, four abreast, and fall into the marching procession all around the arena, following horses and elephants. These forerunners left a pretty rough road on muddy lots for us to follow. The wheels of vehicles left deep furrows, and there were holes we couldn't see for the straw the men had put there to cover the mire, simulating sawdust.

As I turned in the spec costume with my name plainly marked on the wrapping cloth, Rose Wallace had another bundle all made up for me. "A size 1, in tights, should fit you!" she said as she handed it to me. Checking on its contents, I found a set of white cotton tights, the upper part resembling a man's undershirt with tape sewed on at the hemline in front and back to be tied at the groin to keep it from hiking up; a rather crude arrangement, but we all wore hip sashes, which covered up the joining line of the two pieces. Added to this was a coarse white-haired wig with a permanent Psyche-style hairdo, which fitted any size head. Over this went a wide tape tied tightly around the head, which secured it from sliding out of place and at the same time lent it a Grecian effect. Next came a long, flowing white satin cape, to be worn over the tights so as to keep the form covered during the course between dressing room and big top and until getting inside that black curtain called "balloon," where we made ready to mount the revolving table.

This entry, as we walked through the lot and into the arena, presented an eerie sight—like a flock of spectres on Halloween.

Miss Clarens was in charge of the white makeup, which she prepared and distributed to us. This paste, applied generously over the face and neck and then dusted with talcum powder so it wouldn't crack with the heat, seemed to benefit rather than harm the skin—the long sleeves and gloves took care of the arms and hands. The ingredients used were zinc oxide with two parts glycerin to one of water, making it the consistency of cold cream. When the weather was cold and damp, she substituted alcohol for the water. The clowns used lard to mix with their zinc, which made theirs waterproof and durable, since they used the same makeup through the entire performance. They had to use Albolene (mineral oil) to remove it, while ours could be washed off with soap and water.

In addition to the three groups of statuary composed of us girls, equine posing was presented on all four stages, showing horse and rider in various moods. Beautiful white horses remained as still as marble during the poses, some of which were intricate contortion positions for which they were trained especially for this act.

The statue number on the whole was an artistic achievement—one of the features of the show, a relieving contrast after the fast-moving, exciting action of preceding acts. We girls were thrilled to be part of this feature when hearing the ovation of spectators as we marched past them on our way out of the big top.

THE AWE-INSPIRING
MR. JOHN

The Philadelphia stand was followed by a split week between Washington and Baltimore. By that time, everybody with the show had become acclimated to the outdoor life, having gone through the annual spell of the grippe which attacked the majority of the folks during the first week outside but left them practically immunized for the balance of the season.

These long stands at the outset were advantageous for the entire personnel, giving them a breathing spell between moving—a chance to get in practice for the one-day stands that followed thereafter, with few exceptions, in the bigger towns.

This was the season the show was scheduled to go to the West Coast, taking its turn every other year with the Ringling Bros. World's Greatest Show, which was owned and operated by the same firm—the Ringling Bros.—who routed them in territories where they wouldn't conflict with the other and alternated them every year.

Of the five original Ringling brothers, only three remained now: Charles and Alf T. were at the helm of the Ringling show, while John—Mr. John, as he was always referred to—was *our* boss.

Mr. John was engaged in various enterprises, including oil, real estate, and (mostly) railroads, so he spent but little time on the show. But we always knew when he arrived. On that night, our train took quite a beating. We felt the terrific bumps and jolts as the crew coupled on the immensely heavy, specially built steel car in which he traveled from place to place. This private palace-on-wheels, equipped with every modern device, was the last word in luxury for the comfort of this tycoon, who had a mansion on New York's Fifth Avenue, a vast estate in Florida, a yacht, and whatnot. However, it was said of him that he was happiest in the comparatively reduced abode of this car, with only an Oriental couple, valet, and cook to serve him.

At a glance down the line of our old-fashioned wooden coaches, which were painted a gaudy shade of orange, the better to show up the ostentatious lettering of the show's title on each, Mr. John's car stood out like an intruder because of its height and drab, dark-olive color, which might have blended in quite inconspicuously with other Pullman cars of any railroad-company-owned train.

Passing this car—which, by the way, was lettered JOMAR, a contraction combining the two names John and Mable Ringling (Mable was his wife)—I often wondered what mysterious charm and treasure must be hidden behind those peep-proof drapes whose orderly arrangement uniformly screened every window; like an enchanted castle, it intrigued me. Was his wife there with him? I wondered, because she never came to the lot.[1]

The first time I saw Mr. John, I was terribly impressed: his height, towering over all others—six feet, four inches; a handsome man on the portly side, with fine features and a swarthy complexion, just as I imagined he would look. He was talking with Mr. Bradna near the back entrance. Pretty soon, a number of the men performers came ambling along but hung back at a respectable distance from this great personality until he turned from Mr. Bradna. Then, one by one, they had an interview with him. Yes, with even a clown among them, Mr. John listened to each grievance with as much interest as a counselor to a client. The interview must have been very satisfactory to the clown, judging by the alacrity with which he strutted back toward the dressing room. Mr. John disappeared through the big top. The little scene left me wishing I had something with which to approach this amazing king of a showman.

During his absence from the show, a private secretary, Charlie Kennelly, represented Mr. John and kept him posted on all matters of business. Certainly, Charlie must have been the ideal secretary, having been in Mr. John's employment for many years. Charlie and I got to be quite chummy, leaving the train mornings at the same time by coincidence on various occasions, walking to the lot together and talking on this and that. He was mild of manner and a dreamer. Aviation still in its infancy, it had captured his fancy. He had watched me tackle several feats that required courage or nerve as an initiative. On one occasion during these walks, just as a plane flew by and we were both looking skyward, he remarked, "Do you see what I see? That is the most promising enterprise in the near future!" Then grasping me by the hand, he asked, "How would you like to drift into that branch as a career?" He spoke as if in a trance as he went on: "I can see it now. You will be known as the Dare-Devil Doll!" There was fever in his eyes, as if he had hit upon a great discovery. I couldn't for the life of me figure out just what he had in mind to bring about the realization of his dream. Funny thing, but I couldn't at that time share his enthusiasm. All I wanted was to carry out my original plan—to become a great rider and then, through some mishap maybe, join Otto Kline.

I realized I was letting him down, that he had been counting on my cooperation. He was sure of Mr. John's.

11

■ ■ ■ ■

CALIBRATING
FOR A CAREER

Already I had made some progress; several times I had taken the black mare, Kitty, into the big top for practice during the time between matinee and night show. I bought a divided skirt from one of the cowgirls and a pair of boots from another. With the black velour hat, muffler, and shirt of Otto's which I had brought along, I was all set when I asked Dick Shannon if I might have the mare. "You'll have to get Mr. Bradna's permission for that!" he replied.

Mr. Bradna had a smile under his mustache, as he saw me all rigged out to the last detail, even to a quirt, which I had borrowed from Lottie, one of the cowgirls. She was going to teach me some tricks. "Go ask Dick Shannon!" he said, as if passing the buck. I could see that none of them took me seriously, and, almost at the point of turning on the tears, he gave me an okay to take the mare into the arena.

When I finally got her to lope with me hanging onto the pommel and mane, it was quite exciting. I didn't see how they sneered and made fun of me, those whom I thought to be my friends. But it did me some good, after all, because the next day, Mr. Bradna told Cy Compton, the chief of the cowboys, that I was to go in the lineup, riding in before the grandstand while the announcer told the public to take notice of the long line of riders—champions, all of them—who would take part in the aftershow and to buy their tickets as soon as the agents passed among them. The price of admission was "just fifteen cents!"

I soon learned that yodeling hoot the others gave out to make the character realistic. And those horses listened to every word the announcer said. No sooner did he say "fifteen cents," and they were off! This I learned the hard way after my horse reared up and turned around suddenly, leaving me there before an astonished public, while the others dodged me as they galloped by. A couple of ushers helped me up as I put on an act of fainting. Walking out, Mr. Bradna stopped me at the door, concerned as to my fall. I told him the facts—that the horse and I didn't work on the same cue and that I would be prepared for the exit on that magic last line to which the horses were so alert.

Besides the experience I gained in riding in the lineup, which was only a few minutes' work each time, I was paid two dollars extra per week. And although I had to tip the groom twenty-five cents for saddling the horse, it was still worthwhile.

The show had been out several weeks when we hit Newark, New Jersey, a date I've been looking forward to with great anticipation ever since the last issue of route cards. With parade, matinee, and night performance, I'd have little time to spare, but being that it was only a short run to the next stand, I had laid my plans. I'd jump over to New York after the night show and retrieve Shmoontsie. I could hardly wait, for in the interim, I had spoken to Lady Alice, who had an act of mixed household pets: pigeons, cats, albino rats, and mice. I sold her on Shmoontsie's talent. Though all her performers were white, Shmoontsie—black and white—could be the clown in the act. Everything looked favorable. I'd have my pet, after all.

When I arrived on the lot in Newark, rumors were rampant that there might be no show. The parade had been called off definitely. Infantile paralysis was raging in many sections the country over and had reached alarming proportions. The epidemic had taken a critical turn, especially through this territory. Schools were closed, and public gatherings—particularly those involving children—were discouraged. The legal department of the show, entrusted to the eminent law authority, Mr. Cook, was even now in council with the city fathers and would give us the verdict momentarily. I lost no time hopping on the Hudson Tunnel to Herald Square; a cross-town car at Thirty-fourth Street took me almost to the door of the pet orphanage on the extreme East Side of the metropolis. I fairly flew into the Bide-a-Wee. A few minutes later, I left clutching the Brooklyn address of the family that took Shmoontsie on the next day after I had left her there.

With no time to follow through and with an obligation to the show, I could not return to New York until after the night performance. I checked in for the night at a small hotel nearby to get an early start for Flatbush, with my hopes sky-high at the prospect of holding her again. But there was no such a number on the street, nor did anybody in the vicinity know a family by the name I'd been given. I took the train back and arrived in time to make the parade.[1]

One day, after the show had been on tour for some time and I was more at home, my attention was attracted to the Roman riders. I walked over to John Fuller, a year-round trainer of horses, and asked him what it takes to ride Roman. It was plainly evident that one had to be above medium height to stand in a chariot and control all the lines of four horses. Besides, the chariots were seldom used on the road because they couldn't work on a bad track or in a packed house (straw house, when people sit along the track). I was therefore interested in the Roman standing: an event that would run under any condition and was the closing feature of the races, the finale, just before the band struck up "The Star Spangled Banner." As a Roman rider, the public would remember me on its way home.

In my imagination I could already picture myself dressed in long, filmy chiffon drapes which would fly through the air, trailing me, accentuating the speed.

"Why, sure, I can teach you," Fuller said when I asked him how to go about it.

"But . . . do you ride Roman, too?" I asked skeptically, believing it to be a specialty in itself.

"Why, shucks! There's nothing to it! Right now, I'm filling in for the other chariot driver, Jack Foley, till he's able to get on the job again after that spill. He was just lucky that quarter-pole didn't brain 'im! Yeah, I pinch hit for all of 'em! Roman standin'—nothing to it!"

"And when could we start?" I asked eagerly. This sounded too good to be real, but I knew he was sincere about helping me.

"Let's make it Monday between shows. The horses will be in good shape then after their Sunday rest!" he said after a short pause.

So there was something to look forward to. I dreamed it and lived it till Monday came. "I shall be the first woman Roman rider!" I kept thinking to myself, and though I tried hard, it just seemed impossible to keep it any longer, and so I disclosed this great plan of mine to Mabel.

"It's been done before," she said with a shrug of the shoulder. "Only two years ago there was a woman, Marie Elser, a fine, big strapping woman, who rode like a man; yet she didn't set the world afire; in fact, you couldn't tell her from the other two—the men riders. No, you won't be the first!"

If her reply was intended to dampen my enthusiasm, at least one point of her information saved the situation; they'd have to be blindfolded not to see the femininity about me, the way I'd put that act over. My determination became stronger than ever now.

A midi-blouse and black bloomers comprised my practice clothes when John Fuller helped me mount the team. Beckie and Johnnie (my parade horses) were rigged up with the regulation Roman trapping—a small pad attached to the girth of each horse for the rider's feet and the inner halters crossed, so both horses' heads were held together, more or less. There was also a twelve-inch strap between the girths of the two, holding them together in the middle as well. Beckie was used in the Roman races, teamed up with another horse, but—as Fuller explained—Johnnie, used only in parade and spec, would hold her back.

Fuller sat on Johnnie, controlling the speed, while I stood up in front of him, one stockinged foot on each horse; we got started. It was a glorious feeling as he got them on a canter. Everything was fine until one of them, shorter-gaited than the other, changed tempo, so that one went up and the other down, raising the devil with my knees. Coming to the turn, Fuller told me to lean on the inside horse while pushing with my right foot on the outer. It worked! At the next practice I was alone on the team.

I managed to get some practice whenever possible, using the regular team of Beckie and Red Cloud. The first time I asked for the team, Dick Shannon warned me that unless I could stay with it for three times around the hippodrome track I would spoil the team for the rider using these horses in the races. I made it and felt mighty cocky about it. This was soon cured when someone opened the curtain of the back door just as I was passing it for the second time, and though I didn't see it, the horses did. The race was over as far as they were concerned. Unprepared for their sudden right turn, I flew left, injuring the last two vertebrae of my spine in falling against a stake.

This proved to me that horses aren't as accurate in mathematics as they are alert to sensory cues, hearing or seeing. That curtain, which was usually opened to let them exit on the third time around in the races, if opened any other time still signaled a cue to turn out—for which the rider had to be prepared in his balance.

But if horses are short of intelligence, their meanness is not to be underestimated.

I was standing at the side of the pad room one day, tending my own affairs. The sidewall had been tucked up here and there for ventilation. Suddenly I was seized by what seemed a thousand demons as one of the horses, reaching over the halter shaft, nabbed me at the small of my back, holding me for some length, while his bite inflicted piercing agonies. I lost my footing, and he held and shook me as a dog would shake a rabbit. On releasing his grip, he gave me a terrific push, which sent me sprawling. Staggering to my feet, I proceeded to the doctor's tent for treatment. From the excruciating pain, I believed there was a chunk missing. However, the blunt teeth didn't cut through the skin, though the blood had spurted through the pores of the pinched area.

This act of violence without provocation proves my point. Among horses, there are the perverse and irrational, as among all living creatures.

Horse sense? Horse feathers!

CHAPTER 12

BAREBACK

THE ARISTOCRAT OF CIRCUS ACTS

I began to talk horses and watch the equine acts. Bareback riders own the stock they use; no one can borrow any of their horses. It is impossible, therefore, under ordinary circumstances for anyone to learn a certain style of riding unless a family or troupe takes an interest in one young enough to break in. The trick of balance is only a small part in rosinback or bareback. It requires grace, poise, and agility to perform on a horse with powdered rosin as the only trapping under the rider's feet. Ballet technique is the first essential for straight or principal riding; as for comedy, one must be practically born for it. It was Charlie W. Nelson, my late agent and friend, who said, "There is nothing so pathetic as an unfunny comedy riding act."

The true merit of a riding act is lost to the spectator unless given special buildup by the press or the announcer. The public simply takes it for granted otherwise, without making analytical comparison. It is either funny or beautiful to the untrained eye—just part of the circus and no more. Small wonder, then, that they are among the vanishing features.

To mention grace and technique, one is immediately reminded of Ella Bradna. Never again will there be another gracious lady of the circus ring, the typical Columbine, to equal her in charm and perfection. When she appeared, there was nothing left to wish for—yes, the ideal circus lady poets would write about.

There was a romantic legend the older troupers told of these two, Mr. and Mrs. Bradna: how she was born in a circus wagon somewhere in the Alps. Her father owned the circus, and this child was destined to be a prodigy. In early childhood she was taught riding, juggling, and wire walking. Her basic training was ballet dancing. When grown up—a star of the sawdust while touring through that region disputed by France and Germany which was called Alsace-Lorraine—a young nobleman of distinguished background attended the performance. So came love at first sight. And the story had it that he was to have followed the circus from town to town until finally, this titled and impetuous young swain, who had stables and servants at his disposal, chose employment as her groom to be near her because papa insisted she owed it to her public to remain and carry on the tradition—her family name, Bradna, must be kept gloriously in the limelight. The young nobleman acquiesced even to remain anonymous under the name Bradna, Ella's family name. A bit far-fetched, but that's how it was told.[1]

Of course, it all had a happy ending, for here they were: Mrs. Ella Bradna, the bareback rider, and Freddie, as she always called him, our very debonair equestrian director.

Rosinback acts rated top with a circus and commanded the highest salaries. Unlike other circus acts that can adapt their work to the environment of other branches of entertainment, the riding act must have sufficient space for the area marked by the ring curb (which is carried by the act when playing dates away from the circus). Their equipment also includes a coco mat for flooring other than turf, which is not only heavy and bulky but expensive too. All in all, it is a big investment to own a riding act—the aristocrat of circus acts.

Because it was held in great respect for its superiority over other acts in the circus, riding was always considered above levity of humor or comedy. A clown stepping in the ring in some instances, or doing bits of burlesque outside the ring during the pause between routines of the rider, was the only amusing touch to relieve the decorum and seriousness of the occasion—until along came the Hannefords.

The Hannefords, discovered by Mr. John in England, made their debut in this country during the opening of the 1915 season at Madison Square Garden and revolutionized rosinback riding. The family consisted of the mother, daughter Elizabeth (Lizzie to all), and two sons, George and Poodles (the eldest of the three). The fifth member in the act, named Davies, rode in place of the father, who had died recently. But it was Poodles who started a new trend in riding, doing comedy plus.

Ella and Fred Bradna, "A Rainy Day," Barnum & Bailey, 1910. Frederick Glasier Collection, neg. no. 0892; black-and-white photograph, copy from glass plate negative, museum purchase, Collection of the John and Mable Ringling Museum of Art Archives, Sarasota, Florida.

The Hanneford family (L–R): George, Lizzie (Elizabeth), Poodles (Edwin), Elizabeth, and Fred Derrick (ca. 1915–18). Frederick Glasier Collection, neg. no. 0420; black-and-white photograph, copy from glass plate negative, museum purchase, Collection of the John and Mable Ringling Museum of Art Archives, Sarasota, Florida.

By 1916, about 75 percent of the paper (posters) used by the circus showed this family with the phenomenal riding clown, Poodles. Their act stopped the show at each performance. This act with the great Poodles made riding history for all ages.

"It can't last!" cried the other riding acts. "It will cheapen the quality of rosinback!" was their contentious opinion. They followed, disheartenedly, the accounts and writeups of the trade papers and the press. All shared the public's fervor of the novelty and merit of the act and the furor it was creating. The other aristocrats raised their austere voices and eyebrows in confusion over this shocking episode during the first and second season and waited for the excitement to subside. But instead of waning, the popularity of the Hannefords with Poodles grew and grew. So during the winter following the closing of the 1916 season, in many ring barns, there was much practicing going on in secrecy. When spring came, a score of old, established family acts—riders for generations back—sprouted out with an imitation of the character Poodles had created, ready to meet the challenge at the opening of the season. Like an epidemic, they were spreading all over, shamelessly, brazenly, without subtlety. They dressed the character with the same style of fur coat, trying to do some of the grotesque tricks Poodles had made his trademark, such as sitting on the rump of the running horse, nonchalantly reading a newspaper, or perhaps mounting the steed's head, or allowing the horse to drag him along the ground as he hung on to his tail. All were copied from Poodles's routine.

This lowest form of plagiarism only increased the public's acclaim for the original, the one and only Poodles Hanneford.

Riding acts, as a rule, do two turns in the circus. Managers were glad to buy these acts when they found out that the second turn was a comedy act.

The Hanneford's act as I saw it in 1916, my first season with the circus, began with the clearing of the huge eight-pole top, then the announcer—with great emphasis—told the folks what they were about to see. Two grooms came leading in six beautiful horses (two of them pure white, the others white with black spots). A magnificent sight they made, lined up on the track outside the center ring. A hush fell over the big top as the fanfare brought on the troupe. The two ladies, Mr. Davies, and George were attired in formal evening dress, including wraps, capes, and high silk hats for the men. Poodles, who was also wearing a high hat over his strawberry-blond wig, made his entrance wearing a heavy fur coat, which in itself was preposterous in the summer heat. An attendant collected all the wraps but Poodles's, who removed his hat, then put it back on again. After removing his arctic coat, he produced a whisk broom from his pocket after reaching inside his baggy trousers almost to the depth of his shoes. He brushed and brushed the coat, then held it up to an imaginary hook in the air. On finding it would not stay put in the air, he folded it up neatly and placed it on the ground with great care. Then, as unpredictably, he used it as a mat to wipe his feet on.

As the music segued into a fast-tempo waltz, he turned to the other members of the troupe, who just stood there feigning confusion, made a grab for Lizzie's hand, and led her into a whirlwind dance ending it up with butterflies, in which Lizzie's long skirt accentuated their flight through the air in a perfectly horizontal position. This dance always drew a big hand. Following it, two horses were led into the ring, the two straight men doing a routine of principal riding, with Mrs. Hanneford as the ring mistress.

In the next routine, Lizzie proved her ability on jump-ups and riding. She stood so erect, one would have thought the horse's back was magnetized. Poodles clowned all the way through the act, on the horse and off.

They rode with dizzying speed, all four on one horse—off again, on again. Poodles would make a run for a jump-up and, overshooting his aim, land away out on the track. Again he would try, but seemingly too crowded with the other three, he slid off or just stepped off at the rear of the horse. Still not discouraged, he would make a run for it and land on the horse's head backwards, facing the others. Who could forget antics such as these?

Like everybody there, I was keenly interested and asked Mrs. Hanneford how Poodles came about—no, not his unusual name, that would have been too personal, but the character he created. I sensed there was a story behind it even before she started off, saying, "He was just born for it!"

She and her late husband were both famous riders. Poodles, only a tot of four years old, watched them at each performance from the back entrance and made up his mind one day that he would go in the ring with them. The action followed the thought. Nothing they could do would keep him out, so they gave him a part as a page. He was to take their wraps on making their entrance.

Completely happy with the role, he put the hat on his head, the better to handle the other articles. It was quite a load for a toddler. The hat slipped down over his eyes; he tripped over the ring curb, going headlong to the ground and spilling all the fine togs in the mud. Panicky over the mishap, the scolding or spanking he was sure to get—or worse yet, to be taken out of the act—he sat down and tried in his childish way to rub the mud off, succeeding in messing the garments up worse than they were.

No one saw the great riders during that performance. Poodles Hanneford, aged four years, stole the show. And he had stolen it ever since.

A BACKDOOR GLIMPSE OF SUPERMEN AND SUPERWOMEN

Outstanding among the attractive girls in the statue group were the Cinilia sisters, Minnie and Ana. Minnie was pledged to Dave Clark of clown alley. Ana was free and a target for the wolf's whistle, had such a thing been in vogue at that time or possible, with the close vigilance of the wives and the official detectives who were patrolling the straight and narrow paths lest someone stray from them. But, as the adage goes, where there's a will, there's a way. The guys and gals used the mail to solve their amorous problems in making a date for Sunday. With no show on the lot, they could take in a movie or anything open in the way of amusement. Writing to the other was about the only medium of communication that proved safe and above suspicion. And for their rendezvous, they almost always chose the post office, probably because they were always sure of locating that particular place in a strange town, making the date a few days in advance.

And that's where Ana was to meet Harry R___, according to the letter she received from him three days before reaching the town. Harry, a performer rating high in an original comedy act, was married, with the privilege of having his wife on the show.

Ana wasn't averse to dates. However, in this case—whether she had scruples, or this particular Lothario simply didn't appeal to her, I shall never know—what she did have was a great sense of humor. She promptly relayed the message to Mrs. Harry R___, who on the appointed day appeared in Ana's stead at the time and place specified.

We were all in on the joke and laughed at the innocent way she boastfully was showing us the new diamond ring her husband had bought her on the following week—a gift that she rightfully owed to Ana's clever maneuvering of the situation.

Turning now from the ridiculous to the earthy, there was the whimsical Livia Bartoli, married to Seppi Colini, one of the two men she juggled like toys in her inimitable act. This exponent of feats of strength was truly an exciting female to look at. She had an abundance of glossy black hair, which she wore piled high upon her head; her buxom body was bursting with vitality; the overplump legs were tactfully concealed beneath the long folds of her gown, a style of wardrobe she used invariably. The male members, likewise, dressed in formal evening clothes, lending the act an air of distinction. She was the typical Italian beauty with olive complexion, featuring a pair of green eyes that danced seductively as she smiled, acknowledging the tumultuous applause on completion of each intricate trick.

The two men were excellent tumblers, doing somersaults and each landing on one of her shoulders. For a finish, as the men were executing a series of Arabics around the ring, she would catch them by the small of their backs—one on each outstretched arm and balancing them on the palm of her hands. Thus holding them leaving the ring, she carried them down the full length of the hippodrome track before the grandstand—an act hard to follow or to top, and also one of Mr. John's favorites. That was the Livia in the ring.

But once outside the back door, she was a potential siren. Men, married or single, melted like butter at the sight of her. And she was aware of it—she could see right through their subtle attentions. She was a menace to their virtue and a source of envy to their wives, a situation she evidently enjoyed, playing with the drooling males as a cat with a mouse, regaling them with a smile and an occasional short repartee. Men thought of her as the ideal woman with whom they'd want to be shipwrecked on a lonely island—excepting her husband, that is, who was seemingly untouched by his wife's rare charms, leaving her alone in the berth night after night while he would seek a more delectable pastime by joining a few poker-playing friends in some other berth down the aisle. It was plain that their marital life was doomed; they remained together only for the sake of the act, which was a howling success.

Then, finally, came the inevitable change; Livia had come into her element, proving she possessed power, brain as well as brawn. Booked with several other acts for a two-year tour of South America, no sooner did the unit get started on its route than she seemed, all of a sudden, to assert her authority over the others, running the show, laying out the program, and making changes as she deemed fit. Acts of recognized standing resented having one of their equals dictate to them unless there had been an understanding to that effect at the very beginning.

Many tales were told of that expedition by the acts on their return to the United States: How she broke off with Seppi, paid him off, and dispatched him to Italy; how she had taken over the management and finances after winning over the impresario. As his betrothed, she was boss of the outfit and ruled it as no man would have had the audacity to do. When the box-office returns were scant, she commanded the performers to shell over their savings, or whatever cash they had in their grouch bags,[1] in order that the show might move (allegedly with gun in hand), which was something new to American acts, unaccustomed to such oppressive tactics. Those who showed reluctance were threatened with being left stranded. It was a long way from Broadway; in a foreign land, not speaking the lingo, what could they do?

According to later reports, Livia had quite an adventurous and colorful life, finally marrying someone outside of show business and drifting into calmer waters. From recent rumors, she is managing executive of a radio station in one of the neighbor republics.

Intelligent as well as beautiful, this woman merits a profile in my Hall of Fame, among the great and near-great of the circus.

While the performers may control their deepest emotions when before a public, they will give vent to all the pent-up passions in the confines of their privacy. Examples of their will power or self-control are demonstrated in daily occurrences: A high-wire act, the man carrying the unfaithful mate balanced on his shoulders, across the lofty thread of steel, knowing her affections have waned; the bareback riders who continue their act after being divorced and one of them remarried; the ex-spouse working with the former mate as before. In some cases, they even enter into an association—breaking in the successor as a member in the act. It is a heartache each time they enter the ring. Sometimes such methods are used to hold the act together; other times, sentiment is the motive, because it is the only link which holds them together when the heart of one is still pining. They will go on this way for some time until the wound is healed, or the seed of revenge takes root and grows—harbored and nurtured by the torment at the sight of the rival's victory until it can no longer be held in check.

The climax usually takes place away from the audience. After all, this is her or his private affair which is reserved to oneself. All the bitterness is liquidated in a moment of rapture and seldom in a spectacular mode, though it leaves the stigma of the great havoc which ultimately induced the action.

There was Mademoiselle Adgie, the famous lion trainer, of whom I had heard in dressing-room gossip from time to time. From bits of conversation, I gathered she had been on the Barnum & Bailey show quite recently, prior to my advent by a season or two. In referring to her, the gist was always treated as something of a mystery. However, that's nothing unusual when a woman is featured as she was, dressing in a wagon most likely. The ladies in the big dressing room resented such a privilege given to a performer back in those days. And wagging tongues can soon whip up a vicious rumor. "Why does she always wear gloves?" I would hear their conjecture, and, "She is rather dark for a Caucasian! Wonder what nationality she really is?" The discussion would end with these conjectures.

Marie, the colored porteress in the single-girls' car, discussing her one day, said, "You all say what you like, but I know my own race; that Madame Adgie sho' has some colored blood in her!" And that's how it went on, more or less.

Then broke the tragic story of the fatal accident that her assistant met with one Sunday night. Briefly, this is how the story went: Adgie was allegedly in love with him, expecting to be married, but the sudden cooling of the romance on the man's part aroused her suspicions, and soon after she discovered that she had a rival on the show. (I am not certain on which circus this event took place; it was not the Barnum or Ringling show, however.) Enduring the pangs of jealousy, Adgie kept the secret to herself, since she was dependent on his assistance in her dangerous act and could ill afford to lose him.

On a certain Sunday (with no performance), she made an inspection of her cats as the train arrived, declaring that the big African lion was sick and shouldn't be taken to the lot but placed in one of the empty stock cars. The order carried out, she later went into the car to administer some medical treatment to the ailing Nubian. Toward evening she told her assistant to check on the beast.

Some razorback or animal man passing by heard the scuffle and commotion inside the stock car—the cries of a man's desperate call for help mingled with the roaring, jumping, and clawing of the ferocious beast. He summoned the head porter, who in turn called Adgie. When they reached the car, it was too late. There was dead silence. Adgie entered the car with flashlight in one hand and revolver in the other. Shooting blanks in the lion's face, she got him back into the cage. To this day, it remains one of the unsolved mysteries. How did that lion get out of his cage if the door had been closed? It could have been an oversight on her part. The man entered the car unarmed, unprepared to find the cat loose. In the dark, the frightened beast pounced on him, and that was that.

The news account carried in the daily papers regarded the incident as a human-interest story. The headline read: "Jealous Lion Attacks Rival for Love of Mistress."[2]

During the winter of 1929–30, while touring the interior of Cuba with the Santos & Artigas Circus, I met Adgie. She was in her last stage as a performer, with only three skinny female lions which she exhibited as an attraction in a *caseta* (the Spanish equivalent of a sideshow). I found her to be a very interesting and cultured person, had not her general appearance been a counterpoise. She was old, run-down, and tacky; yet, like a good sport, she seemed to keep up her spirits. Having just completed an unsuccessful tour of Central America, looking as if she and the lions had been on a hunger strike, she was returning to the United States. En route she changed her mind and stopped at the port of Havana, where the immigration authorities held her for clearance: it involved not only the red tape of transporting wild animals, but her own papers were a bit irregular.

Although a native of the United States, she liked to pretend she was some foreign personage—having invented so many fables and fantasies regarding her background that they sometimes confused her. Her tall tales were comical, and in spite of people laughing at her, she would stick to her story until now, in her senility, she swore by her fabrications. The name given on the passport read Adelaide Castillo. She said her father was a Spanish *grande* and a pirate. The name Castillo was Spanish enough, but Adgie spoke not a word of Castilian. The authorities, dubious about her origin, held her for investigation. In the meantime, there was the question of feeding her and her carnivorous troupe. They got in touch with the circus owners, bond was fixed, and poor Adgie worked for the *centavos* they paid in those small pueblos to see her lions, which resembled great danes more than jungle royalty.

Striking a strangely fantastic picture as she sat there in a small enclosure, surrounded by the three cats lying at her feet, it seemed unreal. Her face was a wizened mask, the aquiline nose lending it a witchlike appearance. From under the bandana, which she always kept tightly wrapped over her head, gray stubble of hair peered out here and there. The fashion was the short skirt, but hers swept the ground at her feet. But what positively stumped me was that heavy velvet dress which she wore for costume (most likely her own creation) in that tropical heat. Just looking at her caused me to perspire as in a steam bath.

Adgie and I became chummy, but I never asked about her past. A peculiar twist about her as regards celebrities who outlive their feature value, then live in past glory: Adgie never made reference to the days when she was at the top.[3] And, somehow, having met her in the present dire situation, it was hard for me to associate her with the famous character I had known only by reputation. On one or two occasions when casually referring to her past, she mentioned the name of a Mr. Hall, too vaguely for attaching any significance as to the place he occupied in her fabulous history, however.

Each day as soon as my act was over, I'd come out of the big top to visit her, serving as her interpreter—telling the *mozo* how much meat to buy for the lions. Working on a percentage basis on a dime-admission price, some days she barely covered the cost of their food. In the spring, I returned to the States, leaving her there.

About two years later, I ran into her on Broadway; she still wore the bandana over her hair. We stopped in for a cup of coffee and to have a little chat, when she unfolded the pitiful story.

Apparently, she could no longer support the cats; one of them had died, and the Humane Society took charge of the other two, where they were kept in a spacious terrain with other animals.[4] One day, a rural policeman passed by and spied the strange-looking creatures through the wire-mesh fence; he promptly aimed and shot both of them, probably believing he had performed a heroic act that should rate him a promotion.

And so went the last of Adgie's lions. Having received her birth certificate in the meantime, she was given a clear bill, returning to the United States. At the time, she was employed as a chambermaid in a cheap, stag flophouse in the West Thirties. When I ran into her, she was on her way to a tea room on West Forty-fifth Street, which someone had told her could use a fortune teller. I wished her luck in landing the job.

That was in 1932. Nothing was ever heard about Adgie since. She probably died in squalor in obscurity. That's how she would have wanted it—no fanfare, no publicity. But she rates a eulogy from me. I wonder how she made out.[5]

The Reiffenachs' riding act had been the feature in the center ring of the Big Show since their arrival from Austria in 1924. They were a family of five; three daughters and a son did the riding while their mother was the ring mistress: the usual family rosinback act. However, the carrying (or was it principal?) act of two of the girls, Rosie and Mitzie, was the highlight of the show over a number of years. Wearing one-piece tights (union suit) with huge, ribbon-bow bustles as the only adornment of the statuesque forms, all three girls were a symphony of grace.

The girls were young, exceptionally beautiful, and, though many eligible suitors of equal rank aspired to win one of these blond Venuses, mama said "no!" They had to marry riders to carry on the family métier. Only Rosie fulfilled her mother's wish when she married Clarrie Bruce, the clever Australian rider, who proved to be an asset to the act with his original comedy in a character of his own creation. Mitzie, the eldest sister, in spite of the mother's opposition, married a ground comic—a clown—while Bettie, the youngest of the family, fell victim to Cupid's darts the moment she laid eyes on one of the two brothers in the new perch act on the show, the Olveras. Ruben, the one balancing the pole, was the object of her young dream. Though far from the matinee-idol type, this young Mexican swept her off her feet completely.

She loved this dusky Romeo not wisely, but too well. One may as well try to hold back the tide of the ocean as to suppress the burning desire she felt for him. Not even the hornlike callous jutting out on his brow caused by the weight of the perch which he balanced on his forehead seemed to mar the blind infatuation. In her eyes, he was an Adonis. Regardless of the restraint by the older sisters, the advice of the brother, and the vigilant eyes of the mother, love (as always) found a way. And notwithstanding their antagonistic attitude toward these impetuous young lovers, the family finally had to relent and consent to the marriage.

The young couple lived happily enough, but the family never wholly reconciled to the match and plainly manifested a dislike for the new member; their aversion continued even after the baby arrived. Ruben, though hostile to the hostile feelings on the part of his wife's family, tried his best to make a go of his domestic life, but the wrangling persisted till the young husband finally sought release in drinking.

During winter, there were separations owing to the diverse nature of their acts. The units were booked independently: the perch act in one part, while the riding act in another part of the country. Bettie couldn't leave the family; she was needed in the act. The abuse she suffered from them and even the occasional drunken sprees of Ruben seemed as nothing compared to the torment of being separated from him. Four years of this, and then came the beginning of the end.

In 1938, both acts—the Reiffenachs and Olveras—were on the Al G. Barnes show. By then, Ruben, fed up with family ties and squabbles, found a new love interest right there on the show, using little discretion, with utter disregard for the wife's feelings, in courting her. At the closing of the season, he followed the new flame to the West Coast. Later obtaining a Mexican divorce, he married the girl, who, incidentally, was more ideally suited for him, with a closer understanding than Bettie and even as regards geographical distance—she being of Mexican origin also.

The Reiffenach family established their home in Louisville, Kentucky. It was the winter season of 1941–42. The Olveras were touring with Polack Bros. Shrine circus, playing indoor dates. Rubin's new mate now worked on top of the perch in his act. The show was scheduled for a week in Louisville. The Reiffenachs, contracted with another Shrine circus, were to open the same week in some other town.

Bettie, knowing Ruben was with the Polack outfit, on seeing the advance billing plastered all over the town decided that she would see him at any cost. Of course, the family wouldn't hear of it. She belonged in the act and couldn't be spared, even as she insisted she wanted to remain only for the child's sake: little Rosie, now eight years old, had a right to see her father. But the answer was still negative, and so she had to contrive a plan. What could she do to free herself from them? She must see Ruben! She would see him.

The time passed slowly. Two more weeks remained before the scheduled date. In another week, the family, including Bettie, would start out on their impending tour. They had been practicing daily in the ring barn and getting their equipment ready. The mother was sorting out the costumes for cleaning and pressing. Bettie promptly offered to do the dry cleaning, taking the pile of clothes and cleaning fluid to the trailer which Clarry earlier had put in condition for their trouping.

In less than two minutes a terrific explosion and screams brought the family rushing out of the house to see the trailer enveloped in flames. And there, in the blazing inferno, the outline of Bettie's nude figure stood at the open door, screaming in agony and panic in the midst of the conflagration.

When the Polack show arrived in Louisville, everybody knew about the accident, having read the *Billboard*. On the second day after opening, a group of us went to the hospital to visit Bettie. It was a gruesome sight that met my eyes: the first time that I have seen a carbonized human body and still with life. She was propped up inside of what looked like a coffin with tiny lightbulbs burning in the corner—either to keep an even temperature or to show her progress at night. The completely nude form, stretched out full-length, was black, like barbecued meat, presenting a macabre aspect when she spoke without moving the lips—what was left of them. The entire picture, with the box situated in the center of the private hospital room, reminded me of a wake. She seemed to be elevated slightly, like a levitation act—whatever held her up in space?

I remained after the others had gone. Something in her demeanor told me she had something to say. The nurse had explained that the black surface was partially fish skin—a method of treatment. She added that this case was baffling to them all, how she had stayed alive during the twelve days since the accident—a miracle attributed only to the strong will to live, since her physical injury seemed to show no favorable progress. Her face was blank; there was no sign of expression—the movement of muscles for registering mood or emotion were completely destroyed, but I am sure she meant to smile with satisfaction when she told me that Ruben had been there the previous day to see her. And those words spoke volumes. Her mother and the little girl had remained in Louisville to be near her, the others leaving for their destination to fulfill the contract, for after all, the show must go on!

Ruben didn't go back to pay her another visit. Instead, his new wife, Anita, went another day, taking some flowers. How much more they would have meant to her had he brought them! Having given so much for just one sight of him, was it worth it to her? I wondered. She waited the balance of the week for him in vain. The show pulled out. In the next issue of the *Billboard,* the name of Bettie Reiffenach Olvera was in the list under the heading, "The Final Curtain."[6]

Some time had elapsed when the Reiffenachs played in Los Angeles with the Cole Bros. Circus. Ruben went to visit his daughter, but the child's grandmother denied him the privilege, whereupon he consulted a lawyer and found out that he not only had a right to see his child but could obtain custody of her if he so desired. Legal steps were taken, and Rosie (named for her aunt), who had seen or known so little of this man who made a bid for her possession, surprised everyone when she declared her preference for the father to the family that had raised her. Anita, her stepmother, told me not long ago that the girl has never been difficult to handle. At this time I reckon Rosie to be about fifteen years old—a blond replica of her father, as I remember her when she was a toddler.

Contrary to the general belief that children of show folks will, by natural inclination, follow in the footsteps of their parents, the fact is, it usually works in the reverse. Just as those out of the profession are enchanted by the apparent glamor and mysteries of what seems to them another world and become stage-struck, literally speaking, so the offspring of the wandering fathers—by the time they have reached the age of taking cognizance of their environment—long for the normal childhood, living in stationary homes and other advantages stable citizens' children enjoy which is denied them. Little do they realize the immense improvement in their welfare that exists in the present times over the era of only a generation back before the liberal laws banning child labor, and otherwise extending protection to them in all stations and classes—yes, before these had come into prevalence.

Today, parents may no longer impose their will over their children's destiny by duress, corporal punishment, or frightful threats in forcing them to learn the tricks and doing as dictated by them. True, they will try by shrewd methods—easier on the children than in their own apprenticeship—to cajole them into training, but if a child shows strong aversion for the particular line designated by the elders, it is a useless effort and abandoned by the wise parent at an early attempt.

Because of the compulsory schooling the law requires the children have nowadays, they soon learn of their civil rights—that they are free to choose their own vocation—which accounts for the relatively small percentage of sons and daughters carrying on the family act. No more whipping and starving the obstinate pupil to make him turn somersaults, get up on the traps, or walk the wire with blistered feet. Today it is all learned by inspiration of the prospective artist. It is easy to recognize performers of the old school—they will show a definite finish to their tricks, which is difficult to imitate. However, the performers of the new generation display more originality in presenting their act. The unmistakable spirit of spontaneous aptitude, plus the pride they take in their pursuit—all their own—is much in evidence.

With the most enviable opportunity to become a top-notch bareback rider—everything at her disposal—by the time she was old enough to get her preliminary training, Rosie Reiffenach Olvera was already fed up on the business. With all the humoring and pampering by the aunts and grandmother, she wished only for the quiet home life, which she knew was not to be hers following the profession of her parents—for which she seemed destined as far as her maternal family was concerned. The court trial seemed to suggest the only alternative. Her testimony was the point upon which the judge ruled in favor of the father—awarding him her custody.

Colleagues and friends of both sides viewed the decision with no small apprehension, although Ruben proved to the court's satisfaction to have a permanent home established in Los Angeles. These friends, somehow, sized up the situation as mercenary, believing that his chief aim was to exploit the child, breaking her in for the act. But Ruben fooled them all, proving to be an ideal parent. Rosie was given her chance to pursue the life of the average child with what advantage was within the family's means—just a normal life, attending school and playing with others of her age in the neighborhood, with no stardust in her eyes, nor the fabulous show business in her plans.

CHAPTER 14

ELEPHANTS ARE LIKE PEOPLE

Set on making the circus my career, I availed myself of every opportunity to exploit whatever approach seemed open. Established acts sometimes take on new members as the occasion requires, of which something great may develop as a result. I needed fundamentals, yet I was slanting for a solo, knowing that once you enlist with a troupe, you have lost your identity. I still had faith in riding, but I began to understand that the horizon on that sky was limited to a small area for one in my situation.

Then, as if destiny were playing right into my hand, one of the three ladies presenting the elephants was taken ill. It looked as if she might be out for some time. We were on a three-day stand when Mrs. Bradna suggested, "Why not understudy the routine?" It sounded like an impossibility to me at first, but I knew that this kind lady wouldn't instill false hopes in me. With her judgment, she should know that I could accomplish it. Having seen the act from the spectator's angle, it really looked terrific and daring—just my dish.

How to go about it? Yes, there was a slight catch to it. I must act the part of a diplomat: go to the head trainer, Mr. Mooney, offer my efforts to try, and make it appear as though the idea were my own. I didn't understand

the reason for it at the time. I knew that Mr. Bradna had omnipotent authority over everything pertaining to the performance. I realized later that he
respected certain forms of propriety regarding the other head of a department. The elephants belonged to the show, and their training was entrusted
to one who was competent to discharge his duties. The presentation of the
act was actually done by cues given by the trainer or his assistants; one of
them would stand inconspicuously outside the ring, making it appear that
the glamorous gal was the boss of the shebang. Elephants are downright
drab looking, but a girl dressed in colorful raiment adds vividness to the act.
She is agile and strikes pretty poses when mounting, whereas a man would
only sell the tricks he taught the elephants.

It was up to Mr. Mooney to break the girls in, and to broach the subject
as if no one else had had a hand in it required diplomacy. This boss, likewise observing the formalities of courtesy, told me to go ask Mr. Bradna to
give his sanction. This is an example of the tactics used in a high-caliber
aggregation such as the Barnum & Bailey or the Ringling Bros. Circus, and
it explains why, season after season, the same important posts were manned
by the same executives who carried on the business in perfect harmony.

And so it was that at nine o'clock sharp the next morning, I was in
practice clothes, learning to grip the harness and take the tempo with the
elephant as he hoisted me high up in the air. Although most performing
elephants are females (cows), they are always referred to as "bulls" in circus
parlance. In this particular herd, however, a male named Albert did most
of the mount and pyramid tricks. Though male, he was as temperamental
as a prima donna. My hundred-pound weight was like a rubber ball to him,
yet after picking me up the third time with his trunk, he balked. He picked
me up alright but dropped me immediately and with an impact that set off
fireworks inside my head. Then, knowing instinctively that he was in for a
severe reprimand following such behavior, he instantly knuckled down on
his knees, trumpeting and burying his head as in shame. This expression of
remorse is a natural characteristic of the species. Could it be possible that
man, in expressing humility, copied the elephant? In another respect they
resemble humans. The elephant cow's mammary organs are situated in the
forepart of her body between the neck and the abdomen, equipped with
two nipples set independently apart at either side.

So the elephants became half my life. I noticed in particular the methods
employed by that fine, patient man, Mr. Mooney, who had the semblance
of a college professor rather than a chief of elephants. His handling of the
moody giant who had exhibited that tantrum during our rehearsal was

simple. He took hold of Albert's ear, led him out in the menagerie, and then ignored him. The elephant, accustomed to receiving some token of affection or appreciation—a little tickling behind the ear or a squeeze of the lower jaw—was most unhappy when snubbed, a severe punishment, especially since the other members of the herd were still in the ring. It is a general fact that elephants love their trainer. He never has to resort to corporal punishment since they are highly sensitive and their feelings easily hurt. Only rarely does an exasperated caretaker use that hook at the end of the stick elephant men always carry, on top of the ear, the only tender part of the elephant's body.

Every successful trainer I have known possessed a magnetic personality and a soft heart. The one who impressed me as the greatest of them was Walter McLain, of the Al G. Barnes show. Under a rough exterior there beat a heart as soft and kind as a mother's, for he treated his charges with the same tenderness. Those elephants knocked themselves out to do things for him, impossible things. Elephants I learned were also employed in erecting the big top. With their enormous pushing power, they get behind a heavy load or a pole and move it in butting fashion. The ingenious Walter McLain even hitched them up in harness to pull wagons. That was a sight: elephants pulling a train of four or five heavy trucks along the road from depot to lot. Walter is gone now, the victim of an accident while still a young man. He was killed as he stood by the runway while the razorbacks were unloading the train. One of the wagons got out of control and rolled off the flats and over him. His untimely death in 1942 was a great loss to the Big Show as elephant boss.

We had another workout after the matinee, and that same night, I hopped, skipped, and jumped around six elephants. Albert behaved like an angel. He just didn't like rehearsals and let it be known in no uncertain terms.

Because of the great difference in size—Bessie Mainwood, whose place I'd taken, was a good deal larger than I—the wardrobe woman gave me the costume used on rainy days by Albina Hines, who worked with a herd in the center ring; she came nearer my size. After the act, I had to make a quick change for the statues. Rushing down the aisle, I was startled by a voice calling from behind a trunk in the other aisle. "Say!" I looked around and saw Albina who had come in ahead of me. She was furious with rage, judging by her tone, as she pointed a finger at me and screamed: "That's my uniform! Who gave you that costume? Take it off immediately, that's mine!" she commanded.

"Manicuring the Bulls under Canvas," Barnum & Bailey (no date). Frederick Glasier Collection, neg. no. 0018; black-and-white photograph, copy from glass plate negative, museum purchase, Collection of the John and Mable Ringling Museum of Art Archives, Sarasota, Florida.

I was in a hurry, but I stopped long enough to tell her to cool down, that I happened to know that it was the show's wardrobe, and I wasn't going to contaminate it with leprosy. She blew up: the very idea that I—a statue girl— would dare to talk back to her in that manner. I reached a safe distance on the other side of the partition and foe. Turning the episode over in my mind,

I arrived at the conclusion that it wasn't so much my wearing the costume that irked her, it was the psychological point, the fact that I now ranked in the same category with her as far as the audience was concerned. Outside the back door, however, I was still in the low strata and would remain there, regardless of what outstanding feats I might achieve. But not forever.

Fifteen years later, while appearing as a feature attraction at Playland— Westchester County's swank amusement park—a very chic woman came back to my dressing room to compliment me on my act and to tell me how it thrilled her. Yes, it was Albina. I found her so beautiful, so charming behind her smile, I hardly recognized her at first. She said she was out of show business and was a fashion buyer for Best and Company, an exclusive New York department store, attached to their Rye branch. I enjoyed seeing her.

Success sometimes turns tables in odd ways. It was in Playland also that another person (not so attractive) came back with the park director's permission to interview me. I thought her questions were rather impertinent; they were in relation to my work. I told her I'm not giving out trade secrets, whereupon drawing herself up to her full height, my visitor introduced herself with equally haughty mien. I could scarcely believe that before me stood the once famous interpretive dancer, Gertrude Hoffman, who with her group of girls had been headlining every bill on the big time and whose group many years ago I had tried in vain—would have given my right eye—to join. But "Miss Hoffman wouldn't see me." Was this the same beyond-reach personality? It seemed incredible. She was at this time co-producer with the great Hermann, master of acrobatics of Philadelphia. Together they supplied units of acrobatic dancers and aerial ballets which had suddenly become the rage with musical revues.

I still thought she was out of line with her impudent questions. She sought the know-how so she might copy my act. The very cheek of her![1]

Bessie returned to the show but didn't go back in the act. Being the wife of one of the cowboys, she got by just making spec and parade. I continued with Albert and his harem for the balance of the season; the act boosted my salary up by five dollars, so I was drawing a total of seventeen dollars per week.

CHAPTER 15

ENGINEERING
THE WHITE CITY

My curiosity next led me to inquire how it was possible for our train to arrive, let us say, at 7:00 AM at some point, and on reaching the lot, we'd find all four flags waving atop the cookhouse. This baffled me until I found out that the 150 pieces of railroad vehicles—coaches, stocks, and flats—traveled in four distinct sections, each getting a head start of the other as soon as it was loaded. The first to leave, and consequently the first to arrive on the chartered schedule of the four show trains, the cookhouse was the first contingent on the lot, set up by its own gang immediately after the lot superintendent surveyed and laid out the plan of the entire project.

Dinner was the last meal, served on the lot from 4:00 to 5:30 PM. Canvasmen, teamsters, razorbacks, and other help not utilized during the performance usually ate as soon as they saw the flag being hoisted up. Performers also started trickling in as they finished their act. Having removed their costumes and makeup, they would go to the cookhouse. By 6:00 PM, with all the dishes washed and packed in crates, no longer in their immaculate, white coats, the waiters, joined by chefs and dishwashers—all wearing overalls—were loosening guylines, rolling up canvas, and pulling stakes, and the cookhouse disappeared, gone, to be loaded on the first section. And their day's work didn't end there. No, they had to hang around till the show was over for cherry pie, a term they had for little tasks they were obliged to perform [without pay]: fold and stack up all the grandstand chairs and load them in the wagons. This work, for some reason or other, corresponded to the cookhouse gang. In the morning, of course, there were any number of the town's kids anxious to do the job of setting them up in exchange for a pass to see the show. (Carrying water for elephants is a fable: the water wagons supplied that precious liquid, hauled over great distances at times; yet to this day, kids like to boast of that chestnut.) At night, however, it fell to these hard-working fellows, who were the jacks-of-all-trades in the case. They were permitted to go in the big top to pass the time watching the show, but most of them preferred scouting around for a sociable little circle in one of the wagons, where a group of others were down on their knees— and I don't mean praying, but eager to clean them of their weekly tips in a friendly little crap game by the light of a smoky torch.

After they finished the cherry job, they were free to go where they pleased, the only hitch being that by that time, they had to rush for the train, the first section being just about ready to pull out soon after midnight, and they had better be in their bunks if they wished to stay with it. The berths in their car, as in all other workmen's coaches, were built three-high, with two men assigned to each bunk. The management, aware of this element's lack of interest in folderols such as curtains or blinds, had their panes opaqued by a coat of white paint obstructing the view in or out of the windows.

Loaded on that first section was also the menagerie and a detached division of the vast herd of draft horses that did all the moving between train and lot. The same work today is done by tractors—faster and more efficient, but not as picturesque.

The menagerie being torn down as soon as the Big Show got started is a custom still prevalent. During the last show of a stand, by the time the performance is over, only the sawdust and the traces of elephants, zebras, and other herbivorous species—not kept in cages—are left as reminders marking the locality of a zoo that in itself represents a fortune. Oh, yes, here too puddles are left: the pink lemonade that was not sold the butchers had spilt on the ground; the surplus bottled stock was returned to local representatives. Juice is never taken to the next stand.

The wild animals, kept in cages unless used in some act in the arena, were never removed from their confinement—those cells on wheels. Teams of horses hitched to them, they were transported to the train and loaded on flats with canvas covering to protect them against the elements; this precious cargo would be the first to leave and arrive at each stand. When there occurred a delay in transit, the keepers—whose sleeping coaches were attached to the same section—would check on them, going down the line, watering them and administering other soothing aid necessary to comfort them.

Giraffes have specially built stalls for travel, with flooring dropped below the axle line to conform with the regulation height above, yet allowing ample room for the long neck, which is very delicate and sensitive. A broken neck is the most common cause of their death. They usually get special attention, inasmuch as they are mute and can't register their plaint by sound. Unlike elephants, giraffes will breed in captivity.[1] Their extreme shyness is often mistaken for stupidity.

On very long runs, all four trains would stop somewhere along the route to feed and water the livestock and sometimes even pitch a temporary cookhouse—which was like a picnic for us, with no top, just tables set up for a nice hot meal. It is so pleasant to recall those times. But they were very few. As a general custom, we were supplied with dukies for the long trips when the trains didn't stop long enough for a meal. These dukies—box lunches—contained two sandwiches, some hard-boiled eggs, cake, and fruit. On leaving the cookhouse at the last meal, the checker at the door handed the dukies out, one to each individual.

Remembering now this thoughtful gesture of the management, I regretfully say that it was a total waste as far as the performers' treatment of it, at least. In the dressing room that evening, they played ball with the eggs, some practicing juggling with them. None of the contents of the well-meant dukies ever found their way to the cars; the people instead would buy up some silly junk in a nearby store, depending on doing their own cooking on a primus or sterno, while some would hop off when the train stopped at a switch somewhere en route and go to the privilege car for a snack.

From yonder green days, I recall two outstanding figures responsible for engineering the fast construction work of the colossal enterprise. Both men were well advanced in years but so much better seasoned in experience for their weighty tasks: Daddy Lynch, the boss of the teamsters ("hostlers," in circus jargon) and in charge of the countless heads of draft horses, was one of them. Seeing him mounted on his well-groomed bay, he reminded one of a Civil War cavalry officer. His shaggy moustache covered his mouth completely. Maybe that was why his voice came out so soft—it was strained through that gray wad of hair before it reached the ear. Wherever one looked on that vast terrain, there was Daddy Lynch wearing the gray uniform of a marshal, riding up and down the lot, spotting each wagon as it arrived with its load—part of the big top—in its proper place, according to the markers of the layout, a sketch outlined by the other man, of even greater importance than the first. That man was Happy Jack Snellen, lot superintendent and captain of all hands connected with setting up and tearing down the tented city. Even the razorbacks came under his jurisdiction, helping on the big top once they finished unloading the train. Happy Jack was in charge to see that the show went up daily as per schedule according to its tradition while still with his original bosses, Barnum and Bailey. The Ringlings let him have full sway in the matter without any interference. With the wisdom of many years' practical knowledge, this field strategist knew at a glance over the allotted grounds what went where, staking out the general position as on a map, using small red flags fastened to metal pegs stuck in the ground outlining the project. His post required a man of vision, keen judgment, and quick decision—one to apply the vertex of his wit to create a socko display of a location the average citizen would hesitate going to in case of an emergency, much less to visit as an amusement center. Some of those impossible lots were laid out over an old coal yard, a dumping ground, or a swampy hollow. In any of these despairing situations, it took some one with a spark of genius to draw up an imaginary blueprint of such a plot which, in a matter of three or four hours later, was converted into a most resplendent exposition site as if by magic power.

Happy Jack Snellen was that man back in 1916, when I first saw him—a powerful-looking man, too stout for such an active occupation in the face of his approaching old age. Although he threatened to remain permanently in his native Bridgeport when the show folded up that fall, he was the first one on the lot on the following season. They just go on and on with the show. But then, who was there to have taken his place?

He knew the psychological points of the game, this outwardly crude person who worked out problems with the intelligence of a mathematician, giving thought to details and stressing the finer points as by a mastermind. For example: the front entrance or midway was always given the advantageous view to the approach of the grounds from the main highway or transportation system of the town. In many instances, for lack of space, the cookhouse and horse tents had to be set up on a location some distance away, the nearest vacant ground that could be arranged for—sometimes a half-mile away from the main lot. An area of nine acres was required to hold the entire outfit, with the menagerie and big top, six- and eight-pole structures, respectively, taking up the largest portion. Sideshow and concessions were laid out so there would be ample space on the midway to hold the large crowd of people who hadn't yet made up their minds regarding the show. The appeal of the exaggerated paintings exhibited in front of the sideshow plus the high-pressure spieling of the barkers exhorting the merits of the original subjects inside was so great that in many instances it worked out this way: the spectator, who came with intentions of seeing the main show, breaking down not only his resistance but his pocketbook as well, satisfying his curiosity in that emporium of oddities of nature, would go home without having seen the Big Show and all its wonderful collection of rare animals that are awe-inspiring, and free with each ticket purchased. Yes, this still goes on to this day. While the original plan of the management was not intended to compete with the sideshow, or vice versa, but rather to exploit the business from all angles, it tends to confuse quite a few among the public.

Happy Jack's gang—the roustabouts or roughnecks, as they are commonly known—worked with unbelievable speed in building up and tearing down the White City. Collectively, they comprised the largest crew of any group of men there. Perfectly organized, like a well-trained army, whether in unison or divided into small units spread all over the field, they worked with precision and harmony, obeying the command of the straw boss selected from among their own rank, according to seniority or experience.

Among them were canvasmen, trackmen, seatmen, and various specialists. However, at the time of getting started, they all worked together as one unit. One minute, you'd see the center poles being erected—one by one they were raised, horse and elephant power all put to use; next, like so many swarms of ants, groups of men would be rolling out huge bundles of canvas, the various sections of which were stretched out between the poles, laced together, and ready to be pulled up in the air. Then came the quarter poles, et cetera, tapered down to the side poles. The sidewall would be pulled up after all the riggings, seats, and cages with animals were inside.

Stake driving, done by machine today, was one of the intricate tasks when done by manpower, swinging a sledgehammer ranging from sixteen to twenty-four pounds in weight. In groups of seven men (with a section leader in each unit), they started simultaneously at different points around the tents followed by the stake wagons. Standing in a circle, each man in the group took his turn at pounding on the stake in rhythm to the leader's singing. It required perfect timing to keep the sledges in balanced precision, like spokes of a wheel. I often marveled at how they kept up that measured sequence without a split second's variation, which might have gotten them tangled up, knocking each other's brains out—nothing like that ever happened. That was a classic feat, indeed, a great sport, lost to appreciation of its value.

The stakes generally used in the circus are four-foot-long wooden poles of three-inch diameter with an iron band at the top of each to keep them from splitting; driven down, they leave about fifteen inches above the ground for tie-off.

The leader prompted the men for tempo, singing familiar little jingles, as the following: "I had a little dog / His name was Jack, / He got killed / On a railroad track." Sometimes it took a few more beats to get the stake down, in which case, he would just add a musical "hit it hard, hit it, hit it!" When the ground was really hard, it took two choruses to finish off driving one stake.

These one-man philharmonists were poets as well as vocalists, setting the current news of the show and its people in rhyme and singing it to the same tune as the other verses before, thereby making this menial job of the moment so much lighter for the others, accompanied by entertainment, especially with a spicy seasoning—maybe some hot gossip concerning the kinkers (their term referring to the performers). These singers would thus dish out all the topical scandal in calypso style.

In the late autumn, when the season was drawing to a close, the singers would turn to the route card for their lyrics, such as: "Four more weeks / It won't be long; / You'll look for the flag. / But the flag will be gone!" (The flag in reference was the blue field with the silver stars, of course.)

A hillside or a muddy lot always presented a problem. The seats had to be blocked up and rings and platforms leveled off as near as possible for the balancing of riding and ground acts, to whom anything on an angle looks and feels cockeyed. A flooded or muddy lot was miserable for all concerned. The tents went up, as always. However, the entrance rated the choice spot and got a thorough going-over, filled in with cinders and wood shavings. Oh yes, Mr. and Mrs. Public and their little ones were always at the heart of the management. Their comfort was given first consideration. After all, their support was what kept the show on the road. The performers would go through their routines in the best way they could, and it was over, but not so for the poor army of roughnecks. Theirs was a long, drawn-out session from early dawn to dawn of the next day, when they would finally pack up the last top—rolling the mud up with it, and if the sun came out in the next town, hoping to shake it off on their rounds of guying out—heaving and tugging on the ropes in the same seven-men units with their leader singing the tempo, ending each chorus with, "Heave it down!" "Heave it down!" "Next!"

Comprising in its majority colored men such as had a yen for travel and adventure, the big-top gang was the backbone of the show—the hardest working contingent, at least. They were soldiers of fortune at heart, working during the night and early morning in rain or cold, scarcely ever turning in to the bunks provided for them on the train. After the last load was off the lot, they would get aboard their section, riding on the flats or wherever they could hang on. They wanted to see the country from the moving train during the short transit; besides, on arrival at the next stand, they would be routed out of their berths anyway. But once their chores reached an end—when all the banners were hoisted—brother, that was it, free to do as they pleased! Laying around the lot all day, they would stretch out in the sun along the canvas sidewall all around the big top and catch up on their sleep. And even at this they were useful by keeping out the crashers who sometimes managed to escape the watchmen's eyes and crawled in under the sidewall. Seeing a man lying there, they would quickly retreat during these leisure hours; the inclemency of weather and adversity of conditions were completely forgotten. The hardships of tugging on wet ropes and canvas, the misery of last night and early that day, would become remote. They enjoyed loafing in the sunshine; that's all they were aware of.

Having slept through the lunch hour, they turned their gaze in the direction of a certain four-pole top, three of which with flags waving, meaning nothing. The stream of smoke indicated that dinner was cooking. Soon the fourth flag would be seen from the distance, where roast beef and all the trimmings would just hit the spot. Yes, it was a beautiful life, after all.

And some of the Negroes in Happy Jack's gang even got a break to participate in the performance, utilized in the grand Oriental pageant, where, without the use of makeup, they were naturals, representing the eunuchs of the pompous pashas, dressed in ostentatious garments, carrying palanquins wherein sat the beautiful concubines of their master's harem. A few of them, rigged out with colorful adornments appearing as native tribes, toted drums and other instruments of percussion, in which role they were truly in their element, marching around the track in the colorful spec. The glamor plus the couple of dollars' boost in their meager weekly pay made it worth the five minutes' walkaround twice daily.

Provisions were arranged for by the twenty-four-hour man, Mr. Conway. Saying his position was an important one would be repeating the same cliché. Any effort to describe his manifold job would fall short of adjectives. I shall therefore condense it into a brief synopsis: he traveled one day in advance of the show, hence the term—though I often wondered whether he derived his title from the twenty-four hours' work he crammed in daily. Some of the business at hand on his list called for arranging the rental of the lot, a tedious task that requires strategy in cutting down the cost, especially if it happened to be cultivated land with a good crop of vegetables or a strawberry field. It was bargained for and sacrificed for the one-day stand of the circus. He had to obtain the license for the performance and the permit for the street parade (though the latter has been abolished since the early 1920s). No more use for the familiar jargon: "Hold yer hosses, here come the elephants!" called out by the marshals in warning the good country folks along the streets. Besides, there are no more "hosses" either—the farmer loads his family in the old gasoline buggy and drives over in modern style.

With other legal documents for concessions, et cetera, adjusted, he has to procure all the necessities for the mammoth show—groceries for the personnel and feed for the livestock, a staggering quantity for one day's consumption, a list of items too gigantic to enumerate. Just as a figurative pattern: take the average housewife, who does her daily marketing for a family of five, let's say, then multiply that number by three hundred, which should give an approximate idea of the size of his shopping bag. Then there are the animals to provide for—herbivorous and carnivorous—also the sundry items used in general with a circus. The figures are beyond my arithmetical ability to juggle. The bales of straw for bedding: hay and grain by the tons. Milk, fruit, and vegetables for bears and monkeys, each species to its own diet. Old horses and cows for the meat-eating animals, bought alive and butchered on the lot; occasionally some of the show's horses which had lost speed or service value were killed, replaced with new stock bought here and there, as opportunity presented at auctions or county fairs. Bales of wood shavings by truckloads, used for ground covering on the hippodrome track and in rings, which was preferred to sawdust. Water, likewise, had to be arranged for, of which the show used a liberal amount, the water wagons sometimes hauling the precious fluid from miles away.

Wood and charcoal were the fuels employed in the cookhouse then (today they use butane gas). For illumination, calcium carbide was employed, which also had to be marketed (a few years later, the circus installed its own electric plants). The above-mentioned are but a portion of the list of articles the twenty-four-hour man had to have wrapped up and delivered at dawn the next day.

As soon as the first section arrived, Mr. Henry, the cookhouse boss, Happy Jack, and the trainmaster were the first to alight. The trio lost not a moment. They picked up the directions, giving the location of the lot as well as the list of dealers and bills of merchandise, which Conway had left in cars of the stationmaster before he boarded the train for the next town, where he would go through the same shopping routine. Having done his errands at each stand and drawn a diagram of the lot and how to reach it, he made a personal inspection of the route leading from the railroad yards to the lot, chalk-marking with arrows pointing in the general direction the wagons were to traverse on the way over and evading hazardous points such as bridges or weak-surface-covered streets. The town authorities never hesitated in shaking down the circus owners for the full indemnity of broken pavement or the like, occasioned by the iron wheels under the heavy loads. At every turn or intersection, he would mark a fresh arrow on tree, post, fence, or sidewalk, which served as a guide for the first driver; the others would follow in his wake. On the return at night, torches marked the turns along the course of the haul.

By the time the fourth section arrived, we could generally scent our way out to the grounds. However, very often the coaches were switched to an entirely different location; with no runs or wagons to indicate the direction, one would just have to rely on instinct and start walking along the tracks—a miserable course, especially when it would lead over a trestle. It would eventually bring one to a path or street, here again heeding one's intuition in turning right or left until meeting the first person on the way, of whom to inquire: "Which way to the showgrounds?"

Town folks always knew where the circus would set up. Hadn't they been waiting for months since seeing that poster, which the number 1 advance-car billers had pasted on the most conspicuous barn or billboard of their burg? Later came the number 2 advance-car, spreading more paper over the town, covering walls and store windows (all those giving concession and space for billing receive passes to the show). The number 3 car preceded the show by a week; its head billposter usually saw to it that the place was well covered. The press agents in the advance also did their darnedest to sell the show through publicity, cooking up every kind of human yarns about the people and animals of the circus to impress the public. The town becomes alive and humming with activity on the eve of the show's arrival. The baker would have received an order for nine hundred loaves of bread, for instance.

Of course, everybody knew where the showground was located. A number of kids and grownups, too, would have been out there since the previous day taking a look if anything had been started yet. Everyone was astir. Lithographs in multicolors showed a million unbelievable feats to whet their curiosity. The citizens were eager and waiting; they wanted to see those beautiful girls shown on the pictures flying like birds through the air, and also the savage jungle denizens—some posted on pedestals—while others leapt through a hoop of fire their trainer held up.

The field man of the promotion department had done his job well (he traveled in the advance and remained several days in a spot). A sort of business manager, he sold the advertising space in the program and put in the advance order for the large quantities of provisions a week or so before the twenty-four-hour man arrived.

As near as I could gather, the entire roster of individuals connected with the Big Show before the turn of the 1920s numbered some 1,500, of which about five hundred were performers in some capacity, including those in the sideshow. The others made up the staff and working class. It will not be exaggerating to say that 2,500 pounds of choice fresh meat daily was required for the cookhouse alone (not counting the meat for the animals)— that amount was not to be picked up in a small town overnight.

The circus sometimes left more money in a town than it took in at the ticket wagons.

FINDING THE LOT—
A DAILY HEADACHE

I was not entirely sorry to see the season nearing its end. Trudging along in the early morning trying to find that lot, getting there in time to make breakfast so as to feel fortified to ride in the long parade and be able to smile all the way, all became a dreadful nuisance. The monotony of the long, tiresome walk was broken only when meeting someone and then by asking the same question as always. Not satisfied with the direction already given, I'd ask as many persons as I would encounter. It made the labor easier, or so it seemed, until it finally became a habit. With the flags and billowy white tops already in view just a piece ahead of me, with the road leading directly to it, I would still ask the same question automatically.

Transportation in rural districts had not yet developed, and one had to reach town in order to get a streetcar or a jitney (a popular term for cab in those First World War days). Sometimes the walk to town equaled that of going directly to the lot, so there was little choice but to accept it as one of the unpleasant things we find all through life. By the end of that first season, I arrived at the conclusion that it was the phrase most often used in my daily routine. Imperfectly compiled grammatically, it met all the requisitions in its brevity, a question one may ask a passerby without even stopping one's course. Using the term "showgrounds" instead of our own "lot" was a psychological point for the benefit of the layman, who connects it more readily in his comprehension.

I also came upon an odd fact. The show people's common question dealt with a subject of purely personal interest: "Which way to the showgrounds?" They wanted to get there. It is imperative. On the other hand, the first question asked of show people out of sheer curiosity: "Where do you go from here?" I have never known it to miss. So many times I wondered over this. As if by universal vibration in city and country, the question is the same. I know they are aware of our nomadic calling; still there are so many other unusual facts about our lives that would be of greater interest to these folks, such as, "What do you do in the show?" (which is usually their third question); the second, generally: "Where are you from?"

The only logical answer I find for this common phenomenon of thought by these stay-put folks is the secret longing within to see the other half of the world.

I was asking myself a similar, related question, "Where do I go from here?"

ON THE SUNNY SIDE

To a performer of the theater, once having gotten a taste of the circus, in spite of all its hardships, rain, cold, and heat in extreme, it is still the most fascinating and advantageous branch of show business. There is a feeling of security and brotherly love among these folks who live and work in such close association, together twenty-four hours a day. There is great comfort in being relieved of the problems of booking or job hunting, of being sure of the weekly pay and the roof over one's head, be it canvas or the plywood over the berth. But best of all were the three square meals a day—and they were all of that. Breakfast, according to the general opinion, was the best meal—at least, I hated to miss out on it. Where but in the circus cookhouse would performers as well as roughnecks feast on a full-cut sirloin or T-bone steak early in the morning and be entitled to order a second helping if the first one proved insufficient, a bit tough, or not done to a turn desired? Also pork chops, ham and eggs, and liver and bacon enticed the folks to get up early and tear across the lot while the blue flag was still waving. Fruit, cereal, hot cakes, or muffins were included, and tea or coffee were never scarce.

I seldom made lunch, which was usually cold cuts, stew, frankfurters, or chili; on the dinner menu, there was a choice of two meats, ham or beef roast, vegetables, salad, and dessert—pie or cake. On Sundays, it was always chicken. Bread and butter were on the table, all that one could eat, and by chipping in fifty cents per person plus the dollar weekly tip, the waiter would always have relishes, catsup, and jam, which the cookhouse didn't supply. The milk used in coffee and on cereal was the evaporated kind; however, anyone desiring fresh milk could buy it at the entrance.

On the Fourth of July, a banquet dinner would be served—roast duck or turkey with all the fancy trimmings. The partition between the performers' and workmen's side was let down, and colorful streamers were strung across the entire length of the cookhouse as one gorgeously decorated hall of festivity. The tables were weighed down with fruit, nuts, and all sorts of goodies—a veritable feast. The patriotic color scheme was carried throughout, even to the words of the national anthem printed on the souvenir menu card.

The barrier of class distinction was also let down during the entertainment program for all ranks held in the big top immediately following the dinner. Workmen enjoyed equality with the performers for this one day—Independence Day for all Americans.

Men from all groups participated in the sports events: wrestling and boxing, with star performers matched against roustabouts.

On Halloween, another party followed the sumptuous dinner, this time in the dressing room—that is, separately, with the ladies and gents remaining in their respective division. The party was quite informal, a sort of burlesque potpourri with a marked democratic air about it as the aristocrats mingled freely with the untouchables, the statue girls. The bareback riders and trapeze artists let their hair down and loosened up, forgetting their aloof manners; they cut up like we were all palsy-walsy.

Mickey Graves's wife, Judy, who worked manege[1] and posed with a pony in the statue number, was a first-rate guitar player a well as a vocalist.[2] She organized a chorus of girls for singing and dancing. Laura, in the Davenport troupe, was the chairman of the entertainment; word had gotten around that I could shake a wicked hip, and I was immediately drafted for the hen party.

Yes, the whole affair was a success. I was applauded by the nobility, but on the next day everything was back to status quo—I was ignored or treated with the same contempt.

While the women gave way to the merriment, the men on the other side of the partition were having fun of their own; their boisterous laughter indicated they also had something novel to amuse them not intended for mixed sexes.

Again and again, I pondered how was it possible for people to change from one day to another and wondered which side of them was the natural one. Surely that haughty air was all artifice! Lost in meditation over these peculiarities in human nature—the assertion of superiority of one individual to another, with no apparent difference in their general aspect—I began to search for the link dividing us. If it was priority, I was determined to stick to the circus until I acquired seniority. But it wasn't that at all; it was the system of some of the foreign troupes who came here for a season or two, spreading their aroma of caste distinction and polluting the air with their snobbishness, which to most other performers seemed the hallmark of smartness; consequently, they adopted the attitude.

As always, my thoughts reverted to the plans I had made: yes, I shall graduate from the statue class; there is so much one can do in a circus even without copying someone's act. Wait, I'll show them!

I practiced Roman riding assiduously, and just to stimulate my hopes and morale, I went to work on my first costume, following a design as conceived in my imagination: a soft, white, china-silk gown, topped off with a cape of golden brown satin—Grecian lines predominating.

Jimmie Picchiani, of acrobatic fame, had been dabbling in amateur photography as a hobby. I arranged with him to make some snapshots of me in action while riding the team. With this plan in mind, I waited for a smooth, spacious lot. Luck was with me, for in a few days the show was set up on a fairground with a turf nearby. After the matinee, I got all decked out and got the team. Jimmie came out all set with his camera. No sooner did those horses get sight of the grandstand and race track than they were off! All the seesawing on the lines couldn't check their speed. I must have ridden about ten miles before my knees just gave out, and I tumbled off backwards. The team, riderless, slowed down immediately. The groom standing by snubbed and led them back to the pad room. I don't know how many times they took me around the track past the bandstand. The snapshot showed me leaving them in a most unartistic pose. "No good! I can't sell that as an act to Mr. Ringling," I told Jimmie, who thought it was a masterpiece of action photography.

On another occasion, I was more fortunate. Mr. John was visiting the show, so again, I got all dressed—looking like Helen of Troy herself. This time taking no chances, I did my racing in the big top, hoping he might happen to be someplace where he would see me. Jimmie was to try it again, catching me coming out at the back door, but instead of snapping my picture, he told me he had just been talking with Mr. John inside the big top. I got all excited, sure that he must have seen me, which was worth more than a thousand pictures.

"Are you telling me the truth?" I asked him as I fairly leaped off the team.

"Sure, go look for yourself. He's sitting in the reserves near the bandstand."

I slid behind the curtain, half concealed, looking in the direction indicated. I saw for myself: there sat Mr. John Ringling, listening to the scratchy sharps and flats of a one-string violin played by the octogenarian joey, Miaco—a contraption improvised by himself from a cigar box and a broom handle. The music evidently intrigued this big man, for he seemed amused at the old clown sitting next to him. Or was it that it struck a chord of harmony within him from the past when he, too, as a musician doubled in his own band? Or, still farther back, the days when he, as a kid, saw a circus, and Miaco was the first clown he could remember?

How kind of him to show this attention to the old man who during his long career never rose above his lowly rating—a clown. And how happy the old clown must have felt at having this honor to entertain a king—indeed, the king of the circus.

I sneaked out as quietly and unperceived as had been my entrance, satisfied that my riding was as good as on the books for the next season already.

CHAPTER 18

LIFE UNDER THE BIG TOP

PRIVATE, SOCIAL, COMPETITIVE

The season was well under way before I caught on to the customs and habits in the private life of the people in the Big Show, on the lot and in the coaches. I found out that, despite the rigid rules governing their social activities, the boys and girls managed to enjoy a certain amount of freedom for normal recreation, although very little of it during weekdays. With parade every morning, matinee, and night show—and sewing, washing, and practicing in between—the time was pretty well limited to these essential duties. However, come Sunday, well, nearly every unattached man or maid seemed to have some romantic interest.

Being laid out in the single girls' car, I naturally came upon the inside dope on the principals involved in amorous affairs. Some of the courting was carried on boldly, some stealthily, and only a few of the more serious ones with the sanction of the guardians—the bosses of the individual troupes. For instance, in the case of Emily, the niece of the haughty Mrs. Silbon, she had been engaged to Jack Heather of the Four Comrades comedy tumblers. Their courtship bore the stamp of approval. While Clara, working in the same Siegrist-Silbon flying act, madly in love with Alfredo Codona of the same troupe, did not get the blessings of that lady; in fact, the match was looked upon disdainfully by the entire troupe. Like a foreboding of events, they all saw the menace behind it. Alfredo was an excellent flyer; his brother Lalo was the catcher. Clara, though with no special feature insofar as flying to her credit, made a very striking figure in the air (attractive for its symmetrical proportions for the most part); she was an asset to the act just standing on the pedestal. In spite of the opposition and criticism by the heads, these two, ignoring any interference in their wooing, continued their love affair, making no effort to cover it. Clara made coffee on Sunday mornings in the car. Of all the girls there, she was the only one who would dare such brazen behavior as to send a message by someone to Alfredo's car to come and get the breakfast she prepared and placed on a tray. Waiting for him on the platform, the two would have their little repast together out there. Later, they would meet in town.[1]

On Sundays, all the performers leisurely took their time in getting up, putting on their best clothes, and going where they pleased. Most often it would be to the lot—there was always some repair work to be done on riggings and props, maybe a new coat of paint. The appearance of their paraphernalia is important to them. But in the virgin's car, there'd be no cares of business; this was a day of recreation. After their coffee session, the girls would get all dolled up and meet they boyfriends on the lot or in town, take in a show, et cetera—places to go were always to be found. There was Millie Lapell, the girl whom Mr. Bradna dubbed as "Black-eyed Susie" from the first day when she came on the lot applying for a job in the Wild West. Although she spoke to no one, it was general knowledge that she and the dashing Butch were meeting in town.

The strangest pair of them all was the combination of Elisa, the German girl, and Rodriguez, the Spaniard who spoke not a word of English. They both spoke sufficient French to get a start, however. And so well did they progress in the universal language of love that theirs was the first and only marriage that season. When the show hit Los Angeles, they both asked Mr. Cook, the legal adjuster, to help them in their matrimonial intentions. That, too, entered as legal matter, was part of Mr. Cook's responsibilities. He sponsored them as representatives of the aggregation which facilitated the prompt issuing of the license at the local city hall; the marriage ceremony was performed immediately after. Not much fuss was stirred up over the nuptial event. Their status remained the same as far as their accommodation was concerned. She continued to sleep in the virgin's car, while he was to remain in his for the balance of the season. Nothing was done about laying them out together.

Some of the men were members of fraternal organizations: Elks, Moose, et cetera—and the local lodges sometimes arranged for a little blowout and dance for the benefit of the visiting members on the show. These, in turn, could bring along some others as guests—women always included. At these little socials, it would always come to light who was whose beau.

"Lor', I declare, you sho' look pretty today, Gracie!" said the porteress to Grace White as she handed her the new suit out of the locker. The slim, blond-curled unicyclist with the Buck Baker skating and bicycle act was the object of envy of the entire bunch there. We all knew she was going to meet Poodles Hanneford, the most eligible bachelor on the show. His sister, Lizzie, as she was known in general, was being escorted by the tall, dark, and handsome Tony Picchiani, brother to Jimmie, who owned the act of the same name. Doris Davis, in the upper opposite from mine, was also preening her feathers for a date with handsome George Smith, the assistant front-door man. Everybody had somebody if one set out to make something of it. As for me, I was still in a state of confusion—living in the past—and still tagged along with Mabel and Harry Clemings. I was usually up on my shelf asleep when the others came straggling in; that is, those who habitually returned to the car. There were others who preferred going to a hotel to have the benefit of a hot bath.

CHAPTER 19

FINALE OF
THE SEASON

Official route cards listing the entire season's stands as well as announcing the closing date were issued in the commissary wagon. Everybody got excited over this event, stopping to buy one before entering the cookhouse. It was a momentous occasion affecting every living soul with the outfit, playing havoc on the emotions. Some were happy, others sad over the season coming to an end in three weeks. These complete season's route cards constituted the official notice. At the tables, the conversation was louder than usual; the arrogant ones talked in terms of big-time vaudeville bookings which their agents were getting lined up for them. Parents were exuberant with fluttering hearts at the approaching reunion with their young ones. Whether for better or worse, to all it was a welcome change.

It gets awfully cold about November, even in the deep South; then it is miserable to be out all day under a canvas top, which is weather-beaten and offers little resistance against wind. The rain, too, finds all the holes in the patched top overlooked by the canvasmen. To me, therefore, the definite closing date meant relief from such conditions. Inside of me, I already felt the comforts of a steam-heated room with carpet on the floor.

Following the example set by most of the folks in the lower bracket who lived in or around New York or Bridgeport, I also planned to put in a request to ride back on the show train. That was my first interview with Mr. John Ringling. I had already received the contract for the next season at the sum of twenty-five dollars per week for the specialty of Roman riding. Now I spoke with Mr. John. He was holding an unlighted cigar in his mouth, on which he seemed to be drawing; removing it between his fingers, he went through the motions as if spitting in an effort to clear his lips of the tobacco fragments. This and the frequent blinking engraved his personal characteristics indelibly on my memory. He listened as I timidly made my request and replied in his rich-toned kindly voice by recommending that I see the general manager, Mr. Becker, to have my name put on the list.

The trip from Memphis to Bridgeport, traveling on freight schedule, took about six days. The train would stop along the route for hours at a time to feed the stock, switched to a sidetrack in some freight yard.

With the single girl members of the big troupes gone, we of the humble class enjoyed the comforts of lower berths. Although there was quite a substantial number of us left, we each had a berth to ourselves. But after shivering through the first night, we doubled up for comfort by keeping one another warm. As freight, no lights were permitted on any part of the train, and with no sociable card games the nights seemed as long as at the North Pole.

On long stops, we took turns buying provisions for the bunch. Two or three of us made the trip to the nearest grocery, which was seldom less than three miles away. On leaving the train, we would inquire of the first brakeman or section man, "Which way to a store?" or, "How long we gonna stop here?" That was of vital importance—what if the train only stopped to take on water or to switch to another line, waiting for the engine to be coupled on, and took off?

Marie, the porteress, was still in there with us, but she no longer shined our shoes. Anyway, we didn't get them muddy staying aboard the train.

CHAPTER

20

CIRCUS
EXPERIENCE
PAYS OFF

"Girl to present elephants" was the ad that caught my attention in the wanted column in the *Billboard.* Following the directions given, I contacted Frank A. Robbins, the owner of Eva and Babe. The act was playing in the Nixon-Nirdlinger Theater in Philadelphia.

A grand old man, Mr. Robbins was the stereotype of the pioneer circus owner. He told many interesting tales, which I now wish I had listened to with more attention, but instead I just pretended to be a good audience for the sake of politeness and respect while the estimable old gent would recount valuable incidents in relation with circus lore.

Although I had worked the greater part of the season with one of Mr. Mooney's herds of six, my experience with elephants actually began with these two after the old trainer, Thompson, left the act, which happened the same day that Mr. Robbins took me backstage to introduce me. Explaining that the appearance of a girl would add to the presentation and create greater demand in booking the act, he tried to soothe Thompson's injured vanity. But Thompson couldn't see eye to eye with the boss, and without a word of warning, on finishing the last show of the night, we saw no more of him.

The groom attending the elephants, who had worked under Thompson's direction for some time, remembered their routine—as did the elephants, for that matter—but being unaccustomed to take command from him, they balked, especially Babe, whom Thompson had broken in from a green state. She had a mean streak in her nature. The left ear that was almost eaten away by the sore inflicted by constant prodding and hooking attested to the difficulty in handling her. During the rehearsal the next morning, when Thompson failed to show up and neither I nor the bull man could make them budge, Mr. Robbins realized that we were licked. Another act filled in for us for the balance of the engagement, while he got busy. Through his connections, Mr. Robbins by the end of the week had another trainer, replacing the old fogy who certainly didn't belong in show business.

As the new man took over, it was interesting to watch his tactics, the psychology an elephant trainer uses in getting acquainted with his charges. The two gals practically cooed to him in no time at all, showing off their tricks with hardly any prompting. Mr. Robbins and I made notes of the tricks in their successive order. The cues used in training bulls are well-nigh universal—known to all trainers. He tried every one on them to see which ones they'd respond to—a sort of elephant audition which was truly an educational session. He next went over the tricks with me doing the mounts, including those I did with Mooney's herd and one which I recalled Thompson doing with Eva during the show I caught from out front. I remembered how to go for it by taking hold of the collar with the right hand and the tusk with the left. At the command "up!" my body swung in tempo in front of the elephant. By the time she reared up, I was lying across her two front legs—held up like a babe in arms, very effective to the spectator. We got the act in fine shape, ready for the opening of a long list of dates that followed.

That this was a more ideal setup, by far, than would have been the former, we all agreed; at least now I had the seniority by a couple of days. Besides, Old Thompson, so conceited, would have tried to hog the spotlight, a point in direct conflict with the plan. But the new trainer, having family difficulties, was to leave us shortly after. By that time, however, the bulls took command from us.

Not all of the incidents of the tour were pleasant. Babe would not infrequently lower her trunk suddenly in the midst of a swing trick and dump me on the floor. There was no use castigating her; she was just plain ornery.

Eva, on the other hand, was the good old reliable sort: slow but sure. She was on in years then; an Asiatic breed, she was square or, rather, oblong of form. Babe was much shorter, with a back that was rounded like a mountain. She was young and did her work—what she felt like doing—fast, sometimes not even waiting for the cue but anticipating the tricks in the routine. This was all right for individual work, but she killed the effect of the picture when at the finish of the act, both animals were to pick up tiny flags with their trunks and rear up on the tubs set in back of them. Babe would avail herself of the freedom while I was mounted on Eva's head and unable to check her; she'd pick up the flag, rear up, salute, and go down again before I could get Eva up. I finally got the attendant to stand in the wings and show her the hook.

But before I seem to let partiality run away with me, let me say that Eva wasn't altogether perfect. Far from it. She, too, had her playful moments. In one pose, while lying on her side and holding up her hind leg for me to stand balancing on it, while taking a pretty style, some diabolical urge within her to spoil this picture would prompt her, quite frequently, without waiting for cue, to suddenly kick me off. With the impetus she gave me from that position, I always landed on my head—the beautiful plumes of my headgear getting all mussed up, to say nothing of my pride. I took many a bow smiling while tears ran down my cheeks. She must have known it was mischief and probably laughed under her trunk in her own way. I am certain that she knew she had me in a spot from which I couldn't work her over. Proof of that lies in the fact that she never did it during rehearsal (which I put her through immediately after the performance).

A worse feature about her, however, I attributed to physical defect. It would therefore be an injustice to blame her for the grief and no end of embarrassment she caused me during the solemn moment of the lay-over or cover trick so commonly used in bull acts, during which the elephant settles down over the prostrate body of the trainer, covering the figure completely. This feat, though it looks terrifying, is actually tame. There's no danger of getting crushed, for as the bull knuckles down, the forelegs bend like elbows to support the weight from its belly forward. All set for the trick, I would give her the command, but I knew what would follow the instant she started weaving from side to side as if hesitating to knuckle down: Swish-sh-sh!! Down came the deluge, almost drowning me at that tense, dramatic moment when the spotlight focused right on her. No matter how well the attendant worked her out in the alley just before curtain time, the habit was consistent. It was sheer luck when she left it out of the act. Who knows whether it was weak kidneys or a case of elephantine stage fright?

Accommodations for the elephants always presented a problem. Although stables—their suitable housing—could be found in any town, horses had a natural fear for them. Poor Mr. Robbins would use all his guile to get some of those stable or barn doors opened to Babe and Eva. Elephants must have a warm stall, since they are extremely sensitive to heat and cold. Transporting them, it was necessary to have a costly private stock car. The ramp or runway to load them was part of our own equipment. The attendant slept with them in the same car or stable, packing a cot along. Elephants are such busybodies that a sitter must be with them constantly. Even with the man around, they are always up to some prank. One night, they chewed up two hundred dollars' worth of harness hanging near their stall. Another time, they broke loose during the night, walked up a flight of concrete steps, and broke into the office, where they smashed up a desk and files and canceled all pending accounts by chewing them up. Mr. Robbins was constantly settling for damages.

Their stubbornness knew no bounds. They would walk up a flight of stairs in the stable, when doing it on their own initiative, but refused flatly to climb up a couple of steps from the street level to the stage on command. At one place in particular, a carpenter crew worked all morning to construct a covered ramp for them over which they had to be backed in order to get them on the stage. The stage, incidentally, also had to be shored up in many theaters, for if there was the slightest give to the flooring, they positively would *not* appear!

But the following bit I have saved for last because of its unusual nature. Because of the confining obligation required of them, attendants changed with regular frequency, shifting restlessly along to some other job. Mr. Robbins got one fellow who was very cruel or short on patience. At any rate, my costumes were always stained with blood from the bulls' trunks. However, Mr. Robbins tolerated him for lack of a substitute. One day, going for the trick of the babe in arms, I found to my great consternation that there was no tusk by which to hang. Quite bewildered, I went through the act without apparent hitch, thanks to the elephants.

When asked for an explanation after the performance, the man claimed that Eva had tried to spear him. He ducked just in the nick of time, he said, and she hit her tusk against a beam instead, breaking it off with the impact. His statement was obviously false. Eva was playful, but there was not a vicious bone in her massive body. Most likely he had struck her a blow across the trunk with the hook, breaking the tusk.

The most unfortunate part of the incident was, of course, that the broken left tusk was the one I used for the trick. To try it from the other side would have been as awkward as a right-handed person doing a left-handed job. Besides, it would have confused the animal as well. Following the week in

Columbus, we had three days open before the next date in Niles, Ohio. That's where Mr. Robbins found a veterinarian who would undertake the job of clamping the broken tusk onto the remaining stub. A strange request—the good vet probably told of it over and over to his grand- and great-grand-children, for Eva refused to go to the vet's hospital without Babe. However, his laboratory was too small to hold both elephants. We managed somehow by tying Babe to a post in the yard, where they could scent each other. Eva lay on her side, while I sat on her shoulder talking to her as the vet drilled a hole through the stump. During the proceedings, Eva would send messages to Babe with short staccato screeches, to which Babe would respond in kind. The work was finished off by a wide brass-band reinforcement. I tried to hang from it and found it perfect.

Early the next morning, there was a knock on my door. Mr. Robbins came to tell me that during the night, while he was still at the stable, Eva kept worrying the mended tusk, feeling and twisting the small end of her trunk around it. And then—with a vengeance—one yank, and the tusk was dislodged. She held it in her twisted trunk, and then, as with a snap of a whip, she hurled it across to where Mr. Robbins was sitting, as if to say, "Here, you can have it—I don't want it!"

The tusk was broken now at the jawline and bleeding, so Mr. Robbins had remained at the stable all night, watching for symptoms of danger and concerned for Eva's extremely nervous condition. He was quite upset over the whole affair and asked me if I would come to the stable to see if my presence would have a soothing effect on her. I felt guilty, knowing the idea had been my own and had sprung from pure selfishness on my part because I considered the effort too great to practice the trick from the other side. Now there was no alternative.

In time, the tusk started to grow out again: almost two inches of it were showing by mid-March, when Mr. Robbins's daughter, Winifred, took my place, and I returned to New York to be on hand for the call of the Greatest Show on Earth.

AN ANNUAL
SEASON'S OPENING

The European conflict was spreading with ever-increasing force, gaining velocity like a hurricane, involving more and more nations. The spirit of war was influencing our own lives here, affecting the fashions and slang expressions. The theaters, also invaded by the trend, were presenting skits with a patriotic flavor. Songs written in favor of and against the swaying sentiment expressed the voice of the people, their reaction manifesting the general unrest. The topical question was, Will we eventually get into the mess?

Yes, we were definitely headed in that direction. The song (written two years before), "I Didn't Raise My Son to Be a Soldier," had suddenly lost its popularity. Liberty-loan bonds were issued. Drives for their sale were staged with all the spectacular features and glamor that the committees could contrive.

The circus was coming to town, hurray! Only the bright touch of the light-hearted frivolity of the circus, livening up the three-mile parade, could have attracted the tumultuous crowd that gathered on New York's Fifth Avenue, from Eighty-sixth Street, where it started, to Battery Park, where it disbanded. The attendance was, in fact, so closely pressed together, the police had their hands full trying to keep a narrow lane open for the procession to pass.

to tone down the naked truth) suggested not the shepherd, as had been the intention, but something quite confusing.

Seeing him revel in his innocent mirth all the while pointing to the statue, his giggling was so contagious that all of us, though greatly embarrassed, suddenly gave way to uncontrolled laughter, as if exploding after the attempted suppression. Had an august judge sentenced me to die in that instant, I still would have been unable to hold back the convulsive fit of laughter, the urge was so powerful. We all left in short order after that rude behavior. That is the mood in which I best remember Strawberry Red, a benign character, yet he too caused me grief.

Butch Siegrist, the third Roman rider, was a good-looking chap and a natty dresser. He was generally liked on the show, especially by Mr. Bradna, for whom he acted as lieutenant in the parade, rendering him also other little services of confidence which Mr. Bradna appreciated. The Roman race was fixed; I was to win at all times.

Because the track was too narrow for three teams to line up abreast, the two boys would get a head start, while I trailed close behind them till the final turn, when they would pull out slightly, letting me gain the lead on the inside of the curve. But Butch, somehow, resented me; or was it just plain cussedness? In any case, he and Strawberry would get so far ahead of me from the start that the fastest team in the world couldn't make up the distance. At the finish, just as the bell started ringing, both rascals would pull up their teams on the straight stretch, making a farce of the whole thing. Sometimes I fooled them; pulling on my team, bringing the horses almost to a halt, I would yell on top of my voice, "All right, Ezra, you win!"

Mr. Bradna would proceed to bawl me out, blaming me alone. Between the two, I was provoked to distraction.

Then came the war. Strawberry Red was one of the first to be drafted into the armed service; an old clown named Sam Bennett took his place in Roman riding. I was worried at first, expecting the old coot to buckle and drop off any moment, but he stood up as straight as a spike. Amazed at the fortitude of his legs, I learned that in earlier days he had been an equestrian, doing bareback riding. There were no more shenanigans with Sam in the race; he was serious about his work and respected the performance above trifling. Of the thrills and spills, I recall the many tumbles, getting mixed up between eight hoofs whenever the team would lose its footing on slippery, muddy tracks or stepping in a hole covered up by straw.

As a Roman rider I was now eligible to sleep in a lower berth which, of course, I had to share with someone. But I could not fathom how Millie

(Black-eyed Susie) from the Wild West came to be the other to share it, since she had no special qualifications to rate a lower. She rode no broncs and did no roping nor trick riding. It couldn't have been class distinction that led me to resent being laid out with her, but still it griped me. How did she come to be the one?

Dressing in the hooligan, I soon found out that Butch was smitten by Millie's dark charms and, availing himself of the favor in which he stood with Mr. Bradna, wheedled from him this privilege for his beloved. This fact only irritated me more, and because of my aversion to Butch, the feeling seemed to have extended toward the subject of his affection. And I am sure there was no love lost on her part toward me. So profound was our antipathy that all during that season, while bunking together in a narrow berth, we managed to keep our bodies from touching.

But time has a way to alter issues. In 1935, we happened to be in Billy Rose's *Jumbo* together, where Butch and Millie made a snappy team doing a perch act.[3] Incidentally, we worked in the same scene, and the three of us were the best of friends. We often reminisced and laughed over those clashes in the Big Show eighteen years before.[4]

The Big Show of 1917 opened with the pageant prelude, *Aladdin and His Wonderful Lamp,* a Chinese fantasy of dazzling beauty and splendor such as Marco Polo never had the good fortune to witness, I am sure. The entire production was staged by Mr. Bradna during the short snatches of time between other urgent tasks in the three days that the circus got possession of the Garden before the opening. During this time he also reviewed the new acts, timed the various numbers, and arranged the program.

Credit should also be given the eminent master Karl L. King, who composed and arranged the music, described as "conceived in the style and spirit of the Celestial Empire." Nor could the public have guessed that the beautiful princess was the truly beautiful and young wife of Charlie Siegrist:[5] Edie, as he called her, could be gazed upon and admired at close range. There was nothing artificial about her. She was not the arrogant, regal type of Mrs. Silbon, who played the role of the Dowager Queen in the Chinese spec. Edith was a sweet, innocent-looking beauty, the sort anyone could approach.

Something warm about Edith made me feel at home with her, calling her by first name when talking to her. Muzzie Millman visited in the hooligan so she could smoke, while I visited with Edith Siegrist in the big dressing room to gain knowledge about aerial work. The hints and ideas she imparted were later to affect my whole future.

LEITZEL, QUEEN OF THE AIR—OF THE GROUND AS WELL

Verily, this was the era of air-consciousness, and trapeze became the main topic of the dressing-room conversation. Every dizzy dame on the show had visions of an aerial career from the time we left the Garden. It was in the air where that little queen, Leitzel, conquered not only the audience but everybody connected with the show. She was responsible, to a great extent, for the current fad gaining popularity with the entire cast. Spotted in the middle of the program, the entire arena was surrendered to this tiny fluff of blond hair, sheen ruffles, and rounded arms which showed no exertion as she took hold of the web, turned upside down and into a plange, and held the pose for a few seconds so the audience could appreciate the picture; then relaxing, she again placed the free hand high above the other, holding the rope, and turned upside down, repeating this until she reached the top—about sixty feet in the air. Under canvas, the peak working height was limited to forty-five feet, but in the Garden it was possible to reach a height of eighty-five feet to the rafters.

Having ascended to the vicinity of the crane-bar, she went through a short routine of poses on the web—using no loop for hand or foot. Even the performers were astounded at her ability to hang on freehanded. This she followed with a routine on the rings. Perched there, she would pause in between as if she had all the time in the world. The people gaped, for she was interesting to watch even when doing nothing. Reaching inside the front of her bodice, she produced a tiny, white powder-puff, then proceeded to dust the powder on her hands in an apparent act of coquetry. The real purpose, which only aerial performers grasped, was powdered rosin for gripping. She concluded by dropping the cloudlike puff, which floated downward, visible in the floodlight. This, too, was part of the presentation, accentuating as it did for the benefit of the audience the great space between her and the ground below. She began again with a one-armed pullup, followed by a press-up into a handstand. Suddenly, allowing her body to overbalance, she plunged backwards. (Incidentally, the sudden drop which provided the momentum entailed in this trick caused the crystallization and snapping of the shackle that brought about her death.) After the handstand trick, followed by some fast giant-swings involving shoulder dislocations, she reached for the web and started her roll downward—the same motions as in ascending, only now in reverse—one, two, three, and she was back on terra firma.

The ease and skill with which Leitzel worked made her act appear like no work at all. The tricks were amazing yet looked too easy. The audience applauded but expected to see more—something with a sensational climax. And they all wanted to see more of this adorable mite of femininity so easy on the eyes.

While the maid arranged one of the golden curls that bounded out of place or straightened a ruffle on the little mistress's dress, the announcer took over to tell the "ladies and gentlemen" about the one-armed somersaults she was going do in the air, ending with, "Miss Lillian Leitzel, the only living person to accomplish this feat!" (And she was, for at that time no one had attempted to copy the trick.) She now slipped her right hand through a loop at the end of a rope which led through a pulley from above. Then she slid the small safety band down close to her wrist, securing her hand. She was hoisted up in the air till the plunger on the rope reached the pulley. As she did those throwovers, her tiny feet were executing cuts; the picture was thrilling and beautiful. The audience gasped; the drums accentuated each revolution as the announcer kept count: "forty-eight, forty-nine, fifty!" She stopped, and the line of men who held the rope, straining with all their might, started walking back with it—smoothly—till once again she was on the ground. This time her curls were all open from the impulse of the revolutions; her hair looked as if standing on end.

She bowed, bending forward like a mechanical doll. The maid arranged the pink-tulle scarf around her shoulders and followed her across the track; the applause was still audible—like hail hitting a tin roof—as she disappeared behind the exit curtain on the Twenty-sixth Street side.

During this time the Garden was blacked out, and no one could see the eager performers and other employees crowded in back of the seats on every tier of the huge building watching this wonderful act. Three or four days after the opening, the folks get to know how the show is progressing by the music which can be heard all throughout the building. For instance, when I heard a certain tango being played, I knew Fillis's dancing horses were on and that after two more numbers would come Leitzel's act.

The bandleader Karl King, impressed by her work, composed a special piece of music—an inspiration which he dedicated to her and called "The Leitzel Waltz," which is still the property of the Ringling-Barnum combine. The undulations in the composition resembled the ripples of falling water.[1]

This was Leitzel the performer. Now let us peer at the Leitzel behind the scenes.

After leaving her mother and the Leamy act, Leitzel was taken under the wing of Charlie Ringling, who, together with his brother Alf T., was managing the Ringling Bros. World's Greatest Shows. Under his direction, she was built up as a feature of that show. With the other two brothers, Otto and Al, having passed on, John alone was carrying on the Barnum & Bailey Greatest Show on Earth acquisition.

After leaving their winter quarters in nearby Baraboo, Wisconsin, the Ringling people usually opened their annual season at the Coliseum in Chicago, at a later date than the Barnum outfit's debut in New York's Madison Square Garden. Between them, the brothers arranged to loan Leitzel to the Barnum show as a feature attraction for the opening of 1917 at the Garden. After the New York engagement, she was to return to the other circus. Mr. John had already signed up Ruth Budd, who would be strong enough as a feature on the road, for the entire season.[2]

Rehearsal time came, and Leitzel wouldn't rehearse. "That's all right," Mr. Bradna humored her. Ruth Budd put on tights and went through the act as if for an audience, using her own specially arranged music. Leitzel was told to watch and gauge her time, more or less, by Ruth's act, since the two were to work simultaneously. This was shocking news to her, but Mr. Charlie wasn't there, and she didn't feel certain of her authority to speak up as she would have on the home field. The only person here from her own base she had brought along was her private rigging man. He had been looking after her equipment and knew the routine of her act with his eyes shut. He did the groundwork on which depended the smooth performance of this mistress of the air. He knew exactly when to hold the web tight or slack, directing the men who assisted; many years he had been in her employ. Bob was the perfect rigger, always cheerful and patient, but at this moment she needed someone, a confidant, to hear her outbursts—for, as she sat in the loge watching the procedure, inside of her was a smoldering volcano.

Ruth Budd ascended her web, and though not as high as Leitzel's, she did pretty work and sang at the same time. When at one passage Ruth reached a high note and held it as well as an intricate pose at the same time, that was too much! There's nothing like sound to attract attention. Leitzel didn't wait until Ruth finished but sprang up and tore across the arena. She headed directly toward Mr. Bradna, who was watching Ruth's act, and rudely interrupted him. Covering her temper with a smile, she asked sarcastically, "Does she sing in the act, too, or is this just a musical rehearsal for tempo?"

When told that the vocalizing was, in fact, part of the act, she flew into a rage, screaming, "That yodeling and screeching will drive me hysterical. I will not have it!" With that, she stamped out of the arena and into her dressing room.

Ruth's contract was all signed and sealed—a season's work. A conference between Mr. John and Bradna was followed by another, including Ruth's business manager. What they were now negotiating was to pay Ruth for the five-week Garden engagement, but she was *not* to start working till the road. It was Ruth's turn to assert herself. She wasn't going to take that lying down. The New York appearance with the Big Show was worth more than a season's work on the road, as far as prestige was concerned. What to do? Putting them on separately would slow the show down, especially since both acts were of similar nature. More discussions were followed by legal procedure.[3]

When the show opened three days later, there was but the "One and Only Leitzel" featured in the air. For the road, the show had plenty of good aerial novelties; singles, doubles, and small groups. Lupita Perea, who did a sensational half-somersault forward, catching by her heels on a swinging trapeze; the four Daring Sisters, a European novelty on a quadruple trapeze; and several others.

Everything settled to her satisfaction, Leitzel went to the wardrobe department to arrange for someone to attend her—not quite a maid, but to appear as such. Her personal maid was left in Chicago. Mabel Clemings was selected, and so now she didn't have to make spec or go in the statues; her job was to help Leitzel dress, wash her tights, and attend her in the ring by removing the piece of drape from around her shoulders and replacing it again on the finish. Also she gathered up her slop shoes (mules) as the temperamental queen kicked them off her feet, to have them ready for her to step into on her descent.

Sometimes, when she felt really ambitious, Leitzel did an encore. Her rigging man, Bob, dressed in white flannel uniform trimmed with gold braid and wearing white gloves, was always standing by. When given the nod, he would fetch the mouthpiece and trapeze from Leitzel's rigging box. Again she would lock her wrist in the loop, and as she was being hoisted up, Mabel, seated on the trapeze held by Leitzel's teeth, would be lifted up in the air with her, the one arm supporting the weight of both.

This she would do on very rare occasions, and hardly anyone suspected that it was prompted by an impish desire to show off before Clyde Ingalls, the mellow-toned announcer with whom she struck up a desperate flirtation.[4] He usually followed her out of the arena for a chat at the dressing-room

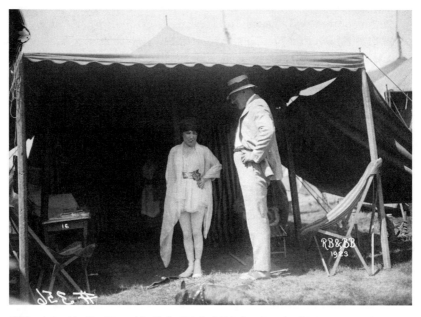

"Lillian Leitzel in Her Tent with Clyde Ingalls," Ringling Bros. and Barnum & Bailey Circus, 1923. Frederick Glasier Collection, neg. no. 0356; black-and-white photograph, copy from glass plate negative, museum purchase, Collection of the John and Mable Ringling Museum of Art Archives, Sarasota, Florida.

entrance. What a contrast they made in size, since he was a powerful figure of six feet, two inches in height, towering over her like a giant.

It was a flirtation and nothing more. There couldn't be—Clyde was married. His beautiful brunette wife, Irene, worked in a levitation act with him in the sideshow. Anyway, it would all come to an end after the New York stand.

But New York was to see more of her. Florenz Ziegfeld signed her up for the entire winter season to appear in his *Midnight Frolics* atop the Amsterdam roof, where Bird Millman was an established feature attraction of the ultra-swank nightspot for the last two seasons. How the famous producer and "glorifier of American womanhood" managed to keep both stars happy, each demanding top billing, is a secret that was never divulged.[5]

Incidentally, in the 1930s, after the death of the great artiste, a sudden surge of imitators began circulating in the white tops and theaters.

Of the many who aspired to succeed Leitzel in her unique one-armed somersaults, only three approached their objective in what might be a token similarity to the original, and each in a diverse way. Janet May did the best arm-dislocation. In thrusting her body straight up in perpendicular position, she actually brushed against the suspending arm at each revolution. Mickie King came closest in charm and appearance, and Irma Ward had the greatest endurance.[6] As a matter of fact, Irma's revolutions only took form at the count of fifty; after that, she could go on indefinitely, as if in an endurance contest, which became monotonous to the spectators.[7] All three were five-footers. Taller girls doing the trick appeared awkward and out of balance.

But, tall or short, none had ever come up to Leitzel's unparalleled style or standard.

CHAPTER 23

PROGRESS, TRENDS, AND CUSTOMS TYPICAL OF CIRCUS FOLKS

Riding in single file, the tandem section occupied a place of honor near the head of the long parade. Classified now as a horsewoman, I was given a team of the beautiful cream-line used in that section exclusively.

The costumes were those depicting polo players, somewhat exaggerated in color, perhaps, but still retaining the feature characteristics: the helmet-shaped hat and gay-colored striped shirt that went with the riding habit, which was ultra-smart. The long-staffed mallet wasn't always carried on my shoulder. That little rascal Whitie in the lead led me a dog's life all through the parade. At times he almost pulled me over my mount's head. The long lines made it difficult to control that frisky, high-spirited liberty horse when he was behaving like a spoiled child. By reaching forward with the seven-foot-long handle, I could just about touch his rump, reminding him I was still with it. He just about wore me out.

The marshal insisted on turning a square corner, but Whitie had other ideas. Sometimes, on seeing the big bandwagon in front of him make a turn, he acted as if he were now in the lead of a parade all his own and decided to keep on going straight ahead. By pulling vigorously on the line corresponding to the turn, I managed to bring him to attention, whereupon he would

Tiny Kline standing atop two horses, Barnum & Bailey Circus, 1918.
Image no. WHi-41680, used with permission from the Wisconsin
Historical Society.

spitefully cut diagonally across the intersection—rules be hanged. At other times he'd stop dead-still. When I touched him with the mallet, he would bring both hind legs into action. I had to hold back the horse I was riding, or Whitie would have kicked his head off. Most amused by these pranks would be the children along the street watching what they thought was a free exhibition. Even the grownups believed it was part of the show. It was indeed an odd spectacle to see a beautiful aristocratic-looking horse of fine breeding standing in a spot acting like a clown-mule.

Yet this same Whitie was the high-school horse trained to pose as Pegasus, reared up against the cart that Mrs. Bradna drove in the ring in the Act Beautiful. Possibly he resented having to make parade, but all the ring-stock of the show was used; even the famous dancing horse Dolly Varden was ridden by one of the marshals. Only the privately owned rosinbacks were exempt, getting their beauty treatment during parade time.

With each day passing, I got more exasperated with parade and Whitie; yet there was nothing I could do about the situation. Or could I? Convinced finally that the course of fate is paved by one's own efforts and that change must result from one's own initiative, I decided to experiment.

And so it was that returning to the lot one day, I went directly to the harness maker and had him cut a form of a piece of leather to fit my mouth for all the teeth to bite on. Making these mouthpieces was a regular sideline of the man in the harness shop; he made all those used by the iron-jaw acts on the show.

It was required of the ladies in the flying acts to participate in a number earlier on the program called Little Aerial, which is the equivalent of the aerial ballet of today. As a result, they all learned to hang by their teeth, since the only rigging it required was a rope and pulley; besides, once the extreme agony of the first two weeks' practice was lived through, the next two weeks would see a gradual tapering off of the pain in the eyes, nose, and jaw, and the temples would also cease that hammering sensation. The vertebrae that made that cracking sound in the back of the neck every time the mouth took the weight of the body would be quite silent by the third week. The obnoxious smell of the strap and the flavor of tannic acid would be the only lingering elements.

In four weeks, there could be a brand-new act in anyone's repertoire. What a boon to the First of Mays; or, as was the case with the flying acts, here they had a second act. Some of them worked singly, others in groups of three or more, as did Mrs. Silbon and her girls. Edith Siegrist also did a double iron-jaw with the girl in the act, and so, as the saying goes, "if they can do it, why couldn't I?" With that slogan, I set out for the task. Hanging the strap over a guyline on the side of the big top, or most anyplace where I could suspend my weight, was good enough. Within a short time, I only felt pain in my neck during the night; the hanging was a cinch.

It wasn't by coincidence that soon after, there were at least a dozen aspirants for the iron-jaw specialty; the bug seemed to have bitten a large number of the girls, from the statue rank up. Wherever one looked, they were hanging like cherries, all over the lot. Wives, heretofore satisfied to make parade, spec, wash their husbands' clothes, et cetera, suddenly turned ambitious for a career. For those who dropped out during the first discouraging days, new ones sprung up. I watched the cavalcade with disdain.

There were those who carried through to a successful finish. Charlotte, from the statue group, had a definite interest to follow through; she and a catcher named Shives, working in one of the flying acts, probably had some plans of their own. I had seen them making goo-goo eyes at each other from their horses when they lined up for parade. Table-rocking Harry Ritley's wife was another. I felt a secret admiration for the guts and consistency of Mrs. Clara Ritley. She was a very large woman, towering over all the others; on the parade, she represented Liberty (and was almost as gigantic) atop the America float. Although well proportioned, she must have weighed . . . well, anyway, it doesn't matter on scales. Rather, I calculated in terms of lifting that much weight from the neck down—oh, mamma!

With everyone trying to get into the act, I lost interest and put the mouthpiece away. The lot of them planned on giving Mr. Bradna an audition, having made their own costumes for the occasion. I remember the crowd that mobbed the back door after the matinee that day to see the lineup of new candidates for next season's aerial display. Bradna arrived and looked them over as if seeing them for the first time; scrutinizing and appraising each one from head to foot, no detail escaped the shrewd eyes of that connoisseur of feminine pulchritude. The smile under his pencil-line moustache indicated he was pleased with what he saw—that is, until his gaze lingered on Doris Davies, his smile changing to a smirk as he turned around muttering to himself, "Cheesescriose! She's got her tits under belt!" The trend in fashion decreed the boyish figure; Doris, rather amply endowed, had carried the vogue a bit too far. Hoisted in the air, they all looked like angels.

Having abandoned the air, I looked around on the ground. Every day, when I saw George Belford's boys roll out the mat, I'd stand by. Lester's two brothers were being broken in for acrobats and risley (foot juggling). Mervin was already working in the act; Buddie, the youngest, was just learn-

Edith Siegrist practicing the iron-jaw act, Ringling Bros. and Barnum & Bailey Circus (no date). Frederick Glasier Collection, neg. no. 0275; black-and-white photograph, copy from glass plate negative, museum purchase, Collection of the John and Mable Ringling Museum of Art Archives, Sarasota, Florida.

ing. Hand-balancing was the primary trick. The old man would take them in turn. Each one of the five boys in his act had to go through a routine of hand-balancing as a preliminary to the other work. After Buddie, I'd get in line for a turn; the old man would hold my feet in the air until I felt my own balance with fingers, wrists, shoulders, and head, all poised. Mr. Belford wasn't very patient; Web's and Delbert's crooked ankles bore witness to the kicks and other abuse they had been subjected to ever since they were Buddie's age—about eleven years old. Taking on his apprentices, the old man would adopt them—figuratively speaking—taking them to his home, Sunny Brook Farm, which was somewhere in Indiana. Having no children of his own, the boys were like his family. Though stern, he was a mighty good teacher and grand performer himself.

He was very helpful, teaching me to turn cartwheels in a circle. He even tried bending me back from a handstand until finally he told me, "Yes, you have the makings of a good, stiff contortionist!" He was right; the only place I bent was in my knees—my back was as level as a table. Well, no use following the rainbow. I was too materialistic for dreams. There must be something I could be adapted for; to find it was my problem. Anyway, my name was already in the program, listed in the racing events; this was something not even the Codona boys could boast of, for their identity was lost working in the Siegrist-Silbon troupe.

The season was in the last half when there were rumors in the air about plans for a double wedding. Involved were: a) Mrs. Silbon's niece, Emily, and Jack Heather; and b) Bella, the blond girl in the same troupe with Emily, who was to be joined in matrimony to Leo Picchiani, the ideal masculine figure, who also played the role of Aladdin in the spec.

It had come as a surprise to all. The sudden decision was arrived at—most likely—on a dare in the men's dressing room, where there was never a dull moment. Whatever its source, Emily wasn't getting any younger. A marriage with Jack looked advantageous from every angle, and they had been courting for several seasons. As for Bella . . . well, she wasn't Mrs. Silbon's responsibility outside the act. Besides, marriage might put an end to the idle talk about her being—let us say—undignified from the ladies' viewpoint, and so it was approved. It just had to be.

Earlier in the season, handsome George Smith and Doris had united, and with events always running in cycles of three, it was inevitable.

As the news broke of their plans, nobody expected it to happen the next day—another surprise. And so, while everybody was congratulating the brides and grooms, this event called for a little merriment—for the clown band to serenade the four principals. They struck up and played such tunes as "There'll Be a Hot Time in the Old Town Tonight!" and others with equally suggestive titles, when actually there was no blowout or celebration in prospect. The same routine as always on a one-day stand; the usual packing up and hustling down to the coaches was the only program the newlyweds could look forward to, at least until Sunday.

Come Sunday, everybody who customarily left our car left. Emily, how-ever, who as a rule would be gone for the afternoon and return by evening, remained in the car, obeying orders from her aunt: "It would be most im-proper for a young woman of your background to give cause for undignified remarks about you. You would surely be the butt for the embarrassing jokes that usually accompany newly married people! I want to spare you from that shame. I forbid you to leave the car this Sunday or the next!" I heard her saying this when talking to her niece early in the morning just as the train arrived. She added that in a few weeks when it will have been forgotten, she could sneak away without the inquisitive eyes of the others upon her. "Anyway, you've got all winter to be together!" she concluded, returning to her stateroom.

While I thought that modesty was being carried too far here, in this case, I wasn't too greatly surprised.

ON A MAGIC CARPET
TO A LAND FANTASTIC

The show—alternating the route with the Ringling outfit each year—closed the season at Richmond, Virginia, from which point the group of acts booked for the Santos & Artigas Circus was to leave on a special party ticket arranged for by that management.

The Cuban impresarios had acquired ownership of Eva and Babe. On a recommendation by Mr. Robbins at the time of their purchase, the agent Charles Sasse signed me up immediately to present them; thus, I was assured of a winter's engagement. The Davenport riding act included on the roster, Orrin was left in charge of the party. The trip was delightful—leaving the cold winter blast, already sampled in Richmond, behind us to bask in the tropical sun at Key West before boarding the ship for the ninety-mile cruise, then Havana—a new world! Everything was so different: the massive concrete buildings, all of a yellowish hue, with their iron-barred windows and tile floors; the language, Spanish exclusively, except for one of the desk clerks of La Flor de Cuba, where we all stayed by prearranged plans of the business manager of the circus, who also served as guide. Both he and the hotel clerk spoke perfect English. The hotel was situated on Monte, overlooking Parque Yndio from the top floor, where my room was. What a thrill to find oneself in a strange land—different food and eating habits, and people seem different, too. You gape at them, and they gape at you. They smile, eager to do things for you, to please you.

Rodriguez, who left his wife Elisa in the States, seemed to enjoy the popularity he had suddenly plunged into; he knew the place and the lingo, escorting all the single women and some married ones, too, promenading up and down the Prado; stopping and sitting down at a sidewalk table in front of El Dorado and ordering a round of piña colada, a most refreshing drink. The hotel was swarmed with acts from various circuses in the United States. Santos & Artigas, having scored a hit on their previous year's venture, now engaged enough troupes and material to launch two units: Circo Rojo and Circo Azul. The Pubillones Circus was also in preparation for its annual debut; with the stiff competition put up by the other firm, the management went all-out in corralling as many novelties and features as were available. La Flor de Cuba was crowded to capacity. Watching the people milling in the lobby, I suddenly spied Clara. Was it because the others were all strangers that my heart leaped with joy at the sight of her? There had never been any leaguing or intimacy between us during the two seasons on the same show, occupying the same car; but now, in strange surroundings, I felt a sudden alliance with the person whose face was familiar. Formed as if through sympathy, I became conscious of a friendship that never existed, and there we were, talking and sharing confidences as if we had years of kinship of the past to discuss—and to think that only a week before, when passing the narrow aisle of the virgin's car, we ignored each other's existence. Briefly, this was her account: she, Alfredo, Lalo, and George—another boy in the troupe—left the Siegrist-Silbons and formed their own flying act, complete with rigging and net. They were signed up with Pubillones Circus, after which they were planning to tour South America.

The following week, she and Alfredo were married.[1] The ceremony was officiated right there in the hotel. I've seen their act once, when Circo Azul played date-to-date with Pubillones in Pinar del Rio. I finished my act with the elephants and tore over to the other end of town as if to see someone very near and dear to me. Like a happy family reunion, we all enjoyed visiting together. Alfredo was so attentive. I didn't fail to notice how gently he handled her rope on the iron-jaw act. Their flying act was a knockout. It gave me a contented feeling to see them so happy and this interest so recent. It was definitely the strange environment which has that effect on people.

Having completed the Havana engagement at the Teatro Payret, the Circo Azul was the first unit to go on a tour of the interior, opening in Regla, just across the bay. Checking on the location of my berth in the office car, the director told me that some difficulty had arisen over the distribution of the staterooms; would I go to a hotel for the night until they were straightened out? This is what I learned later: two persons were to share a stateroom all the way through the train—no partiality was shown; they were all feature acts as far as the management was concerned. But to make things more congenial for the acts, they grouped them according to their former association; since man and wife naturally shared a room, the tact applied only to the single persons. The Davenports were from the Barnum show, with Laura as the odd number; they promptly jotted me down in the same room with her. Aiming at harmony, single members were paired off with associates hailing from the same show wherever possible; pains were taken to set up the list. However, when the Davenports arrived, the arrangement had to be changed. Los Pachecos, an acrobatic act that came from Chile, had a single girl who was already layed out with someone from another troupe. They had to see how it could be worked out and juggled around. Yes, it worked out for Laura; she shared the room with the Pacheco girl. I never could arrive at a reasonable conclusion as to what the objection could have been. It was not against my character, I am sure, so it must have been that the statue-whiting was still showing. That next season, the other snobs might find out that she and I slept in the same stateroom, breathing the same air, with her losing something thereby. It certainly didn't elevate their standing in the eyes of the director, especially when he found out that there was no personal grudge—on my part, that is.

It all turned out for the best in the end. Juggling the list around, there was an act, a single, that came from the John Robinson show: Minnie Fisher. No, I didn't know her, but that mattered little. She was the most congenial person I ever met. She looked older than her years but was oh, so young in spirit. That season was all the more pleasant because of Minnie. Having been in Cuba before, she spoke enough of the language to get along in the *bodegas* (cookhouses). We cooked our meals in our stateroom over an alcohol burner, as did the other performers, since—according to the custom of the ruralists—it was improper for a lady to go out to eat in a *cantina*. Within a week, we palled around, forgetting the difference in our ages, tramping over to tobacco plantations and sugar mills, drinking the *guarapo,* the sap after it is pressed out of the cane. There was never any matinee, and Minnie always knew where to go and what to see.

Cuba Bella, as the natives refer to their beloved land, is to this day my conception of the Garden of Eden, with its eternal summer, out in the open country where people live contentedly in a hut with dirt floor, eat beans and rice and *yuca* and *ñame* (starchy roots that taste like potatoes), and where the children go not only barefoot but bare all over till the age of eight. In school they have to dress. This was the life of the average *guajiro* (farmer or peasant), and it seemed a carefree, good life.

Alacranes, or Alfonso XII, was the official name of the town according to lettering on the station sign. The train stopped, then started switching to a sidetrack. Those stops and starts, using no air brakes, were enough to tear the entrails out of one. I grabbed my bucket and walked on ahead to the engine to get hot water for a bath, ignoring the hissing that came from the curious by-standers to attract my attention. They always awaited us in every town, peering in wherever they'd see an open curtain to see the *artistas* and screaming with delight when they recognized a favorite clown: Pepito or Guerrerito. Manolin was the newest of these native products, who did practically everything their high-priced European prototypes could do.[2] But Santos & Artigas spared no expense. They had contracted a team of those *comicos* or *payasos* (as they call them) at fabulous salaries. Their patter must have been as good as their tumbling. In addition to the dialogue, juggling, sleight-of-hand, ventriloquism, and what-have-you, they were also versatile musicians, playing various instruments. With their large repertoire, they could remain for several days in a town, changing their act, drawing the same crowd—truly a one-man show, any of those Spanish *payasos*.

Another feature—a must with any Cuban show, whether it be *variedades* (vaudeville) or *Caballitos,* the common term for circus (a derivative, most likely, from the old-fashioned merry-go-round, the granddaddy of the circus)—was the popular *rumba* (pronounced room-bah) team. No show was complete without them. They were referred to as *negritos;* usually impersonated by white people, the men used blackface makeup, the women, a light mulatto shade of makeup. Their act consisted of dialogue of the spicy variety, song, and dance. They cut each *entrada* (entry) short, making about ten to twelve entries and exits during their turn, which was the finale of a performance. There was always the wrangling between the parents and the children just as the *negritos* were announced. The parents would want to take them home; the kids would want to remain. And it was the old story: the kids always won. They loved it!

The dance is interpretive. Each finger means something. They remain in their respective distance, dancing not with but rather before each other. The rumba is a ritual dance of African origin; its motive: to exhaust the dancer to a state of unconsciousness. There is no movement or grinding of hips involved, though they shake their shoulders vigorously. The dialogue is the only suggestive part of the presentation.

Now, let me see. Just what was it I had to go and buy in that *botica?* It must have been iodine—about the only drugstore item I had need for. A few drops added to the bath water when sponging down kept the mosquitoes from eating me alive. No, I'm not going to drift away from my story.

That's right, it was in Guira where I heard the voice, ere I had time to take notice of the young chap sitting behind the glass showcase with a book before him: "Can I be of any help to you?" he said, in perfect English. Quite startled, I could scarcely believe my ears. One would expect an English-speaking clerk in the Internacional next to the Hotel Plaza in Havana, but not in this dinky, one-street hamlet. And only one side of that street was built up; the other side was the railroad track. He was so boyish looking. I sized him up as possibly being a student, more than likely the only one in town who spoke English and wanted to show off. For wherever the show people went, those *Criolos*—the term native Cubans use referring to themselves—could spot an Americana at a glance. Rising from the high stool as I approached, I was amazed how tall he was when standing. We got into conversation, asking the usual questions to suit the occasion: where he had learned the language? and so on. To my astonishment, he informed me that Dr. Jorge Hernandez y Fonte—the name on the sign above the entrance outside—was his own. Having graduated from the Massachusetts College of Pharmacy, he was the *regente* of the business.

He seemed rather loquacious, which left me in a state of confusion as to whether it was genuine enthusiasm to strike up acquaintance with me, or whether he was just given to braggadocio. However, I tried to understand his side. Not often did he have the opportunity not only to speak the language but to discuss the locale as well, for having been in Boston many times, I knew the points I played in the Howard Theater where he saw all those naughty shows, referring to burlesque.

"Where do you go from here?" he asked quite casually, not realizing that even then he was quoting a cliché of a typical American. Since the show issued no route cards, it was by mere chance that I happened to remember the *mozos* mentioning the next day's stand. He remarked that by coincidence he had to go to Union de Reyes on a matter of some legal business, something about listing the establishment since Guira lacked municipality; while the *botica* belonged to another, legally it was his responsibility, registered under his title.

Not giving the matter another thought until the next day, looking out the window, I spied my newly made acquaintance on the station platform. "Come over here, Minnie; take a gander at my boyfriend!" I said jokingly to my roommate, in a casual way—at the same time deliberating whether I would go out to meet him or not. "No, I shan't, after all. I have no obligation to him and no inclination to start something that might, eventually, lead to some unpleasant adventure." Besides, he said that he had business to look after. Then why didn't he mind that instead of hanging around the show train? With this syllogism, I went about preparing my breakfast, never giving him the benefit of the charitable conclusion that it was already eleven o'clock; that most people in other walks of life have already accomplished half a day's work; that he might have finished his business in the courthouse and was now waiting for a train to return. No, I didn't think of that.

After about an hour, I peered through the curtain again, seeing him walking slowly back and forth almost in front of our coach, probably having inquired which was the elephant lady's car. Well, such patience should not go unrewarded. It must be genuine interest on his part. And with Minnie inciting me to go—"What can you lose? He might show you a good time, spend the day pleasantly! Go! Live a little!"—I got ready, putting on my white linen suit for the occasion.

It wasn't business that brought him to Pedro Betancourt the following day. He was a little bolder now, sending a note by the porter to inform me that he was waiting inside the station. I needed no urging from Minnie this time; my ego flattered by this assiduous attention, I lost no time in dolling up to meet him.

He was a likeable fellow—and so good looking, with refined demeanor and extremely polite manners. He wasn't—as Minnie and I would have him—the son of a wealthy sugar or tobacco plantation owner but came from fine Spanish ancestry, though that didn't justify the soft blue eyes, the honey-colored hair, and fair skin—yet, according to his account, his father was born in Andalucia, Spain. On his maternal side, however, the lineage could be traced to the Huguenots, who fled from their native land, France, in the eighteenth century to escape religious persecution and whose descendents have remained Protestants to this day.

Indeed, with each moment, he just grew on me. We took a walk to the showground, where he saw the elephants at close range. We then went to the dressing room. He was as impressed as a small boy. I opened my trunk and showed him some pictures of Otto, the only thing in this world I have been absorbed in—a beautiful memory. As I check back to that incident now, I am still puzzled at the way he reacted. It didn't discourage him, which was really remarkable considering the act—like throwing cold water on someone. No, he was still patient and sympathetic.

"He must have been wonderful, like you say, to deserve your love!" was all he said as we closed the album.

The last passenger train to Guira scheduled for the day having already gone by, he got aboard the caboose of a freight train back. We waved good-bye. The next day, I received the first of what was to be a series of daily letters thereafter. He came again in Jovellanos, a big town. The show remained three days there. We were together most of the time—playing dominoes in one of those large coffeehouses, drinking café con leche or café solo. I missed him after that parting and looked for his letters with anticipation. I found that our thoughts and perspectives seemed to be attuned in perfect harmony. We were compatible, our views coinciding as cog-wheels do.

During the ensuing weeks, Minnie was to hear a lot about Jorge. I didn't care to tramp around to see the sights any more; I just wanted to stay in and write to, or dream about, him.

The show was scheduled for Santiago. In a letter, Jorge informed me that a classmate of his, Federico Perez, would come to visit and take me around to see the sights—he granted him the privilege, and if it would afford me some pleasure, it would be his as well. This gesture, too, proved his generosity and noble thoughts, in which I was considered first. The friend proved worthy of his confidence. Federico was a jolly good fellow—very correct—and he showed me all the highlights of the town. Driving a car, he was in position to go—not to town—but out of it.

It was nearing March—time to think of the other world, with its hustle-bustle and competition. The Big Show, as always, was opening around about the end of that month. So it had come to an end. This island paradise would soon be just a dream, to recall and relive during the few leisurely moments I would find. The happy days always pass too soon.

The Davenports had already left; with stock, one has to allow for possible loss of time in case of some delay in their transportation. I had also given in my two weeks' notice and was showing Señora Pacheco how to do the tricks with the elephants. She was a hefty woman—twice my size. I could see Eva blinking her small eyes each time she went to mount her. Babe just went about her business unconcerned. She would do as she pleased under anybody's command. Old Julio, their caretaker, was quite efficient; I felt confident they would carry on without a hitch.

From a point somewhere in Camagüey Province, I boarded the train for Havana, which I should rename as Heavena, because that's where I imagined myself to be during the two days spent there before boarding the ship that was to bring me back to earth. Jorge was now to be my powerful incentive to forge ahead—to start climbing, rung by rung, the ladder of achievement. Be it ever so tedious, I must do things to hold his interest.

When the S.S. Morro Castle pulled away from the wharf, most of me—the spiritual part—was left behind on shore with him as a souvenir. I took with me never-to-be-forgotten mental pictures of a land as mysterious as it is beautiful.

Sr. Dr. Jorge Hernandez y Fonte would be the way to address my letters to him. It sounded so exotic and important, too. Fonte was his mother's family name. The proper form to address her would be Sra. Concepcion Fonte Viuda de Hernandez—the wife retains her maiden name in marriage. For legal purposes, both parents' names are used, which establishes the legitimacy of the individual.

I could hardly wait to see the bunch in New York—to tell them I was in . . . no, I had better not tell them. Yet, I was just dying to talk to somebody about him—how wonderful he was, his immaculate clothing, aristocratic carriage. No, I had better not tell them that he keeps his change in a small, silver-mesh bag. They'll misunderstand—how should they know that it is to protect the white linen suit from getting all grimy at the pockets?

I realized suddenly that I was no longer free. There was a constant sweet yet painful ache tugging at my heartstrings as the ship was nearing the mainland—the port of New York.

CHAPTER 25

BACK TO THE MATERIAL WORLD

Mr. Cook was at the dock to meet the ship; the reentry of the Chinese troupe, returning from the Pubillones Circus, could not be effected without his intervention. Often I wondered what sign or symbol he used for a password that seemed to open all doors and let down barriers—he never flashed any badge to establish his identity nor presented other credentials, at least not to my knowledge. Yet he was recognized as an authority of the law, with sufficient power of attorney to act in any strategic situation. A brilliant man, indeed, was he. Moving in line with other passengers, as my turn came for passport examination, there—seated with the immigration officials—I recognized Mr. Cook, almost the same instant as he noticed me. How glad I was to see him—the first person from the show—while stepping on good American soil. It was a grand feeling—one of exhilaration—to be back home in the land of opportunity; to hear English spoken all around me; to, well, just one continuous thrill, difficult to describe in words: one's heart could tell it more eloquently. Such was my reaction after an absence of little over four months, which now seemed like ages.

Back on the show. That season the grand entry was a repetition of the previous, minus the pantomime. Among the new features, one that merits special mention was the aerial act of Dainty Marie, a shapely female clad in one-piece white tights; a veritable Galatea that would have aroused any Pygmalion's romantic interest. She did rings and web. Her sister—on the plump side, wearing black tights—counterweighted the web for her. Yes, Marie also vocalized while posing on the web; it seemed to be a trend.[1]

The ladies in the dressing room regarded this new member with some disdain. She wasn't exactly as orthodox in her comportment as had been the standard set up by them. For one thing, she expressed herself too frankly—using common slang and no discretion—but still, she was a feature, working alone in the arena and rating special announcement, so what could they do about it?

Some of the big shots in the front plainly showed their admiration toward her, and she didn't turn down an occasional invitation for supper with any of them. At one place, she and Mr. Black missed the train—the whole show knew and talked about it the next day, but, of course, she didn't care. Marie was quite modern that way. But what about Mr. Black, the head of the rules and order with the show?

She had her stateroom redecorated and some other alteration done on it to suit her artistic taste, which gave the others something more to talk about. But most brazen of all her indelicate actions of conduct was her addressing Mr. John without the prefix—not another person on the show would take that liberty. To this day I wonder how she got away with it.

Her act was very artistic, well presented, but nothing extraordinary, so to speak. Incidentally, she didn't last out the season, having left the show a few weeks before the official closing. As I recall, there had been some rumpus, and she was made to pay for the rearrangement of the stateroom to its former state and color.[2]

Riding Roman and standing and posing with a pony had become boresome. I knew there must be something else that could be done, something that nobody on the show was doing—but what was it?

The show was still in the Garden when I went to confer with Edith Siegrist. Counting implicitly on her having some suggestion, I was tingling with excitement as she said quite casually, "Why don't you try the 'loop-the-loop'? No one's doing that. Ella Hackett, who got killed a few years ago while practicing it, didn't have the proper safety device—using straps to hold her feet on the bar when turning upside down!"[3] Saying this, she started sketching a diagram of the apparatus, explaining at the same time that it consists of a metal trapeze which revolves over a crane-bar. The original had been brought over some years previous by a Frenchman, who also met with death in a fall when his feet slipped from between the two bars he used. Since then, her husband Charlie had been working on the idea, improving on it by cutting slots in the foot-bar; the performer would wear shoes with small knobs attached at the arch, which when slid inside the slots practically locked the feet onto the bar—the same as used in foot revolves—and one may hang upside down, immune to gravity.

It all sounded like a super enterprise, and within a few days, I started acting upon the plan. Without stopping to question my ability to carry out the undertaking, I consulted with Charlie Siegrist for further details. To build it, he recommended Tom Simmons, the man who made most of the riggings and trick bicycles for the performers. Tom's shop was a dingy basement room on West Thirty-ninth Street. There, he and I got together and figured out what I needed, including a clamp holding the iron-jaw swivel. Already I had a mental picture of the act, which would run about three minutes—of which every second had to be filled with action. Only an audience can appreciate how long three minutes can be if an act is monotonous. I also had a collapsible chair made, one that I could fold and pack in my trunk. I would open the act balancing a chair in my teeth while doing an Oriental dance, the same as I had seen Princess Rajah do years ago when I was with Lew Fields's "Fun in a Barbershop" act in vaudeville, and she was on the same bill.[4] The ideas came to me faster than I could fit them in.

With all the paraphernalia neatly packed in one rigging box, I was all set for the road—to practice during the season and show the act before closing. But not always do things happen as one plans. No sooner did I get the rigging assembled for the first time than Mr. Bradna told me it was definitely out. Mr. John had tabooed the looping trapeze. Others had tried it since the Hackett girl's death, but he just wouldn't permit it on the show.

My enthusiasm thus dampened, I was a disheartened and disconsolate mortal till Mickey Graves renewed my hopes, offering to set it up for me in a gym after the closing of the season: "Don't you fret now, gurrlie!" he said in his good old Irish brogue. "I'll have you going 'round that thing in three days! 'Pon my wurrd!"

It sounded incredible, but coming from Mickey, it cheered me up. He was no performer, but he understood riggings and their operation.

I practiced every day. Unpacking the chair and leaving the hooligan, I could hear the remarks: "There goes the nut!" When I told them that next season I'd hold a spot in the center ring, the women snickered. But from the men's side came ugly noises of blowing air with the tongue between the lips, the well-known raspberry or Bronx Cheer, after which they'd all join in the shrieks of laughter, yelling, "Whoop an' did 'e!"—the meaning of which I never could figure out.

Life was rather unpleasant that season. My strong will to conquer had been the only stimulus that kept me going—and, yes, not forgetting the letters from Cuba which helped to make the situation bearable. They came with unbroken regularity—something soothing to look forward to each day.

All my workout so far had been on the ground till one day when I decided it was time I tried climbing up on a rope. Eventually, I'd have to get accustomed to it. Remembering Leitzel's ascension, I thought that would be the way I should like to reach my trapeze. Since that first trial of getting hold of the rope, I knew that climbing up gracefully is the most difficult task in trapeze work. Hanging on with both hands I tried to turn upside down but just couldn't make it. What was there about it that I didn't seem to grasp? Chinning myself was a cinch, I could pull my weight up several times, yet I couldn't get my feet up over my head to save my life.

What happened next seems like fiction. The girl journalist who had joined us temporarily to gather material for a feature article on the circus saw me struggling with the rope without getting anywhere with it. So did some aerialists, for that matter, who just laughed, enjoying the situation. The noble scribe, however—though not an aerialist—knew a little about its principles. Coming straight toward me, taking the rope, explaining at the same time as demonstrating how it is done, she said, "See here, if you want to whip up, you've got to throw your head back before your feet can go up!" And that was the first time I accomplished what I had been trying for days to do. As I look back now, I recall that only a scant number of people are cooperative when seeing someone new invade the field.

Nearing the end of the season, I had a routine of sword whirling, a chair dance, cartwheels around the stage, and iron-jaw swivel, all set in smooth sequence. Except for the loop, the act was complete.

Then came the flu epidemic. Entire weeks' routes were lost—dates canceled owing to the enormity of the spreading of the disease. Yet, strange as it may seem, of the 1,500 people, not one case broke out on the show. All the while in the towns through the South (where the show was at this time), folks were dying like flies. Evidently, the rigorous and rugged outdoor life had immunized us against contagion. The show would be halted on the outside of the approaching towns. We had to keep on going or be quarantined, since the malady was dangerously transmissible. And so the season came to an abrupt end. Out in the freight yard of the line, where they stopped to feed and water the stock, we heard the men, walking down the length of the train, calling out before each car for us to come and pick out our trunks, which were already unloaded along the tracks. The office wagon was also unloaded, and we got what money was coming to us, including the two weeks' hold-back, which was a life saver in many individuals' cases. More than the usual quota of people rode the show train back east that trip.

AN ACT IS BORN

Mickey Graves made good on his promise. After he stowed away the show's props in winter quarters, he came to New York and rigged up my apparatus in Grupp's Gymnasium, where a lot of acrobats worked out in the mornings, and pugilists took over in the afternoons. He and I, on finishing our workout, would remain to watch Benny Leonard train for the championship.[1] And just as Mickey had said, in three days I was looping the loop. Before returning to Bridgeport, he gave me a few points on how to handle the rigging myself: hanging it, guying it out straight, et cetera. Thereafter, I was on my own.

The next step was to get the proper music and have it arranged for theater orchestras. Costumes were also taken care of, and without a showing, I got Pete Mack, an agent for United Booking, to handle the six-minute Novelty Aerial Presentation. I opened a week's engagement at the Harris Theater in Pittsburgh.

Billy Lamont, a wire act from the Big Show who was at the Davis—the big-time house—doing two a day, came over to catch my first show. Remembering that he was assisting Ella Hackett (his sister-in-law) at the time she met her death, he was probably as nervous as I was during that performance; no wonder the report sent to the book office on my act read, "Fair."

With four shows daily (five on Saturday) before the week expired, I was well broken in, a veteran at it. The route Pete sent me following the Pittsburgh date included a split-week between Ithaca and Syracuse, New York. With only three acts on the bill, I opened in Ithaca like a seasoned trouper, using the full stage. Next came another single, working in one. While striking my rigging in back of the drop, I couldn't help hearing the disorderly way the audience was behaving—practically killing his act. The young comedian cut his song and went into his telephone dialogue, supposedly with his mother at the other end: No, he didn't take the quarter she left on the bureau, and about the aunt in a hospital. "Three of them! Well, well, think of it! Three fingers cut off!" And by then, the din started up again, and he went into his closing number, a song: "Why Do They Call Them Babies, When They Are Grown-up Ladies!" While he was singing this song, the audience, Cornell College students in its majority, struck up a song of its own, drowning out the performer on the stage completely.

It's funny how one will remember the minute details at the outset of one's career! Third and closing was Brown, Hall, and Brown, novelty bicycle act. The "femme" member of the trio started with a whirling dervish using swords—probably the only two whirling sword dancers in the United States, and here we were on the same bill of a three-act program! The audience immediately reacted by calling out, "The other girl already did that!"

It was a dejected young man who spoke to me down in the basement, where the dressing rooms were, telling me how big he goes over in the Bronx. A few years later, this same young man was starring on Broadway with his name up in lights over the marquee: "George Jessel in 'The Jazz Singer.'" Such is show business!

Armistice had been declared, but cantonment shows were still going strong as I joined a unit. Later, I got a break in Proctor's Fifth Avenue Theater, where all the bookers caught my act, and *Variety* gave me a writeup that sold me— not just to the theatrical agents but to John Ringling.

It was early in March. Pete Mack had an offer of a long route lined up for me, but I held off.

After the passing of Alf T., with only Charlie and John Ringling left, according to rumors, the two shows were to combine. There was nothing that could induce me to leave New York or even sign anything that might encumber my liberty for the next couple of weeks. So I waited and stalled the agent.

At last came the call in the *Billboard,* and finally the show took over the building. I reported at the office, where I met Mr. Charlie, stating who

I was and what I had. He didn't seem impressed with my description of the aerial act, but looking over the list, he told me I was bound by option to the show as a Roman rider—that any other arrangement would have to be worked out with his brother, who wasn't there at the moment. I sat around all day, then returned again the next day with my paraphernalia. I got to see Mr. John and showed him some of the press notices, especially the one from the green sheet reviewing my routine, which finished with, "Tiny is a finished performer and goes through her act in a businesslike fashion." I am sure that's what turned the trick, the fact that I had already worked the act without a mishap. He called Mickey and told him to put up my rigging, that he wanted to see the act. I wonder what gave Mickey the idea to hang it over the center ring? And he put it up so high that when the trapeze reached the perpendicular point, upside down, it just cleared the beams above. Just before starting, I looked up and felt sick in the pit of my stomach, all the time telling myself, "This is your big moment, now don't be a chump. What difference does height make, anyway?"

Long ago I learned always to dress the role properly, for the costume will determine the nature and quality of an act. While I realized this was only a rehearsal, I put on the gaudiest colors I had in wardrobe, to dress up the drab setting of the barren place. Mickey acted as my property man, and his gang pulled me up in the air suspended by my teeth. I couldn't see the space below me as I neared the trapeze.

Taking hold of the swivel attached to the bar, I executed a fast spin, but with no background to guide me, I got confused swinging up to the bar and found that I was facing in the wrong direction, with my back to Mr. Ringling. However, I thought, by working fast it would make no difference. I was aware of my knees knocking against each other as I looked down the eighty-two feet below me, and I started pumping that swing furiously, as if my life depended on it. Reaching the peak, I balanced it—upside down— before making four revolutions forward. Then, balancing again, I pumped in reverse, making three revolutions backward. Pulling one foot out of the slot and catching it against the rope which Mickey held ready for me, I broke my momentum. Then, taking hold of a hand loop, I was free to come down as fast as the men let in the rope. When I reached the ground, I bowed to the most distinguished audience I have ever performed for, Mr. John Ringling.

He kept turning the cigar round and round in his mouth, then removing it, turning his face sideways, going through the motions as if spitting in clearing his lips of the particles of tobacco—all the while blinking his eyes violently, the rhythmic tap-tapping of his cane registering his mood of satisfaction.

CHAPTER 27

CIRCUS HISTORY
IS MADE

*MERGING "THE GREATEST SHOW ON EARTH" AND
"THE WORLD'S GREATEST SHOW," THEREAFTER TO
BE KNOWN AS "RINGLING BROS. AND BARNUM
& BAILEY COMBINED SHOWS"*

I went downstairs and inquired about the horses. There was a beautiful team of chestnuts with a white diamond marking their faces, perfectly matched—they were Ringling stock. The new boss of the pad room was also a Ringling man. This was the team he recommended I use, since they were fast and could gain the lead anytime I'd let them go. They looked bigger than the other horses, and even their names—Tom and Collins—sounded so masculine. I took them into the arena. No sooner did they get past the entrance to the hippodrome track than both made a lunge as if taking off on wings—leaping an eight-foot gap without touching the ground. But they were smooth runners and tender at the mouth: just perfect.

Again, the opening spec was just a procession without the pantomime—and no wonder, with all the different floats and other vehicles they had incorporated in the tournament, such as the Cinderella coach, for instance, which the Barnum show didn't have. Yes, and they brought their own Cinderella too: Jenny Rooney, voted as the most beautiful gal on the Ringling show. She and her husband, Ed, did a double trap act in the little aerial number. Of course, we of the Barnum faction still had Edith Siegrist as our choice for the title. She was, again, the beautiful princess in the grand entry which, now intermingled with other subjects, seemed to have lost its characterization and become just a gorgeous, dazzling eye-opener—what mattered the title or libretto?—a long line of everything imaginable, of breathtaking surprises without geographical or historical origin.

There were many changes in the heads of the various departments, having sifted out the choice of each show in the combine. Mr. Mooney had been replaced by Deafy Denman[1] as boss of the bulls, but Mr. Bradna still held first place as equestrian director, while John Agee, from the other show, was his assistant.[2] Rose Wallace, from the wardrobe department, was out; George Hartzel was now the head clown, his wife in charge of the wardrobe. The announcer was a man named Graham, also from Ringling fame. It was a keen competition when those posts were under consideration—no one knew who would be in or out. Even now, with the performers, there was plenty of excitement all over the place. The two Clarkonians, the extraordinary flying team, were to work over the center ring; the Siegrist-Silbons, after years of center feature, were to be shifted to an end ring. The Upside-Down Milletts—father and son—also had competition in Hilary Long, who not only did head-balancing on a trapeze but also slid down on rollers attached to his cap over a steep incline, leaping a gap and then landing on his head some distance away.[3]

I was to see for the first time the much-publicized lady principal rider, the "One and Only" May Wirth, also a Ringling luminary. She lived up to her publicity.[4]

The Hanneford family still worked alone; later, in another number, the Wirth family did their second act. The Davenports—Orrin, now combined with his sister, Lulu, and her troupe—left Laura out, who was doing a boomerang-throwing act with her husband between the latter's clown entries.

Strawberry Red had been released from the service and was back at the old stand—Wild West and Roman—while Butch, who had also been in the armed forces with an officer's rank at the time of discharge, was now balancing a perch for Frankie Silvas. I got along very well with Mickey McDonald as the other Roman rider, who, by the way, was also from the other show. Incidentally, Butch had married Millie before he left for camp, and it wasn't long after this season when the two, having left the show, did a terrific perch act. Millie could mount that pole as well as she did the horse. Under the name of France and LaPell, they were a well-established act.

With feelings running high from front door to back, the greatest controversy between the opposite factions was behind the scenes in the dressing rooms—not the small private rooms allotted to Leitzel or May Wirth and family, but the large rooms, where mixed acts from both shows were laid out.

Not a day passed by without some excitement, arguments over trivialities. We, the Barnum people, felt that the other gang was there by the grace of kindness from us, whereas the Ringling bunch was under the illusion that we were the poor orphans who needed adoption, letting us know it in no uncertain terms. It was confusing. During the first week, the Garden was like an arsenal of explosives, where everyone trod lightly. Then, gradually, each got bolder and stood his ground, maintaining that his side was in power. All the grief of getting into the routine of the show was compounded by the political strife.

The combination of the Greatest Show on Earth with the World's Greatest Show proved to be the acme of anything that has ever been attempted in amusement enterprise, superseding creations of the wildest fancy and imagination, exhausting all superlatives and adjectives in its description—it would still be only half-covered, resplendent, stupendous, from every angle. It was to one's credit to be with it.

Merle Evans was the new bandmaster.[5] Leitzel was down with the grippe and couldn't make the Garden opening; however, plans were being made for her to join the show in Philadelphia.

It was during the dress rehearsal—we were lined up for the little aerial, including the Cromwells, Rooneys, Tybells, the ladies from the flying acts, and others, working single—when Mr. Bradna came to tell me to hold the loop part of my act until after his whistle. Quite unprepared for what followed, I was almost beside myself with exultation when—after all the others had left the arena—I was waiting for the next whistle. But instead, I heard the announcer directing the attention of the ladies and gentlemen to the rigging, high above the center ring: "Miss Tiny Kline, the girl that keeps you guessing!" I knew that was my cue to take it away, and when I got through, I heard the sound, like rain on the roof, as I reached the ground. The audience seemed so far away, I thought they couldn't see me in the ring, so I made a run for the ring-curb and, standing on tiptoe, I took my bow from there.

It was a few days after the show had opened when Mr. Bradna called me to one side to tell me not to stand on the ring-curb to take my bow, that

May Wirth used that styling and to her should go the exclusive, or maybe he said "preference." Thus I found that even with the new people who just came on—those who didn't see me wriggle out of the worm-state of the statues—even in their eyes I was still an interloper, notwithstanding that my salary was now on a par with the better-grade singles, not counting the twenty-five dollars additional pay for Roman riding.

I noticed that every time I walked out of the arena, the entire cast participating in the number would still be standing in the exit, watching till I finished. Not that they admired me so; no, they wondered how come *they* didn't get the break. They were now watching. The ice was now broken; anyone might come along with the same rigging, now that the hoodoo and prejudice were lifted, and I wondered how many would put in their bid for next season. It was ever thus. Just let someone start something. Yes, they found my bare legs shocking the first year I rode Roman. I was ridiculed: "What decent female would appear without tights?" Now my costume was truly shocking: "A bare midriff, for shame!" But I risked all their criticism for the success of the act which was based originally on the Oriental dance, the theme of whirling carried out in various phases. It was a novelty, and the style of the costume was an accessory to the theme. Following an axiom that show business is ballyhoo, then let's give 'em ballyhoo, and make it mean something. One doesn't need to be lewd to be original. I suppose thirty years ago a bare midriff was something to be seen at stag parties, yet there I was, selling it as a novelty for the ladies and children—something geographical and therefore educational. Mr. John recognized its merit after seeing it, when he had the program compiled, listing the act: "An Oriental revolving trapeze novelty, performed at dizzy heights: Miss Tiny Kline."[6]

Mr. Charlie issued the copies of the rearranged program for the road, which were distributed to the various departments to be posted as reference. I noticed a change: I was to appear all alone during the pause while the balloons that shield the statues during their grouping were erected. With those huge, black shower curtains (as they appeared) plus the line of ghostly figures marching down the track, the sight of these would naturally detract from anything else, let alone a solitary trapeze in the air. Consequently, the act fell flat, as if it hadn't been on at all. The show had been in Philadelphia three days when Mr. John arrived and reinstated the number as it had been originally presented in New York, with my act as the climax, which didn't please the brother one whit; he wanted nothing in the air outside of Leitzel.

Certainly I was no competition for her incomparable work; nevertheless, the thrilling sensation, the tantalizing play of balancing the swing upside down with the canvas top touching my feet, took some of the edge off, at least for height—which all goes to prove that an act can be a knockout in one spot of the bill and a flop in another. Mr. John was the better business-man of the two—he wanted to sell the public the show as a whole and not compete against the merit of anyone's act in particular. During all my career—while with the show or after—I have never known or heard that Mr. John ever had picked out a favorite or had shown any partiality to anyone in any other way; his interest was strictly business. He kept aloof of petty flirtations—always the correct and respected gentleman.

Leitzel had a private dressing tent with platform floor and carpet. Mabel Clemings had by now officially accepted the position as her attendant or maid, devoting all her time to this little mistress of the magic power. The salary she got from Leitzel was more than double what the show had been paying her for statues, and it was said that she had a soothing effect on this temperamental little artiste, to whom practically anything she desired was granted.[7] The announcer, Graham, with clear tone and perfect diction, didn't suit her, and Clyde Ingalls had to leave the sideshow for the duration of her act to do the master-of-ceremonies honors for her. Soon after, Clyde's wife, the stately and beautiful Irene, left the show, and there were rumors that a divorce was pending.

If things didn't always go right, at least one department gave me equal prestige with others of my present standing. Ollie Webb, the Ringling cook-house boss, took over and, as I found by comparison, put on a much better fare than the Barnum man had. His tables were smaller, accommodating twelve persons each, and he grouped the performers according to their work, more or less. Singles or doubles with similar acts he would seat at the same table. That's how I was at the number 2 table seated opposite Leitzel. At the same table were also Bird Millman, Muzzie, Bird's recently acquired husband, Tom-mie Thomas, Hilary Long, the Rooneys, the Cromwells, and the Hartzels.

Since Leitzel seldom came out to the lot till around noon, dinner was about the only meal she ate in the cookhouse; seated opposite, we soon got to chatting a bit. She was very pleasant, though at times quite moody. She didn't have to ask me the second time to come over to her tent; since Mabel was a good friend of mine, I was a frequent visitor. She always had ice and refreshments and could be a very gracious little hostess—except when news reporters or publicity men came. Then she wanted the show all to herself, and I had better scram before she would have to treat me rudely.

I soon noticed that she would wait for Clyde immediately after her act, with her hair all fuzzed out while she was still short of breath, to hear him adulate her, spoil her, tell her how marvelous she was—she never tired of his compliments. He sent her flowers every day and showered her with expensive gifts. She was especially fond of jewelry. Being the highest-paid single of her epoch, she had acquired enough precious stones to cover her from head to foot. Clyde had a diamond—a huge stone—which intrigued her, so he had it remounted in a ring to fit her finger. She loved to boast of all the attention that six-foot-tall giant bestowed upon her. She got anything she wanted.

Now that I owned an act, I could have argued my way out of parade by insisting I had to look after its setting up, but I felt I'd be taking advantage of Mr. John, who had done so much for me. Besides, I knew no one would understand Whitie like I did. Some other rider might abuse him. To me, he was just a spoiled little scalawag, and I loved him even when he'd stop to show off by kicking his hind legs up several times in rapid succession. I also realized that having gotten this far, I had to keep that precious place and must produce something to add to the act, something that would not be easy for others to copy—not because Leitzel was doing rings and the year before, Dainty Marie; I simply found rings more interesting than the bar and ordered a set from the blacksmith on the show. I rigged them up between shows using long, fine wire, so they looked almost invisible. Even as I practiced, I visualized the possibility for an act I could copyright. Tom Hart, my old standby from the early days, taught me one good trick; then—out of a clear sky, and who would ever believe it?—came none other than Leitzel herself and taught me another trick which was worth a dozen combined. It was not any that she was doing but one that she may have done in her earlier career—a very unusual trick, to be sure. I use it to this day as one of my features. Thus the summer got under way.

When Buck Baker fired Gracie White, he didn't realize how it would all turn out to her advantage, for Poodles, quite serious in his interest in her, immediately intervened to ensure that she remain on the show, and he taught her riding. Theirs was the first marriage of 1919. The Hannefords left the show in the middle of that season from Chicago to fill an eastern engagement.

One day, while practicing my routine, Herbert, the tall blonde flyer with the Siegrist-Silbon troupe, stopped to watch. Suddenly, as if exasperated, he came over and told me where I break my swing-tempo. He was so earnest—I admired his aggressive manner, the way he bawled me out when I didn't do the tricks his way. "Gosh!" I thought to myself. "Where has he been all my life?" There I had been almost four seasons, and this is the first time I discovered him.

After that, I watched him during every show, making it my business to run into him on the lot—accidentally, of course. He didn't make parade, as he had to see about the setting up of the big flying act, so I got ready a few minutes ahead of time and ran in to the big top, pretending to be looking over my rigging—a likely story, as if any rigging Mickey was handling needed looking over.

As a matter of fact, I fell head over heels for that bossy fellow, who could do a double-pirouette from bar to catcher that would make a ballet dancer sit up and take notice. Pretty soon, the folks began to knock him, referring to him as cockeyed, saying he was blind on one eye—but that didn't matter, and neither did the fact that because of overdeveloped muscles, he appeared round-shouldered. His associate flyer, Enrique Diaz, with whom he traveled around constantly, told me one day that Herbert had serious plans to teach me flying. And who knows—he might even . . . well, that was too premature at this time.

I found out he played a guitar and sang fairly well. At night he'd pass by the virgin's car, on the side he knew that my berth was, and whistle, "I'm Forever Blowing Bubbles." That was a cue. I'd open the curtain, and from the window of the car, we'd ogle each other. One day, he told me that I ought to have someone to handle the act for me in the winter; I just couldn't figure out what he meant. "Handle the act for me in the winter"—was he proposing or just looking for a meal ticket? It is a fact that owing to the enormous height and space required, flying acts can't work in theaters. I noticed that on Sundays he was nowhere to be found. Why didn't he ever ask me to go to a movie, as other boys and girls would do?

Then, one Sunday night, I caught up with him. It was in a theater, across the aisle from where I sat. There was my friend Herbert with a married woman and her husband—courting the wife, all the while pretending friendship. It was discouraging—I'd have to make him jealous to bring him to his senses.

The show was somewhere in Texas when Mickey came to the hooligan to tell me that when guying out the rigging, the end bolt holding the shackle broke off, and that he had already put up my rings to work on for that afternoon and night. The rigging could be fixed, but not before the next day. So I worked on the rings that afternoon, finishing together with the other acts in the same number. Mickey pulled my rings off to one side, while Bob, Leitzel's propertyman, set up her equipment. Leaving the big top, I went to inspect the damaged crane-bar. Then turning, I saw Leitzel as she stood at the back door waiting for her turn, with Mabel fussing with a tiny end of a loose thread on her little skirt, trying to break it off. Suddenly, Leitzel spied the set of rings dangling on the side; she promptly sent Mabel inside to summon Mr. Bradna. If she saw me standing there, she ignored my presence. Pointing her finger in the direction of the rings and gasping with fury, she demanded of Mr. Bradna, "What's that?!" When he explained what had happened—that it was only a temporary setup for me so I wouldn't lose the day's work—she almost screamed with hysteria: "Have that stuff taken down immediately, now before my act, or I don't go on!"

I suppose she was incensed over the fact that her rigging-man couldn't touch anything beyond her own equipment, though at the moment she was furious enough to have torn it to bits with her bare hands had she gained access to it. Mr. Bradna told Mickey to drop the rings; at the same time, he told that *fine lady* that she was behaving like a child and that a real trouper would consider the circumstances. It is difficult to fathom such behavior.[8] She would come and teach me a trick on the rings, yet when I was in a tight spot, she'd see me out first before she'd have my rings there. What little I did on them wasn't noticed. I'm sure none remembered it. My rings were hung in the center ring because my falls were on those poles, which couldn't be shifted on a minute's notice. I kept dwelling on the incident until it had taken on a momentous aspect. After this sample of getting pushed around, how could I ever hope to get a break with what I had been dreaming and planning—the long swinging rings on invisible wires, flying over the audience like a huge bat?

I began to see now why she told me that time long ago in her dressing tent, "You have a square neck—you are cut out for iron-jaw work, specialize on that!" Did she mean to help me? No, she wanted to discourage my ambition to work on rings. "My mother has a square neck," she had continued, "and she is Europe's greatest iron-jaw artiste!"

She admitted that her own neck was square, but having developed this phenomenal arm strength, she got greater results from that pursuit. And even *hers* were only human arms of flesh and bone that could take only so much punishment. Her right wrist was everlastingly bruised and chronically abscessed from the pressure of the loop holding her while she did those marvelous throwovers.

Remembering all this, I no longer held any grudge against her, but rather a feeling of deep reverence possessed me. She became *divine* in my estimation of her. Adjusting that band over a bruised, black-and-blue wrist and sacrificing so much, enduring the torture of live tissue being torn from her, she must have been a saint.[9]

I didn't practice that day or the next. My mind finally made up, I sat down by my trunk and wrote a letter—an ultimatum to Jorge—that there was someone on the show interested in me, in marriage; that I owed this to him—the preference—if he wanted to think it over, to let me know his decision in the matter.

In the meantime, I spoke to Herbert, acquainting him with the fact that I was pledged by promise to someone, and since a showdown was inevitable, what would be his suggestion on handling the situation? I said I would abide by whatever his opinion might be.

I was throwing all my irons in the fire. It was immaterial which would heat up first. The reason for it was my indecision as to which course to follow. The last time Mr. John had been on the show, he had caught my routine. Charlie Kennelley, in the office wagon, had told me of the new contract he was drawing up for me next season.

"Evidently the boss was impressed," he said in his genial way, "because your salary is to take a big jump!"

When he told me that, I knew big things were expected of me. Whatever fate deals, I shall have to play accordingly. My trip to Cuba was a certainty. Charles Sasse had sent me the contract already signed, not with elephants, but for the aerial act. It just seemed too fantastic; yet, now that I was nearing my goal, it somehow didn't fully gratify my ambitions. Or was I losing my ambitions?

A cable reached me from Cuba: "Sailing on next ship. Defer decision till my arrival. Love, Jorge."

Everything was piling up. Would I be able to handle the situation wisely? Now that I had one's reply, I would rather have had the other's decision. Or was it a draw between them?

CHAPTER
28

PRIDE VERSUS
VIRTUE

The show was in Greenville, Texas—a dinky little town—when Jorge arrived. We gave only one performance, as the train was leaving early to make a long jump. I scarcely had time for a decent visit with him when he boarded a passenger train for the next town, and thus he followed the show for a week.

At least he made a good impression on the folks; everybody thought he was much too handsome, too fine a chap to be considering anything like marriage with me; already they were making wagers that I'd never land him. What more proof of his serious intention could he possibly give than that already given when risking his life in making the trip via Florida during that disastrous hurricane?

But it was Herbert who put the fly in the ointment. True, he had once told me he'd not give me up, but I just took it lightly, as idle talk, almost as a flattery. In a joking way I asked what he proposed to do about it—never dreaming he'd resort to treachery. He had prevailed upon his boon companion, Enrique Diaz, to call Jorge to one side and do the damage, saying in his native tongue: "Hear me, my friend. This girl is making a fool of you—everyone here knows she's been running around with this Herbert, and they plan to work together. We Latins will not tolerate a woman of light morals.

We are too zealous of our honor to sacrifice it in a moment we shall too soon repent. Show people are for show people; they are no good for others! I am telling you this because we Latins have sentiment for the other. Think it over, *amigo!*"

These were venomous words that poisoned a noble mind. Jorge left and didn't come back for several days. In the interim, everybody was giving me the merry, "Ha-ha, I told you so!"

A few days later, our section pulled slowly in along the depot of a small town where we were to show the next day—Monday. I was leisurely reclining in my berth; there was nothing noteworthy to distinguish this from any other Sunday morning. The same ordinary routine: the girls that customarily left the car for outside diversions were busily primping, decking themselves out in their Sunday best, notwithstanding the gloomy sky with the heavy, gray clouds hanging overhead threatening to ruin all that finery. Rain or shine, they couldn't break a habitual course (or maybe a date), and they wouldn't. I was glad for a day I might stay in, especially in weather as wet as mid-October can be throughout the deep South. The show went ploughing through muddy lots every day; the canvas never had a chance to dry. It just rains and rains in that territory, with never a sunny day at this time of year.

Suddenly, I was roused by the vibrant outcry of one of the girls which was pitched above the other voices in the washroom as she exclaimed, "Dear me, there's Tiny's boyfriend!" and in the same breath, with increasing vigor, "Tiny! Tiny! Come quick, look who's out there on the station platform!"

Although the tone lacked nothing of genuine excitement, my first impulse was to ignore the matter. I had grown accustomed to their raillery and wasn't going to bite into this one. Still, my curiosity got the better of me, and I looked through my own window. Sure enough, at a single glance I saw it was none other than Jorge himself.

I sprang to my feet. In my delight I lost my head, and forgetting everything except that my loved one was out there, I slipped on a coat over my lounging pajamas and fairly flew out to the car steps. From there I beckoned to him. He started over, but his steps were slow and faltering as if with embarrassment. We exchanged greetings, and during the brief conversation that followed I noticed the lack of his usual glow—the warmth of his enthusiasm was not there somehow. What was behind this reserve? I bade him wait inside the station for me, where I joined him after I got dressed.

I know of nothing so desolate as a small burg on Sunday; this was such a place, topped off with chill and dampness to add further to its somberness.

In search of a spot where we might be together, we headed for the town, where the one hotel offered the only haven for distraction—the focal point of interest—for those who habitually sought to break the monotony of the jibber-jabber in the coaches. Having no alternative, Jorge and I followed the beaten path of the others. Inside, the spacious lobby with its modernistic array reflected an air of dignity and comfort one didn't expect to find in a drab, one-horse town. The charm in decoration extended to the dining room as well, which, for immensity, could well have served for banquet or ballroom; the oak-paneled walls and white-linen-covered tables lent it a cozy atmosphere.

On entering the hotel, I noticed it was filled to near-capacity exclusively with the show's people. The entire personnel—from executives to ticket sellers and ushers—was assembled there as at a convention. They were scattered in groups about the lobby, and as Jorge and I passed, some of them leered at us. But if the lobby seemed crowded, the dining room was packed; we managed to find two vacant places and ordered breakfast. Looking about me, every face a familiar one, for a moment I imagined being in the cookhouse, were it not for the luxurious setting and Jorge's presence.

Presently we returned to the lobby and settled down on two overstuffed chairs in a secluded corner, from which we viewed the activities of the people milling about. Some of the folks just coming in were wearing rubber boots, indicating that they'd been out to the grounds and the lot was a mudhole. We were stuck for the day with no place to go. Seated there with a large rubber plant directly before us, we were partially screened off from the mob that invaded the place, which, buzzing with chitchat, resembled a beehive.

I observed that Jorge was extremely nervous, lighting one cigarette after another on which he would draw once or twice, then press it into the dirt at the base of the plant. Here we were, seated side by side, straining under a tension that seemed relentless. Neither of us spoke, just gazing into space as if each waiting for the other to lead—a most awkward pause, to be sure.

I knew it was his turn to say what there was to be said. The fact that he had returned at all was evidence of his decision. Why was he hesitating? Surely he knew what the deal was, and he didn't have to deliver it in a flowery speech. Whatever it was, he must have been turning it over in his mind, laboring under difficulty. Tempted to use pliers to extract the words, I finally asked him where he had been the past week and said that I was under the impression he had possibly returned to Cuba.

There was a strange expression on his face which alarmed me when he asked: "Would that have pleased you?" I was at a loss to know how to meet this odd situation.

I almost said, "Quit your teasing and get to the point!" It was aggravating, to say the least. Instead I meekly replied: "No. As a matter of fact, I have been quite upset over your strange behavior. It is not justified. You should understand, now that you have seen for yourself, that the social liberties are limited with a show such as this. If I haven't been more demonstrative of my feelings toward you, it is due to these silly restrictions. Take me away from this show, and you will find the real me once again!"

Again he looked at me with that enigmatical countenance. I loved him in this mood. A tenderness came over me; I felt like throwing myself in his arms if I had dared. But his attitude was forbidding. I knew there was something eating him, and I must convince him that his suspicion is unfounded. True, I had written to him that there was someone interested in me, but I didn't say I was interested in him.

As if he were reading my thoughts, he asked: "And just how far has your affair progressed before I appeared on the scene?"

This came as a jolt I wasn't prepared for, leaving me stunned for the moment. A ticklish situation indeed, for no matter which way I tried try to exonerate myself, I would only go deeper into the labyrinth. I chose to flatter his ego rather than boast of my conquest.

"There has been no 'affair,' not even an interest—it was all just a scheme to test your own interest in me. My letters should serve as a fairly good guide to how my feelings have grown toward you with each day of the year and a half since we parted. You have never revealed what plans—if any—you have outlined for the future." He lit a fresh cigarette and listened in silence as I continued now that I had regained my confidence.

"This business is glamorous, fascinating, even glorious at times," I propounded, "but it affords little stability. I long for a quiet home life, which I know is not to be mine as long as I stay with the show."

At this, his mood seemed to soften, and puffing on his cigarette, he gazed upward as if reading a message in the zigzag lines of the smoke. My attention was glued on his next words, but some moments elapsed before he spoke: "In the event had my decision been negative, have you made any preparation for an alternative?"

This question seemed too deep for me to grasp immediately; it smacked of the technicality of a cross-examination, and that's exactly what it was, though I was unaware of being on the stand testifying at my own trial. I did know harshness would defeat my cause. This was a time to be humble and submissive, to go along with him on his own terms. After all, this was a serious step, one that required vital consideration. I was certain that once we reached an accord, I should have no regrets. I was sure Herbert could never mean anything to me after today—even at this trial, with the coolness and dignity Jorge maintained, I simply worshipped him. There was nothing on the show I wanted as much as I wanted him.

Gradually, we were arriving at the desired point. His trip could have no other object. Therefore, it was no surprise when we finally touched the subject of setting the date. He would go to New York and wait for me there, but I insisted on getting it over with right there and then. Why wait? He thought awhile, then asked if I had any special motive for wanting to marry on the show—he considered marriage far too sacred to drag it through the profanity of a public exhibition. That part we settled also when I told him there was no publicity or exhibition connected with a marriage—it would be performed by a clergyman or official, with the same reverence as the ceremony of any respectable resident of the community and not on the showgrounds.

I knew Mr. Cook was around somewhere, for I had seen him in the dining room earlier. Excusing myself with the pretext of going to the powder room, I really made a hurried survey of the lobby to locate him.

"Well, well! What is the occasion, seeing you in a hotel?" was his greeting to me. I explained the situation, stressing the point that my fiancé was rather shy—would he sort of intercede, or arrange things in a way as though taken for granted, so it seemed that I had taken no part?

Leaving him, I returned to Jorge, who seemed to be in such deep meditation that he didn't notice me till I sat down. If he were as happy as I, he certainly didn't show it. We talked on matters of no relation to the momentous event that was to take place on the next day, Monday morning. He made reference to the towns, to the people, as he found conditions in general while making the jumps from one place to another.

Mr. Cook obliged; he came over where we were seated. His approach was tactful, casual, like that of an old friend. After I introduced them, he said, quite informally, "Well, I suppose you two want to get married and need a sponsor?"

I felt a flush of shame come over me, for the words seemed to have a quality of brazenness wielding an imaginary shotgun, but my faith in this super-diplomat was so firm that I knew there were no other words that would serve better yet retain the same meaning. I waited impatiently through what seemed a long, consuming suspense, for although the question was indirectly aimed at both, it was up to Jorge to give the reply, to make the final decision by which hung the fate of two. He was taking his time. At long last (or so it seemed to me), he spoke, but the words that fell on my ears stunned me. Did I hear him accurately? "No, thank you. We'll just leave well enough alone."

I couldn't believe it—that sentence, the content of which proclaimed the doom to my contemplated dreams, uttered in such calm, matter-of-fact tone. Could it have issued from the lips of the gentle Jorge? No, it couldn't have. And as I looked at him in my astonishment to see if he might be joshing, even though he never clowned, I was shocked to find his face quite sober, and I became completely bewildered; ruled by emotions and blinded to reason, I could neither think straight nor grasp the enormity of the situation for the moment.

What happened? Was this stage fright? What could have prompted him to change his mind after we had gone over every detail? My face burned with mortification. It took me some time to regain my self-possession. One thing was clear: he deliberately made me an object of ridicule. And what about Mr. Cook? After I had requested him to do us the favor, about which he was so complaisant—how will I ever live this down? What was there left whereby I could save face and pride? During this mental storm, I didn't notice when Mr. Cook had quietly slipped away, till gazing forward I caught a glimpse of him as he disappeared in the crowd.

For the moment I was at a loss as to what to say or do. Nothing seemed to make sense. Should I just disappear? But where could I go? Since he was lost to me beyond all hope now, anyway, let me salvage from the wreckage what I may—redeem myself in the eyes of others—yes, even at the price of humility! I sat there with my brain in turmoil; I thought of any number of plans, each one more ingenious than the last, but none that promised to cover the awkward situation. Several times I opened my mouth, but words refused to come. In a trance I was waiting for something to happen, wishing for some merciful act of divine Providence to render me invisible. At last I found the courage. Pushing my chair closer to his, I spoke. "Listen, I am placing myself at your mercy. Now please hear me out—what I have to say." His gaze was away from me as he fumbled for a cigarette. At least he remained seated as I said, "I wouldn't marry you now anymore than you would me, believe me, but—I implore you—save me from this unfortunate . . . this humiliating predicament I am in. The mortification of having to face these people as a jilted bride is far greater than my frustration at being left 'waiting at the church.'"

"But what do you want me to do about it?" he interrupted impatiently, yet with a coolness that rebuffed me before I concluded my plea. Folding his arms, his mien remained cold and indifferent. How could I possibly expect any concession from him, now that we seemed worlds apart? Although prepared to pay whatever the price to gain my point—even before he assumed this *difficult* attitude, knowing him as I did (his character, his views on such matters)—I somehow surmised that anything not on the up-and-up would be no inducement to strike a bargain with me; nevertheless, he had to be made to realize my drastic plight, and yet, who can tell?

Finishing the loop on my descent, Merle Evans's band struck up "Here Comes the Bride."

What a farce! The tears streamed down my cheeks; no one, excepting Mr. Cook, knew there was no bride—that the young man watching the show from a seat in the reserved section, a place of honor given him by Mr. Bradna, was nothing more than just another spectator to me now. I took a bow, acknowledging the cheers and applause of the attendance. The back end was jammed with our people. After all, to them I was the heroine of the day. My tears were quite in order too. It is proper for brides to weep.

After the races, they all gathered around me. The rice shower and clown-band frolic, which I evaded earlier by arriving on the lot just at the sound of the first bugle call, caught up with me now. Though there was no point in it—the groom having left the lot immediately after the performance, they serenaded me in the ludicrous fashion that had been their custom on such occasions, playing old familiar tunes such as "When I'll Get You Alone Tonight!" and "There'll Be a Hot Time in the Old Town Tonight!" Even as I offered apologies for Jorge's absence, they seemed to understand. He, being a nonprofessional, wouldn't relish these frivolities so typical of show folks' way of celebrating the nuptials of a comrade. Besides, they seemed to get a kick out of playing the tunes, anyway.[1]

At the last minute, I decided to forego the night show and the confusion, take the rigging down, pack up, and get away as soon as possible; Mickey ordered Joe Allen (one of his assistants) to lower it. I told him to leave the falls on the poles; what did I want with four hundred feet of ⅞-inch Manila rope? The blocks were left also.

While dismantling and packing away the bars, I spied Herbert approaching but pretended not to see him. He—who had turned my world upside down—now had the audacity to walk up close to me, and without the slightest trace of emotion or sentiment in his voice, to say, "Well, you could at least leave me your rigging. I don't suppose you'll have any use for it anyhow."

With all the contempt that welled up inside of me toward him in that moment, I was afraid to open my mouth lest I say something to betray my wounds. Even at this point I was grateful to Providence for having delivered me from possibly a worse fate with him; I smiled and said nothing. The friendly advice delivered by his Spanish-speaking confederate, Diaz, which

Jorge mulled over in his mind (and told me about later), had destroyed me. And now he wanted my rigging!

Going out to the wagon to collect my money, I was to run into more aggravation. For all the good things the Ringling outfit contributed to the combine with the Barnum show, there were equally vicious ones. Fred Worril, the general manager, was one of these. Even his appearance was something to grate on the nerves. His overbearing manner and heavy walrus moustache typified the villain behind them. This was the person I had to deal with, as if I hadn't already been through enough purgatory. This character, looking for all the world to be a cheap carnival grifter, refused to sign my release from the show, holding my salary for the current week as well as the two weeks' hold-back. I had counted on that money for my expenses. The only ready cash was a few dollars—not even sufficient at this time for the tips I should distribute among those who had so faithfully cooperated with me during the season. The only satisfaction I got out of telling him off was that the others heard me do it. I told him he was a detriment to the honorable and upright names of the Ringling Bros. and Barnum & Bailey, none of whom ever resorted to petty tactics such as holding their employees' wages. The season was too near the closing to hold me to the contract, especially since I wasn't going to joint out with a competitive firm. In fact, according to my story, I was not to work at my profession at all.

Neither of the Ringlings was on the show at the time, and so there was no one to whom I could turn.

Needless to say, the money was forwarded to me as soon as it was known that I had been signed up with Santos & Artigas Circus. It was in care of that firm that the letter was addressed. Upon receiving it, seeing the gay-colored heading—so familiar to me—I was gratified in full measure for all the grist I had gone through. The check enclosure was of small importance compared to the personal message, which sent congratulations and wished me happiness and success. Another paragraph reminded me of the contract for next season and asked if I would be interested in signing it (a function usually taken care of during the closing week). The letter was signed: John Ringling.

Because of so many unhappy memories still fresh in my mind, I deferred the matter of signing, even though Mr. John cabled me just before the Garden opening of the 1920 season, asking me to come only for the New York engagement and allowing me to name my own terms. I had lost my ambition. Now that I could have the opportunity to really go places—the only chance in a lifetime—I reckoned the odds. The mental anguish and strife seemed to outweigh the rewards of success.

I had been in Havana exactly a month when the circus season—always a gala event—opened. Santos & Artigas at the Teatro Payret; Pubillones just across the Plaza de Marti at the Teatro Nacional.

Despite my bitterness toward those whom I directly or indirectly associated with the drama that had such an unhappy ending, I was glad to see the folks that came from the Big Show. Among the first acts to arrive were the Pallenbergs, who brought me up to date with news and events to the time of the windup: May Wirth had married Frank, the manager of the act;[2] Leitzel and Clyde, following their example, also set sail on the sea of matrimony. Leitzel was booked with the Pubillones Circus and would arrive on the following day—just two days before the debut of the show. Significant, though having no apparent bearing at the time, was the coincided appearance of the Codonas—Alfredo, Lalo, and Clara—on the same program. Their venture during the two years' tour had been most successful, and they had carved out an enviable niche for themselves as the foremost flying act in the business. We had many things to hash over—events that had occurred since our last visit.

The Payret stage had a slanting angle downward; during rehearsal, while spinning with the chair in my teeth, I kept gaining space forward till finally, losing my equilibrium, I went over the footlights and landed in the orchestra pit. The chair was in better condition than I when a stagehand picked us up. As a result of the injury I sustained, I was out of the show during the entire Havana engagement—leaving me with nothing to do but to visit back and forth between the two shows.

MISERY— LIKE DEATH— KNOWS NO CLASS DISTINCTION

Though married but a few short weeks, Leitzel and Clyde seemed already headed toward dissolution. Having planned this trip as their honeymoon, and leaving Bob and Mabel behind, Clyde was to take care of the rigging and hold the web for her. What could be more romantic? Or so it seemed. In actual practice, however, it became a chore very distasteful to the dignified sideshow manager of the Circus Colossal. Although Clyde had no experience as propertyman, Leitzel expected of him the same service she did of Bob, such as covering the rings with fresh tape daily—a task at which he was as clumsy as others involved. Lacking patience and forgetting her poise at such times, Leitzel would fly into a rage and rant at him before the others standing by. It was a calamity. They clashed and quarreled constantly.

However, regardless of any rancor between them, her act didn't suffer as a consequence. The audience made a big fuss over her. To acknowledge the lusty enthusiasm of foot-stamping and whistling, she would step over the footlights to the top of the piano in the pit. This heightened the people's acclamation still more, and they wildly cried "Bravo!" and "Muñequita!" for she truly looked like a doll standing atop the Steinway.

Oddly, in all the days I went backstage, not once did I get to see the show through. As Leitzel made her exit, she would grasp me by the arm and drag me into her dressing room to pour out all her grief to me. In their room at the Hotel Plaza, where I was a frequent visitor, each had a different side to the story in relating their marital difficulties. My role was that of a diplomat: to remain neutral. Their bathroom was cluttered with wet tights and pumps, which Leitzel would bring back with her after the show and put to soak, but not used to washing them, she expected Clyde to do it. Showing me a black and blue wrist, swollen with poisonous fluid oozing out of it, she indicated that it was impossible for her to do washing. A pile of silk shirts—custom-made and costing thirty-five dollars each—which Clyde didn't entrust to laundry men lay heaped on a chair in a rough-dry state. Pointing to them, he lamented, "You'd think she would at least iron them for me after I washed them myself!"

One day she told me he threatened to leave her. She was terrified at the thought of his possible desertion or annulment of their marriage, for her citizenship was derived from her marriage. The prospects of being left stranded hung over her head like the sword of Damocles.

What had seemed an ideal mating ended soon in disaster. These two wanted to be shipwrecked on a deserted island together in order to prove their love for each other. Neither of them was accustomed to hardships. In their attempt to rough it they actually dealt the death blow to romance.[1]

Weaning was the order before me—to break away from the nurturing breast of the Big Show, a painful ordeal, to be sure.

By the time the last acts, returning to American circuses, left Santos & Artigas, we were already on the second-rate route, playing return dates around Havana Province. The show was comprised for the most part of local talent with only a handful of Americanos—acts with no definite bookings in the States—who hung on despite reduced admission prices and reduced salaries.

When March passed, I felt like a migrating bird with a broken wing; not to return to the Big Show created a conflict within me which required courage to fight. But I knew it was just a seasonal habit; like spring fever, it would pass, just as my romantic interlude had passed. And if I felt miserable and restive, it was only by comparison with other seasons, when at this time I would be making vigorous preparations, getting ready for the Garden opening.

I settled back and became a drifter with no fixed plans. When Santos & Artigas finally closed the season, I joined a small itinerant outfit that played the summer through. I worked at an undetermined salary on a percentage basis. On nights when the business was poor, I owed the company money. Expenses of the show were charged up against the co-ops. Taking things in their natural stride was soothing to my nerves: no hustle-bustle, no competition. I was getting top billing as "La Reina del Aire." Sometimes "La Unica!" (the one and only) was added.

Whatever gave me the impression that there was need for a new fad, one that might turn into a successful career? The idea occurred to me one day while in a fairly populous borough, although throughout the day it seemed like a ghost town, as if all its residents were asleep. Not a soul was to be found on the streets. Then it dawned on me: "The Cuban women need waking up; they are too inert!" With this reformation of the land in mind, I returned to the States to take up physical education—a teacher's course, which took almost a year.

I might have saved myself the effort and money invested not only in the scholarship but also the equipment in getting established. Naively, I was pioneering in a field that is frowned upon by the general public. In Cuba, no decent woman would go outside her house alone—much less to a gym. Strenuous exercising is just not on their curriculum, not even for the sake of health or losing some excess weight.

And so once again I came up with an idea, slightly different this time: to become a dancing instructor. Everybody likes dancing!

FATE FOLLOWS HER COURSE—STRANGE, MYSTERIOUS, TERRIFYING

It was in 1926 when the Codonas again played Havana. Having completed my multiple dance course, I was established in a cozy little studio and catering to ladies and children exclusively. Clara, in the spirit of good fellowship, immediately enrolled in my morning class. She was so much fun. The entire group enjoyed her company.

One day, when I had the trio over for dinner, Alfredo asked me if I'd care to sell my rigging now that I wasn't using it. He wanted the loop for Clara as a second act. He went on to say that Charlie Ringling had signed them up when he caught their act in Spain. The Codonas were a big attraction all over in Europe; elated over this good fortune, they were now looking forward with anticipation to that Garden opening as their crowning glory, coming back to the Big Show with their name on the program and working over the center ring, which they demanded to be specified in the contract at the time of signing—as if by ominous intuition. Once they had the agreement in black and white, Charlie Ringling died within weeks. Their former bosses, the Siegrist-Silbons, would be working over an end ring—a strange turn of fate.

I kidded with them, saying that Madison Square Garden had been moved to Eighth Avenue and Fiftieth Street just so they might continue calling the new building Madison Square Garden. I told them of the improvements in the modern structure, including many private dressing rooms along the corridor—nothing like the firetrap the old one had been.

I recounted to them my trip of the previous spring, when I had been to New York and had seen the show with some friends. Unknown to my friends, we had sat in Mr. John Ringling's private box. I suppose it sounded vain even to the Codonas, yet this was an honor conferred upon me which seem too excessive to hold within me. Incidentally, that was the last time I was to speak with Mr. John.

Seated in his office, with the man who not only owned the world's biggest circus but was co-owner of this building housing it, I was making just a social call. We talked on this and that. He seemed interested in my activities and said that if I created something original, he would give it first consideration. I knew he meant it. Always the thoughtful gentleman, before I left, he asked me if I would like to see the show—and who else but Mr. John would have the quality to add, "Do you have any guests with you?"

His last words that I recall, turning to Charlie Kennelly: "Give Mrs. Kline (to him I was always 'Mrs. Kline') five complimentary tickets with my compliments!"

In the following three years, he acquired ownership of the equipment and title of every major circus on the road. By 1928, every outdoor show, including Hagenbeck-Wallace, Sells-Floto, John Robinson, Al G. Barnes, and others—was controlled from one main office.[1] This central control eliminated competition in routing, kept shows some distance apart, and made possible a monopoly over salaries, a sort of wage control. With all the programs set up in the same office, the acts had Hobson's choice if they wished to troupe with a circus. Amusement parks and fairs offered the only alternative. By now, winter quarters and the central office of the Ringling enterprises were in Sarasota, Florida.

I read the account of the Big Show's 1927 opening with avid interest. The Codonas fell in for their share of publicity, getting some marvelous press-notices. I kept thinking how gratifying it must be to them to be zoomed into stardom overnight. On the other hand, how many there must be who envied them! I wondered where Clara's trunk would be situated in the dressing room. She would be bound to incur the ill-feelings of the others over her specially built wardrobe-trunk. It would require some tact on Mr. Bradna's part to settle a possible controversy among the performers; the use of square trunks had been enforced almost without exception. The reason for it? They stack up better.

While I didn't hear from them directly, occasionally I'd run across an article in a magazine or in the pictorial section of the news showing photographs of the highlights in which the Codonas were always included. One syndicate news feature showed a picture which immediately arrested my attention: a three-column cut in a daily paper always has some significance. It showed Alfredo with Leitzel seated face to face at a small table. The caption read: "The King and Queen of the Air, Having Tea Together behind the Scenes."

Just a clever press agent's dream, of course—a human-interest story on the romantic side. It's got to have punch, or the papers wouldn't print it. It somehow brought to mind the time—not so long before—when the trio looked at a collection of pictures on my studio wall. Referring to one of Leitzel (she was posed with a balloon balanced on her hand), Alfredo remarked: "There is the most graceful performer I ever saw. Her every move a picture!"—a compliment to a colleague and nothing more.

In the nine years he and Clara had been married, his love for her had intensified, if such were possible. He would call her on the phone at my studio during class in the morning to check if all was well with her. They were ideally suited for each other. Now, he and Leitzel were posed together.

My business continued in the red; I was glad now that I held onto the rigging, for soon I was back in show business.

Booking agents are short on memory. An act that's out of circulation is soon forgotten. Not one would give me an opening without a showing, so I was glad to get on the Folly Marcus time, a circuit comprising two-and-a-half split weeks. From Lebanon, Pennsylvania, I stopped off at Philadelphia, working some independent time. The offices of Frank Wolf, Eddie Sherman, and Harry Biben became my daily beat. There was a favorite phrase among the performers when meeting in the outer offices or halls: "Booked up for five consecutive Saturdays!" I crossed that Camden Bridge so many times, I thought all roads led from there. Having played just about everything around, including a place called Manayunk, which Eddy Sherman gave to those performers he had a grudge against, I accepted a week in a burlesque house on skid row, which wasn't as bad as I expected, and only two shows a day.

I had been set in the Girard Theater for Thanksgiving week when the Shrine Circus, composed in its entirety of the Big Show's acts with Mr. Bradna as the equestrian director, opened at the Met. What with getting my rigging set up, orchestra rehearsal, and the usual grief of the first day, followed by four shows, there seemed to be no time left to get over to the Met for a visit. But on Thursday, I managed it after the three o'clock show. I arrived at the Met just after the matinee got under way. I started my round of visiting with the first room I came to: Leitzel's. She seemed in high spirits, beaming with rapture, happiness written all over her face as she talked to me while getting ready for her act. This was their first of a twelve-week tour—all week stands. They would be stopping at first-class hotels and really living. Mabel, too, was glad to see me. It made me conscious of the fact that I didn't look as prosperous myself when she showed me her beautiful fur coat. "A gift from Leitzel!" she boasted, "and it's genuine mink!"

Number two was the Codonas' dressing room. It had the effect of a tonic on me to see them. They were more like my own people. I felt quite at home with them. But, during the five-minute talk with Clara, she bared her heart by revealing the sorrowful news that she had lost Alfredo to Leitzel, who practically had him under a hypnotic spell. "He does everything *she* asks him!" she lamented sadly. It was a painful scene. Clara, usually so jolly, was looking dismal. I noticed that the dressing room was screened off. Alfredo, who ordinarily would be dressing on Clara's side, was now dressing with his brother Lalo. This might have escaped my attention had not Clara mentioned it as an example, saying, "You see how we are laid out here; the same situation exists in the hotel. He shares a room with Lalo, while I occupy one all by myself. We are man and wife in name only because *she* told him that *she* wants him for herself!"

Clara had no tears as she related these intimate details of her domestic relations, which only a few short months ago had seemed unshakable.

I didn't take time to watch any part of the show. Instead, I looked over the list of performers of my acquaintance, saying hello to them and waving a salute to the Bradnas from the wings.

The show was over before I realized. On my way out I met Leitzel again. Wrapped in a luxurious fur cape, she looked like a princess. Only then I noticed she seemed more mature. Her hair had been allowed to grow long. The blonde, braided tresses draped in halo fashion around her head had the appearance of a crown. We walked out together. She stopped before the huge black Packard parked by the stage entrance. The liveried chauffeur seated at the wheel, on catching sight of her, promptly got out and opened the door for her. She stalled, waiting for the others in the party. They were going to a Thanksgiving dinner.

"Come along, join us, and have some fun!" she said to me.

"Thank you, Leitzel, but you see, I'm just a small-timer; while you'll be having your turkey, I'll by doing my frolic."

As I spoke, I saw the Codonas come out—Alfredo, Lalo, and Clara—all dressed for the occasion and in seemingly gay spirits. They got in the car with Leitzel and drove off along Broad Street. I hailed a cab, giving the driver the direction: Sixth and Girard.

The last time I saw Clara, in the spring of 1932, she was at the Policlinic Hospital with a broken pelvis and other injuries of lesser degree which she had sustained while attempting to do the Leap of Death: making a dash from a board rigged up high in the air, as if to aim for a trapeze bar. Missing it, the performer—as seen by the spectator—falls on an angle and is stopped just short of hitting the ground by two wires attached to the board above by one end; the other is fastened to the strap around each ankle. The act was first presented by a French girl, Mlle. Gillette, in 1929 and again in 1930. When La Gillette returned to Europe, Clara wanted to try it. She would have succeeded had not one of the wires snapped, lowering her original trim and bringing her into contact with the ring-curb.

And there was Clara! Always the good sport, her cheerful spirit was evident even as she lay there, part of her body encased in a plaster cast while one leg was being rigged up to a contraption above the bed to stretch it to the length that would match the other. Her face lighted up in a broad grin as I neared the bed.

"Why, Clara, what kind of an act is this you're practicing?" I asked to keep her in the mood.

"Don't be funny; and pass me the nail polish," she said, pointing to the cabinet drawer beyond her reach. The polish she applied not to her finger but to her toenails.

In her room were flowers galore, but the bunch she kept on her bedside table was the one from Alfredo. She said he had been up to visit and had assured her that the hospital bill would be taken care of.

She didn't have to tell me—I could guess—that she was optimistic about the accident. In fact, she looked upon it as a blessing in disguise, feeling that perhaps it would awaken Alfredo's interest in her once again. His sympathy seemed so genuine, so spontaneous, it was convincing. She could almost forget that there had been anything ever to disrupt that bliss which lasted almost ten years. She could forgive and forget the bitter dose she had to swallow as he grew more distant day by day—days which brought them closer together only during their act as they stood side by side on the pedestal, smiling at each other for the public's benefit. She would even have been willing to continue as they were—married in name only. But he was impetuous, impatient like all lovers. He was thriving on the publicity linking him romantically with Leitzel, the Queen of the Air. Why not then live up to it in reality? She seemed responsive enough to his overtures. And so it was that on the following season he divorced Clara and married Leitzel. Clara still continued to wash the tights, keep up the wardrobe, and work in the act during the entire season—still throwing the bar to him with just the proper impulse at the right time as always, though he was now Leitzel's husband.[2]

Then came an offer from the Bertram Mills Winter Circus in London, England.[3] Both acts, Leitzel's and Codona's, were to be on the same bill. And they were not going to take Clara. He'd have to get someone to replace her. It was Leitzel herself who picked out a girl from among a group doing some minor aerial work. He didn't need a flyer—he did the flying himself. She might do one trick, a bird's nest maybe, to justify her presence up there on the pedestal.[4] He needed her principally to throw him the bar. Vera, the sister of Clarence Bruce, the Australian bareback rider, seemed to be a likely prospect for the job. She was just a plain girl with no outstanding features, neither in talent nor looks. She was tried out, and she filled the bill, if not the tights (strictly along the boyish lines).

And so they embarked for Europe. Clara, now left to her own devices, was doing a double-trapeze turn with another girl at the time we met again in Cuba. As I recall, she took the whole messy deal philosophically. Still making excuses for him, she said that Alfredo offered to let her choose whatever she wished of the collection of jewels they had acquired in Spain. But she—sentimental little goose—kept only the original engagement and wedding rings. The other precious items went to augment Leitzel's already prodigious dowry. Returning to the show in the spring, she played the role of a Pollyanna, even starting a flirtation with Bert Beeson, the wire act. But only another woman can appreciate the futility of make-believe. In her heart, Clara carried a torch. On the following winter, the King and Queen again were signed up for abroad. From that trip Leitzel never returned. Alfredo brought her ashes back with him.

That had been over a year ago, Clara reasoned. He must have about re-covered from the shock, reconciling to his fate by now. Maybe he had even forgotten the short interlude—his alliance with Leitzel. Why couldn't she and Alfredo start anew from where they had left off? This mishap now was just the stimulus for an opening. She was brimming over with hope.

But later, as I spoke with Alfredo in the Garden, I knew the whole affair was a cold as the Thanksgiving Day turkey on Sunday night. He was gone, head-over-heels for the little Russian trapeze artiste, Tamara. She was a neat little package, doing a single trap act, well presented but nothing sensational.

She had been sold to the show by the Cliff Fischer office in Paris. I had met Tamara in Paris and knew she was dearly in love only with *Tamara*. Married to an Italian nobleman, she treated him as a slave, serving as her property-man. She evidently left him behind; at least, she arrived in New York alone. She had met Alfredo in London, when on the same bill with him and Leitzel. Oddly enough, she resembled Leitzel: small and blond. No doubt she had watched the Queen often enough at the Palladium to acquire certain little mannerisms of the late artiste, which she had now put to use in beguiling Alfredo, who, dressed in a white-flannel uniform, held the rope for her in her ascent, then picked up her mules which she deliberately kicked far off to make him give her extra service hunting for them. Oh, she was a clip! I visited the show again under canvas in Brooklyn. Alfredo had the privilege of a wagon for a private dressing room, which he relinquished to Tamara. Seated therein snugly, she pointed to an oil heater: "Also, Alfredo's!" she bragged. And while I sat there, he came in carrying two buckets of water for her. I was disgusted!

The RKO Circus unit was being whipped into shape. Vaudeville was about to get a shot in the arm. The Palace on Broadway would be the first of the chain of Keith-Albee houses to present the stupendous unit of all-star circus acts. The list, comprised in its major part of Ringling-Barnum features, read like a circus version of "Who's Who." The idea for the extravagant unit was conceived in the imaginative brain of the enterprising Larry Boyd, who has at one time or other dabbled in every phase of show business—as a singer in opera and minstrel shows, as a theater manager and carnival owner, and now as a booking agent.[5] In cooperation with Phil Wirth, of bareback riding fame, the two associates developed the idea to practicability and sold it to RKO Corporation, stirring these austere heads out of their dignified lethargy. An all-circus bill had not been their concept of high-class presentation of big-time vaudeville, but they bought it, nevertheless.

Now to put over a deal of this magnitude needed a new approach in selling it to the public. The show would have to be publicized. Terry Turner, head of the department, remembered an act he had seen at Rye Beach and in the newsreel: a girl who rode down from a tower on a cable, suspended by her teeth. Why couldn't she do a ballyhoo outside the Palace building?[6] The two promoters, Boyd and Wirth, were called for a conference. It was Boyd who said, "Not only outside the building. This girl will fly across Times Square, landing on the Palace roof. That ought to draw a crowd!"

But New York turns thumbs down on drawing a crowd, especially on

Times Square, where the general traffic is one continuous crowd. Regulations are strict on any public display that might cause congestion.

Putting their heads together, one came up with a brilliant idea—an angle the law has no jurisdiction over. The next day I was called to the RKO publicity department, where all parties concerned were gathered, press agent Washburn among them.[7] They told me what they had in mind, and I grasped the idea immediately. We were on the eleventh floor of the Palace as I looked across and spotted the Paramount Theatre three blocks away. But that would involve a competitive house. I then spied the Hotel Edison on Forty-seventh Street, between Broadway and Eighth Avenue. This seemed the better choice. The gap of the two avenues, Seventh and Broadway, running parallel is widest at this point.

Even as I pointed to the sign atop the twenty-seven-story building for a tie-off at the starting point—about three hundred feet up—the nattily dressed gentlemen mopped their brows with their fine linen handkerchiefs and gasped with awe. They didn't believe it. I signed a six-week contract with option of extended time to work in the stage show and to put on one publicity slide at each town in which we were to appear.

Leaving the office, I immediately stepped out the distance between Edison and Palace to check for length of cable needed. The next move was getting the height of both buildings to see how much pitch there would be on the descent. I had a fairly clear picture of the setup outlined in my mind when I left to join the other acts.

For some reason, the Big Show had closed earlier than usual that year. At any rate, by the Twelfth of October, all the acts with the unit which came from the Big Show were lined up with the others in the unit for pictures at Roeder's backyard studio and gym on West Forty-seventh Street. I knew almost everybody there, and we were having a reunion when in came Alfredo and his troupe of two. I was almost floored when he came over to me and introduced his wife—Vera.[8] They just dropped in for a visit. He told me they were set for a European tour for the winter and were sailing the following day. But I could hardly get over the surprise of his marriage.

What actually had taken place, I could only piece together. Most likely, he realized how Tamara was taking him in, giving little herself. Vera, at least, was fulfilling the duties of a member or helper in his act. Perhaps this much-confused young man, accustomed to adulation, had grown to depend on her for moral support, overestimating the value she represented. Vera, in turn, seeing her opportunity, played her trump card. Catching him off guard when at a low ebb, she dealt him from the bottom of the deck:

giving him the ultimatum either to marry her or she would leave the act. It was a crucial moment. He had just signed a contract for a European tour again. He needed Vera. She was an essential in his work. He couldn't break in another girl on short notice to throw him that bar, which had to be timed exactly or his wonderful work would be a total failure. He was too proud of his work to risk his reputation. Besides, Tamara had a husband in Europe, which might embroil him in a skirmish he had no desire for. He married Vera on the impulse. Tamara was thunderstruck! The news was such a shock to her ego that momentarily she became berserk, obtained a gun, and shot herself. Whether she intended to kill herself or not remains her own secret. She most likely adored that gorgeous self too much to destroy it. The bullet just barely grazed her shoulder.

Discussing with Alfredo the project I had in mind—a Slide for Life over Broadway—I pointed to the location. The slide would take me from the sign on top of the Edison Hotel to the Palace Theater roof. Alfredo predicted that I would never accomplish it. However, having a practical idea of rigging skill myself by then, I could see no reason why it couldn't be done—the engineering part, that is. Ten days later, he must have read the account of it in the European edition of the periodicals. The story made worldwide news.[9]

But alas! The reigning days of the King were, even then, already numbered. Not long after, the circus world was to learn that Alfredo's arm ligaments had gone haywire from the excessive stretching his work required. The flyer—now grounded—took on an associate in the person of Clayton Beehee, to whom he was to teach his technique as well as that famous two-and-a-half somersault to the hands of Lalo. The Codona name now was synonymous with flying. Why not carry on? All the time he was hoping that the ligaments would adjust themselves if nature were given a chance. A performer never gives up.

With Clayton taking Alfredo's place in the act, they were set on the Hagenbeck-Wallace program. Alfredo, getting a break as well, was appointed as equestrian director. But, with a new member in the act—and making good—it was no longer a family affair. The new flyer wanted recognition. Nor did Alfredo's wings mend as he had hoped. So the prospects looked bleak. Moreover, Lalo had married, and now with a wife and child, it was time to plan for a more solid future. No use struggling with a proposition which, through any dispute between associates, might blow up on a minute's notice. The brothers finally retired from show business and entered into an auto-machine shop with another brother, in which all three owned joint interest, and took up residence in Long Beach.[10]

It was not so for Vera, however. Asserting herself, she wished to continue trouping. The lure of the show was too great as against the home life and love for husband—had she been capable of such emotion—so she signed up with Hagenbeck-Wallace, back in the ranks where she had been found for Alfredo's act a few years before.

After a period of separation when the Hagenbeck show hit Los Angeles in July 1937, Vera decided to come to some agreement with her estranged spouse. Although she had no part in amassing whatever goods and property he possessed, she was aware that, according to California state laws, she could demand community property settlement in equal shares. She was already in possession of all his jewelry, which he had given her for safekeeping in her grouch bag, and Leitzel's as well, even the huge diamond that once belonged to Clyde Ingalls.

From the apartment she had rented for the week, Vera, accompanied by her mother, who also traveled with the show, drove over to the lawyer's office in Long Beach, where she was to meet Alfredo to discuss the settlement and start divorce action. Whatever his inner emotions, on the surface Alfredo appeared composed as he requested to have a talk with Vera, alone. In the next instant, the mother and barrister were shocked by the sound of shots fired in rapid succession. Horrified, rushing into the antechamber they found Alfredo sprawled across the floor, the gun still clutched in his hand. He had died instantly. Vera, mortally wounded, died in the hospital some hours later.[11]

PART
2

SARASOTA—
LAST STOP

When the men lowered the big top that night, it marked not only the last stand of the season but the folding up, for evermore, of the grand banner of the Al G. Barnes Circus as well as my final appearance under canvas. Closing night with a circus is one of great confusion; lacking the sentiment of the stage-production units or amusement-park organizations, there is no weeping to the strains of "Auld Lang Syne." In fact, by the time the band gets around to play it at the finish of that last performance, quite a number of the troupes have already left for the depot.

The disbanding of a circus happens simultaneously with the performance. As the show progresses, the acts, having done their turn, dismantle their own riggings and props, pack them away in crates and trunks, and arrange for transporting them to whatever point their destination may be for the winter. Special agents representing the various railroad lines have been on the lot all day booking passage for the performers to all points; from that night on, they're on their own. Early that morning, on leaving the show's sleeping coaches, they will have gathered up all their effects, such as toilet articles and suitcases, and lugged them to the lot—the first step toward their separation from the base they have enjoyed from six to seven months.

Once the performers have left, the workmen of the various departments, having packed up and loaded the show's paraphernalia on the train, are mustered out and paid in full—including the two-weeks' holdback in salary the show has kept as bond since the start of the season. Only a skeleton crew is left to take the show into winter quarters. That was the usual procedure. In this instance, however, the show was on its home grounds; rather, it had been taken to the Ringling quarters to bury it.

Although the Ringling Corporation had purchased the Al G. Barnes title and equipment—as well as a group of other competitive shows—back in 1929, it had kept it in its original territory on the West Coast during the ensuing years, managing it by remote control till this closing of the season of 1938, when the corporation wrote finis to it.

All in all, it had been a hectic season—a season to make history. Even the closing day left something to be remembered: Florida, with its usually balmy weather at this time of year (November 27), suddenly turned unusual—the temperature dropped below freezing. Earlier in the day, I had arranged passage for New York, but late that night, when I changed trains at Tampa, the thermometer registered twenty-four degrees Fahrenheit, so I changed my mind instead and had my ticket exchanged to read "California." I nearly froze in the baggage room while getting all my belongings rechecked.

What did it matter if I had prospects for winter dates in the East? That cold frightened me! And though I wanted to get away from the cold, I wanted even more to leave behind the mental anguish that had been my lot during the last half of the season. I wanted to be far away, to lick my wounds like an injured dog. It was only now—when I was free—that all the grief and humiliation I had been exposed to were fully felt.

True, I could have gotten away from it at any time. No one was stopping me. But a stubborn pride made me stick to the dismal finish. But now it was over, and I was on my way to . . . somewhere, to regain my bearing and poise. So it's California! With its climate always on the mild side, I decided to establish my base in the southern part of the state. Having covered the United States from border to border and coast to coast, I was sure it was my choice of the forty-eight.

With winter quarters at Baldwin Park, California, the Al G. Barnes Circus opened its annual official season at San Diego. On the mend after a recent major surgical operation, I went to visit with the performers, for there are always people with a circus whom one, being of the trade, is bound to know. Sure enough, there were! And not only in the dressing room but at the front as well, for it was Ben Austin, the grand old showman whom I knew well, at the head of the show. Talking with me, he gathered that I was available, and two days later, I received an offer (by telegram) to join the show. He specified that it was only for the Los Angeles and Hollywood stands. Having worked at a big promotion under his direction previously, he knew I could cover that weak spot in one of the numbers which was too obvious to the spectators, especially on a week-stand.

He explained later that all the acts were contracted by the Sarasota office, where the program had been set up; however, for this short engagement he would pay me from the petty cash, provided I wouldn't be too pretentious. Though scarcely in condition physically, I accepted the offer. And by the end of the week, I was installed permanently for the season.

In my contentment, I was fairly walking on air. It was like a dream come true to be eating in the cookhouse and with a berth assigned to me on the show train after so many years. True, my salary was in the low bracket, since I was engaged as a special by Mr. Austin probably without the sanction of the eastern headquarters, but I enjoyed certain privileges granted only to high-caliber artistes, such as a berth to myself and not having to go in spec. Oh yes, I even rated announcement on doing that breakaway—the finish-trick in my act. Acting like a First of May, everything thrilled me!

How strange! During the years of freelancing, with some choice front-page and newsreel publicity as a daredevil, doing stunts from a blimp at Atlantic City's Steel Pier or a slide high above Times Square—yes, even working in Billy Rose's *Jumbo*—none of these could measure up to the glorious feeling of being back where I had started and then abandoned in 1919: with a CIRCUS!

There seemed to be no great evolution that I could notice even after nineteen years away from the sawdust and straw, except for a trend toward democracy among the distinct ranks. Stars and features mingled more freely now with the lower class of performers. Statues were no longer in vogue, and the girls now were doing swinging-ladder routines in the air and manege acts on horseback along the track. They also doubled in the Dance-Revue Concert after the regular show, as the Wild West aftershow had given way to a touch of Hollywood glamor, which proved to be a success not only economically, but also by reducing space and equipment needs.

The rules restricting performers taking children or pets on tour had been laxed. The barrier had been lifted in the late 1920s when the Yacopi troupe of acrobats, hailing from South America, refused to sign up unless the infant son of one of the members could be taken along. The act was of such importance to the show that the precedent was established.[1] Thereafter, children could accompany their parents in exceptional cases and in a limited number.

The laboring class had also moved up a notch insofar as accommodations were concerned. Social restrictions, too, had been noticeably broken down. A groom could talk on current topics to the fair lady while giving her foot a boost in mounting, or even on personal matters if she encouraged it. While the morals of the people in general, even now, remained at a high standard, there wasn't quite so much snooping and gossiping about who waited for whom after the night show for the walk back to the coaches. The place of the trunk lost its significance as to rating, and bathing in the nude was now approved in the dressing room. These were the only deviations from the old dogmas on chastity and virtue.

As a whole, the tour seemed like a pleasant vacation trip to me. I enjoyed every phase of it. And although this was but a branch of the mammoth one in the East—The Greatest Show on Earth (or whatever the current billing on the Ringling-Barnum combine)—I was thoroughly satisfied to be where I was for the time being, at least.

Then one day, we read in glaring headlines that the Big Show had been halted at Scranton, Pennsylvania, by labor trouble. There they were, man and beast, stranded on the lot for days with no way of moving. The union had stopped them. After much controversy and bickering, protests from the offices of City Health Ordinance, SPCA, et cetera, and the innumerable obstacles and difficulties arising as a result, it was finally arranged to load the show on the train and run it into winter quarters at Sarasota, Florida.[2]

Regarding the performers, I don't know how the acts were covered by contract; the conditions varied. There was a clause specifying something to the effect of, in the event of "an act of God, beyond the control of the management, et cetera," it shall not be liable. Whether this conflict entered under that ruling . . . (anyway, I never read a contract; I would just sign and hope for the best). But the management is definitely liable for its foreign importations—acts that are bonded in—according to the immigration laws. Looking at it from any angle, the closing of that show—almost at the start of the season—was a major catastrophe without precedent.

Our show was sailing along smoothly enough, excepting at a very few spots where we were picketed at the entrance to the grounds. I remember an incident in one town in particular, in the state of Washington. I know it was bitter cold, and a group of us were circled around a log fire which some of the razorbacks had started outside near the dressing room. It was just about time for the first bugle call before the night show that we heard great excitement emanating from around the front. Seeing people on the run, we all started running in the direction of the midway. What I saw was hard to believe, yet there it was. Two elephants, Ruth and Modac, were wielding ten-foot poles with their trunks, and directed by their trainer, Walter McLain, they were charging for the mob of pickets like angry parents getting after their unruly young. They didn't hurt anyone, but they broke up that line in short order. The pickets, seeing what was coming, dropped their signs and scurried in every direction away from the premises in double tempo.

The show went along with the usual routine until the day rumors ran through the dressing room that some of the big shots from Sarasota were in the grandstand watching the show. Everybody was putting on his or her showiest wardrobe and turning extra flip-flaps for the visitors' benefit. What a show they put on! As for me, well, my heart was turning the flip-flaps as I wondered which one of the big shots counted so much now that Mr. John was gone—as were Frank Cook, the legal adjuster with the show, who was a big daddy to everyone: French, German, Chinese, or Indian alike were his wards; Clyde Ingalls, with his stentorian voice for announcing that would never have needed aid of a microphone; Chick Bell, Hathaway, McIntyre, and Kennelly were all gone, doing business at the main entrance of the Golden Gate with Saint Peter as head usher. Who can be holding their posts now?

Well, I soon found out, but it didn't stir me out of my skin. And I can't remember if the finish of my act ran smoothly or not. I wondered whether they took the interest to watch me for the one minute while I held the audience's attention alone. At any rate, no one came back to say hello to me, and I certainly didn't break through the line of performers encircling the party to express my greetings. After all, I hadn't been officially signed up by them; I maybe wasn't even supposed to be on the roster, as far as they were concerned. Instead, I remained cool, confident that my participation in the show was an asset rather than a surplus expense, especially since the 25 percent cut in salaries had gone into effect a few weeks previous. The cut affected everybody with the show; everyone accepted it, but some grumbled about it, still. Well, the chow was pretty good and the work steady—no care of transportation and loss of time of the freelance status. I didn't even grumble. One consolation about a small wage: when there is a cut, one doesn't stand to lose so much.

The visiting big shots were Johnnie Ringling North, president of the Ringling Corporation; the personnel director (whose name I shall not mention); and other dignitaries I didn't know. After the matinee performance, they stayed only an hour or so, talking to the various heads of departments and performers that encircled them, and departed before the evening show's bugle sounded. And everything went on as before.[3]

Now came the big day, July 4—always a grand celebration on a circus. It had remained so. Starting after the matinee in the cookhouse with the deluxe dinner, from soup to nuts; with the patriotic trimmings—the works—which puts everybody in a festive mood; the jolly activities swung into session in the big top: contests, vaudeville, and dancing till the head usher announces, "Doors!"

The party was an event of gaiety and pleasure for the show's entire personnel—some nine hundred strong, according to the census taken by immigration authorities on our recent tour in Canada. Cares and grief were forgotten as all took part in the festivities. Joy was the spirit of the occasion! I was exhilarated in my triumph, having won the cracker-eating contest. It was about the last happy moment I knew with the show.

Arriving at Redfield, South Dakota, on Sunday (July 10), while switching our train to a siding in the freight yard, I noticed strange-looking cars—sleeping coaches, stock cars, and flats painted dark red and lettered: Ringling Bros. and Barnum & Bailey Circus. This sight filled me with misgivings. None of us performers knew what the score was; it just had to develop gradually. Looking across the ravine in the distance, I could see the tents up, but somehow the outline didn't portray the picture I was so familiar with. Yes, I began to see the light—a merger schemed up to work both shows. Then, on leaving the coaches, I saw the facts when reading the first poster along the way:

Al G. Barnes and Sells-Floto Combined
Circus
Presenting
Ringling Bros. and Barnum & Bailey
Stupendous New Features

That explained everything.[4] Arriving on the lot, the first place the performers looked for was—you guessed it—the cookhouse. Golly! Was I seeing double? There were two of them; yet not one had the friendly emblem up—the blue flag signaling "It's open: come and get it!" Here it was, 1:00 PM, and with the long run we just had made from the last town, all I had was a cup of coffee under my belt, which I got in the privilege car earlier, while still en route. "What goes on?" I thought. Others were standing around, as much at bay as I; no one seemed to know the answer. There was the tantalizing smell of food in the air, but the flap was closed.

What actually was in progress was a feud between cookhouse bosses, each waiting for the headman to settle the question, Who stays? One had to go. But who was the *headman?* That also would have to be settled.

There were a lot of new people all about, swaggering cockily hither and thither as if they owned the joint. I turned toward the big top to see what they had brought in the way of rigging. One look at the interior, and my heart sank. It was a four-pole top, like ours had been, but much higher. My anxiety was fixed on the predicament I found myself in as a result. All my guylines, trimmed for a lower loft, would have to be lengthened. But that was only a small item. The breakaway setup would also have to be retrimmed, and that involved a lot of mathematics. I went to look for Blackie, my property man, but with so much confusion, the new people monopolizing every inch of the back end and all of them with a chip on their shoulders, I couldn't find him or my rigging box. Then it occurred to me that with the new arrangement, I had better wait until whoever was in power first told me where to set up. I didn't see my falls hanging from any of the poles.

Passing along the track, I heard Mr. Austin's voice. Turning in that direction, I stopped as I saw him talking with a youngish dark and handsome (but not tall) man, attired as if he were fixed to play polo. I gazed spellbound at his face, for had he been higher in stature, I would have sworn, "There's John Ringling!" Nor would Mr. John have worn sport clothes around the show; he always dressed in conservative business suits, like a banker or professional man. "He must be some member of his family!" I reflected, seeing him bearing such a marked resemblance. He was! A nephew, son of the only sister of the five famous Ringling brothers. What a disappointment it must have been to them that none of the male members should have descendents eligible to carry on the name in managing the circus. But John Ringling North (using his maternal surname as middle name) was doing quite well as far as carrying the business was concerned. He and his brother Henry were at the head of it now.[5]

I didn't mean to eavesdrop on their conversation, but I stood there transfixed, fascinated by the young man's striking resemblance to his uncle. Presently, I heard Mr. Austin saying, "But you already have six men here to do my job!"

With this remark, caught at random, my skies turned gloomy, forecasting storms. Recovering, I quickly turned and walked away and ran smack into George Smith. Handsome George—who used to be an assistant to Chick Bell, the head usher—was now swinging a cane as he walked around in the capacity of business manager of the outfit. Where was Mr. Bradna, the debonair equestrian director? No, he didn't come! There were several of my contemporaries, Tom Haines and others. Yes, there was Merle Evans, the bandleader then and still the leader. He got quite a kick out of my singing the tune of "Can You Tame Wild Women?" the music he used to play during my act so long ago, as it seemed. It was so good to see him again.

Going through the back door, I noticed a glass-enclosed cage wagon with an ape inside. A man close by, with miniature cookhouse equipment under the same canopy, was chopping up some vegetables. Always interested in monkeys, I inquired about the act. He told me this one did no particular tricks. In fact, he was never removed from this air-conditioned glass house but exhibited to the public drawn by a six-horse team around the track with "Bring 'em Back Alive" Frank Buck as his master of ceremonies.[6] This keeper—a pleasant man named Kronen—explained that his charge was the famous gorilla, Gargantua, whereupon I took a closer glimpse.[7] This ape in no way resembled the two beautiful specimens of their genus that I had seen in the San Diego Zoo, where I watched their capers in that massive steel-barred cage, above which a plaque informs the public that they were captured by Martin and Osa Johnson in the Belgian Congo.[8]

This one's skin, what could be seen of it, was almost black and covered with hair for the most part. He—if its sex may be determined (owing to a physical phenomenon in the arrangement of the species' genital organ being completely concealed in the interior of the body, leaving little trace for an expert to determine whether it is male or female; at any rate, chances being even, I'll go along with the press agent in referring to it as "he")—possessed rather ordinary apish features with a pointed snout (what was left of it) badly scarred about the nose and upper lip. I learned later the tragedy that left its mark on Gargantua for the balance of his baffled life. While being transported from Africa as a baby, the ship's captain took quite a shine to him. One of the hands aboard, to avenge a grudge against the chief, took his spite out on this helpless little ape by throwing acid in the face of the unfortunate victim with the intent to kill him. However, he survived, and except for the horrible disfigurement of face, was none the worse for it. When the captain later made a gift of this creature to a lady of his favor, the little darling proved to be quite a pet until he grew to be too heavy to sit on its mistress's lap or light on her shoulder in a playful mood, and so she sold him to the show.[9]

By now I lost my shyness and was reconciled to making the best of what might follow. When the question of meal serving was temporarily settled, we all ate in the Al G. Barnes cookhouse, with George Tipton as boss. But in the morning, instead of coffee, there was trouble brewing. The Blood brothers, who had come from Sarasota with the others, wanted a showdown. After all, they were from the Big Show and should have the preference, but Tipton had all the cookhouse gang on his side. They refused to work with the new bosses. Again they compromised, with Tipton as head, the Blood brothers his assistants. When the latter started to make up the menu, Tipton walked out, and with him went the entire gang: cooks, waiters, and dishwashers.

Mr. Austin had left the show the previous night, joining his capable assistant and director of personnel, Paul Eagles. Mr. Eagles had sized up the situation from the car platform and didn't even dignify the heads of the directorate with a trip to the lot for the conference but gathered all personal belongings in his stateroom and took the first passenger train leaving for his home in Los Angeles, where he owns a feed and grain business of considerable importance.

With these two—our bosses—gone, I was at a loss as to whom to turn. There seemed to be so many chiefs, yet I couldn't seem to get any satisfactory direction as regards where and when to set up. With no rehearsal and no program, the show got started. Of course, it wasn't the Al G. Barnes show. Most of our acts were used as fillers, and we had to dance to the tempo of the new music.

I had no heart to watch the show. There under the grandstand I strung out all my hanging wires, ropes, and guylines to be ready for setting up as soon as the matinee let out. I inquired of Bob Thornton, our equestrian director, if he knew anything of the plans. Again I was told to wait; it would take a few days to adjust the program. That he no longer had any authority I could plainly see. The one who had the say-so was evasive and didn't bother about my problems. I waited, pulling out the apparatus every single day, then packing it away at night. After two weeks of this, I didn't have the spirit to continue. There were others who had lost their feature spot, but at least they were doing something, even if only working out on the track or doubly in a ring with another act. These alternatives, by the nature of my work, were not open to me.

Mabel Stark, the lady who "Holds That Tiger!" had started on her hazardous career working on the show when it was owned by its original founder, Al G. Barnes.[10] The enterprise, founded on the West Coast, was known and billed as a Wild Animal Show. Later it developed into a typical circus. Mabel's undisputed skill in training tigers, the most treacherous species of cats, was the result of many years' patience and courage.[11] With all the art of the showman in the ring, this sprightly wisp of femininity, besides possessing the qualities and charm of a star, was a very interesting conversationalist, and I went to discuss the situation with her.

Mabel, one of the features of the show in its former state, had been shifted to the opening spot to save time and labor. She dressed still in a wagon, and it was there I found her and asked how she felt about the whole affair. With all the fervor of an evangelist, she threw up both arms, her voice pitched high as if singing a hallelujah: "Oh Lord, it has come to pass! Mr. Al G. can rest in his grave now! He predicted this would happen; he said it all the time—whenever one of the other shows would cut in on his territory and poke slurs at the size of his show by sticking up posters reading: 'Why see the minnow when you can see the whale?' He prophesized then what is happening now: 'Mine will be the last show on the road!' Now look at the posters, and tell me if anyone can dispute it!"

As I watched her, she presented an exalted figure, her face all aglow, reminding me of a priestess. The second bugle call had sounded, which meant just fifteen minutes before the show. Mabel adjusted her cape and, giving her nose a last pat of the powder-puff, we both left the wagon. She headed toward the tunnel where the beasts passed from cage to arena, while I sadly sauntered toward the dressing room, which had become another arena to me with all the new members crowded in. I knew some were wondering why I should be taking up trunk space when I contributed nothing to the show. They didn't know me or the circumstances and had never seen my act, so I could forgive them when they inquired just what I did when I do. It was humiliating to give them any kind of reply to vindicate myself in their eyes. A few of them, First of Mays doing little ladder routines they learned in three weeks while breaking in for the show at winter quarters, felt themselves superior and seemed to be conferring a favor by talking to me. My humiliations were endless.

On a rainy day, with puddles in the dressing room, trunks were shifted helter-skelter for high places. The intruders thought nothing of blocking or even moving my trunk if it happened to be on a dry spot, and I had no comeback.

In the coaches I received the same treatment. A clown and his wife occupying the lower berth below my roost went to the one in charge to petition shifting me so that their young daughter, who did a chambermaid's frolic on a swinging ladder and was sleeping in the single-girls' car, might have my berth or share it with me. This would have been the proverbial straw that broke the camel's back—an affront to me. The very cheek of those lowly people! This pair that only a few days ago had looked up to me with respect now presumed to have a vote on my status. It was too big a lump to swallow! The management considered me, and the shift was not made.

From the very day of the combine, the Barnes performers were given to understand that regardless of whether or not their acts were used in the show, none should be dismissed. However, if they were not satisfied with the new direction, any of them could leave voluntarily without notice or red tape. Being aware of this, I always felt as if I were accepting alms when payday came. When my name was called from outside the dressing room, I felt that all the others were deriding me, looking askance as if to say, "And what have you done to earn that check?"

To be doing something useful with my time, I turned to looking over my costumes, mending the old ones and designing new ones. I sewed on spangles the blessed day long. "Should I land some winter dates, I'll have a new array of wardrobe!" With this thought in mind I found some consolation.

I was doing this one day when the wardrobe woman approached holding a costume on a hanger. She stopped before my trunk and informed me that I was to wear it in spec.

"But I don't make spec!" I answered with finality. I wasn't prepared for the rebuff when she told me that it was by order of so-and-so. I knew it was done with some definite purpose; therefore, why debate over it? Glancing after her as she walked down the aisle of trunks, I couldn't miss seeing the sneers and leers. Ignoring them, I put on makeup and dressed; the costume was a perfect fit, rather pretty, depicting a Mexican hat-dancer. With the entire cast assembled at the back door just before the start of the spec, I found the group (by matching costumes) with which I was to march afoot. Forcing me to walk in that procession—was there also some motive, some insult intended when they must have remembered the intrepid rider I was? I wondered. Then I spied Frank Buck atop one of the elephants, right in his element as if on a safari. "Well, if he makes spec, why shouldn't I?" I simmered down.

"May as well take it philosophically!" I said, remembering the old Spanish adage which translated would read: "There is no evil lasting a hundred years; nor body that could endure it!"

Calloused now to the unsavory situation, I started counting the weeks until the season ended. Occasionally I'd put on practice clothes between shows, hang my rings under a ladder, and go through a routine, carefully omitting whatever tricks I had of genuine value, with all the performers constantly working out new acts and always on the lookout for something original. Well, there is little honor when it comes to material. Almost anybody is a potential suspect in the eyes of one who has conceived an idea, only to find it has been copied. It is impossible to protect new tricks.

Resting between routines while practicing one afternoon, I looked about me. There were acts practicing in every available space, from one end of the big top to the other. One act, in particular, had caught my attention as it practiced on the track nearby. It was the Canastrellis training their young daughter, Tosca, on a bounding rope. She seemed the acme of grace, every move the expression of art. Yet no one else was interested in watching her as she bounded on the rope from sitting to standing position, or left the rope to turn a somersault in space and make a perfect landing on the rope as if it were a magnet. To the others, the act was no longer a novelty. They had seen it for five years in the making, from the time Tosca was a second-grader in school. I wondered why she hadn't already presented this unique act, a girl doing bounding-rope. But the parents—grand performers themselves—didn't deem the act quite finished. Nevertheless, I wished that I might see this rare achievement when produced with full effect. It promised to be one of the outstanding features of the time.

In the ring next to me, I saw a trio of the Christiani family (fourteen in number, counting the wives of the married boys). They were riders, primarily, though some of the members doubled and trebled in ground acrobatics and perch acts. The three girls, Cosette, Chita, and Hortense, were now practicing an aerial act. It was Cosette who broke the ice by coming over to talk to me. Because the family had a private top I had never seen much of them.

"I've been watching you, and I think you do nice work!" she said in a way of a compliment. Ever conscious of the awkward situation I had assumed since the new people had come to monopolize the principal spots in the show, I was in doubt whether the remark was meant truly as a compliment or just a sop to my injured pride. Always striving to redeem myself in the eyes of those who patronized me, I replied: "Oh, this isn't anything but to keep me in shape—to get my arms and wind back. I am expecting word from my agent about signing up with . . . oh, he told me to keep it under my hat. Besides, I might be called to put my act on here, any day—I hope."

I could tell by her expression that she didn't believe me, and as if trying to console me, she blurted out just what I feared all along: "Oh, I'm quite sure they wouldn't discharge you here. Mr. North said so. I heard him mention one day that he remembers you from the old Garden; he was only a little fellow, but even then he thought you had a great act. And you can stay here as long as you like."

I was stunned! Now I knew that it was sentiment that kept me here and that it was up to me to leave. But why should I feel humble now, having stayed on for most of the season? That would be admitting that I had accepted charity. No! I had an act, a feature act. If they threw it away, it was their own loss.

The joke was being carried too far, I thought, when on another day, I again espied Margaret Graham, the wardrobe woman, approach my trunk. This time she had a bundle of tights and stuff which she said I was to wear in the revolving-ladder group, substituting for one of the girls absent that day. I believed it to be a rib and laughed to show them I still retained a sense of humor. On finding she was in earnest about it, I could feel the ground rocking under me. I said a very emphatic "No!" Of all the degrading humiliation they had already heaped upon me, this one I wasn't going to take. I told her what she could do with the bundle.

I expected repercussions from the incident and braced myself. I made spec, removed my makeup, then packed my trunk. I sat on it, waiting for something to happen. But nothing did. As a specialty artist ("principal," in show lingo), I had *not* signed the kind of contract that obliged me to be available for general utility, as directed by the management. I owned an apparatus. I was boss of my own act and was classified as a private contractor. Two days later, as I arrived on the lot and paused to read a letter the mailman had left on my trunk, one of the girls came up and told me I was wanted outside. Instinctively, I knew what was up. My face was flushed with shame and rage at being placed in this mortifying situation. I was told that I was uncooperative, a term I sorely resented. Through my career I had established and followed a principle of protecting the interest of the show with which I was connected. This was not an exception. Being unfamiliar with the routine I was asked to fill, I would have spoiled the picture by being out of step with the others. I explained this, swallowing my humble pie and keeping cool in spite of the storm that raged within me. For, in those brief moments, I remembered all the indignities I had been subjected to ever since that day in Redfield, when the show went on without my act, and I simply tagged along.

To live that down would not be easy! En route to California, during the next two days, I turned the events over and over in my mind, wondering if my age could have been the cause of, or at least a contributing factor to, the pushing around I was accorded. Could be! I knew that my ability to deliver had still been terrific at the last stand in Jamestown, North Dakota. After making a careful scrutiny of the acts and people that were brought on, I arrived at the conclusion that the accent was on youth, and the emphasis on the feminine sex. Although the Barnes show already had a prodigious number of gals, glamorous ones—picked up in movieland, where they were a dime a dozen—the Big Show had brought its own bunch. As with coffee, date seemed of primary importance; talent counted second.

What rankled me most was that this was the first time to my knowledge that personal feelings had weighed against my professional ability.

I should have sat back, relaxed, and enjoyed this trip as a passenger—free of care and no one to disturb me. But my thoughts ran wild, and because there was no distraction or anything to occupy me, I kept dwelling on the gloomy events in my life. Recalling only the inauspicious features, I couldn't shake off that morbid mood.

Even now, I tried to distinguish which one of the many calamities to befall me was the most appalling. Unquestionably, it was the one which in one brief instant almost destroyed me, the one which left a scar of lifelong endurance. Broken bones have a way of haunting the victim every time there's a change in the weather for chill or dampness, and I have many spooks inside me—reminders of unlucky breaks. But this particular break is a constant reminder.

It happened in Hartford, Connecticut, a few years before the great fire of the Big Show top in that same town. The date was February 23, 1933; the place, the Shrine circus at the Armory. Roy, one of the two fellows holding the strip of cloth in my path to stop my momentum just before reaching the low end of the wire, let go of his end, leaving the other fellow holding the bag (to use a figure of speech). Flabbergasted, and with the cloth still in his hands, he became bewildered at the crucial moment as he saw me streaking down at eighty-five miles per hour. He stood aside, not knowing what to do. There was not much he could have done alone, but he was the best eyewitness to the event to tell me later all that took place in that split-second.

Confident of everything going as well in the ensuing performances as during the preceding days of the week's engagement, I went about the act on Thursday night as ordinary routine—hanging on by biting the leather bit attached to the pulley. The height of the Armory tended to make the speed greater than usual. The men had been knocked off balance a couple of times, and Roy had seen me fasten a clamp on the wire after the matinee, so if the two went down, the pulley would stop before hitting the jack—he thought the idea made their effort unnecessary and walked off at the moment I approached. With no men to intercept me, the pulley stopped at the clamp but my body swung upward with the impact of the sudden stop, disconnecting me from the mouthpiece and with enough momentum to hurl me forward right through the bipod in a half-somersault, landing me upside down fifteen feet away near the seats at the back end.

It all happened in a flash. It was impossible for me to get a clear picture of the situation as I scrambled to my feet wondering what hit me on the nose. Why did I fall to the floor—and so far from the apparatus? How did I get there? And why had I let go of the bit?

The questions puzzled me. It was then that I noticed blood trickling from my face. A fine rain of blood before my very eyes! I reached up with my hand to clear my vision, while at the same time my tongue felt a vacant space. What was this? There, under my nose, was nothing but a big hollow. Too fantastic to be real. "I must be dreaming!" was my thought. But instantly recovering from the hallucination, the gravity of the situation flashed to my brain. That part of my jaw which doctors later called the maxilla, involving six frontal teeth and part of the hard palate, was missing. Panic seized me, and I rushed to the jack; my first thought was, illogical as it may sound, that it might still be biting the mouthpiece.

It fills me with sadness now as I recall that first reaction. There was the pulley still on the wire, wedged against the U-clamp, the mouthpiece dangling from the black but no sign of human giblet on it.

Desperate by then, I started looking on the floor, raking the sawdust with my fingers all around the scene of the tragedy, bent on recovering the fragment holding those precious teeth which had been a great asset to me and of which I had been so proud; nothing else mattered. The other performers standing by, seeing me with my head bleeding from every angle, were so horrified that none came near me; they just stared at me at a distance—fascinated, as if seeing an apparition.

The show, of course, went right on according to program and tradition. Very few spectators realized what had happened—those few who witnessed it at close range soon forgot it with the next act. The Hanneford family of riders took their attention. But the director, Frank Wirth, and some of the committee members with ring seats, immediately swung into action. Rushing in my direction, they picked me up and carried me behind the section of seats in spite of my remonstrations. None seemed to grasp what I, terror-stricken, tried to utter: that my jaw was out—lost! I pointed, telling it in pantomime. Looking closer at the gory spectacle I presented, they gave me the first news to cheer me up. No, they couldn't see me smile—with that portion of my anatomy so mutilated it gave a grotesque impression of a perpetual laugh—on being told nothing was missing. Actually, the fragment was still in my mouth, held only by the gum tissue on one side of the fracture, but the gap on the left side between lateral and canine teeth was so wide, it had given me the illusion that part of my face was gone.

Those Shriners went overboard in getting me patched up, calling in the most eminent specialists in town despite the difficulty in contacting them at their homes. (Most of them were probably at the Armory watching the show.) It seemed ages had passed while I was waiting. At last, the ambulance carted me off to the Hartford Hospital, where I remained unattended while the medicos debated whether I was a surgical or dental case. The clock in the emergency room ticked on, already past midnight—it was bitterly cold out, and the heavy snowfall had made the roads impassable. "They'll never come!" I thought hopelessly, when all of a sudden the place livened up. I counted no less than eight dignitaries who came past the stretcher, giving me a fleeting glance, and then went through a door to join the others— taking their time in consultation. So far, no one had even given me a towel to wipe the blood away. When finally a nurse came to undress me (I still had my makeup and costume on), I told her "never mind," that I was "all right from the neck down!" She didn't laugh. I had trouble articulating with my maxilla split wide open, but still I retained my sense of humor. Up until then I felt no pain—the shock took care of that.

Once on the operating table, they all went to work on me. I still babbled on, trying to be funny, and those austere men of medicine seemed puzzled. Besides the jaw injury, there were a broken nose and a jagged cut on my forehead (caused by jamming against the pulley), and also a laceration on the scalp, sustained when landing on the wrong end. This skull wound seemed to be of greater concern to them than the damage to my mouth; while my anxiety was focused on nothing else but. I could live with a hole in my head, but I needed my jaw and teeth to earn a living.

I made the front pages and was a heroine for a while.[12] Private room, nurse day and night, fan mail, visitors, and flowers in abundance. But I could not forever evade a day of realization. It looked like curtains on my career. No! No! I couldn't accept it! The fragment was forced back and wired into place but was very slow in adjustment—growing back to be part of me again. The teeth are still there now, permanently devitalized.

Yes, all the wounds healed, but I have never been the same afterward. My physiognomy was slightly altered (not improved, to be sure).

It took all the determination I could muster to start all over again. I had to do it somehow! And I doff my fez to those Nobles of the Sphinx Temple for the way they have seen me over that hump, defraying all expenses of medical intervention.

I also remember with profound gratitude a kindness of a fellow artiste, Renie Howard, of "Howard Sisters–Ironjaw" fame, who in my darkest hours brought me light. Like a beacon to a ship lost, groping for bearings, came Renie on hearing of my predicament. She was to impart her secret for a gadget she herself used: a vulcanite mouthpiece with impression for only the molars to grip, leaving the front teeth free, which her dentist made for me. This was the solution to my problem.

That same season of 1933, I was set at the Steel Pier, performing from a blimp at great heights. It was here that the publicity director Volk coined the line referring to my teeth suspension, "And here is proof that a woman can keep her mouth shut when she has to!"[13]

The train rambled along, and my mood mellowed with the climate as we neared California.

CHAPTER 32

AN ELUCIDATING INTERLUDE

Although I had officially retired from the road during the spring of 1943, I still accepted local engagements offered to me at occasional intervals, even if I didn't solicit them. I preferred to devote my time and energy to improving my home. However, one can never be completely cut off from what has been one's whole life, as show business has been mine. Time and again I would run into old associates such as the Loretta twins, Ora and Polly, who had been famous horizontal-bar performers featured with the Big Show long ago. Like myself, they still filled engagements here and there, besides working steady for Uncle Sam as riveters in a defense plant.

Yes, there was a war to be won, and why wasn't I out there pitching in? I suddenly felt conscience-stricken. Why not, indeed? What did I have to offer—two or three foreign languages? I applied and qualified for service in one of the branches of the federal government best suited to my ability. It was nice clerical work where I had the privilege of meeting people like Mrs. Mary Sumner, for example. At last, I had a taste of the average citizen's life. To be on equal footing with those whom I used to envy because they had no rigging troubles and never felt butterflies fluttering in the pit of their stomachs just before appearing in front of an audience that was to judge them most critically.

Oh, yes, getting up at 5:30 every morning, being pushed and jostled on bus and streetcar for a full hour, to be at one's place at 8:00, sharp—it wasn't much different from making parade. And I thought it excelled show business in many respects, particularly in one: professional jealousy was nonexistent here, or, at least, I was under that impression until I found out that steel doors can't keep out the demon. Here, too, favoritism played a part, if only in a small way. I was greatly disillusioned to discover one day, quite by accident, that our DAC (the abbreviated title of the chief's assistant), through partiality to one of my colleagues, had given her the credit for a certain assignment I had worked on. Granting that there was purely merit entailed, since neither pay nor position were affected, nevertheless it gave me a formidable jolt. Thereafter, I realized that there are obstacles to be found in any way of life; it is the general scheme in the race to get ahead of the competitor. The game is not always played fair; it is the same in any field because we are all made of the same clay.

With the end of the conflict in 1945, censors were no longer needed, and we were all honorably discharged. I returned to doing stunts. And even though I wouldn't consider trouping as a steady diet, it was very complimentary to my ego and a boost to my morale to find myself in demand. I could give my very life to hear that applause! Yet when my business manager, Eddie Gamble, came to tell me of a movie offer in the picture, *Till the Clouds Roll By,* the first thing that came to my mind was my snow-white hair: "But I will positively *not* dye my hair!" I said to him resolutely, even at the risk of losing the opportunity I had been praying for for ever so long.

When he took me over to the Metro-Goldwyn-Mayer studio for an audition, on seeing me, the directors promptly decided that my hair would photograph well in Technicolor, taking a hue of platinum blonde—the same effect given the audience when I made one of my rare appearances in the Coliseum, the Rose-Bowl, or the Shrine Auditorium.[1] While suspended by my teeth, my face turned upward, it is hard to tell whether I am sixteen or sixty (though closer to the latter). That's what I told Leroy Prinz, the dance director at Paramount in 1940, when he called for two girls to do iron-jaw work in the picture, *Road to Singapore,* with Bing Crosby, Bob Hope, and Dorothy Lamour.[2] I remember agent Al Wager gave me directions to the studio and also a friendly little hint, saying, "And honey, dress up to look like a million dollars!" That's how Al Wager dispatched me, confident that I would fill the bill.

But, instead, that gentleman with the royal name bluntly and with no consideration for my feelings informed me that he wanted two young girls—emphasizing the *young.* When I explained the effect while in the air, he still wouldn't buy. I couldn't understand it. I wondered if I should remind him of the American Legion show he directed in Havana, Cuba, in the early spring of 1927, in which I also participated. I decided against it and left.

For the first time I felt age being cruel to me. It had never occurred to me that I looked or acted any differently—I was the performer I had always been. Enter: Gloom.

Three days later came a telephone call with an offer to play a return engagement at the Million Dollar Theater, and I snapped out of that morose lethargy I'd let myself slip into after that morale-killing encounter. I leaped with joy at the chance to prove that I was still good at my specialty. The fact that they wanted me for a return date was proof of it. Not yet would I have to step aside to make way for youth. (Incidentally, the iron-jaw specialty was most conspicuous by its absence in the picture when it was released.)

My vindication came some years later when I appeared at an outdoor celebration at Malibu Beach—another American Legion show promoted by the residents of the movie colony, who were for the most part participants as well as spectators. On terminating the artistic work, as was my custom, I immediately donned overalls and tackled the business of striking and packing up my rigging, even before the audience had dispersed. Hustling from one end of the terrain to the other in releasing the anchorage of the eight-hundred-foot project, I ran past the manager, Mr. Joe Bren, who, standing by the bandstand talking with friends, stepped in my path, saying, "Say, Tiny, a friend of mine here, Leroy Prinz, wants to talk to you—he's sold on your act!"

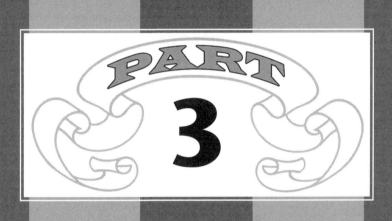

PART
3

THE CIRCUS,
TO DATE (1948)

It was ten years after the collapse of the Barnes Circus before I again visited the Big Show, and as a visitor only. The lot was near the Pan-Pacific Auditorium. After my visit I was filled with nostalgia but glad to come back to my little haven of rest and independence. My head was not in the clouds, and for the first time in my life, while visiting a circus, I did not wish to be with it. I felt no envy for the others, no desire to put on makeup or share in the glory of the applause.

I was content to do as I had been doing, appearing at various local shows from time to time, leaving it up to my business manager's judgment to select only the more desirable dates, with sufficient time between each for me to recuperate. But it so happened that for Labor Day, he sold me in two different spots: the Coliseum, with a star-spangled spectacle, and at an amusement park at one of the beaches near by. I protested that it was too much for me to handle, but he has a way that is quite persuasive. Aside from the money, the knowledge that my work should be in such demand built up my confidence.

"I shall put on a good show at both places!" was my resolution.

There is not a branch in any business, trade, or profession where the party of the second part—the employee—will give so much as in show business. Give a performer a little encouragement, and he or she will give even blood. It is traditional. So conscientious are most performers that when asked to cut their act, the performers usually resent it.

Eddie Gamble got me to sign two contracts for September 6, assuring me of his cooperation so that the time of appearance would not conflict at either place. Being the director of the show at the Coliseum, he could arrange to put me on early or late to suit the time of availability. He also helped me to procure an extra windlass from a shipyard, since I had to set up two separate riggings.

Coincidentally, the Ringling Bros. and Barnum & Bailey Circus hadn't been in this territory since 1942, but with railway transportation now eased up and labor shortage no longer an obstacle in making the long jumps to the West Coast, the Big Show was scheduled to open an eight-day stand in Los Angeles starting September 4.

By a special arrangement, the movie colony had bought the show at a flat rate for one day; the proceeds were to go to enlarge a local hospital. Screen actors were doing all the publicity and making personal appearances in the show to stimulate the business on behalf of this benefit performance on the eve of the circus's official debut. At one hundred dollars a seat, the funds raised amounted to nearly a quarter-million dollars and gave publicity to the show of equal value. The business was sensational during the entire stand: the public out here was hungry for circus, especially the Big Show after a six-year absence.

With all the goings on during the week, the town was ablaze with posters. The publicity campaign was on full force. The Thrill Show scheduled for the day in the Coliseum received its share of attention. Press agents also had arranged a couple of guest appearances for me to be interviewed on the popular radio programs. The beach was also publicizing its special added attraction on the occasion of its closing day and ran ads in the dailies with a picture of me suspended by my teeth. At any rate, I was properly in circulation during that week.

But the biggest stunt the Coliseum pulled off was to televise the entire performance. It had been announced over the channels in advance (and this hurt the attendance badly). With a seating capacity of over 110,000, there were lots of vacant spots. It always dampens the spirit of a performer to see blank sections. And when I checked on my rigging just before the show, I felt somewhat dejected seeing that the place wasn't packed. On my return toward the dressing room, I noticed a familiar face. Wracking my brain to place him, I knew the instant he spoke to me that it was Carlton Winckler, the great technician and stage director with Billy Rose's productions. He was now directing the lighting effects for television.

Something about Mr. Winckler's demeanor at once inspires the love and respect of those who come into contact with him, as I knew from the pleasant association with those well-conducted and disciplined organizations under his supervision. I was rather proud of the fact that he recognized me—so elated, in fact, that I had completely forgotten how weary my body was after the incident of coming in contact with a wall too suddenly only a little while before. During the matinee performance at Ocean Park that day, as I made the descent over the tops of concession buildings, I failed to clear completely one of the parapets. As I slammed against it, the impact almost knocked me cold, my limbs taking the brunt of the punishment. Though badly bruised all over, I was greatly relieved when emergency care and X-rays at the Santa Monica Hospital revealed no broken bones, and I was permitted to fulfill my obligation of two more performances that evening. My lacerations and cuts were invisible from the height and distance at which I worked. Having done my act at the Coliseum, a waiting car drove me back to the beach for my last frolic.

The next day I attended to tearing down the rigging at both spots, and, while I was bent on visiting the Big Show, I kept postponing it from day to day till the end of the week, the final day of the Hollywood stand. When Eddie Gamble told me that a certain party from the Big Show had been over to catch ours at the Coliseum, I was beside myself with . . . what was it, and what did it matter? Well, just that, had I known it in advance, it would have been easier on the committee's budget—yea, I would have gone on just for the satisfaction I'd have derived from it; more, I would have paid my own expenses! There are times when money is of no importance.

With events breaking in the foregoing succession, it seemed as if all my prayers had been answered. No longer hindered by that inferiority complex, I could now walk up to any of them with my head held high, my self-confidence restored. Surely they must have heard of my success through some channel!

I planned my trip so that I might have time to visit with the folks—my contemporaries and others whom I knew—before the show would start. It was about 6:00 PM when I approached the lot and headed straightaway for the back end. The lot seemed unusually small to hold the Greatest Show on Earth, but times had changed since I'd seen it last, taking a terrific leap over the last decade. New industries had sprung up during and after the war. With industry came people, and soon all the vacant lots were disappearing as gigantic factories were built over them and whole towns were built up around them. Housing projects and community settlements spread out over the vast terrain on the outskirts of the towns to accommodate the ever-increasing populace. The influx of human stream! Where do all these people come from? Surely, they must have left vacancies in their former habitations, these folks who had migrated into the state as if by mass exodus from somewhere. The availability of lots for the circus was getting scarcer and scarcer, and the circus was gradually forced to get in step with the times, cutting down on the size of the tents: the big top had been reduced from an eight- to a four-pole structure.

With the dressing room as my first stop in mind, I circled the big top, but except for some small tents for the band and wardrobe and a wagon stationed here and there with a curtain drawn across and a stepladder hooked on at the rear, presenting the old familiar sight of a star's or boss's private dressing or retiring room, there was nothing to be seen indicating what I was after. The pad room was much reduced in size, and as I looked in, its occupants—excepting the grooms—were 100 percent equine. "No dressing-room top!" said an attendant when I inquired as to its location. "They all dress under the seats in the big top!" he added, on seeing the puzzled look on my face.

Come to think of it, I had noticed the sidewall tucked up here and there, with groups of people seated or standing around trunks, which I had taken for rigging boxes. Well, this was something to cause consternation! I walked over to the nearest of what appeared to be cave dwellings, where a young woman was removing some tights from a cord stretched between guylines. But what shall my question be? I hesitated before speaking to her; I had to think quickly of something pertinent to the private lives of these nomads so that she might recognize the trouper in me rather than shy away as from a curious townie. "Yes, I've got it!" I said to myself. "I'll ask for someone on the show; but who do I know positively to be with it after so many years?" Somehow, the name Paul Jerome flashed to my memory—the first acquaintance I had made the day I began.

I was in luck! Paul was indeed still with it. The girl told me to walk around to the opposite side of the big top from where we were standing. "You will find most of the men there, clown alley, too!" she said. The women had evidently been given the side nearest the back door for protection.

It was a happy encounter between Paul and myself. True, I found him slightly changed, but who of us hadn't? He was still the same Paul to me, however, the one I have always held as the model of the circus gentleman.

Though only a clown, to me he symbolized the type of men—decent, upright in character—connected with that branch of show business. It flattered me to be recognized at once by him. "Here's Ira Millette; you remember Ira, and Albert Powell!" he said, pointing to the two comrades of many years' association.[1] Holding me by the arm as he did long, long ago, he called out a number of performers from adjacent caves he was sure would know me. Some old and some newer acquaintances were revived at this special reunion. He was about to show me how this newfangled dressing-room idea worked when a trio appeared.

"Hello, Paul!" said the taller of the two men of the trio.

"Hello, Red! Hello folks!" said Paul to them, then, "Red, meet a friend of mine, Tiny Kline. Tiny," turning to me, "Meet Red Skelton!"[2]

"Tiny used to be with the show," Paul continued, "And she was a great little performer!"

Always touchy on the subject of reference in the past tense, I promptly cut in: "What do you mean by 'used to be'? I still am. Why, only this past Monday, I took part in a show at the Coliseum!"

"What does your act consist of?" asked the comely young woman with the two men, who was introduced to me as Mrs. Skelton.

"Oh, I slide down a cable, hanging by my teeth!" was my modest reply.

"Are you the one who did that stunt going through a ring of fire? I've seen it on television; it was one of the. . . ."

By television one is known. I left them to look around for some others I might know. Somehow, it never occurred to me to inquire into Paul's intimate affairs. I simply accepted it as a fact that he never had any—that is, except that one which was to warp his entire perspective on romance forever. That one time when he brought Frances, the pretty, willowy blonde girl, on the lot to arrange for the privilege of having her travel on the show until they reached an agreement as to whether she would marry him in the Catholic faith or he would have to turn Protestant. There was no difficulty in getting her on—she could fill in wherever girls were used: in parade, spec, statues, or in Mrs. Bradna's "Act Beautiful" of posing horses, dogs, pigeons, and pretty girls holding garlands of roses around the ring. Frances was a sweet, innocent small-town girl, young and beautiful but with a will of her own. They had been debating on the subject, both holding out for the other to give in.

Imagine the surprise of everyone when, three weeks later, she and the bashful kid, Bobbie Fisher, a flyer in the Charlie Siegrist troupe, announced that they were married. It was a surprise to all but Paul; to him it was a tragedy to last a lifetime. He had never married.

My thoughts reverted to the huge trucks—as Paul described them, like immense floats. They had been conceived, probably, from the small-time medicine show mounted on wheels. Standing side by side, they unfolded huge wings which were braced up by poles to form the grandstand and reserved sections. While seating the audience on top, they served as dressing rooms underneath, accommodating about eight persons with ample room for their trunks, buckets, chairs, and what-have-you. While I felt nostalgic for the big dressing room where I could see the entire ensemble at a glance, my admiration went out to the one with the ingenuity to design this revolutionary invention. I didn't have to ponder long who it could have been when I remembered the stake-driving device run by motor; the safety chain-stringers which prevent the jacks from spreading and the seats from collapsing; the giant spool on which to wind and unwind the big top canvas and roll it with facility to any determined place on the lot. The name popped up from the past—Cap Curtis, the lot superintendent and big-top boss of the Al G. Barnes show back in 1938. Of course! Who else but him? All those back-breaking, labor-saving implements were his brain children—and now this baby.

A thought flashed to me: "Why, he must be here!" Simultaneously I set out to find his wagon, which I knew must be close to the stake and chain division—the roustabouts' hangout and gossip-exchange. As I ran between props and wagons, dodged stakes, and ducked under barrier-ropes, I could see ahead a group of the roughnecks surrounding this captain who was issuing orders. The show was to move after this, the last performance of an eight-day stand. Probably a large percentage of them were new hands, replacing those who had taken a liking to the Southern California climate and left the ranks of the big-top gang to become private citizens. The remaining hands had to be briefed on handling the task of striking the gigantic project, all the more difficult in the face of heavy traffic (in the midst of the movie capital). It was necessary to instruct the new buddies, who for the most part didn't know a bail-ring from a gim-pole.

It was like old times as Cap and I compared notes, happily chatting away. I didn't ask him about the seat trunks—there was no need to. I remembered a sketch he showed me ten years before, when the thing was still in the theoretical stage. While talking with him, it occurred to me how hard it would be to replace this man, a great genius in his field, yet so unassuming and calm—a man who never used a cuss word or raised his voice in handling difficult situations. He remained a gentleman while battling the elements against great odds and with an acute shortage of men; a man who spends his brief hours of relaxation in designing contrivances to meet the present-day demands for speed. In the midst of the crucial moments of raising the big top, he was never too tense to sneak up and say "boo!" when he'd see me standing somewhere with my back turned. He seemed to get a kick out of watching my reaction to having the wits scared out of me. I always gave a better performance when I saw him in the seats opposite my rigging. He was one of the people I was most glad to see again, Bill Curtis.

On my way to the back door again, I saw a huge figure of a man loom into view as he stepped down from one of the wagons.

"Well, Bob Reynolds! Bless your big heart!" was my greeting to him. What a pleasant feeling overtook me at the sight of this fellow, the boss of the propertymen, an able successor to Mickey Graves (who had also joined the departed big shots). Just how able he is, I should know, for it was he who set up the cable spanning Times Square for my big stunt back in 1932: a rigging job that required more nerve than the business of sliding across. Bob Reynolds was the only person I ever trusted with my rigging for security and judgment of angle without first checking on it before I performed.

"Whose wagon is that one, close to yours?" I asked Bob. "That's the bandmaster's—Merle Evans. You should know him," he said as if searching the past. And I did, indeed.

I hurried away to catch him before he left to take his place on the stand in the center ring for the concert. But there was no need for the rush. The band no longer plays the overture. Instead, there's an electric organ concealed at the far end of the big top that emanates the soft music—which struck me as more suited to a sacred concert than a circus. Yet strangely enough, it was soothing to the nerves of the agitated crowd, as kids scrambled for seats and agents proclaimed their traditional, "Peanuts! Popcorn! Soda-pop!" and sold balloons, toy monkeys on a string, and whips which the small-fry would flagellate over the heads of those seated around them. Soft music was needed.

All the years I have known Merle Evans left no trace of age on his face. This man seemed to have the secret of eternal youth. Not only physically but spiritually as well, for later, as I followed the progress of the performance, I realized the amount of energy he put into his work, not to mention the creative ability to select the proper music for each number to suit the tempo of the action and give it the proper atmosphere or dramatize the highlights. Without his musical interpretation, which intensified the high points, many acts would have fallen completely flat. Although he used the latest popular songs and dance music, his arrangements contained many shifts of musical moods. His artistic taste provided accompaniment that complemented each act to its highest degree. It was easy to understand why there had been no change in bandleader or musical director (as it is called today) during the last thirty years.

"Oh, Merle! How good to see you!" I exclaimed as he opened the curtain at the end of the wagon and stepped down.

"Well, Tiny! You old sonovagun, how are you?" I heard him say while his long arm spanned all of me as he squeezed me in a gesture of greeting. We began comparing notes. We recalled the days of ten years ago, when the acute labor situation forced us all to double in extra chores, including working in the cookhouse.[3] Merle was an expert pantryman, while I was one of the many waitresses. Some of the ladies—stars in the rings—washed dishes at mealtime. After finishing their act, the man on the flying trapeze and other kinkers had to sit it out till the end of the show at night for cherry pie and juggling—not balls—but trucks in the loading and unloading.

"Have you seen Margaret yet?" he asked presently. "She'll be tickled pink to see you. Just wait till she finds out you're around!"

For a moment, I had to consult my memory. Margaret? Of course, Margaret Mays, the English girl who had been the top model of the statue group in ring number three back in 1916. She was Margaret Evans now. He led the way to a shady little enclosure between two wagons; there sat Margaret, knitting as usual, only now it was Argyles for her maestro husband instead of the khaki socks we all worked on, in those days of World War I, as members of Circus Chapter of the Red Cross.

Visiting with Margaret, I saw Lizzie Hanneford, the widow of Ernie Clarke of the once-famous Clarkonians.[4] Her prodigious daughter Ernestine was around the grounds somewhere, a young matron herself now and retired from the circus since her recent marriage to a radio emcee. "Ernestine was just eating it up," in Lizzie's words, "to be on the lot again!" Ernestine was almost literally born in the ring and was in her own element here. Lizzie felt lost since her daughter's marriage and retirement. At heart she was still with it, taking her life at ease reluctantly. Both her brothers were carrying on the family tradition in separate units. Poodles, the once-famous comedy rider, now featured his daughter Gracie in the act. And the elder Mrs. Hanneford, the matriarch of this grand family unit of yesterday's fame, still carried on as the ring-mistress for her son and granddaughter. Poodles's wife Grace also participated. However, George, the other boy, did the most in perpetuating the family act and the name as well, boasting of two sons and a daughter who did all the riding. George filled in with clowning on the ground, with his wife as ring-mistress. Since both units used the same billing—"The Hanneford Family of Riders"—the public was often confused. Both were perfectly legitimate.[5]

I covered a lot of territory in a short space of time, visiting not only with the people on the show but other visitors like myself. For instance, I met Everett Hart, one of the Hart Brothers, a comedy tumbling act of long ago. In fact, his late brother, Tom, used to be my official guide during the first weeks after I joined out, when I wasn't with Mabel and Harry Clemings. Tom had taught me that half-somersault forward catching by my hocks while I was struggling to become an aerialist. Everett had turned to business here, but the circus had drawn us together. I had inquired of another clown who joined us for my favorite people, the Bradnas, and learned that they were spending their eighties at Sarasota, where Mr. Bradna passed most of his time fishing—his Sunday recreation in circus days, when the Chinamen usually benefited from the success of the catch. I wondered what his feelings must be when the show pulls out of winter quarters each spring for that grand opening in the Garden, like a retired admiral who stands on shore, watching the fleet weigh anchor. I learned that his retirement was actually forced upon him by an injury he sustained in a fall which crippled his back, and that he had finished that season on crutches.

That fabulous character, Mr. Bradna! Were I writing a novel instead of a memoir, he would be, without hesitation, my choice for the hero.

"By the way, who's the equestrian director on the show now?" I asked. Our friend, looking around, pointed in the direction of a figure conspicuous for the regalia he was wearing, which was a fairly good replica of the antiquated type of storybook ringmaster. "There he is, that's him—Springer!" As he mentioned the name, it had a familiar ring. "Springer?" I repeated after him. "Wasn't he the announcer with the Al G. Barnes outfit in '38?"

"He might have been, but I wasn't there. This is my thirty-sixth consecutive season on the Ringling show!" In his tone it was hard to distinguish the boast. But of course it was a boast. They were all proud of setting a record for continuance. After all, wasn't this the first in rank, the Big Show?

I left my two companions and proceeded in the direction of the top hat, red coat, white breeches, and black boots. The man wearing them was busily engaged chatting with a rather charming young girl—too absorbed to notice me as I approached, which gave me a chance to survey him at close range. Yes, it was the same man. I recognized him even with the mustache, which completed the character he was portraying. "I'm sure he'll remember me too!" I thought. "The time he used to tell 'em about me, in Ring One, saying, 'Watch her!'" I waited for the break in the soft slush he was slinging, too soft for a man his age. He finally turned around and we said hello.

Time was nearing for the show to start, and I wanted to pay my respects to the head of this big enterprise. That's what I would have done had Mr. John still been at the helm. Well, why not his successor—his illustrious nephew—who looks enough like him to bring back the pleasant memories?

At the office wagon, I was informed that Mr. North was touring Europe in search of new talent.

"What about his brother, Henry?" I asked, willing to settle for anybody of the same blood of the Greatest Showman That Ever Lived.

"He is visiting with friends out in the Valley!" was the reply. Craning my neck through the window, from white wagon to red wagon, not one familiar face did I see.

Now I had to see about getting in to see the show. There is an established custom to extend courtesy to the ex-troupers, admitting them through the back door without the requisites of complimentary tickets, but one must go to the general director in charge of the back end of the show and personnel to obtain his permission, which is usually granted. Still, this promised to present some complication; for one thing, the show was a sellout, and I was reluctant to ask a favor.

Running into Everett again, I explained my predicament. He said, "Why, it's a cinch. Just see Pat. He's over in that wagon."[6] He pointed to one with an awning attached. Under the extension on a cot reclined the kingfish in reference. "He'll take care of you!"

"But the house is packed," I told him. "They are turning them away out front—I've seen it!" I hesitated.

"Oh, don't let that discourage you. It's been like that every show. Still, I've managed to squat down someplace here," he said, taking me by the hand. "I was just going to see Pat myself. You'll see this show, or my name ain't. . . ." (At this point we arrived at the wagon.) "Hi, there, Pat! Look who's here!"

Pat himself escorted me through the door. The crowd was jammed on the blues. Every seat in the grandstand and reserves was taken. "Terrific business, Pat!" I remarked, wondering how he was going to conjure a place for me. He stopped in front of the reserves and told the usherette to have a chair brought in and placed on the bandstand for me. This was indeed an honor. And though the view was greatly obstructed by the cages transporting the beasts during the wild-animal act, I enjoyed sitting close by the performers' entrance, watching them come on and exit and occasionally flirting with Merle, who was standing almost within reach.

Near me I saw Springer, leading his fair companion to a chair which was placed next to mine. He wore the black cord around his neck, from which the shiny little whistle was suspended, and discharged the duties of both announcer and equestrian director. The whistle was blown per cue-sheet rather than giving the command. The program was expertly laid out and planned. It didn't take me long to arrive at the conclusion that the acts were synchronized with the music. No more muffing of tricks made to appear accidental in order to sell them to the public as intricate feats when accomplished. One act, however, got quite obnoxious in overdoing, taking more than its share of ad libitum to the point of imposing on the patience of the spectators. This was the ascent and descent of the lad in the highwire act. A similar hullabaloo over little merit was the swaying-pole. The applause that followed the conclusion of the latter was *positively* meant for Merle Evans; the musical accompaniment was a classical masterpiece for which he and his band should have taken the bow, not the man on the pole. As for the rope-walking to the wire, the audience applauded, glad it was over after so much horsing around. But here I dwell on what is insignificant as compared with the dazzling show as a whole. The first thing I noticed which added to its color was the usherette. She was gentle, neat, and trim in her natty uniform, presenting an eyeful to the spectator even before the show got under way. Although not an original idea, it was in this case economical, since these cuties, after the audience is calmly settled, leave their posts in charge of a small staff of male ushers and double in the aerial ballet.

For one accustomed to give the show rather than watch it, it is difficult to relax and enjoy it as a spectator. Knowing the countless details behind each presentation, one is interested in the technical points involved. Watching the setting and striking of riggings and props, I missed the clever gags of the clowns covering up that pause between acts.

I wished I might have seen that dusky-skinned animal trainer go through his routine with the cats. Judging by the applause, this Hindu was no slouch. The fact that he worked nude from the waist up, exposed to the sharp claws, added to the merit of his intrepid feats. Unfortunately, only the grandstand side could see this part of the performance. On the opposite side from the reserves, it was a blank because of the cages. But, as I understand, it was a step forward in public safety. The old-fashioned tunnel blocking the hippodrome track was really a menace in case of a disaster of fire or blow-down.

The jungle act over and the track cleared, the show got off to a fast pace. As it progressed, I became conscious of the fact that this was no longer the show as a *circus*. It was now a *production*. Not the show as it was whipped into shape in three days back at the Garden but one that showed many arduous weeks of rehearsal. It bore the stamp of the producer of a musical, a technique that's unmistakable.

"Why, this is *Jumbo* I'm seeing!" dawned on me all of a sudden. And as in a dream, everything had undergone a strange transformation.

Even the costumes: the show now dresses the entire cast, from the features down. No longer may the performers express their individual artistry in apparel, which sometimes drew the audience's attention to an otherwise mediocre act. Now the list of features is set up, and a special art designer is contacted. He looks over the style of wardrobe each act favors for its particular specialty, depending on the nature of the work, of course. The artist will then design the sketches following the original idea of the performer, but elaborating to compliment the wearer. The sketches are submitted for approval to the producer, after which they reach the costumers. Each member of the cast is measured for size; the costumer follows the design of the sketches. The acts of less importance, as well as the chorus ensemble, have to accept the creations as conceived by the artist or the producer, a theme to correspond with some idea in relation to the number or scene. This has been the procedure of stage productions until recently, when the glamorizing bug bit the circus. All this marked improvement over the old custom of leaving the acts to furnish their own costumes according to each one's taste and choice. No longer would it be a source of bad blood among performers aroused by copying another's ideas of a particular style in wardrobe.

The acrobats made a very effective display as the various troupes marched in a long line, dressed in brightly colored costumes, all exactly alike. They took their places in the rings and finished simultaneously. The same method was followed through every number, except when there was a special motive for featuring an act among others. They were identified by the lavishness of the costume. This arrangement, plus strong lights focused on the select subject, naturally faded out the other acts. For instance, an aerial-novelty number featuring a trio working above the center ring was dressed in an attractive, light wardrobe and tights. Four other acts appeared in the same number, including Albert Powell in a swinging-trapeze contortion and Ira Millette, head-balancing specialty, all wearing drab-blue overall effect. As they passed where I was seated, I mistook them for propertymen. Not until they were aloft did I realize who they were. The only act that received the attention was the trio in the center. The others . . . well, *I* knew they were there.

There was a familiarity to this staging. Behind such skilled production I knew there must be a great mastermind. With this sudden thought, as if by art or a genie, there before me stood Barbette. The very *unique* Barbette, onetime idol of Paris, who was featured at the Empire over eleven other acts doing a female impersonation in a very clever aerial act (I've seen the billing myself). Later, he was also one of the features in the *Jumbo* production at the New York Hippodrome. Now an instructor, he was in charge of the aerial ballet. Having heard that I was in the seats, he came over to say hello.[7]

As we talked, he told me I was a witch to have guessed that John Murray Anderson was responsible for directing and staging the entire presentation except for two numbers which, he proudly boasted, were his own creations.[8] One of them, the aerial number, was more than exciting—it was breathtaking. And though he was standing there beside me on the ground, I saw Barbette on every web, trapeze, ladder, and loop-the-loop.

While with *Jumbo,* whenever his trapeze needed new rope, he always called on me to change it. Feeling sorry for him having to depend on others one day, I offered to teach him the knack of splicing. He left me quite befuddled when he said that he didn't care to ruin his hands. We've had a good laugh over this every time we've met, when I remind him of it. Collaborating now with his sponsor, Murray, they made an ideal team; both were artists—first, last, every inch of them. It was gratifying to see him. There was something about this individual: "extraordinary" doesn't quite describe it. He was as enigmatical as the smile of the Mona Lisa. In his presence, one was conscious of a mystery shrouding this person, who, with his Oxford accent, also spoke French and German fluently and was rather tall, possessing a feminine softness, having unusually small hands and feet. Yet this Continental, as he would impress you, was actually a native of a small Texas community who got his start in show business as an adolescent by joining out with a troupe known as the Aerial Orfets doing iron-jaw and trapeze. My former agent, Charlie Nelson, told me the story, adding, "Barbette was the prettiest 'girl' of the troupe!" (He should know, since he was the troupe's agent at the time.)

Not only a great trapeze performer but also a wire-walker of grace and quality did Barbette turn out to be. Europe proved to be a fertile ground for his endeavors. There, he was built up as a feature not only for his talents but as a fashion plate in feminine finery for which he was unusually adapted.

From the first moment we met during the *Jumbo* production, there seemed to be a mutual feeling of friendship that sprung spontaneously between us. It must have been propinquity—both of us were engaged in the same line of work and interested mainly in our work. He was grounded now, yet in his proper element with the circus, taking the bow on his present act.

During the show's progress I began to draw up a summary of what it had to offer to make it stand out as first and greatest. Highest honors, of course, went to the juggler, Francis Brun. He was truly marvelous, and the musical accompaniment, a piece by Khachaturyah, was so well suited his fast and furious movements that it seemed the composer was inspired by this wizard's work to write it especially for him. I chalked up the juggler as the highlight of all the other acts.

The Christmas spectacle was tops in artistic achievement. Very elaborate and impressive, but it came too late to compensate for the void created by the absence of the grand entry—the proverbial spec—that used to start off the performance, as well as every heart a-bumping. Nothing could replace the first blow of the equestrian director's whistle, which caused the curtain at the back door to be drawn aside, followed by lights, the sound of the trumpets at the entrance of trumpeters on gorgeously caparisoned mounts, heralding the awe-inspiring procession of kaleidoscopic colors and designs beyond the wildest fancy of the imagination. The effect of this entry could be judged by the "ahs" and "ohs" emanating in waves from the spectators young and old. The weird-sounding music would send one and all to the faraway lands not to be found on any map: a never-ending stream of Oriental splendor with fantastic features, each different as if in competition attempting to outshine the other in richness. Next came rare species of beasts of burden with brilliantly adorned trappings, carrying the beautiful women of exotic charm, a spectacle which the clever lighting effects, makeup, and costumes helped to perfect as if touched by a magic wand. This is the feature that was sadly lacking to start off this 1948 edition of the Greatest Show on Earth. At long last, coming as it did in the middle of the performance, it fell short of the proper appraisal. Most of the audience—especially the moppets, who were already half-weary and half-disillusioned—were fidgeting in their seats, ready to go home. Before, it was always the spec that sold them the circus, putting them in the proper mood for watching the rest that followed.

And somehow I missed countless other items that go to make up the real spirit of the wholesome entertainment. The spontaneous and unpredictable capers of the clowns were now, too obviously, measured for time and action. Everything was done mechanically to so many bars of music.

The elephants' presentation that followed was, on the other hand, startlingly effective. For being daring, as far as the exhibition was concerned, I will say that it left me frozen in my seat. The march of the long line of bulls got under way along the track. They formed an endless chain with each one's trunk hooked onto the tail of the one in front in an extended row that any Rajah would have been proud to own, though I doubt if he could by any stretching of his imagination ever have conceived the idea of dressing up the procession as this line was, for the magnificent animals were adorned with scantily attired gals with bare legs, straddled on the necks of the elephants. That was certainly a new twist, for not even the bullmen rode them in this fashion; they always sat on the beasts' heads, with their legs together as on any seat.

Aside from the girls mounted on their necks, the elephants had no covers or trappings to detract from the attraction (if it was intended to be that). The jogging and rolling movement—the natural gait of elephants—caused the girls to appear to be doing bumps all the way around the track. Their faces were directed toward the audience in a perpetual smile—the old stage-smile—and their hands held to their hips heightened the effect, leaving no doubt in anyone's mind that it was anything but deliberate and definitely so: burlesque transposed to the big top. And these very changes I saw in the Big Show were the influence of Broadway and Billy Rose, who is Mr. Broadway in person, and, of course, John Murray Anderson, who had done all of Billy Rose's shows.[9] Now the Big Show has gone Broadway under his direction.

I had barely recovered from the shock of the elephant entry when, almost on its heels, followed the next jolt to fairly lift me out of my shoes. This time my doubts were aroused whether I might be a prude or just too old-fashioned to accept drastic modernization. There may have been a difference of opinions and views relative the spectacle in reference, but I have only caught it from the angle described in the following lines.

The Circus Ball, a colorful potpourri with the entire cast participating in the dance frolic, spread out over the big top from end to end—in the rings and on the track. The scene as a whole resembled a Mardi Gras or Carnival. The tall showgirls were dressed in "Gay Nineties"–style evening gowns with plunging necklines, which showed up their amply endowed flaming youth. Each one danced with a dwarf partner, who reached up to her pelvis in height. This too seemed crudely obvious. As if that were not pointed enough, however, there was a burlesque facsimile of glamor girls, impersonated by the taller clowns using their white makeup and wearing the same-style gowns with built-in padding to simulate breasts of exaggerated proportions, ridiculously overlapping the décolleté bodice. While it is true that such farce isn't new, having been used innocuously by buffoons before, this situation became suggestive in the confusion. It was difficult to discern at some distance the straight from the travesty, presenting a rather risqué caricature for children or older people with impaired vision.

Whatever there was of beauty and merit in the spectacle had been counteracted by the crude effect it created for the average attendant, in whose mind the circus is established as an institution of clean fun and entertainment for all the family. I sat there dumbfounded, wondering if what I saw marked the general trend the circus shall follow in the future, or if this alteration was just a miscarriage of a new idea as an experimental venture. It is my opinion that it was a lamentable state of affairs—almost a sacrilege to the noble institution, so typically American and so dear to the heart of every child and grownup who remembers the circus as the first big thrill of his life.

It is lamentable indeed to infuse the chaste and easy-to-follow entertainment as it has hitherto been known with newfangled, sophisticated bits of olio suitable for the Folies Bergere or an ultra-blasé Broadway extravaganza where out-of-town sightseers or tired businessmen go in search of recreation and spice to pep them up. And no matter how subtly it is dressed, the slip shows.

Not having seen the Big Show for a number of years, the change—positively revolutionary—was difficult for me to accept. The circus had always been the one big event of the year which season after season brought the greatest joy in the way of amusement to the people in the big town and the small hamlet alike. I felt a lump in my throat realizing that it was passing—this circus that had captured the imagination of kids from the great metropolis to the western farmland. It had now been streamlined and overhauled beyond recognition and interspersed with innuendoes that tended to confuse the impressionable minds of the small-fry.

The street parade had been eliminated some years back. The draft horses had disappeared, giving way to powerful tractors to haul the paraphernalia between train and lot. There wasn't much left to see of the Big Show for free, but the circus itself, under the big top, had remained a bona fide show of a quality and standard that characterized it for over three generations and had taken many years of bitter struggle on the part of the early pioneers to build.

With the circus gone high-hat and *mondaine* on par with any musical production, what was there for the child to look forward to in the way of a treat? The circus—as I had just seen it—was certainly not planned to amuse the innocent mind.

The circus heretofore was unique in its construction; with all the other shows and amusements of many varieties in New York City, the stockbroker and pushcart vendor alike waited for the coming of the circus to give the family a treat to watch their young ones' eyes open wide with wonderment at the sight of that big parade, the rapture almost bursting their little chests. Well, the circus was growing up; it had been learning about the birds and the bees.

The circus should never have to grow up but eternally remain a myth, a Peter Pan,[10] a symbol of purity—to let us live again for the duration of the three hours of each year in the happy joyland of childhood as we watch the beautiful lady dancing on the back of the white horse; the strong man holding up a three-high; the elephants carrying the beautiful queens and princesses seated in a houdah under a gold minaret; and the clowns doing funny things ad lib, without counting the eight bars of music allotted to complete some gag.

It would be an injustice on my part if I failed to mention that while looking around the lot earlier, I noticed another innovation added to the multiple changes: septic tanks on wheels, individual trailers stationed in strategic points here and there on the lot with conservative lettering: "Men," or "Women," on each. This I found to be the greatest improvement, modernizing the old-fashioned donniker of the Chick Sale model, where one had to share this intimacy with three others—leaving much to be desired, not to mention the discomforts of having to wait for its construction on days when the show was late in arriving. These private tanks are now the first on and the last off the lot; and no doubt the workmen count it as a blessing. This improvement very likely extends to the connection (the passage between menagerie and big top) as well, for the public's comfort—so clean and sanitary, especially for big towns where the show remains several days on a stand.

The show was over! Nothing but the sideshow was open for those who cared to linger longer on the midway. No more concert—another tradition in circus history gone with yesterday. But then, with the basic factor, the slow, primitive way of tearing down, the cause for its original existence now removed, this aftershow would only slow up the pace in getting off the lot but pronto. The crowd dispersed in no time. Each section had an emergency exit at the top row, descending by steps on the outer side, and most of the spectators availed themselves of the convenience, leaving by that medium. The sidewall already dropped, I went to visit some more—that is, it had been my intention to, but alas! Not a kinker was left on the lot; they had gone. Indeed, the dressing rooms had already disappeared: the seats on top turned down, the giant wings folded against the sides of the trucks on powerful hinges, the vans started off. As if by magic, everything just vanished—before my very eyes—leaving me confounded with wonderment at this lightning speed. The lights went out, and the big top was being lowered when I looked again: nothing but a line of trucks, rolling, gradually leaving the lot.

It is significant, I think, that it never occurred to me to ask of any of the folk *where they went from here.* The answer seemed to be nowhere. The real Big Show was dead.

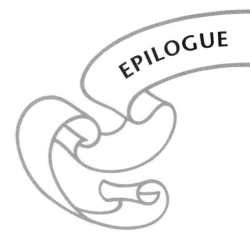

THE SHOW—
THE PUBLIC—
UNTO THE END

Mrs. Corning, in the next house, heard the crash as I came tumbling down when the nail I was trying to dislodge from the canopy over the back door suddenly gave way under the clawhammer.[1] I went east, the ladder, west—both in a race downward. Looking across over the low picket fence separating our properties, one glimpse presented the picture. Like the good neighbor she was, she rushed over immediately, finding me moaning while sitting on the ground leaning against the cement porch to which I had fallen. Badly shaken up, still I was conscious of having landed upright like a cat—my right foot hit the cement floor violently before I buckled and rolled over backward off the edge I was now hugging.

"Are you badly hurt, Mrs. Kline?" she asked with concern. "Had I better call a doctor?"

"Oh, no, no! Just let me revive, I'll be alright." And even as I said this, I felt sick in the pit of my stomach, aching from head to foot.

By now, Mrs. Boone, from the other side, had also come over. She was trying to help me to my feet—in vain. Meanwhile, Mrs. Corning got her car, and we were off to the emergency hospital.

"Just like old times!" I thought, remembering all the accidents of the past.

"Now, this isn't going to hurt!" the doctor assured me, and with that, he proceeded to probe the injured area with fingers that gripped like tourniquets. Wincing with pain, I tried to control my grimaces—still showing off my valor, if only before a doctor.

"No bones fractured!" was his consoling report. At the same time, he told me that it would be some months before I would be able to walk on that foot.

"But why didn't you give your full name and state your former occupa . . . I mean, your occupation?" asked Mrs. Boone the other day when she visited me. (She had heard me answer the questions the nurse asked when filling out the report: "Mrs. Kline—housewife.")

A smile crossed my agonized face as I continued flexing the stiffened ankle—the exercise recommended by the medico, which was extremely painful. Yet I couldn't help smiling. My imagination was working overtime. There, before me, I could visualize another ridiculous situation I might have been placed in, had not my presence of mind intervened, averting it—and just in the nick of time.

Those reports are turned over to the authorities; anything newsworthy reaches the press. Always hypersensitive, I used to wilt at the derision of associates but abhorred most of all the press agent's slant at satire in connection with my work. The reaction of the public, its opinion—that's what counted. Today, no longer in the profession, my publicity value has diminished to the minimum. However, there is a humorous angle to this incident, not likely to have escaped the triggerlike wit of the news reporter.

How should I have felt reading in the local news (yea, probably even picked up by the syndicate)—I can see the headline as plainly as day: "Ace-Woman Aerialist Falls from Five-foot Stepladder—Is Seriously Injured."

And would my face be crimson with shame!

The End

APPENDIX A

SUPERSTITIONS

Even in this day of enlightenment, superstition among show people is too deeply ingrained to shake off as so much humbug. The list of premonitions is endless. However, by giving a few examples of their significance, the layman may get a proper perspective of the impact these have on the believers and why. In each example the omen is italicized.

No further proof of appreciative value is needed when one checks back to Leitzel's fatal fall on *Friday the Thirteenth*. Or Otto Kline's last ride—wearing a *yellow* shirt and expiring in ward number *thirteen,* where he was placed for medical aid at Bellevue Hospital. Canaries were always banned as pets to be taken on tour because of their color.

Forgetting something essential to the act, in the dressing room or elsewhere, is another ill omen. Returning to retrieve it, one usually sits down long enough to count to ten to thwart the jinx; but in my experience the antidote never worked. Conscious of the slip all during the performance, some mishap was bound to occur.

Whistling in the dressing room absentmindedly one day resulted in the snapping of a guyline, jarring my trapeze during the performance to the extent of injuring my back—a displaced vertebra is mute testimonial to the incident. The evil supposedly affects the one nearest the door; I was alone in the room. Leaving the dressing room, I turned around three times and expectorated, which is supposed to counteract the hoodoo; it didn't! However, on other occasions, I have forestalled many a disaster by taking extra precautions on ominous days and signs; a last-minute check of the rigging revealed dangerous flaws, which proves there is some basis to these creeds.

Someone looking in the same mirror over one's shoulder is as bad as breaking one. A colleague sharing a dressing room with me couldn't resist the urge to peek at herself in my mirror over my shoulder when passing; the next day I received a death notice of someone dear to me. *Peacock feathers* were tabooed for ages in some shows.

Singing "Marble Hall" or "Home, Sweet Home," behind the scene by any member of a stage production was a sure sign that the show would fail and fold up soon afterward.

Unlucky month: everybody has one. Misfortune strikes at a specific time of the calendar; February is my nemesis. The dateline of every serious accident to befall me bears out this fact.

There are good omens also, as when the time Gracie White (later Poodles Hanneford's wife), on the night of her debut in the riding act, entered the ring and smack, dab! She *stepped into horse droppings,* soiling her nice clean pumps; the elder lady Hanneford jubilantly portended it would bring her luck. She married Poodles that same season.

Some beliefs are national, others international, while still others remain regional. At one time, while with a small circus in Cuba, I used "La Paloma" as musical accompaniment in my act; the manager requested me to change it for another piece. Another time business had been bad for a spell and continued so even after weeding out and dismissing all *crosseyed members.* I was quite puzzled one day at seeing the workmen lower the big top, reverse the canvas, and then set it up again—inside out—as a measure to offset the *hard luck* which had been stalking the show. Strangely enough, the business improved immediately after this operation; it would be unfair of me to say that the changing of territory had not been a contributing factor, in part, at least.

John Murray Anderson, famous producer and director of shows and extravaganzas such as the Ziegfeld Follies, Billy Rose's presentations, and of late having been responsible for the lavish arrangement and display of the glamor department with the Ringling Bros. and Barnum & Bailey Circus, will wear the same suit of clothes all through the time of rehearsal—be it one or three months—that he wore on the day he was summoned by the management to discuss the plans of the show. Although a person of extraordinary refinement and otherwise a man of good taste and fastidious dresser, he *will not change that attire until the show has opened,* after which he will dispose of it by burning it. At these rehearsals he gradually assumes the characterization of a tramp-comedian, especially when the time drags on as it did with the production of *Jumbo*—over six months. By then, his pants were almost in tatters, and one couldn't tell the original color of the material for the dust and grime it had collected, first in the dingy Manhattan Opera House and later in the Hippodrome, where the construction work of changing the building from theater to arena was in progress. But he staunchly stuck to his superstition. Needless to say, his shows were always successful.

NOTES

Abbreviations

The following abbreviations appear throughout the notes:

BB	*The Billboard*
BRTC	Billy Rose Theatre Collection, New York Public Library for the Performing Arts
BW	*Bandwagon: The Journal of the Circus Historical Society*
CWM	Robert L. Parkinson Library and Research Center, Circus World Museum, Baraboo, Wisc.
NYT	*New York Times*
V	*Variety*
VO	*Variety Obituaries,* 8 vols. (New York: Garland, 1988)

Introduction

1. "Shrine Circus to Honor Allies," *Los Angeles Times,* September 8, 1942, A12.

2. Ship Manifest for *Ultonia,* arrival date: January 31, 1905, Ellis Island, retrieved August 17, 2005, www.ellisisland.org; Tiny Kline, "My Will and Testament," January 28, 1963, Superior Court of the State of California for the County of Los Angeles, County Records Center, Los Angeles; Editor's telephone conversation with Sheila McKay Courington, May 10, 2004.

3. My thanks to Bob Cassens, Dessa Cassens, and Kalman Incze for their generous help in trying to track down Kline's birth records in Budapest. Kalman Incze of Budapest also contacted the Hungarian Association of Acrobats to no avail. Based upon the ship manifests at www.ellisisland.org, I thought that Kline might have been born in Mateszalka, Hungary, not Budapest. However, I scoured the Mateszalka birth records at the Church of Latter-Day Saints Family History Center and, alas, found nothing.

4. Elizabeth Ewen, *Immigrant Women in the Land of Dollars: Life and Culture on the Lower East Side, 1890–1925* (New York: Monthly Review Press, 1985), 21.

5. "Tinker Bell Brings Never-Never Land to Disneyland," *News from Disneyland* (press release), 1962, 1 (courtesy of Rebecca Cline, Walt Disney Company Archives, Burbank, Calif.); Ship Manifest for *Ultonia*; Editor's telephone conversation with Sheila McKay Courington, May 10, 2004.

6. Kline's status as a child immigrant without a guardian serves as the biggest

clue to concluding (tentatively) that she arrived at Ellis Island on January 31, 1905. The ship manifest for the only other possible arrival date—August 29, 1904—notes that Helen Deutsch, age fourteen, met her father Leopold Deutsch in New York City. Furthermore, nearly illegible notations next to Helen Deutsch's name on the 1905 manifest suggest that she arrived with a group of performers. Although Kline's grandniece remembers her grandmother, Fanny Tabory, telling her that she and Tiny arrived in America together, there is no record of the two traveling together from Hungary. In addition, a manifest for Fanny Deutsch, also hailing from Mateszalka, Hungary, and also departing from the Croatian port of Fiume, dated January 25, 1906, shows that the thirteen-year-old "Hebrew" tailoress was to stay with her sister, Helen Deutsch, in New York. Ship Manifest for the *Slavonia,* arrival date, January 25, 1906; Ship Manifest for the *Kroonland,* arrival date, August 29, 1904, retrieved August 17, 2005, www.ellisisland.org; Editor's email correspondence with Sheila McKay Courington, August 17, 2005.

7. Kline, "My Will and Testament."

8. Jenna Weissman Joslit, *The Wonders of America: Reinventing Jewish Culture, 1880–1950* (New York: Henry Holt and Co., 1994), 35–36, 172–75; Joslit, *A Perfect Fit: Clothes, Character, and the Promise of America* (New York: Henry Holt and Co., 2001), 107–8.

9. Nancy B. Sinkoff, "Educating for 'Proper' Jewish Womanhood: A Case Study in Domesticity and Vocational Training, 1897–1926," *American Jewish History* 77.4 (June 1988): 576.

10. Clara de Hirsch, the German Jewish baroness who founded and provided major funding for her eponymous charitable organization, had never been to the United States.

11. *Clara de Hirsch Home for Working Girls,* pamphlet, "Extract from Certificate of Incorporation of the Clara de Hirsch Home for Working Girls," 1897, p. 4, Ninety-second Street Y, New York, courtesy of Steven W. Siegel, library director and archivist.

12. See Louise Levitas Henriksen with Jo Ann Boydston, *Anzia Yezierska: A Writer's Life* (New Brunswick, N.J.: Rutgers University Press, 1988); and Carol B. Schoen, *Anzia Yezierska* (Boston: Twayne Publishers, 1982).

13. Anzia Yezierska, *Bread Givers* (1925; reprint, New York: Persea Books, 1999), 162.

14. *Clara de Hirsch Home for Working Girls,* pamphlet, 12.

15. Sinkoff, "Educating," 580–85.

16. Riv-Ellen Prell, *Fighting to Become Americans: Jews, Gender, and the Anxiety of Assimilation* (Boston: Beacon Press, 1999), 24.

17. Ibid., 52–53.

18. Ibid., 37.

19. "First and Final Account, Report, and Petition for Distribution, for Statutory Attorney's Fees, and Extraordinary Attorney's Fees, and Approval of Sale of Properties," p. 9, Tiny Kline Probate Records, Los Angeles County Court Records.

20. Editor's telephone conversation with Sheila McKay Courington, May 10, 2004.

21. See Kathy Peiss, *Cheap Amusements: Working Women and Leisure in Turn-*

of-the-Century New York (Philadelphia: Temple University Press, 1986); Harvey Green, *Fit for America: Health, Fitness, Sport, and American Society* (Baltimore: Johns Hopkins University Press, 1986), 246.

22. Robert Allen, *Horrible Prettiness: Burlesque and American Culture* (Chapel Hill: University of North Carolina Press, 1991).

23. Laura Browder, *Slippery Characters: Ethnic Impersonators and American Identities* (Chapel Hill: University of North Carolina Press, 2000), 3.

24. "The Circus Colossal, Combining the Two Unequaled Institutions of the Amusement World, Ringing Bros. and Barnum & Bailey Combined Shows," *Magazine and Daily Review,* road ed. (N.p.: Powers Engraving Co., 1919), CWM.

25. Helen Duchee and Otto Klein, Certificate of Marriage, March 17, 1915, Clerk of Orphans' Court, Marriage Record Department, County of Allegheny, Pittsburgh.

26. M. Alison Kibler, *Rank Ladies: Gender and Cultural Hierarchy in American Vaudeville* (Chapel Hill: University of North Carolina Press, 1999), 1–21.

27. Janet M. Davis, *The Circus Age: Culture and Society under the American Big Top* (Chapel Hill: University of North Carolina Press, 2002).

28. Bob Gettemy, "Aerialist Tiny Kline Thrills Crowds at 71," *Los Angeles Times,* July 23, 1961, OC1.

29. "Tiny Kline Uncorks 1,000-Foot Descent Thriller at Playland," BB, week of August 1, 1931, 34.

30. Leonard Traube, "Tiny Kline Laments," BB, February 13, 1932, 61.

31. "Seeks Job by Aerial Feat," NYT, October 22, 1932, 17.

32. Qtd. in Gettemy, "Aerialist Tiny Kline Thrills Crowds at 71."

33. Marcello Truzzi, "The Decline of the American Circus: The Shrinkage of an Institution," in *Sociology and Everyday Life,* ed. Marcello Truzzi (Englewood Cliffs, N.J.: Prentice-Hall, 1968), 315, 319.

34. Editor's telephone conversation with Sheila McKay Courington, May 10, 2004.

35. See Elaine Tyler May, *Homeward Bound: American Families in the Cold War Era* (New York: Basic Books, 1986).

36. "City History," City of Inglewood, retrieved August 19, 2005, http://www.cityofinglewood.org/about/city_history.asp.

37. "Inglewood Demographics Census 2000" (sidebar), City of Inglewood, retrieved August 19, 2005, http://www.cityofinglewood.org/depts/pw/gis/default.asp.

38. "Blockbusting" refers to a particularly devious practice among realtors that contributed mightily to postwar white flight: agents would approach white homeowners to inform them that their neighbors were selling their houses to people of color. In the tense landscape of American race relations, such comments were frequently enough to trigger panicked residents to sell their homes to the realtor far below market value. The realtor, in turn, would sell these houses to people of color far above market value, thus earning a hefty profit. See Thomas Sugrue, *The Origins of the Urban Crisis: Race and Inequality in Postwar Detroit* (Princeton, N.J.: Princeton University Press, 1997); W. Edward Orser, *Blockbusting in Baltimore: The Edmondson Village Story* (Lexington: University of Kentucky Press, 1997).

39. Editor's telephone interview with Olivia Grieco LaBouff, August 16, 2005.

40. "Inglewood Demographics Census 2000."

41. Editor's telephone interview with Olivia Grieco LaBouff, August 16, 2005.

42. Ibid.

43. Ibid.

44. Qtd. in Gettemy, "Aerialist Tiny Kline Thrills Crowds at 71."

45. Editor's telephone interview with Olivia Grieco LaBouff, August 16, 2005.

46. Frank Waters, *Of Time and Change: A Memoir* (Denver: MacMurray and Beck, 1998), 2.

47. Ibid., 11–13.

48. "First and Final Account," 6.

49. Editor's telephone interview with Olivia Grieco LaBouff, August 16, 2005.

50. Editor's email correspondence with the Disney archivist Rebecca Cline, March 30, 2004.

51. "Tinker Bell Brings Never-Never Land to Disney Land," 1.

52. Qtd. in Gettemy, "Aerialist Tiny Kline Thrills Crowd at 71," 7.

53. Anthony Lane, "Lost Boys: Why J. M. Barrie Created Peter Pan," *New Yorker,* November 22, 2004, retrieved November 1, 2006, http://www.newyorker.com/critics/atlarge/articles/041122crat_atlarge?041122crat_atlarge.

54. *Peter Pan,* dir. Clyde Geronimi and Wilfred Jackson (Walt Disney Productions, 1953).

55. Qtd. in Steven Watts, *The Magic Kingdom: Walt Disney and the American Way of Life* (Columbia: University of Missouri Press, 2001), 329–30.

56. To wit, another reference to the strange sexual reach of Tinker Bell: Bill King, who was convicted of capital murder in the dragging death of James Byrd Jr. in Jasper, Texas, mentioned in an interview that he has a Tinker Bell tattoo on his penis. Ricardo Ainslie, *Long Dark Road: Bill King and Murder in Jasper, Texas* (Austin: University of Texas Press, 2004), 101.

57. David Nasaw, *Going Out: The Rise and Fall of Public Amusements* (New York: Basic Books, 1993), 254.

58. "Tiny Kline," V, July 15, 1964, 53; "Rites Friday for Aerialist at Disneyland," *Los Angeles Times,* July 7, 1964, A2.

59. "First and Final Account," 8.

60. Josh Getlin, "Ball Has Dropped on Seedy Times Square," *Los Angeles Times,* December 30, 1998, A1.

61. Thomas J. Lueck, "A Group Tries to Attract Stores to Serve Times Square Residents, *New York Times,* March 7, 2005, 1B.

62. Getlin, "Ball Has Dropped."

63. Qtd. in ibid.

64. Pradnya Joshi, "Times Square Gridlock: With City Tourism on the Upswing, Civic Groups Seek to Ease Growing Foot Traffic," *New York Newsday,* June 2, 2005, A49.

65. "Episode #316: Ripley's Believe It or Not! Episode Guide," retrieved May 11, 2004, http://www.sonypictures.com/tv/shows/ripleys/database/ep_316a.html.

66. Kline, "My Will and Testament."

67. Editor's telephone conversation with Thomas Nebbia, June 2006.

Prologue

1. Kline never identifies this heinous book or its author.

2. Circus parlance for a candy vendor.

3. A "propertyman" is a versatile person whose multiple jobs can include setting up the performers' equipment (trunks, rigging, harnesses, etc.) or selling supplies on the lot.

Chapter 1: The Bend in the Road

1. Clyde Noble, the aerialist brother-in-law of Minnie Fisher (a.k.a. Minnie Noble), claimed that Minnie was the first to perform the iron-jaw act in the United States after witnessing the stunt in Mexico. However, this is likely an overstatement. The circus historian Steve Gossard notes that Mademoiselle de Granville, an aerialist with the Great International Menagerie and Circus in America in 1874, was described as "the lady with the jaws of iron." It is unclear whether her act involved lifting and suspension using (as Kline puts it) "teeth power." Performing with the W. M. Harris Nickel-Plate Circus in 1886, Monsieur and Mademoiselle LeStrange were described as "human butterflies" hanging by their teeth. And in 1879, the English aerialist Emma Jutau streaked down a cable while hanging by her teeth, reportedly reaching speeds of seventy-five miles per hour. England was also the location for the earliest reference to an aerialist lifting a heavy object by the teeth. Mademoiselle Senyah reportedly "held and swung a man" by her teeth in 1867; in 1868, the Coutellier Brothers spun each other around by the teeth at Tony Pastor's Opera House in New York. In the early 1880s the British Parliament considered the Dangerous Performances Bill, which listed a number of difficult acts—including women hanging by their teeth—that arguably should be banned. Although no such legislation was proposed in the United States, there are numerous references to the dangers of the iron-jaw act: "Accident at a Circus: Lottie Watson, the Woman with the Iron Jaw, Seriously Injured," NYT, July 1, 1885, 1; "The Iron Jaw Failed Her: Mlle. Anna's Terrible Fall from a Tight Wire," NYT, February 23, 1887, 1; "Trapeze Girl Breaks Neck in Fall," NYT, May 3, 1937, 21; Steve Gossard, *A Reckless Era of Aerial Performance, the Evolution of the Trapeze,* 2d ed. (Normal, Ill.: Self-published, 1994), 2, 16–19.

2. Kline defines the iron-jaw act accordingly in a footnote: "For the benefit of those unfamiliar with the term; it applies to (a) holding one's grip by the teeth bulldog-fashion, suspended in the air; (b) lifting another person's weight; (c) juggling furniture or tugging an automobile—in short, any work involving teeth-power. Best described when referred to in Spanish as 'fuerza dental.'" Tiny Kline, "Showground Bound," manuscript, CWM. Unless otherwise noted, subsequent quotes from Kline in the notes are from this manuscript.

3. The first Shrine Circus was performed on February 26, 1906, in Detroit. The show was sponsored by the local Shriners of Moslem Temple as a way to draw new members and to raise money. Attracting three thousand patrons in a small one-ring arena, the show was successful. Within a year, other local Shrine temples across the country sponsored their own circuses. The circus proved to be an ideal vehicle for the local orders, all of which were part of the Ancient Arabic Order of the Nobles of the Mystic Shrine, a fraternal organization founded in 1870 that was devoted to amusement, fellowship, and philanthropic pursuits. The Shriners were founded by two Thirty-second-Degree Masons, William J. Florence, a comedian, and Dr. Walter M. Fleming, a Masonic scholar and physician who was smitten with exotic and mystical orientalist imaginings about the Arab world. Consequently, members wore fezzes, governing structures bore quasi-Arabic titles, and temple names were based on Arab locales. Because Shrine shows performed in the winter, they provided a perfect job opportunity for temporarily unemployed circus performers. Local Shrine temples often sponsored circuses. The Polack Bros. Circus was created in 1931 by the impresario Louis Stern and Irving J. Polack, a former carnival and vaudeville operator. By the mid-1940s, Stern and Polack were so successful that they formed two units—Polack Bros. Eastern and Western. After Polack's death on July 13, 1949, his widow, Bessie Polack, attempted to keep the shows afloat with Stern, but both units eventually merged in 1958. John H. McConnell, *Shrine Circus: A History of the Mystic Shriners' Yankee Circus in Egypt* (Detroit: Astley and Ricketts, 1998), 1, 15, 134.

4. Historically, drag has been an integral part of clowning. In 1786, for example, the English clown Baptiste Dubois performed an act called the "Metamorphosis in a Sack," in which he seemingly transformed himself into a woman while tumbling around in a sack. See Janet M. Davis, *The Circus Age: Culture and Society under the American Big Top* (Chapel Hill: University of North Carolina Press, 2002), 169–79.

5. Joe Grimaldi (1778–1837) came from a theatrical family. According to a profile in the *New York Times,* Grimaldi's Italian grandfather first came to England as dentist to Queen Charlotte but became famous as an acrobat nicknamed "Iron Legs" because of his superlative leaping skills. Grimaldi's father was ballet master and "primo-buffoon" of Drury Lane Theatre and Sadler's Wells. When Joey was only one year and eleven months old, his father introduced him to audiences for the first time as a toddler tumbler. As a Little Clown in later Robinson Crusoe pantomimes, a monkey, and star of Mother Goose "buffooneries," he was immensely popular with English audiences for his comic acrobatic stunts and pantomime. The historian David Carlyon notes that the generic name "Joey" for clowns was likely a writer's creation years after Grimaldi's death, reflecting the nostalgic, child-centered turn of the Gilded Age circus (a dramatic departure from the raucous, adult-focused circus of the antebellum era). "Clowns of Then and Now," NYT, September 25, 1927, X6; David Carlyon, *Dan Rice: The Most Famous Man You've Never Heard Of* (New York: Public Affairs, 2001), 412.

6. "Trap" is short for "trapeze." The "cloud swing" is another name for the single trapeze, while a web act is an aerial performance using vertical rope (as opposed to the high-wire horizontal slack rope). The circus historians Steve

Gossard and Stuart Thayer speculate that the trapeze probably represented a synthesis of earlier aerial materials: the horizontal bar, the web, ring acts, and the slack wire. Gossard, *Reckless Era,* 8; Stuart Thayer, *The Performers: A History of Circus Acts* (Seattle: Dauven and Thayer, 2005), 138–39.

7. According to Kline: "I learned about 'tie-off' from a crafty old stagehand long ago. It is a safety measure against possible skidding of the endless rope through the bite or brake of the lever-lock under sudden jar or pressure. It consists of twisting both—up and down—ropes into each other (three or four twists will do it), inserting a peg in the center, and tying the peg against the shaft of sheaves."

Chapter 2: As Mrs. Private Citizen

1. Born in Breslau, Germany, Leopoldina Alitza Pelikan, a.k.a. Lillian Leitzel (1892–1931), was raised to be an aerialist. Her mother, Elinor "Zoe" Pelikan, and her aunts, Toni and Tina, performed in an aerial troupe known as the Vandis Troupe. Classically educated, fluent in five languages, and a concert-caliber pianist, Leitzel first tried her hand at aerial work when she was twelve years old after her grandmother took her on an annual visit to watch her mother perform. Leitzel began performing at age thirteen as part of her mother's aerial act. Upon arriving in the United States in 1908 to work with Barnum & Bailey, Pelikan's troupe decided to adopt the name of their American agent, Edward T. "Ted" Leamy. Known as the Leamy Ladies, the five aerialists performed their acrobatic routines on the trapeze, and Leitzel specialized in the stunt that would soon make her famous: the one-armed plange (or arm-swings) routine. In the winter season, after her mother and the other Leamy Ladies returned to Europe, Leitzel remained in the United States and played vaudeville, Broadway, and additional circus dates. She became a star after she signed on with Barnum & Bailey for the 1915 season. She remained with the show for the rest of her life. Fred D. Pfening Jr., "Lillian Leitzel: A Circus Diva," BW 47.3 (May-June 2003): 3–10; Gossard, *Reckless Era,* 24–26.

2. Leitzel's fatal fall in Copenhagen was big news around the world. See, for example, "Lillian Leitzel Injured: Circus Performer Falls 50 Feet as Trapeze Breaks at Copenhagen," NYT, February 14, 1931, 15; "Lillian Leitzel Improves: Circus Acrobat Has Concussion of Brain from Fall in Copenhagen," NYT, February 15, 1931, 8; "Circus Fall Fatal to Lillian Lietzel: Famous Circus Star Dead from Fall," NYT, February 16, 1931, 11; "Leitzel Burial to Be in California," NYT, February 18, 1931, 10.

Chapter 3: A Flight on Gossamer Wings

1. The correct spelling of the show's title is *Hip-Hip-Hooray.*
2. Simply known as Charlotte to her fans, the German-born teenaged skater was Charlotte Oelschlagel (not Oelschlager). Born in Berlin, Oelschlagel (1898–?) took up ice skating as an eleven year old on the advice of a doctor who recommended fresh air and exercise for the sickly child. Her health was immediately restored, and she eventually became a famous skater. Charlotte arrived in New

York at the age of seventeen in 1915 to star in the cabaret-style *Hip-Hip-Hooray* at the Hippodrome; she worked in the United States for the next seven years. Although she never competed, she was a pioneer in pairs skating with her later partner and second husband, Curt Neumann (Charlotte was previously widowed). Oelschlagel and Neumann applied several ballet maneuvers to ice, including the classic "dying swan" number. Charlotte also originated the eponymous "Charlotte stop" (a.k.a. the "Charlotte"), with leg held vertically. "Who's Who on the Stage," NYT, January 10, 1926, X4; Benjamin T. Wright, "The Best, from Henie to Albright," NYT, February 6, 1994, S08; Michelle Kaufman, "Gaining an Edge," in *Nike Is a Goddess: The History of Women in Sports,* ed. Lissa Smith (New York: Atlantic Monthly Press, 1998), 161.

3. R. H. Burnside (1870–1952) was a prolific producer, stage director, playwright, lyricist, and librettist. He also served as director of the Hippodrome from 1909–23. He entered show business as a callboy for Gilbert and Sullivan shows at the Savoy Theatre in London. He debuted as an actor playing a dog in *The Bohemian Girl.* Arriving in the United States as a stage director in 1894, he enjoyed a long career on Broadway and beyond. He also organized a cowboy spectacle for the New York World's Fair in 1939. He died when he was eighty-two years old. "R. H. Burnside," VO, vol. 4, n.p. (originally in V, September 17, 1952, 75).

4. Reviewers took note of the copious numbers of chorus girls in *Hip-Hip-Hooray.* According to Heywood Broun, "On the stage of the Hippodrome last night there were chorus girls enough to insure every freshman in Yale, Harvard, and Princeton a supper party. . . . There are folk, some of them theatre goers, who would rather have the shadow than the reality. There is no dream stuff in 'Hip-Hip-Hooray.' It has not an iota of scenic restraint. At worst it follows the notion that if you can get a certain fine effect with ten girls a ten times finer effect may be gained with one hundred." Heywood Brown, "Best Big Show at Hippodrome," October 1915, "Hip-Hip-Hooray" Clippings Book, BRTC.

5. Charles Bancroft Dillingham (1868–1934) was one of the premier theater producers during the first three decades of the twentieth century. Dillingham began his career as a journalist in his hometown of Hartford, Connecticut. After working in Washington, D.C., and Chicago, Dillingham entered the world of the theater as a drama critic for the *New York Evening Sun.* Dillingham tried his hand as a playwright in 1896 with *Ten P.M.,* which debuted at the old Bijou to unfavorable reviews. However, he established close relationships with influential figures in the theater business and consequently abandoned journalism to become a theater advertiser. Eventually he joined with Florenz Ziegfeld and Abraham Ehrlanger (who had since parted ways with his former partner, Marc Klaw) to form a powerful, multimillion-dollar triumvirate. Dillingham and another business partner, Howard Gould, built the Globe Theater at Forty-sixth and Broadway in 1910 and enjoyed nearly thirty years of virtually constant success in their oft-called "house of hits." Dillingham also ran the Dillingham Theater Group for solo ventures. He managed multiple famous acts such as Irene Castle, Dave Montgomery, and Fred Stone. Dillingham took over the Hippodrome from 1910–23. Handsome, kind, generous, and funny, Dillingham maintained excellent relationships with his actors and fellow producers. He was best known for his

NOTES TO PAGES 63–67   323

musical comedies, which one journalist characterized as "smart . . . beautifully dressed, nicely tuned, and with clean and clever dialog." Moreover, the same journalist noted that Dillingham "refused to smut up his shows to meet the growing trend toward the risqué." However, the Depression ravaged the theater business, and in 1933, the multimillionaire Dillingham went bankrupt—in no small part owing to his generous support of his financially troubled partner, Erlanger. Dillingham enjoyed a brief comeback later that year with *New Faces* but died of arteriosclerosis at the age of sixty-six. "Charles B. Dillingham," VO, vol. 2, n.p. (originally in V, September 4, 1934, 61).

6. David Montgomery (1870–1917) and Fred Stone (1874–1959) were hugely popular musical-comedy partners from 1895–1917. First appearing in blackface in vaudeville, they worked their way up to headliner status, earning approximately $150 per week in 1900. Their first musical comedy was *The Girl from Up There* at the Herald Square Theater in New York in 1900; in 1903 they starred in Hamlin, Mitchell, and Fields's production of *The Wizard of Oz* in New York after a highly successful run in Chicago in 1902 (Stone played the Straw Man [Scarecrow], while Montgomery played the Tin Woodman [Tin Man]). In 1906, they began their long-term business relationship with Charles Dillingham. Stone and Montgomery were also founders of the White Rats, an actors' union, in the 1910s. The partnership was cut short by Montgomery's untimely death at age forty-seven. Stone, however, enjoyed a sixty-four-year career in show business. He was born in a log cabin in Longmont, Colorado, and was an athletic, theatrical child who began performing a tightrope act with his brother at age ten. He joined the circus, where he honed his acrobatic skills. In addition to his later success in musical comedy, Stone also was an accomplished dramatic actor on stage and screen. His first Hollywood production was *Alice Adams,* starring Katherine Hepburn, in 1935. Stone's obituary in 1959 remembered him as an amazingly versatile performer: "Not only was he an accomplished acrobat, but he could cut a slick figure eight on the ice, do fancy rope tricks and even ride bareback, among other feats." "Obituary," VO, vol. 1, n.p.. (originally in V, April 27, 1917, 14); "Fred Stone Dies at 85," VO, vol. 5, n.p. (originally in V, March 11, 1959, 76).

7. Fred Thompson (1873–1919) was also the architect of Luna Park at Coney Island. His marriage to Mabel Taliaferro ended in divorce. See Woody Register, *The Kid of Coney Island: Fred Thompson and the Rise of American Amusements* (New York: Oxford University Press, 2001).

8. Reviewers likewise observed the plethora of chorus boys in *Hip-Hip-Hooray:* "And there were chorus men enough to keep the employees of a sport shirt factory working night and day shifts for one week and eight hours. That was the one sad thought we took away from the Hippodrome. We had never realized that there were so many chorus men." Brown, "Best Big Show at Hippodrome"

9. The homosexual performers whom Kline worked with in the early twentieth century were all part of a larger thriving urban world of "fairies," "inverts," "female impersonators," and "traders." The historian George Chauncey argues that homosexuals were generally more tolerated during the first third of the century than in later years partially because homosexuality had not yet been

rigidly codified as a pathological condition that was diametrically opposed to normative heterosexuality; rather, popular and scientific notions of a flexible "third sex" rendered homosexuals virtually unthreatening to established gender codes. George Chauncey, *Gay New York: Gender, Urban Culture, and the Making of the Gay Male World, 1890–1940* (New York: Basic Books, 1994), 9, 57.

10. Further information on Moctezuma remains elusive. Newspapers do not mention his participation in the Indian Village at the 1935–36 San Diego Expo. The Indian Village was eventually closed and turned over to the Boy Scouts owing to lack of public interest—a striking contrast to the Panama-Pacific Expo in 1915–16, where the Indian Village was a major hit. In 1935–36, the nudist colony at Zoro Gardens provided the exposition's biggest draw. Women "nudists" clad in brassieres and G-strings and elderly men cloaked in long beards and baggy trunks lounged about the exhibit. Despite protests from local churches, the Braille Club, and the County Federation of Women's Clubs, the titillating show remained. Richard W. Amero, "San Diego Invites the World to Balboa Park a Second Time," *Journal of San Diego History* 31.4 (Fall 1985): 261–79, esp. 265, 271; "Blind Protest Nudist Colony," NYT, January 24, 1936, 21.

11. John Philip Sousa (1855–1932) was the nation's best-known bandmaster and composer of marches in the late nineteenth and early twentieth century. Born in Washington, D.C., he enlisted in the Marine Corps, played in the band, and later became the Marine bandmaster. His compositions, "Stars and Stripes Forever," "Semper Fideles," and "El Capitaine" (among others) made him famous. During World War I, Sousa was assigned to take charge of all bands at the Great Lakes naval training station and was promoted to lieutenant commander. Even as an elderly man, Sousa displayed his vigorous showmanship in performance tours across the country. "John Philip Sousa," VO, vol. 2, n.p. (originally in V, March 8, 1932, 63).

12. Reviewers echoed audiences' enthusiasm for the "Ballad of the States" (or "Ballet of the States" or "March of the States," as the number was variously called), particularly in the patriotic milieu preceding the nation's entry into World War I: "And when they [Sousa's band] began to crash out the 'Stars and Stripes Forever,' there was a demonstration of cheering that almost lifted the roof off the house. The final effect shows the entire company covered as if by one huge star-spangled banner that spread over the entire stage." "The Theatre," *Globe and Commercial Advertiser,* October 1, 1915, "Hip-Hip-Hooray" Clippings Book, BRTC.

13. Not all audiences were enthusiastic, however. One Georgian who witnessed the "Ballet of the States" left angrily after seeing what he thought were the dancers representing Georgia. He told the *Macon Telegraph* that the Georgia dancers were wearing dresses depicting men hanging from trees. Newspapers across the South reprinted this article and vigorously denounced this Yankee show for supposedly poking fun at the southern lynch mob. Yet the Georgian had mistakenly thought that the Nevada dancers—who played happy-go-lucky divorcees wearing dresses containing effigies of their respective husbands while the band played, "I'm on My Way to Reno," and "Good-bye, Sweetheart, Good-bye"—represented Georgia. The actual Georgia dancers, unbeknownst to the Georgian spectator,

wore dresses depicting cotton in full bloom. "How Georgia Was Offended by the Unconscious Sousa," *New York Tribune*(?), March 15(?), 1917, "Hip-Hip-Hooray" Clippings Book, BRTC.

14. Publicity materials for Charlotte Oelschlager marketed this popular ice skater in a similar fashion, adding that ice skating was an androgynous sport: "This little book is intended as a stimulus and encouragement toward ice skating among Americans. It is intended as much for women as for men. There are no physical reasons why women should not skate quite as well as men. Skating is a matter of balance and grace, not strength. Young girls often become very expert skaters, doing all the difficult feats that men accomplish." "Charlotte, Hippodrome Skating Book, Souvenir," Three Hundredth Performance, March 22, 1916 (New York: Hippodrome Skating Club, 1916), MWEZ x n.c. 28,811A no. 19, BRTC.

15. Armando Novello, a.k.a. Toto the Clown (1888–1938), filed a libel suit of fifty thousand dollars against the *New York Daily Mirror* in late November 1938 for falsely writing that he had died a pauper after allegedly working as the highest-paid clown in the nation. Ironically, shortly after signing all paperwork concerning the lawsuit, Novello was rushed to the hospital for an abdominal obstruction. He died eleven days later on December 15, at the age of fifty. "'Premature' Death Libel Suit Ended by Toto's Demise at 50," VO, vol. 2, n.p. (originally in V, December 21, 1938, 47).

16. The composer Raymond Hubbell (1879–1954) got his start as a pianist, band leader, and staff composer in Chicago before coming to New York around 1902 to compose musical spectacles for the Hippodrome, the Schuberts, and the Ziegfeld Follies from 1911–14, 1917, and 1923–24. Hubbell was a founding member of the American Society of Composers, Authors, and Publishers in 1914. "Raymond Hubbell Dies at 75; Last Survivor of Group Founding ASCAP," VO, vol. 4, n.p. (originally in V, December 15, 1954, 71).

17. Gaby Deslys (1884–1920), the flamboyant French actress—perhaps best known for her romance with King Manuel of Portugal—died when she was thirty-six years old. "Gaby Deslys Dies after Operation," NYT, February 12, 1920, B1.

Chapter 4: In Pursuit of a Mirage to Yesterday

1. In Kline's words: "An unwritten law is practiced by show managers: intercepting and opening telegrams addressed to members of the cast received during the performance and withholding anything of a morbid or tragic nature, having tendency to interfere with the presentation, until after the performance is over. A measure of precaution taken to protect the interest of the audience, averting the confusion or panic as a result of the shocking news to the performer."

2. In addition to other newspapers, the death of Otto Kline was front-page news in the NYT, "Circus Rider Killed in Ring before 5,000," NYT, April 22, 1915, 1.

3. Cy Compton (1876–1944) was born in St. Joseph, Missouri. He joined Buffalo Bill's Wild West Show as a cowboy when he was eighteen and ascended the

ranks to become head man of the cowboy department. During Cody's second European tour (1902–6), Compton met and married his wife, Lillian (Lily), also a performer. After Cody's show disbanded, Compton was in charge of the Barnum & Bailey's Wild West aftershow concert in 1914, a position he kept for the next twenty-one years. From 1935–43, he performed at parks, fairs, and rodeos. He also produced Wild West shows for the Russell Brothers and Beatty-Russell circuses the year before he died suddenly of a heart attack at the age of sixty-eight. The cowboy actor Tex McLeod (1889–1973) achieved great success as a "Will Rogers–style rope-spinning monologist" in England, where he lived the majority of his adult life after performing at the Victoria Palace in London in 1919. He was born in Austin, Texas, and began a vaudeville career at the age of seventeen, winning acclaim as a rodeo rider in Wyoming, Oregon, and at the Calgary Stampede in Alberta. In addition to his work at the circus, he performed two seasons with Buffalo Bill's Wild West Show. McLeod died in Brighton, England, at the age of eighty-three. There is little readily available information on Sam Garrett. BB, January 26, 1935, Cy Compton Scrapbook No. 14, p. 35, CWM; "Tex McLeod, a Monologist in Style of Will Rogers, 83," NYT, February 14, 1973, 44.

4. Guy Weadick (1885–1953) was born in Rochester, New York. The youngest of five children, Weadick was thrilled to learn about life in the West from the scores of circuses and Wild West shows that passed through town, in tandem with stories his uncles told upon returning from the West. Weadick left home as a teenager and traveled to Alberta, Wyoming, Texas, and Oklahoma, where he worked as a rodeo announcer and a trick roper. In March 1912, Weadick and his wife, the trick rider Flores LaDue (Grace Bensell), returned to Calgary, where Weadick and a businessman friend organized the first Calgary Stampede, held from September 2–5, 1912, with twenty thousand dollars in prize money. This was the first of several stampedes that Weadick organized in Winnipeg, New York, North Dakota, and Arizona, among other places. According to Col. Bailey C. Hanes, Weadick "did more than any other to promote genuine rodeos." Col. Bailey C. Hanes, *Bill Pickett, Bulldogger: The Biography of a Black Cowboy* (Norman: University of Oklahoma Press, 1977), 53; Donna Livingstone, *The Cowboy Spirit: Guy Weadick and the Calgary Stampede* (Vancouver: Greystone, 1996), 2–3, 9–19, 32–36, 39, 45, 58–72, 117, 122.

5. Placed in the center of the page, the initial plea for an Otto Kline memorial ran as follows: "The grave of genial, magnanimous, kind-hearted, generous, open-handed, cordial Otto Kline is unmarked by any memorial from his professional friends and associations. This is not a reproach—yet. But the weeks and months are speeding by rapidly. What is to be done about it?" BB, August 14, 1915, 23.

6. For more coverage of the Otto Kline monument fund-raising efforts, also see BB, August 21, 1915, 23, and October 2, 1915, 6, 9.

Chapter 5: A Tour behind the Platforms of Those Strange People

1. Also known as the "opener" or the "talker," the spieler spoke to the crowds outside the sideshow tent as a way to induce them to buy tickets to the show.

2. Edward Arlington (1878[4?]–1947) was the son of the showman George Ar-

lington. Raised in the milieu of the circus and the theater, Edward worked as a traffic manager for Barnum & Bailey in 1903–4, in addition to other managerial positions. He purchased a half interest in the Frank A. Robbins Circus after James Bailey died in 1906. Like other showmen of his era, Arlington invested widely and frequently in the amusement business. After selling his interest in the Robbins Circus in 1907, he worked with Gordon Lillie (of Pawnee Bill's Wild West fame) and Buffalo Bill Cody. In 1908 he became half-owner of the Miller Brothers 101 Ranch Real Wild West. From 1913–15, the show was at its largest and featured celebrity attractions like the world heavyweight champion boxer Jess Willard and Buffalo Bill Cody. The Millers sold their portion of the show to Arlington in 1916. According to the circus historian Chang Reynolds, the Millers probably sold out because they were fearful that America's impending entry into World War I meant that transportation networks would be disrupted. Moreover, their ranching operations in Oklahoma (along with oil exploration efforts) were booming. Arlington remained an outdoor showman but also became owner of a lucrative New York City hotel. Michael Wallis, *The Real Wild West: The 101 Ranch and the Creation of the American West* (New York: St. Martins, 1999); Notes on Edward Arlington, George L. Chindahl Collection, CWM; *Miller Bros. and Arlington 101 Ranch Real Wild West, Magazine and Daily Review* (Cincinnati: Strohbridge Lithograph Co., 1914), n.p., Chindahl Collection, CWM; Chang Reynolds, "Miller Bros. & Arlington's 101 Ranch Wild West Show, 1907–1916," BW 13.1 (January–February 1969): 4–21.

3. The colorful Sam Gumpertz (1868–1952) was a central figure in the outdoor amusement industry. Born in Washington, D.C., and raised in San Francisco, Gumpertz was an athletic and musical child. He joined the Jackley family of acrobats at age nine as a top mounter; injured within months of his appointment, he returned to school. By age twelve, he was starring in stock-company productions at the Tivoli Opera House in San Francisco. Three years later, Gumpertz headed to Texas, where he became an accomplished sheepherder and cowboy. He then joined Buffalo Bill's Wild West Show as a cowboy and acrobatic rider. In his early twenties, Gumpertz became an advance agent with the Colonel Hopkins vaudeville show during the winter season and worked on the management staff of the Buffalo Bill or Barnum & Bailey in the summer. At the turn of the century, Gumpertz became an immensely wealthy amusement-park, theater, and minstrel-show impresario, first in St. Louis, and then assuming a major role in constructing Dreamland Park at Coney Island. He served as the park's general manager until it was destroyed by fire in 1911. Thereafter, Gumpertz purchased additional property at Coney Island and Brighton Beach and ran an amusement syndicate until 1932, when he became general manager of the Ringling Bros. and Barnum & Bailey Circus. His tenure was controversial, and he resigned in 1937, when the show was returned to the Ringling family. "Sam Gumpertz," *Banner Line*, October 15, 1971, 6–8, Periodicals Collection, CWM.

4. The Miller Brothers located their first 101 Ranch on the south bank of the Salt Fork of the Arkansas River in Kay County, Oklahoma. Eventually the ranch stretched over 110,000 acres and encompassed three working towns: White Eagle, Red Rock, and Bliss. At its height, the ranch contained twenty-five thousand head

of cattle, 250 employees, a zoo, and the largest bison herd in the world at that time. The show expanded wildly in the 1920s, employing 1,700 people and six hundred horses, but finally went bust in 1931, closing in Washington, D.C., amid the Great Depression. Wallis, *Real Wild West;* Hanes, *Bill Pickett,* 8, 49, 163.

5. According to Kline: "Annie Oakley, famous sharpshooter with the early Wild West shows, used to ballyhoo her act by shooting at bits of paper, for which the crowd would scramble to retrieve; any holder of a bullet-perforated stub would be admitted gratis at the entrance to the show."

6. Lucille Mulhall won the title World Champion Woman Roper, and her good friend and mentor Will Rogers called her "the world's greatest rider." In 1916, Homer Wilson was also the publisher of the *Wild Bunch* magazine in Mulhall, Oklahoma. In 1920 he won the multiple roping category at the Dewey Roundup. Hanes, *Bill Pickett,* 58–59, 147–48, 153.

7. Texas "Tex" Cooper (1876–1951) was a versatile cowboy, trick rider, sharp-shooter, and stage and screen actor. Cooper shot glass balls with bullets while riding a horse in the 101 Ranch and Wild West Show and starred as a cowboy on the New York stage. He was featured on Broadway in *Whoopee* and as a deputy federal marshal—a role he also played offstage in real life—in *Green Grow the Lilacs,* which dramatized the history of the Oklahoma Territory at the turn of the turn of the twentieth century. The busy actor appeared as an extra and in bit parts in hundreds of B-Westerns, including his last film, *King of the Bullwhip* (1950), in which he played Buffalo Bill Cody. In the vast majority of his films, Cooper received no on-screen billing, but as the movie critic Hans J. Wollstein notes, he was clearly recognizable by his "long white hair and florid mustache." "For the Guild and Good Old Oklahoma," NYT, March 1, 1931, X3; *NYT All Movie Guide,* accessed August 22, 2006, http://movies2.nytimes.com/gst/movies/filmography .html?p_id=14858.

Chapter 7: A New Leaf

1. Emil and Katherine Pallenberg were a husband-and-wife team of bear trainers and handlers. When the aerialist Lillian Leitzel complained that the bears were too close to her when she exited the ring and in their cages near her dressing tent, Pallenberg stolidly told Leitzel that "unmuzzled Russian bears have the right of way." This was, according to Robert Lewis Taylor, one of the few times that Leitzel acquiesced. Robert Lewis Taylor, *Center Ring: The People of the Circus* (Garden City, N.Y.: Doubleday, 1956), 239–40.

2. Arnold "Mickey" Graves (?-1944) was one of the most versatile people behind the scenes at the circus, as Kline makes clear throughout her memoir. According to his granddaughter, Michele Graves, Mickey immigrated to the United States from Ireland at age sixteen in the late nineteenth century and made a living doing odd jobs for about three years before he joined the Adam Forepaugh Circus. He worked as a stagehand and a boss propertyman for approximately thirty years. Editor's email correspondence with Michele Graves, May 23, 2003.

3. The transience of the workingmen (also known as "roustabouts") was such that show owners practiced a "holdback" system of pay, whereby circus manage-

ment would hold back a portion of the worker's wages each week until the end of the season. Given the strenuousness of life as a circus laborer, many looked at the job as a temporary one, a way to travel and see the world for as long as their bodies would hold. Circus routebooks often noted that muddy conditions could prompt dozens of workingmen to quit. Consequently, shows hired laborers wishing to "run away with the circus" throughout the season.

4. John and Charles Ringling were virtual opposites in terms of their management styles. John was more concerned with systemic circus operations, while Charles was deeply involved in the daily operations of the show. Both had their passionate supporters. By 1919, the two brothers were bitter rivals, and the family became factionalized. David Lewis Hammarstrom, *Big Top Boss: John Ringling North and the Circus* (Urbana: University of Illinois Press, 1992), 21–22.

5. Paul Jerome played a clown in "grotesque whiteface" with large, gaping buckteeth. LaVahn G. Hoh and William H. Rough, *Step Right Up! The Adventure of Circus in America* (White Hall, Va.: Betterway, 1990), 204.

Chapter 8: Where Caste Is Observed

1. Described by the equestrian director Fred Bradna as the "most beautiful performer" in the circus, Bird Millman (1890–1940), a dainty white woman with dark hair and fine features, was the first wire-walker to perform without constant use of a balancing umbrella. She also worked a wire seven feet off the ground and thirty-six feet long rather than the usual eighteen feet, which gave her ample time to dance, skip, and run while singing a range of popular tunes. Always "vivacious, charming, and a flirt," Millman saucily sang, "How Would You Like to Spoon with Me?" She serenaded and danced to other numbers, like "Aloha," with a chorus of eight voices singing from the ground. She finished her act with a flourish by running the length of the wire and jumping through a paper hoop. Millman was born Jennadean Engleman in Canon City, Colorado, into a circus family. Her mother, Genevieve M. Patton Engleman, and her father, John Dyke Engleman, were wire-walkers and flyers who toured with circuses and big-time vaudeville while young Jenny remained with her grandmother. (Apparently, John decided to change the family name because of its difficult spelling. He reportedly opened a dictionary and randomly placed his hand on the page. The name Millman stuck.) John taught young Bird wire-work and iron-jaw, a painful process accompanied by much crying. Jenny became "Bird" because of the chirping sounds she made and the naturalness with which wire-walking came to her. Bird performed with Barnum & Bailey from 1913–19, Ringling and Barnum from 1919–20, and with the Ziegfeld Follies during the winter season. Bird retired from the circus at the end of the 1920 season but continued to play vaudeville and on Broadway until she married a Boston businessman, Joseph F. O'Day, in 1924. After O'Day's sudden death in 1931, Bird moved back to Canon City to live with her mother and raise turkeys on her ranch. In early 1940, Bird was diagnosed with bone cancer in her spine. On August 5, 1940, she died—reportedly just as a flock of white doves fluttered away. In April 2002, the Fremont Civic Theater of Canon City memorialized Bird Millman in a musical bearing her name. Frank

D. Robie, "The Real Bird Millman," BW 42.6 (November–December 1998): 44–46; "Bird Millman," *The White Tops* 13.8–9 (June–July 1940): 17–19, Bird Millman GP File, CWM; Fred Bradna and Hartzell Spence, *The Big Top: My Forty Years with the Greatest Show on Earth* (New York: Simon and Schuster, 1952), 307, 313; Dexter Fellows and Andrew A. Freeman, *This Way to the Big Show: The Life of Dexter Fellows* (New York: Viking, 1936), 232; "Hopes to Cross Niagara on Tight-Strung Wire," *Washington Post,* April 1, 1923, 56; John Moore, "'Bird Millman' Flies Again in New Musical," *Denver Post,* April 7, 2002, 10F.

2. Zip . . . What Is It? was born William Henry Johnson (1857–1926) in Bound Brook, New Jersey. According to the historian James Cook, Johnson was likely the third man to play the role of What Is It? for P. T. Barnum, even though others have asserted that Johnson performed as the only Zip. Cook states that the first Zip was Hervey Leech in 1846 in London—where the fur-clad act's raw meat–eating performance of "savagery" was unpopular. The second popularized the act and was likely a mentally disabled African American man perhaps suffering from microcephaly. In 1867, an astonished Charles Dickens reportedly exclaimed, "What is it?" when he saw Zip perform in his shaggy savage suit and spear. Thereafter, the name stuck. Although press agents spun tales about P. T. Barnum supposedly rescuing Johnson from slavery as a child, Johnson's sister, Sarah Van Duyne, recalled that her parents and neighbors pressured her brother to work for Barnum's circus in 1877. Furthermore, federal census records show that William Henry Johnson of Bound Brook, New Jersey, was born in 1857. Sideshow scholars such as Robert Bogdan characterize Johnson's utter silence and oddly shaped head as signs of mental retardation, but as Kline suggests, Johnson was probably, above all, an excellent actor. Likewise, the showman Barry Grey remembered that Johnson had a superior memory and was able to recall precisely acts he had performed decades earlier. Johnson worked with Barnum & Bailey his entire career, but as he aged, he only worked New York–area dates, supplementing his income with summer gigs at the Coney Island freak show. After a career of performing in silence, the popular performer died at Bellevue Hospital in New York after a bout with bronchitis in 1926. James W. Cook, *The Arts of Deception: Playing with Fraud in the Age of Barnum* (Cambridge, Mass.: Harvard University Press, 2001), 126–29; Robert Bogdan, *Freak Show: Presenting Human Oddities for Amusement and Profit* (Chicago: University of Chicago Press, 1988), 134; "Zip, Barnum's Famous 'What Is It' Freak, Dies of Bronchitis in Bellevue; His Age Put at 84," NYT, April 25, 1926, 1.

3. Poodles Hanneford (1891–1967) also appeared in silent films with Mary Pickford and Charlie Chaplin during the 1920s. The Hanneford family has had a long and illustrious relationship with horse acts. One ancestor, Michael Hanneford, reportedly performed an equestrian act as early as 1621. Sy Syna, "A Family that Really Manages a One-Ring Circus," NYT, August 10, 1980, 19; Lisa Prue, "300 Years of Circus Tradition," *Omaha World-Herald,* December 5, 2002, 11GO.

4. Orrin Davenport represented the fourth generation of a family of equestrians that stretched back into the eighteenth century. At age eighty in 1916, his father was still actively training his family-based troupe of equestrians near Chicago, while Orrin's eight-year-old son was learning the family trade. "Pre-Natal Power in Big Circus Acts," NYT, April 23, 1916, 14.

Chapter 9: Equestrian Director Par Excellence

1. Born into a wealthy Strasbourg family with considerable brewing and banking interests, Fred Bradna (1872–1955) was an excellent gymnast and equestrian as a young man. See chap. 12 n.1 for more information on his entry into the circus, in addition to his romance with his future wife, Ella Bradna. Joining the Ringling Bros. in 1903, Bradna remained with the show for the rest of his long circus career. Wearing a silk hat, Prince Albert coat, white tie, whistle, and thin moustache, Bradna cut a striking and ubiquitous ramrod figure as the show's equestrian director. His precise commands punctually choreographed hundreds of animals and performers. In addition, Bradna was able to converse in multiple languages. Unfailingly disciplined and kind, he was enormously popular both on and off the circus. The Circus Fans of America, for one, named several local chapters after him. Bradna died at home in Sarasota, Florida, at the age of eighty-three. "Fred Bradna of Ringling Circus, Its 'Field Marshall,' Dies at 83," NYT, February 22, 1955, 21.

Chapter 10: The Awe-Inspiring Mr. John

1. Mable Ringling (1875–1929) was married to John Ringling from December 1903 until her death from diabetes and Addison's Disease in 1929. A "beautiful and well-dressed woman," Ringling was an active part of the social scene in Sarasota. She loved Italian architecture and played a central role in researching the design for the lavish family home, Ca' D'Zan, which was styled after a Tuscan villa. Fred Dahlinger, "1907: The Season That Set the Course of Circus History for the Next Century," conference paper presented at the 2006 Circus Historical Society Convention, Sarasota, Florida, May 7, 2006; David Chapin Weeks, *Ringling: The Circus Years, 1911–1936* (Gainesville: University of Florida Press, 1993), 25, 119–22, 167.

Chapter 11: Calibrating for a Career

1. In November 1916 (the same year Kline tried to find her beloved Shmoontsie), the SPCA accused its smaller rival, the Bide-a-Wee Home for Animals, of housing sick animals with healthy ones and feeding rancid meat to its shelter occupants. At a subsequent trial, the Bide-a-Wee was found not guilty of all charges. "After Bide-a-Wee Home," NYT, November 26, 1916, 4; "Clears Bide-a-Wee Home," NYT, November 25, 1916, 4.

Chapter 12: Bareback

1. Kline's version of the Bradna romance is surprisingly tamer than other published accounts. Ella Bradna (1879–1957) came from a distinguished Bohemian circus family and was an equestrienne star by the age of ten. Riding with the Cirque Nouveau in Paris in 1900, Bradna was standing on her tiptoes when her horse bolted after being hit by a large floral bouquet tossed by an appreciative fan. Reportedly, Bradna was thrown into the lap of a handsome Alsatian cavalry lieutenant named Frederick Febere. They were later married in Cologne, Germany.

Frederick relinquished a prestigious career as an army officer to join his wife in the circus. His family was outraged: Frederick gave up a large inheritance and changed his name to Bradna. In 1902, James Bailey invited them to join Barnum & Bailey in the United States for the 1903 season. Ella Bradna became an accomplished center-ring equestrienne with her "Act Beautiful," comprised of equine dancing and birds. Fred eventually became the show's equestrian director. They retired in 1945 and lived in Sarasota for the rest of their lives. Ella Bradna died there at the age of seventy-eight. "Ella Bradna, 78, Circus Rider, Dies," NYT, November 13, 1957, 32; Bradna and Spence, *Big Top*, 15–18.

Chapter 13: A Backdoor Glimpse of Supermen and Superwomen

1. Performers kept their most valuable belongings (such as cash and jewelry) in their grouch bags—small, purselike pouches that could fit easily in a pocket.

2. The death of Adgie's assistant and fiancée, Emerson D. Dietrich, received much attention in the press. Although the circumstances of the attack remained suspicious among circus people, a coroner's jury ruled that the death was an accident. Adgie maintained that her lions were jealous of her fiancée: "Lions are just like dogs or cats. They know when someone else shares the affection of their owner. Now that I think of it, it was only a few weeks ago that Emerson put his hand caressingly on my shoulder on the stage at Salt Lake City. I looked over at Teddy, one of the lions. His eyes glittered, and he snarled. And it was Teddy that knocked Emerson down and killed him." "Lions Jealous of Dietrich," NYT, June 23, 1914, 20.

3. Indeed, Adgie was such a big star with the Barnum & Bailey Circus in 1915 that she was featured in a full-color circus poster reclining among lions in skimpy, diaphanous garb in one scene and dancing the tango with one of her charges in another. "Great Groups of Trained Wild Beasts Including M'lle. Adgie's Acting and Dancing Lions," Poster Collection, CWM.

4. Animal-welfare activists in the early twentieth century wielded enough political clout to influence animal-care policies in the amusement industry. The Palace Theater in New York and the Keith vaudeville circuit nationwide enforced rules of animal kindness to avoid trouble with humane organizations. Consequently, Adgie was rebuked for using force to discipline her lions in 1914: "Adgie was told that her lions must be treated with kindness, no matter how violent they became." NYT, September 20, 1914, X5.

5. Fred Bradna remembered Adgie as the unattractive trainer of "four toothless, moth-eaten, senile lions." Despite Adgie's fame in the 1910s, there is no media record of her death in V, NYT, BB, or other publications. Bradna and Spence, *Big Top*, 204.

6. According to the *Billboard*, Betty Reiffenach Olvera died on April 17, 1942, "of burns sustained in January when a stove exploded in her trailer." "The Final Curtain, Mrs. Betty Reiffenach Olvera," BB 54.17 (April 25, 1942): 28.

Chapter 14: Elephants Are Like People

1. Gertrude Hoffman (1898–1955) was born in Montreal. She danced with the Ziegfeld Follies, worked as a screen actress with the Vitagraph Company, and

was a star in the *Broadway to Paris* revue in New York in 1917. From 1938 until her death, she worked as a clairvoyant in Washington, where her husband was an official with the Republican National Committee. "Gertrude Hoffman," VO, vol. 6, n.p. (originally in V, June 15, 1955, n.p.).

Chapter 15: Engineering the White City

1. Kline is incorrect. Elephants first successfully bred in captivity at the American circus in 1880, when the elephant Hebe, belonging to the showmen James A. Bailey and James Hutchinson, gave birth to Baby Columbia.

Chapter 17: On the Sunny Side

1. "Menage" riding (often corrupted in the American spelling as "manage" or "manege," as Kline does here) has its roots in the elite Italian and French dressage, or *haute ecole,* tradition. Riding sidesaddle, the menage performer instructs her horse to execute a series of intricate and elaborate steps and kicks in a display of what circus people call "high school" riding as a reminder of the act's privileged origins. Stuart Thayer, *The Performers* (Seattle: Dauven and Thayer, 2005), 110–11.

2. Judy Field (Graves) immigrated to the United States from England to perform with the Ringling circus as part of a Russian dance troupe. She became a showgirl with the circus, met and married Mickey Graves, and had four sons. When she was not with the show, busily taking care of three of the four sons, the fourth son (Glenn, the father of Michele Graves) stayed on with the circus under the care of various show folk, including Lillian Leitzel, who sent Judy a card saying that Glenn was fine and "getting fat." Editor's email correspondence with Michele Graves, May 23, 2003.

Chapter 18: Life under the Big Top

1. Alfredo Codona (1893–1937) was part of an illustrious family of aerialists. Born in Hermosillo, Sonora, Mexico, to Hortense Buislay, an English trapeze artist, and Edward Codona, a Mexican circus owner, Codona's education in becoming perhaps the best flyer in circus history started in infancy. His family toured across Mexico and Cuba during Alfredo's childhood. The nomadic family worked for the Wirth Bros. Circus in Australia in 1913 and then signed on with the Siegrist-Silbon troupe of flyers. In 1917, they joined the Ringling Bros. Circus. Taylor, *Center Ring,* 244; Gossard, *Reckless Era,* 151.

Chapter 21: An Annual Season's Opening

1. "Strawberry Red" Wall hailed from Washington. In 1924, he signed on with a traveling rodeo outfit organized by Pete Walsh that was, according to the historian Donna Livingstone, Calgary's first competitive traveling rodeo troupe. Livingstone, *Cowboy Spirit,* 93.

2. Ken Maynard (1896–1973) was a "cowboy film hero" in approximately three hundred movie Westerns yet died in virtual anonymity—falling from a life of

wealth and living in a mansion to a precarious alcohol- and tobacco-addicted existence in a San Fernando Valley trailer park. Maynard lived on a Texas ranch until he was twelve, at which time he ran away and joined a wagon show. His father retrieved him and enrolled him in military school, where he became an expert horseman. After graduation in 1914, he joined the Kit Carson Show and then worked on the Hagenbeck-Wallace Circus. After serving in the army in World War I, Maynard returned to the amusement business as a cowboy rider in the Ringling Bros. and Barnum & Bailey Circus. His friend Tom Mix connected him to important movie producers in Hollywood in 1923, where he eventually starred in a long string of films. Poor and forgotten, he died in 1973 at the age of seventy-seven. "Ken Maynard," VO, vol. 7, n.p.. (originally in V, March 28, 1973, 78).

3. Billy Rose (1899–1966) was born William Samuel Rosenberg in New York. He became a famous lyricist (primarily as a collaborator), Broadway producer, and theater and nightclub owner. He produced *Billy Rose's Aquacade* at the New York World's Fair in 1939, starring the Olympic swimmer Eleanor Holm (whom Rose married after divorcing his first wife, the comic actress Fanny Brice), Esther Williams, and Johnny Weissmuller of *Tarzan* fame. Rose also produced the well-received *Carmen Jones,* an all–African American adaptation of Bizet's *Carmen,* which became a motion picture in 1954 starring Dorothy Dandridge. Answers .com, accessed on July 1, 2005, http://www.answers.com/topic/billy-rose.

4. After over a year of preparation and weeks of delay, Billy Rose's "musical circus extravaganza" (in Kline's words) opened at the Hippodrome on November 16, 1935. Written by Ben Hecht and Charles MacArthur and scored by Richard Rodgers and Lorenzo Hart, *Jumbo* featured Jimmy Durante and Paul Whiteman in addition to a bevy of past and present circus celebrities, such as the bareback rider Josephine De Mott Robinson and the animal dealer and trainer Frank Buck. The production contained a real elephant named Rosie (who formerly played a sacred white elephant) and was inspired by P. T. Barnum's famous elephant, Jumbo, who was killed by a train fifty years before in 1885. The theater critic Walter Winchell praised the show's visual flair and 250 talented human and animal performers but noted (along with other reviewers) that the musical contained little in the way of a plot: "It is a thread of a tale this 'Jumbo,' certainly not a speedy one, or attention-arresting saga—but every bit of it agreeable and it serves the plan." Winchell also praised Kline's performance: "Tiny Kline, the slide for life girl, is another thriller." The show ran profitably for months and garnered offers of up to two hundred thousand dollars for the film rights. Rose brought the production to Fort Worth for the Texas Centennial exposition in July 1936. But despite Rose's concurrent production at the fair, Sally Rand's "nude ranch" (a strip show), the show lost money, and by October 7, a headline in *Variety* declared: "'Jumbo' Disintegrates into 50–Cent Circus; Texas Date Another Flop, Ran Show $30,000 Further into Red." By this time, Rose had decided to drop the production's dialogue, leaving it "little more than a one-ring circus," according to *Variety. Jumbo* was shuttered and returned to storage in New York. The production came back to life as a film in 1962 starring Jimmy Durante (again), Doris Day, and Martha Raye. Walter Winchell, "'Jumbo' Thrilling Spectacle at Hippodrome," *New York*

Daily Mirror, November 18, 1935, 79; Willard Keefe, "Billy Rose's 'Jumbo' Has N.Y. Gasping," *St. Paul Press,* November 24, 1935, 85; Richard Watts Jr., "Sight and Sound," *New York Herald Tribune,* November 24, 1935, 85–86; E. K. Titus, "A Pachyderm with a Past," *New York World-Telegram,* December 13, 1935, 105; Billy Rose, "Billy Rose Lambasts Those Envious Rivals," *New York World Telegram,* December 14, 1935, 106; Lloyd Pantages, "Cattle Barons of Dallas Bid for Talent," *New York Journal,* July 2, 1936, 134; "Jumbo Disintegrates into 50–Cent Circus," V, October 7, 1936, n.p.; Jumbo—Hippodrome Show Production, Clippings Book, MWEZ n.c. 4651, BRTC.

5. The circus historian Steve Gossard calls Charles Siegrist (1880–1953) the "greatest all-around circus athlete in history." Born as Charles Patterson in a covered wagon and abandoned by his widowed father as a child, the young Charlie eked out a living selling newspapers on the streets of Portland (or Seattle) in the 1880s, using showy acrobatics to attract customers because a severe speech impediment made him nearly unintelligible. A minstrel-show proprietor recruited Charlie in 1889, and James A. Bailey hired him nine years later to work as an apprentice with the Siegrist Silbon aerial troupe. Patterson changed his name and remained with the circus for the rest of his career. Standing five feet, five inches tall, Siegrist speedily replicated acts that took others years to cultivate. In addition to his formidable aerial skills, Siegrist worked as an acrobatic rider, a tumbler, and a slapstick prizefight performer. He had unbelievable stamina, particularly in the aftermath of a bad fall in 1931, when he broke his neck. In 1933 he was fully recovered and performing vigorously once more. Although he worked as a flyer well into his sixties, Siegrist remained frustrated because one giant plum eluded him: a triple somersault to a hand catch on the trapeze (Ernie Clarke of the Flying Clarkonians achieved this feat around 1909). Fred Bradna argues that Siegrist never received the sort of recognition that other legendary circus athletes received because he never created original acts, instead focusing on imitating the tricks of others. Siegrist died in Normal, Illinois, at the age of seventy-three. Gossard, *Reckless Era,* 10, 162–65; Bradna and Spence, *Big Top,* 177.

Chapter 22: Leitzel, Queen of the Air

1. The bandleader Merle Evans recalled that he frequently had to improvise during Leitzel's performances because she was prone to adding impromptu parts to her act. Accordingly, Evans told the circus author Robert Lewis Taylor that he "feels today that Miss Leitzel aged him in disproportion to his years." Taylor, *Center Ring,* 216.

2. Ruth Budd (1895[?]-1968) performed in an acrobatic act, the Aerial Budds, with her younger brother Giles, in fairs, circuses, and on vaudeville. After Giles was injured in 1915, Ruth became a solo act. Working briefly on the Big Show, Budd was better known for her performance in silent film (as Darwa, "the female Darwin," in *A Scream in the Night* [1919]) and as a singing aerial act on vaudeville until she retired in the 1930s. In 1921, Budd was scandalized, accused of being a "sexual deviant" during her brief engagement to the female impersonator, Karyl Norman. She settled permanently in Fort Wayne, Indiana, in 1927, after marrying

an electrician and stagehand, Ray Hanna. Along with her parents, the couple managed a small grocery store. M. Alison Kibler, *Rank Ladies: Gender and Cultural Hierarchy in American Vaudeville* (Chapel Hill: University of North Carolina Press, 1999), 143–70, 204.

3. According to Fred Bradna, the feud between Leitzel and Budd occurred in 1919. An examination of the show programs, however, does not support Bradna's recollection, as Budd and Dainty Marie were likely not employed with the combined Ringling Bros. and Barnum & Bailey Circus in 1919. Bradna and Spence, *Big Top,* 185.

4. Clyde Ingalls (1876–1940) worked as the manager of the Ringling Bros. and Barnum & Bailey sideshow for more than twenty years. He was born in Rice Lake, Michigan, and joined the circus after laboring in lumber camps. "Clyde Ingalls," NYT, March 18, 1940, 17.

5. Known as the "glorifier of the American girl," Florenz Ziegfeld (1869–1932) created his flashy, spectacular Ziegfeld's Follies in 1907 after spending four years in Europe, where the Folies Bergere served as an inspiration for his lavish American revue. Ziegfeld was the son of Dr. Florenz Ziegfeld, who organized the Chicago Musical College. A talented dancer with a keen musical ear, Ziegfeld was surrounded by the works of Beethoven, Bach, and Schubert as a child. He was also deeply interested in theater, a passion his father helped nurture by hiring him as a talent scout in Europe to find acts for the Chicago World's Fair in 1893. Although all the European acts he hired failed, Ziegfeld quickly became famous at the fair when he became the theater manager of Eugen Sandow, whom he successfully marketed as the "perfect man." In 1927, Ziegfeld temporarily abandoned the Follies for musical theater, producing wildly successful shows like *Sally, Rio Rita, Show Boat, Kid Boots, Show Girl,* and *Smiles.* He and his wife, the actress Billie Burke (who starred as Glinda the Good Witch of the North in *The Wizard of Oz* in 1939) lived extravagantly, reportedly traveling with a hundred trunks at a time. Ziegfeld died of complications from pneumonia in 1932 at the age of sixty-three. A tribute to Florenz Ziegfeld in 1932 argued that Ziegfeld should not be remembered as simply an adaptor of the spectacular, sprawling French and German "girls-and-music" shows. Instead, his claim to originality lay in his ability to transport his audiences into an imaginative realm of sheer spectacle. "If his productions were, on the whole, florid and lavish, they had also their moments of delicacy. They came nearer to transporting an adult to an unreal, charming fairyland than anything since the vivid shows of childhood. His best had a special magic about it, apparently inimitable. . . . It was a subtle but quite recognizable characteristic. Anyone who has gone regularly to the theater in New York for the last 20 years would almost certainly be able to identify a Ziegfeld show without looking at the program or knowing what theater he was in." "Florenz Ziegfeld Dies in Hollywood after Long Illness," NYT, July 23, 1932, 14; "Florenz Ziegfeld," *Washington Post,* July 26, 1932, 6.

6. The correct spelling is Mickey King. King (1905–2004) was born to a large French Canadian family in Sutton Hoo, Quebec. Named Marie Florida Gertrude Comeau at birth, her nickname "Mickey" stuck for life. At the age of thirteen, she fell five stories after a fire-escape railing broke. According to Steve Gossard,

the accident made her fidgety and nervous. At age fifteen in 1920, she ran away from home, took a series of odd jobs—from textile worker to nanny—and eventually landed at the circus. While visiting a circus, she and a friend met the animal trainer Terrell Jacobs, who introduced them to Joel L. Myers, the show's ballet director, who hired showgirls. Mickey joined the Sells-Floto Circus at Greenfield, Massachusetts, at the age of eighteen. That same season, Eddie and Mayme Ward (of the Flying Wards) invited Mickey to join their troupe. They trained her well for a range of aerial feats: single trapeze, rings, web, cloud swing, flying-return act, and wire-walking. Although Mickey left the Wards for nearly three years after her marriage to the animal trainer Alan King in 1924, she rejoined them in 1927. After Eddie Ward died in 1929, Mickey began training for a career as a solo aerialist and soon perfected turning one-armed planges (swinging rotations). For many years, King held the record for turning 276 one-armed swings at one time. Her sister, Antoinette Concello, is regarded as one of the most accomplished trapeze artists ever. Finally retiring in the town of Peru, Indiana, where the winter quarters of the American Circus Corporation were located, Mickey King died on January 4, 2004, in her ninety-ninth year of life. Steve Gossard, "A Conversation with Mickey King," BW 47.2 (March–April 2003): 27–30; Gossard, *Reckless Era*, 27–28. Mickey King's death date courtesy of Steve Gossard.

7. Irma Ward (spelled Erma in other accounts) was slated to attend a music conservatory after finishing high school in Peoria, Illinois, at the age of sixteen in 1920. However, Erma Hubble (as she was then known) joined Eddie Ward's aerial troupe in Bloomington, Illinois, renamed herself Erma Ward, and became a famous aerialist who held the record for one-armed swings (two hundred consecutively) in 1925. Gossard, *Reckless Era*, 26–27.

Chapter 24: On a Magic Carpet to a Land Fantastic

1. In 1917 Alfredo Codona married his first wife, Clara Curtain, in Havana.

2. Kline refers to Pepito Perez as a "native product" of Cuba, but according to *Variety*, he was born in Spain and came to the United States, where he was billed as "Pepito the Spanish Clown" in the 1920s. He appeared in the prologue for Charlie Chaplin's stage production, *The Circus*, at Grauman's Egyptian Theater in Hollywood in 1928 and thereafter did pantomime and appeared in movies and on television. He died in 1975 in Santa Ana, California, where he had lived for fifteen years. "Pepito Perez," VO, vol. 8, n.p. (originally in V, July 23, 1975, 71).

Chapter 25: Back to the Material World

1. Marie Meeker performed under the name Dainty Marie. Raised in Leavenworth, Kansas, Meeker first performed in vaudeville (along with Julian Eltinge), where she established her headliner act of sitting high on a swing, singing clearly and powerfully to the crowd below. She was also famous for her "ripe and undulant figure" and scant dress in "flesh-colored, one-piece tights," according to the journalist Robert Lewis Taylor. Taylor, *Center Ring*, 236–38.

2. The "rumpus" Kline refers to has been well remembered. Dainty Marie Meeker feuded publicly with Lillian Leitzel, who viewed Meeker (along with Ruth Budd, who likely appeared on the show during the same season) as a threat to her own solo performance and center-ring star status. John Ringling sided with Dainty Marie, while Charles Ringling backed Leitzel—whom he rightly recognized as the bigger star. Both stars periodically threatened to walk off. The Meeker-Leitzel feud finally resolved itself when Meeker threatened, once again, to not go on. Fred Bradna gave her an ultimatum at Coffeeville, Kansas: "Either you go on, or you're fired. I've had all of your temperament that I can take." Dainty Marie opted to leave, with "no hard feelings." Later, Meeker became a devout Christian Scientist. She still performed, but now only sang religious songs. She and Bradna reestablished friendly contact while she worked in the Midwest.

There is a discrepancy in terms of Kline's recollections and the dates of both Meeker and Ruth Budd's employment with the show. Kline remembered Dainty Marie Meeker from the 1918 season, while Fred Bradna distinctly remembered that Meeker was on the newly combined Ringling Bros. and Barnum & Bailey Circus in 1919, along with Ruth Budd (whom Kline remembered from her 1917 season with the Barnum show). According to Steve Gossard, who has graciously perused all pertinent show programs from 1917–19, it is difficult to establish an accurate timeline. Neither the Ringling Bros. nor the Barnum & Bailey programs for 1917 mention Budd or Dainty Marie by name. Budd is not mentioned in the 1918 Barnum & Bailey program, even though a photograph of a "Belle of the Flying Trapeze" bears a striking likeness to her. Dainty Marie, "the charming queen of the air," was featured in display 11, along with several other acts. In the 1918 Ringling program, Leitzel performed a solo act: "The entire arena is surrendered to M'lle. Leitzel, Queen of Aerial Gymnasts who has amazed all Europe with her wonderful feats of strength and endurance. Suspended at dizzy heights this miniature marvel of mid-air breaks every law of gravity casting her body over her own shoulder scores of times without pause." The 1919 combined-show program mentions neither Budd nor Dainty Marie. Editor's email correspondence with Steve Gossard, December 20, 2004; Taylor, *Center Ring*, 236–38; Bradna and Spence, *Big Top*, 185–88.

3. Ella Hackett's accidental death while practicing a trapeze act was well covered in the press in 1914. In a front-page story, the *New York Times* reported that she slipped and fell during a practice session between the afternoon and evening performance of the Barnum & Bailey Circus at Madison Square Garden. Working a dangerous double trapeze act in which she twirled around the bars of the larger and smaller trapeze which were attached to each other while the whole unit swung through the air, she wore no protective safety belt and fell head-first onto a stage used for the show's opening spectacle, "The Wizard Prince of Arabia." The nineteen-year-old performer was dead within minutes. "Girl Trapeze Flier Killed at Circus," NYT, April 2, 1914, 1.

4. Lew Fields (1868–1941) and his stage partner, Joe Weber, were popular vaudevillians and theater producers at the turn of the twentieth century, specializing in Dutch comedies that burlesqued contemporary dramatic hits. Fields got his start as a blackface comedian in the 1880s and soon turned to burlesquing white

Euro-American dialect. Weber and Fields helped launch the careers of actors like David Warfield, Anna Held, and Fay Templeton in their lavish revues. Fields died in Beverly Hills at the age of seventy-three. "Lew Fields Dies in Cal at 73, Joe Weber at His Bedside," VO, vol. 3, n.p. (originally in V, July 23, 1941, 62).

Chapter 26: An Act Is Born

1. Benny Leonard of Harlem became the world lightweight boxing champion in 1917. "Leonard in Ring Tonight," NYT, July 17, 1917, 8.

Chapter 27: Circus History Is Made

1. The influential elephant trainer George "Deafy" Denman (1871–1937) joined the Barnum & Bailey Circus when he was seventeen, where he worked in the menagerie. Denman succeeded his boss, Harry Mooney, to become superintendent of elephants in the newly merged circus in 1919. During his long circus career, Denman trained some of the most illustrious elephants in the business, including Modoc and Yasso. His obituary, however, paid special attention to another, more humorous, episode in his life: when Denman caught one of his elephants tiptoeing into a feed shed in the middle of the night, opening the lock with her trunk, helping herself to a snack, then relocking the door and tiptoeing back to her stall. Denman had been mystified when feed repeatedly disappeared at night, so one night he staked out a spot near the feed and stayed up all night to catch the culprit. "George Denman, 66, Elephant Trainer," NYT, October 1, 1937, 21.

2. The conflicted employment status of Fred Bradna and John Agee illustrates well the awkwardness of merging the two circuses. John Ringling promised Bradna that his job was secure as equestrian director. However, Charles Ringling hired Agee for the position. Ultimately John Ringling prevailed, and Agee promptly quit the show and moved to the West Coast. Shortly thereafter, Bradna became ill with encephalitis; Agee agreed to return and fill in for Bradna. After Bradna recovered, Agee remained as equestrian director, while Bradna was promoted to general equestrian director. Although Agee disliked this arrangement, he stayed with the circus for the remainder of his contract. Bradna and Spence, Big Top, 96–100.

3. In 1919, the New York Times noted that Hilary Long performed "what is perhaps the most dangerous feat of this year's circus. He wears a tin hat with a groove in it. He climbs to a high perch in the western end of the Garden from which a slender solid steel wire is stretched a fourth of the way across the Garden. On this wire he stands on his head and in that position, while the audience gasps, he slides to the ground." "Super Circus Draws Crowds to Garden," NYT, March 30, 1919, 25.

4. The Australian bareback rider May Wirth (1894–1978) was the daughter of poor, nomadic circus performers. (Her father, John Edwin Despoges, reportedly escaped Mauritius for Australia when his family was charged with embezzlement.) After her parents separated when May was seven years old, the circus owners Marizles "Rill" Wirth and John Wirth adopted her. Raised in the colorful milieu

of Australia's largest circus, May quickly adapted. Her biological father, who changed his name to Johnny Zinga (derived from the Italian word for Gypsy male), had trained three-year-old May to tumble, to walk the wire, to fly on the trapeze, and to perform as a contortionist. However, under the careful training of her parents and other accomplished riders like Orrin Davenport, May became a famous bareback rider. As a teenager, she became the only woman rider ever known to have accomplished the feet-to-feet forward somersault on the back of a cantering horse, as well as a "back-backward" somersault, where she stood facing the horse's tail, somersaulting and twisting so that she landed facing the horse's head. Arriving in the United States in 1911, Wirth practiced her riding at Josie DeMott Robinson's estate on Long Island, where she auditioned for the Ringling Bros. Circus in front of John Ringling. She opened as a center-ring star for the Ringlings in 1912 at the age of eighteen and settled in the United States permanently. The bareback rider Orrin Davenport taught Wirth the incredibly difficult "back across," which required the rider to execute a clean somersault from the back of one horse to the back of another cantering directly behind. Wirth also accomplished the highly dangerous feat of jumping from the ground to a cantering horse's back with large, clumsy market baskets attached to her feet. May performed as part of the Wirth Family—which also included her adoptive siblings Phil and Stella Wirth. During the winter season, the family worked the Keith vaudeville circuit, among other "big-time" syndicates, a pattern that continued for the remainder of May's career. She married the booking agent Frank White (who took her name professionally) in 1919. Wirth retired comfortably in 1934 at age forty. In 1964 she was inducted to the Circus Hall of Fame in Sarasota, widely recognized as the most accomplished woman bareback rider ever. Wirth died at the age of eighty-eight. Mark St. Leon, "An Unbelievable Lady Bareback Rider May Wirth," BW 34.3 (May–June 1990): 4–13; Davis, *Circus Age*, 95, 263 n.54; "Mrs. Marizles Wirth, Circus Equestrienne," NYT, April 1, 1948, 25.

5. Merle Evans (1892–1988) led the all-brass band for the Ringling Bros. and Barnum & Bailey Circus from 1919–69. Born in Columbus, Kansas, Evans taught himself to play the cornet at age ten. When he was fifteen, he left home to perform with itinerant medicine shows, Buffalo Bill's Wild West Show, and, in his words, "every vaudeville pit in the country." While playing his cornet with Gus Hill's minstrels, Charles Ringling recruited him to lead the newly combined Ringling Bros. and Barnum & Bailey band. Playing roughly two hundred different pieces of music in a single three-hour circus performance, Evans's band incorporated waltzes, marches, gallops, tangos, operatic numbers, and pieces by Wagner, Tchaikovsky, and Sousa, among many others. Known fondly as "Toscanini of the Big Top," Evans also directed and recorded bands around the United States and Europe, where his concert program included works by Bach, Beethoven, and Brahms. Although he first announced his impending retirement in 1955, Evans did not actually leave the circus until 1969—fifty years after he began with Ringling Bros. and Barnum & Bailey. Even then, the indomitable Evans still performed frequently. In 1987, at the age of ninety-five, Evans worked as guest conductor for band workshops. Merle Evans died in Sarasota at the age of ninety-six. Wolfgang Saxon, "Merle Evans Is Dead; Former Band Leader at Ringling Brothers," NYT, January 3, 1988, 26.

6. Kline received high praise in the *New York Times* review of the opening night of the combined show: Kline (along with the Cromwell trapeze troupe) was singled out as one of the two "stars" of the aerial acts that evening. "Miss Kline performs at the very top of the Garden. She uses a metal swinging trapeze, and brings the act to a close with a series of giant swings in which the trapeze itself revolves around the bar, while she stands rigid within it." The review made no mention of Kline's scant "Oriental" dress. "Super Circus Draws Crowds to Garden," NYT, March 30, 1919, 25.

7. According to Robert Lewis Taylor, the statuesque Mabel Clemings "towered over [Leitzel] like a colossus." Still, Leitzel bullied Clemings constantly and hit or threatened her with regularity. Thus Clemings's good salary was hard-earned. The temperamental Leitzel reportedly fired and rehired her on a daily basis; furthermore, Clemings had to rush into the ring during each performance to lift Leitzel as she "fainted." Taylor, *Center Ring*, 215, 220, 233.

8. Merle Evans often braced his band for Leitzel's temperamental outbursts. She commonly stormed the bandwagon after her performance, and Evans would yell, "Drummers take cover!" because Leitzel's ire was usually directed at the drummers, who frequently produced what Leitzel thought were unsatisfactory drum rolls. Taylor, *Center Ring*, 216.

9. Indeed, Leitzel's outbursts were tempered by periods of enormous generosity. She was a wonderful hostess and played her piano in her stateroom for her many visitors. She loved children and animals, particularly her pet bulldogs. Fred Bradna recalled Leitzel going to great lengths to care for strays: "Once while shopping between performances in Cleveland she chanced upon a mongrel puppy with a broken leg. She lifted the dog from the gutter, took him to a veterinarian, and remained there until she had assured herself that the victim would live and be cared for. So absorbed was she in this act of mercy that she almost missed the evening show. Only the fact that her act was last on the bill permitted her time to make an entry." Bradna and Spence, *Big Top*, 183.

Chapter 28: Pride versus Virtue

1. Rumors of Kline's supposed marriage to Jorge even reached the *Billboard*, which reported the union on October 25, 1919: "Dr. George Menendez [*sic*] and Tiny Kline . . . were married recently. Mrs. Menendez will retire from the show business. They will make their home in Cuba." BB, October 25, 1919, 75, Periodicals Collection, CWM.

2. May Wirth's marriage to the theatrical manager Frank White was reported in the *New York Times*. The wedding was a gala affair with a big reception of circus and theater performers, managers, and owners at the Astor Hotel and a wedding cake with a white frosting model of May's favorite horse. "May Wirth, Circus Rider, Weds," NYT, November 28, 1919, 3.

Chapter 29: Misery—Like Death—Knows No Class Distinction

1. After Leitzel and Ingalls divorced, Ingalls married Mrs. Henry P. Baines, a widow of a Canadian businessman who had been killed in World War I. At the

time of her marriage to Ingalls in 1925, Baines was in charge of showing the gorilla, John Daniel II. Incidentally, Ingalls's obituary lists Nell Holesteen as the name of his first wife, not Irene (as Kline lists it in the text). "Clyde Ingalls," NYT, March 18, 1940, 17.

Chapter 30: Fate Follows Her Course

1. John Ringling's purchase of the American Circus Corporation holdings (comprised of five circuses: Sells-Floto, Hagenbeck-Wallace, John Robinson, Sparks, and Al G. Barnes) occurred in September 1929—not 1928. Alas, the timing of this major acquisition could not have been worse. Six weeks later, Black Tuesday marked the beginning of the Great Depression. Circus attendance fell sharply, and in 1931, the Big Show was forced to close on September 14, the earliest date in its history. Jerry Apps, *Ringlingville USA: The Stupendous Story of Seven Siblings and Their Stunning Circus Success* (Madison: Wisconsin Historical Society, 2004), 211.

2. Leitzel and Codona were married in 1928. Called the "Douglas Fairbanks and Mary Pickford of the circus," Leitzel and Codona represented the most glamorous circus coupling of their day. Gossard, *Reckless Era,* 151–52.

3. Bertram Mills (1873–1938) resuscitated the flagging English circus by hiring fresh international talent and by instituting special by-invitation-only performances around Christmas in 1920 called "opening lunches" at the Olympia for select members of the press and high society. The press immediately hailed the show as the "Great Circus Revival." Although Mills raised ticket prices, audiences flocked to his show, and a hit circus was born. A far smaller show than the sprawling American railroad circuses, Mills's circus was still large by British standards in the mid-twentieth century, traveling with approximately 250 people and one hundred animals. Antony Hippisley Coxe, *A Seat at the Circus* (London: Evans Brothers Ltd., 1951) 35, 120; PeoplePlay U.K., accessed July 19, 2006, http://www.peopleplayuk.org.uk/guided_tours/circus_tour/the_modern_circus/default.php.

4. The "bird's nest" position (also known as the "crab") on the trapeze involves the flyer swinging with his or her head up, chest thrust outward in a backbend, and holding the bar simultaneously with both hands and feet. Gossard, *Reckless Era,* 122.

5. Larry Boyd (1892–1934), an ebullient promoter and former vaudevillian, also worked for George Hamid as a field-man booker. Plagued with obesity, the three-hundred-pound showman lost one hundred pounds and promptly suffered a heart attack. He never fully recovered and died months later at the age of forty-two. "Larry Boyd," VO, vol. 2, n.p. (originally in V, January 2, 1934, 109).

6. The press agent Terry Turner (1892–1971) created Kline's traffic-stopping stunt of gliding by her teeth across Times Square. Throughout his career, Turner had a gift for stunning ballyhoo. In his obituary, he was credited with creating the flagpole-sitting craze. As the exploitation director for RKO Radio Pictures during the early 1930s, Turner also promoted the career of Frank "Bring 'em Back Alive" Buck by creating a miniature mechanical jungle menagerie atop the marquee of

the Mayfair Theater, where, in a prelude to *King Kong*, "lions roared and elephants trumpeted, while automated gorillas beat their breasts." While working for the Loew circuit, Turner managed and marketed the conjoined twins, Daisy and Violet Hilton. After planting a rumor that a medical separation was imminent because one of the twins was in love, the public outcry against Turner was so fierce that he reportedly went into hiding. Turner died at the age of seventy-nine. VO, vol. 7, n.p. (originally in V, December 8, 1971, 55).

7. Charles Washburn (1890–1972) was an author-playwright and a renowned press agent in the twentieth century. His client base included Billy Rose, John Barrymore, Sonja Henie, and Mike Todd. Originally a police reporter at the *Chicago Tribune*, he entered show business in the Chicago nickelodeons. His Broadway productions included *All Editions* and *Come into My Parlor*. As a press agent, he coined the term "platinum blonde" to describe Jean Harlow's glowing hair color. Washburn died at the age of eighty-two. VO, vol. 7, n.p. (originally in V, January 12, 1972, 78).

8. Codona married the Australian aerialist Vera Bruce on September 18, 1932.

9. Humorously enough, the *New York Times* reported that Kline performed the spectacular slide across Times Square as a way to find work (even though she was simply performing ballyhoo for her employer). Thousands of people gathered to watch Kline's 1,300-foot slide. She was reportedly arrested on a charge of disorderly conduct "for endangering the lives of persons on the street," but Magistrate Katz in West Side Court dismissed the charges. On episode number 316, airing on October 9, 2002, "Ripley's Believe It or Not! TV" featured the iron-jaw performer Tavana Luvas, who slid by her teeth across downtown Las Vegas in homage to the seventieth anniversary of Kline's slide across Times Square. "Seeks Job by Aerial Feat," NYT, October 22, 1932, 17; "Episode #316: Ripley's Believe It or Not! Episode Guide," accessed May 11, 2004, http://www.sonypictures.com/tv/shows/ripleys/database/ep_316a.html.

10. Lalo Codona retired permanently from the circus in November 1937 after a debilitating injury that dislocated his shoulder while performing in Paris. "Lalo Codona Is Hurt in Paris Circus Act," NYT, November 14, 1937, 26.

11. The couple's divorce on July 1, 1937, precipitated the horrifying chain of events on July 30, 1937. According to Vera Bruce's mother, Anna, Alfredo asked the divorce lawyer to step out of the room and then quietly told his ex-wife, "Vera, this is all you've left for me to do." Codona pulled a pistol out of his pocket and fired it five times before turning the gun to his head. He died instantly. Despite surgery and repeated blood transfusions, Vera died the next morning at a Long Beach hospital on July 31. The murder-suicide made headlines across the nation. See, for example, "Codona Kills Self, Shooting Ex-Wife," NYT, July 31, 1937, 4; "Bullets of Codona Fatal to His Ex-Wife," NYT, August 1, 1937, 4.

Chapter 31: Sarasota—Last Stop

1. Fred Bradna referred to the Yacopi Troupe as "unquestionably the finest tumblers of modern times." Using a teeterboard, a troupe member would catapult into the air, somersault several times, and land on a chair balanced atop a

ten-foot pole. The Yacopis also tailored this act so that the acrobat landed at the top of a pyramid of three men standing on each other's shoulders. Bradna and Spence, *Big Top*, 162, 165.

2. After joining the American Federation of Actors (a union affiliated with the American Federation of Labor) in 1937 and signing a contract with the president of the Big Show, John Ringling North, workingmen collectively protested when North imposed a 25 percent pay cut as a way to avoid bankruptcy. Under the leadership of Ralph Whitehead, a former actor, the AFA refused to accept this concession and consequently walked off the job at the union-friendly town of Scranton on June 22, 1938. Although performers voted with an 85 percent majority to break ranks with the striking roustabouts, their actual numbers were puny compared to the gargantuan masses of roustabout labor (some nine hundred strong). The strike made international headlines. On June 24, two photographers were killed in an airplane crash near the Scranton showgrounds after they tried to take aerial photographs of the strike scene. Mayor Fred J. Huester ordered the circus to leave town, declaring that the "wild animal aroma" wafting from the stalled circus was a "menace" to Scranton's health. To accelerate the show's departure, the mayor levied multiple fines on the circus for the costs of police protection and "sterilization" services, among other things. A few days later, the circus shuttered its wagons, boarded its 1,600 employees on the rails, and rumbled toward show's winter quarters at Sarasota—an unprecedented event in the history of the Ringling Bros. and Barnum & Bailey Circus. Ralph Whitehead was thoroughly vilified in the national media for destroying the circus, while the Circus Fans of America began a national "Save the Circus" campaign to bring back the Big Show. "Circus Stays Dark: Workers Bar Cut," NYT, June 24, 1938; "Two Fliers Killed at Circus Strike," NYT, June 25, 1938; "'Big Top' May Yet Carry On as Heads Confer, Encouraged by Nation's Protest at Its Closing," *Washington Post*, June 29, 1938; "Victory!" *New York Herald Tribune*, June 28, 1938; Sidney M. Shalett, "But the Show Didn't Go On," NYT, July 3, 1938; "Save the Circus!—It's a National Movement," *Philadelphia Enquirer*, n.d., 1938, 4, Roland Butler Papers, CWM.

3. John Ringling North (1903–85) was the firstborn son of Ida Ringling (the sister of John Ringling) and her husband, Henry Whitestone North. John Ringling, the last surviving Ringling brother, had no children and therefore no heir to his circus business. Ringling's nephew, Johnny North, adored his uncle and was saturated in the world of the circus as a child. North worked as a candy butcher at age twelve and then as a billposter. However, as "Mr. John" aged, his relationship with his handsome, carefree nephew (whose unfinished education at Yale Ringling had paid for) faltered. Ringling questioned Johnny's seriousness and commitment to the circus. Consequently, in 1935, Ringling wrote a codicil to his will that prohibited Johnny and his brother Henry from handling Ringling's estate (moreover, Ringling substantially cut his nephews out of his will). After Ringling's death in 1936, there was protracted legal wrangling (the estate remained in probate for several years), and North eventually was appointed executor. Hammarstrom, *Big Top Boss*, 12, 22; Weeks, *Ringling*, 250–58; Davis, *Circus Age*, 254 n.97.

4. See "Circus Plans Coup to Salvage Show," NYT, July 3, 1938; "Ringling Sends

Third of Circus to Barnes Show," *Tampa Morning Tribune*, July 5, 1938; "21-Car Ringling Train Goes to Join Barnes," NYT, July 5, 1938, Roland Butler Papers, CWM.

5. The circus historian David Lewis Hammarstrom contends that John Ringling North ultimately saved the Ringling Bros. and Barnum & Bailey Circus. This was no small task, given the show's volatile finances, family squabbling, labor unrest, and the devastating impact of the big-top fire at Hartford, Connecticut, on July 6, 1944, in which 168 people died. Hammarstrom argues that North saved the circus in part with exciting innovations: working with industrial designers like Norman Bel Geddes in 1939–40 to modernize the show's midway and lithography, and commissioning George Balanchine to choreograph a ballet for elephants in November 1941 and Igor Stravinsky to write the "Circus Polka" for Balanchine's "Ballet of the Elephants" in 1942. Moreover, in the midst of a violent confrontation with the Teamsters' Union (which was trying to organize the show's laborers), North made the difficult decision to abandon the canvas tent in July 1956 as a way to cut costs and save the circus. Lastly, to the chagrin of his fervently anti-Communist colleagues, North imported scores of highly talented performers from Eastern Europe beginning in 1965 as part of his "bold" Slavic period. The weary North sold the circus in 1968 to the brothers Irvin and Israel Feld, who had made a fortune in the drugstore business and record industry. Hammarstrom, *Big Top Boss*, 76–77, 94, 193; Davis, *Circus Age*, 294 n.8.

6. Born in Gainesville, Texas, Frank Howard "Bring 'em Back Alive" Buck (1884–1950) was an avid animal collector as a child. He dropped out of school after the seventh grade and left home, working as a cowpuncher, bellboy, and a "music man" for a Chicago music publisher selling tunes to vaudeville singers—all while learning how to read and write. After winning $4,500 in a poker game in 1911, his career as an animal dealer began: he traveled to Brazil, bought exotic birds, and then went to New York, where he sold them for a profit. Thereafter, he expanded his scope worldwide, particularly during World War I: the dominant force in the global wild-animal trade, the Hagenbeck family, was shut out of key African markets with Germany's loss of its African colonies. The British naval blockade further disrupted Hagenbeck's animal business by preventing access to important European ports. Anti-German sentiment in the United States further damaged Hagenbeck's business. With consequently little significant competition, Frank Buck became the world's leading animal dealer. In an age before tranquilizing darts, Buck captured his animals with creative traps and snares (with critical help from scores of native people who worked for him). He wrote about his experiences in eight wildly popular books, starting with *Bring 'em Back Alive* in 1930. He also enjoyed a highly successful career in radio, film, and as the impresario of Frank Buck's Jungle Camp at the Chicago World's Fair in 1934 and then at Amityville, Long Island. He was so famous in 1938 that John Ringling North hired him as a feature attraction to introduce Gargantua the gorilla. Despite a career of extreme danger, Buck did not perish as the result of an animal attack: he died of lung cancer on March 25, 1950. Steven Lehrer, introduction to *Bring 'em Back Alive: The Best of Frank Buck,* ed. Steven Lehrer (Lubbock: Texas Tech University Press, 2000), vii–xviii.

7. The full name of Gargantua's keeper was Richard Kroner.

8. Martin Johnson (1884–1937) and Osa Leighty Johnson (1894–1953) were renowned explorers, wildlife photographers, filmmakers, and authors. Born in Rockfort, Illinois, Martin left home at age fourteen on a cattle boat to Europe. Later, he traveled with Jack London to the South Seas, working as a cook on London's ship, the *Snark*. He began his career as a photographer and filmmaker on the voyage, and upon returning to Kansas (where his family had moved), Johnson opened a theater to exhibit his films. As a successful theater owner, he started other theaters in Kansas. In Chanute, he met and married Osa Leighty. With the profits from Martin's theater business, he and Osa traveled to Africa, where they made the highly lucrative film *Hunting Big Game in Africa*. As prolific authors and filmmakers, the Johnsons also helped develop exhibits for the American Museum of Natural History in New York. Imbued with the racist ideologies of the "white man's burden" and Social Darwinism, the Johnsons represented people of color around the world as "savages" who were incapable of self-government. Martin Johnson was killed in a plane crash in Burbank, California, in 1937. Osa survived the accident. "Martin Johnson," VO, vol. 2, n.p. (originally in V, January 20, 1937, 62).

9. John Ringling North purchased Gargantua in 1937 from a Brooklyn-based animal fancier named Gertrude Lintz, who opted to sell her pet gorilla after he jumped into bed with her. Despite Gargantua's reticence to perform at the circus, he was still famous primarily because of the press agent Roland Butler's clever publicity campaigns. In 1938–39 (similar to other celebrity primate pairings of the past, such as the chimpanzees Chiko and Johanna in 1893), Butler crafted a "marriage" between Gargantua and a female gorilla named M'Toto. As part of his efforts to modernize the midway with a streamlined aesthetic, the industrial designer Norman Bel Geddes had plans (which never materialized) to construct a cage in which "Mr. and Mrs. Gargantua the Great" could mate under the public eye. The bandleader Merle Evans remembered that audiences were forever confusing Gargantua's name: "Once in Jackson, Tennessee, out from Memphis, we were unloading the circus. . . . There were these two guys came up and said, 'We sure would like to see that 800-pound guarantee you've got.' A lot of people could never pronounce Gargantua." Gargantua made the news in 1938 when he seized John Ringling North and pulled his arm through the bars of his cage. His keeper, Richard Kroner, beat Gargantua off with a club. The gorilla celebrity died at the end of the 1949 season with the Big Show. Hammarstrom, *Big Top Boss*, 41, 67–68, 76–77; Henry Mitchell, "For Circus Maestro, the Band Plays On," *Washington Post*, July 12, 1985, D1, D9; "Gorilla Bites Circus Head," NYT, February 16, 1938, 23.

10. Al G. Barnes (1862–1931) was raised on a farm in Lobo, Ontario, where he developed keen relationships with his animals and was reportedly able to break horses by talking to them. In 1895, he sold the farm and started a wagon show with the proceeds. For years he exhibited wild animals at fairs and carnivals before he created a full-scale circus. Hoh and Rough, *Step Right Up!* 218–19; William L. Slout, *Olympians of the Sawdust Circle: A Biographical Dictionary of the Nineteenth-Century American Circus* (San Bernardino, Calif.: Borgo, 1998), 18.

11. Even as a child, Mabel Stark (1888–1968) knew that she would eventually join a traveling show after she saw a circus in Princeton, Kentucky. Thereafter, she spent her spare time at the zoo watching the animals. As a teenager, Stark felt alienated by the world of traditional courtship, knowing that a traditional life as wife and mother would not be hers. Working as a nurse as a young adult, Stark "ran away" to California, met the showman Al Sands, and joined the Al G. Barnes Circus in 1913. She became one of the best big-cat trainers in the business, even though she faced occasional obstacles on the basis of her gender—including occasional dress requirements that compromised her safety in favor of sexual titillation. Mabel Stark as told to Gertrude Orr, *Hold That Tiger* (Caldwell, Idaho: Caxton Printers, 1938), 28–30, 50–55; Davis, *Circus Age*, 83, 102–3.

12. Kline's injury and hospitalization were also covered in the *Billboard*. See "Tiny Kline Injured," BB, March 4, 1933, 52; "Tiny Kline," BB, March 11, 1933, 43.

13. George Hamid Sr. (1896–1971) was a manager at Steel Pier when Kline performed there. One of the most colorful figures in the outdoor amusement industry, Hamid's biography represents a classic bootstraps narrative. Born in Lebanon to an impoverished family, Hamid's education ended with only a couple years of school. Instead he worked as a child, performing acrobatic stunts for pennies. His mother died when Hamid was three and a half; thereafter, his grandmother was a central part of his upbringing. With her blessing, Hamid immigrated to the United States in 1906 at age ten to work for his uncle, Ameen, who managed a troupe of acrobats. Hamid traveled to Marseilles in a rat-infested steerage compartment. Upon arrival, he saw Buffalo Bill's Wild West Show (which was touring in Europe). He looked for his uncle on the showgrounds, did not find him, but was hired by the show. Although Hamid's act was popular, he was slowly starving owing to a usurious manager. Alarmed at his emaciated condition, the sharpshooter Annie Oakley demanded that Hamid and other children in the acrobatic troupe be fed sufficiently, and conditions improved. Upon arriving in the United States in 1907, Hamid went to work for his uncle Ameen, who quickly proved to be a wretched boss, withholding pay and beating young Hamid. Ameen abandoned Hamid when Cody's show went bust in 1913. Although Hamid returned to Ameen sporadically (most famously working as an acrobat with the actress Eva Tanguay on her vaudeville show), eventually Hamid broke off with his uncle for good. He wandered to Atlantic City, slept under the boardwalk, and practiced his acrobatics on the beach until one day he was hired by a booking agent. Working as an acrobat and a blackface minstrel, among other acts, Hamid became friends with Sam Gumpertz and other influential amusement figures. In 1916 Hamid worked as an acrobat for Howe's Great London Hippodrome Circus. The show's owner, Jerry "the Terrible Turk" Mugivan, was a ghastly boss who beat his employees, cheated them, gambled, and occasionally "red lighted" seemingly disagreeable workers (throwing them off the moving circus train). Hamid left the show, telling Mugivan that he would own his own show within a year. And he did: Hamid's Oriental Circus, Wild West and Far East Shows Combined, opened in 1917 and struggled from the start. The show did not last the season. But in 1918 he was offered a job to become booking manager for Alexander "Uncle Alex" Pantage's vaudeville circuit. Hamid opted instead to join Frank Wirth to open Wirth and

Hamid Fair Booking Company. In 1925, Hamid opened a solo agency, the World Amusement Fair Booking Association, and became a powerful presence in the outdoor amusement business in the eastern United States. Hamid again tried his hand at running a circus with his friend Bob Morton with the successful Hamid-Morton Circus. In 1925, Hamid became a manager at the Steel Pier, which he eventually purchased in 1945. From the 1920s onward, Hamid brought sensational features to the Pier, including Doc Carver and the Diving Horse, Alvin "Shipwreck" Kelly, the record-breaking pole sitter, and Kline, who was called the "Zep Girl" as she hung by her teeth from a blimp. Hamid's rags-to-riches success prompted his induction into the Horatio Alger Association of Distinguished Americans in 1948. Hamid died at the age of seventy-five. His son, George Hamid Jr., a Princeton University graduate, was also a successful showman. See George A. Hamid with George A. Hamid Jr., *Circus* (New York: Sterling, 1950); "George A. Hamid Sr. Dies: Steel Pier Owner was 75," *Philadelphia Bulletin,* June 14, 1971, MS 5, VI: B (Personnel), William F. Cody Collection, Harold McCracken Research Library, Buffalo Bill Historical Center, Cody, Wyoming.

Chapter 32: An Elucidating Interlude

1. Kline appeared several times at the Los Angeles Memorial Coliseum over the years, including performances at a rodeo and a halftime show during an annual Los Angeles Rams–Washington Redskins charity football game. The enormous arena, with its distinctive peristyle arches, was completed in 1923 and was meant to serve as a memorial to fallen soldiers in World War I. Hosting college football games, the Olympics in 1932 and 1984, Super Bowl I in 1967, and home to the Los Angeles Raiders from 1982–94, the Coliseum also hosted nonsporting events such as addresses by President Eisenhower and a sermon by Rev. Billy Graham, which shattered all prior attendance records with an audience of 134,354. The facility was designated a state and federal historical landmark in 1984. Chris Epting, *Images of America: Los Angeles Memorial Coliseum* (Chicago: Arcadia, 2002), 7–8, 13, 15–18, 58–63, 97; "Throng of 50,000 See Rodeo, Thrill Circus at Coliseum," *Los Angeles Times,* June 23, 1941, A9; "Circus Act Featured at Rams Game," *Los Angeles Times,* August 10, 1958, C4.

2. A writer for the *New York Times* remarked in 1945 that the life story of Leroy Prinz (1895–1983) "reads more like the script of an Errol Flynn adventure, the chief difference being that a script writer wouldn't dare cram as much action into a single Flynn picture as Mr. Prinz claims to have experienced." Born in St. Joseph, Missouri, Prinz was so rambunctious as a child that his father sent him to St. Mary's School in Kansas City for some "Jesuitical discipline." Seven years later, Prinz "hopped a freight," where he met an African American teenager who became his partner in a song-and-dance team, Prinz and Buck, in 1911. A couple of months later, Prinz left the partnership and became a cabin boy, shipping off to France, where he worked for the next two years as an itinerant dance teacher. He joined the Foreign Legion as a bugler, then became a mechanic and pilot in the French air force at the onset of World War I. In 1917, he switched to the American military and joined the Ninety-fourth Aerial Squadron, First Pursuit

Group. He claimed to have survived fourteen crashes, and while convalescing, he organized shows for the troops. After World War I, Prinz returned to the amusement industry and worked for Al Capone, who hired him to book shows at Chicago nightclubs. Vengeful rival mobsters tried to kill Prinz for stealing their acts, so Prinz retreated to Mexico and then Nicaragua, where he worked as a pilot for the Nicaraguan rebel leader, General Sandino. In Prinz's words, "[I] ferried ammunition by plane and occasionally dropped some small bombs." After the Marines landed in Nicaragua, Prinz hastily returned to New York and show business. In 1931, Prinz moved to Hollywood at the request of Cecil B. DeMille, where he became a leading screen choreographer. In 1945 he was dance director at Warner Brothers. Occasionally he returned to aerial stunt work, piloting (for example) the aerial sequences for the film *God Is My Co-Pilot*. Thomas M. Pryor, "The Peripatetic Mr. Prinz," NYT, June 17, 1945, X3.

Chapter 33: The Circus, to Date

1. Albert Powell was a contortionist and a trapeze artist. Fred Bradna describes his profound flexibility as he lay on the trapeze bar, "looking for all the world like a set of long underwear swinging on a clothesline in a high wind." Able to double over backwards touching his toes to his head, he would release his hands from the trapeze bar and swing his body in circles around the bar. Bradna and Spence, *Big Top,* 314.

2. Born in Vincennes, Indiana, Red Skelton (1913[?]-1997) frequently claimed that his father once was a circus clown (even though there is no historical evidence to support this story). Skelton did, however, leave school before the age of fifteen to perform in multiple traveling shows, including a minstrel show, a river showboat, and a circus, where he cultivated his comic skills. Thereafter he worked as a radio emcee, a comedian, hosted his own radio program on NBC, performed at President Roosevelt's birthday celebration in 1940, and then became a film star. Skelton entered the television business in 1951 when he began his twenty-year tenure as the star of the "Red Skelton Show" on NBC. Skelton died of pneumonia at the age of eighty-four. Wesley Hyatt, *A Critical History of Television's Red Skelton Show, 1951–1971* (Jefferson, N.C.: McFarland and Co., 2004), 6–10, 16–17, 156.

3. Kline is referring to the circus strikes of 1938, which she discusses vividly in chapter 31.

4. Ernie Clarke was born in England and was a sixth-generation circus performer. Ernie was the eldest of six children. He and his brothers Charles and Percy became successful circus performers. Called the Clarkonians, the troupe joined Barnum & Bailey in 1903 at Madison Square Garden. Ernie Clarke debuted a unique act in which he performed a double somersault with a pirouette. Three years later, the Clarkonians executed a tricky back somersault that twisted into a forward somersault. Ernie Clarke's greatest claim to fame lay in being the first to complete successfully a triple somersault to a hand catch on the trapeze around 1909. The Clarkonians enjoyed a long and successful thirty-plus-year circus career. Gossard, *Reckless Era,* 130, 134; Bradna and Spence, *Big Top,* 167.

5. Tommy (1927–2005) and George (1923–) Hanneford ran their respective circuses until 2005, when Tommy died and George was evicted from a long-standing show site in Fort Lauderdale. As young men performing together with rest of their family, George played the straight man to Tommy's comic riding routines. Known as "the funniest man on horseback," Tommy Hanneford and his wife, Struppi Hanneford, a German émigré and former trapeze artist who worked a tiger act, formed the Royal Hanneford Circus in 1965. In later years, the show performed frequently as part of local Shrine circuses. Tommy was also active as a technical adviser for television programs and for the film *Barnum*. Since Tommy's death on December 5, 2005, Struppi has assumed full management of the circus. George Hanneford—aged eighty-three—and his wife, Victoria George Hanneford, operated the Hanneford Family Circus. Victoria was an outsider to the circus when she married George in 1952, but she quickly adapted to show life and became an accomplished trapeze artist. She later settled into raising baby elephants in addition to looking after two young children, Cathy and George III, and running the circus with her husband. George and Victoria's son, George III, has appeared in several recent films. For sixteen years, the Hanneford Family Circus performed at the Fort Lauderdale Swap Shop until the Swap Shop's owner, Preston Henn, forced the Hannefords off the property over an ugly dispute concerning workers' compensation and back pay. The Hannefords moved their stock to their family quarters in Myakka City, Florida. Hildegard Scheibner, "Equestrian Co-Owned Royal Hanneford Circus," *Sarasota Herald-Tribune,* December 9, 2005, BS10; Evan Benn, "Circus, Customers Left Fuming in Florida," *Miami Herald,* August 13, 2005; Sy Syna, "A Family That Really Manages a One-Ring Circus," NYT, August 10, 1980, 19; Prue, "300 Years of Circus Tradition"; Sahib Shriners; Hanneford Circus, accessed December 29, 2004, http://sahibshrine.org/circus/hanneford .htm; http://hanneford.8m.com/family/geovicky/gandv.htm.

6. Pat Valdo (1881–1970) worked at a variety of jobs during his long career with the circus—from a lowly candy butcher to a top-ranking managerial position as supervisor of performance and personnel for Ringling Bros. and Barnum & Bailey. Christened Patrick Francis Fitzgerald at his birth in Binghamton, New York, in 1881, Valdo longed to be in show business as a child, even though his father, William J. Fitzgerald, dearly wanted him to enter the family trade of cigar making. Smitten by traveling shows that passed through town, young Pat learned how to juggle and entertained his classmates with aerial displays of inkwells, chalk, erasers, and apples in front of the blackboard. Pat left school in the tenth grade and joined the Walter L. Main Circus as a candy butcher. Months later he got a job with the John Robinson Circus for ten dollars a week as an apprentice clown. On the advice of a veteran performer, he changed his name to Pat Valdo, and in 1904 he joined the Ringling show, where he remained for the rest of his career. With his white face, broad red lips, and black eyebrows, Valdo crafted several distinctive and popular acts, including the midget fire brigade that raced into the arena and assaulted the burning building and a trick wig that would spin atop his head when pulled by a string in his pocket. After his marriage to the equestrienne Laura Meers in 1914, he joined his wife and her brother in a wire-walking act. He also assisted the equestrian director Fred Bradna. In 1929 John

Ringling made Valdo director of personnel. In 1969 Valdo became the show's first director emeritus. Always remembering the significance of the clowns in promoting the cohesion and fluidity of the overall performance, Valdo was quick to "send in the clowns" if there was trouble during the show: "The clowns are the pins that hold the performance together. They can always stall until things are straightened out." Pat Valdo died in Sarasota in 1970 at the age of eighty-nine. "Pat Valdo, Retired Supervisor of Circus Personnel, Is Dead," NYT, November 12, 1970, 46.

7. Barbette (1899/1904[?]–1972/73[?]) was part of a long line of female impersonators at the circus—following in the footsteps of the bareback rider Sam Omar Kingsley (a.k.a. Ella Zoyara) and the acrobat Lulu Farini in the nineteenth century; and the bareback rider Albert Hodgini, the wire-walker Berta "Slats" Beeson, and the comic Fred Biggs in the twentieth century. Born Vander Clyde Broodway, Barbette grew up in Round Rock, Texas. After he graduated from high school at age fourteen, he answered an advertisement in the *Billboard* and joined the Alfaretta Sisters' "Famous Aerial Queens" as a female impersonator-cum–wire act. Eventually changing his name to Barbette, he worked in vaudeville and circuses before traveling to Europe, where he became a popular trapeze artist and wire-walker. He also became close friends with the French poet and dramatist Jean Cocteau. Injuries sustained in 1938 ended his performing career, but Barbette worked to great acclaim backstage as an aerial director. In 1943, for example, he worked with the director John Murray Anderson on the Ringling Bros. and Barnum & Bailey Circus to stage the opening spectacle, "Hold Your Horses." In 1949 he staged the *Monte Carlo Ballet,* synchronizing forty female aerialists aloft. Barbette died in Round Rock on April 5, 1972 (or 1973). He has been memorialized by a French bistro in Minneapolis, "Café Barbette," which opened in 2002, and by an award-winning play, *Barbette,* which toured in 2002. Fred D. Pfening Jr., "Spec-ology of the Circus, Part Two," BW 48.1 (January–February 2004): 3–21; Elaine Liner, "Swingers: Barbette Soars to Greatness with the Tragic Tale of a Trapeze Artist," *Dallas Observer,* accessed January 5, 2005, http://www.dallasobserver.com/issues/2002–06–13/culture/stage.html; Matt and Andrej Koymasky Home, accessed January 5, 2005, http://andrejkoymasky.com/liv/fam/biob1/barb7.html; Footlight Notes, accessed January 5, 2005, http://footlightnotes.tripod.com/Barbette.html; The Handbook of Texas Online, accessed January 5, 2005, http://www.tsha.utexas.edu/handbook/online/articles/CC/fc154.html.

8. John Murray Anderson (1887–1954) was a producer and director who worked in New York theatrical productions and at the circus. Born in St. Johns, Newfoundland, Anderson came to the United States as an antiques dealer. He produced his first Broadway show in 1919, *Greenwich Village Follies,* which went through six different editions. He produced, directed, wrote, and/or created thirty-four musicals, twenty-nine of which were shown on Broadway, including *Fanfare, Life Begins at 8:40,* the *Ziegfeld Follies, Jumbo,* and *Music Box Revue.* Five of his shows were presented in London. He produced the first all-color film, *The King of Jazz,* starring Paul Whiteman, in 1930. He also was involved in producing seven different circuses for Ringling Bros. and Barnum & Bailey. Many circus people, Kline included, credited Anderson with making the circus more theatrical with

standardized costuming and synchronized numbers. Furthermore, Anderson's reach extended into productions for world's fairs in New York and San Francisco. Anderson died in New York of a heart attack at the age of sixty-seven. VO, vol. 4, n.p. (originally in V, February 3, 1954, 75).

9. Kline relates the following in a footnote: "I remember that during the *Jumbo* production, Billy Rose, dean of 'piquant' nightclub show producers, was very particular about keeping *Jumbo*—a musical circus extravaganza—absolutely free of suggestion whether in line or action. He boasted proudly that *Jumbo* was the cleanest show on Broadway; a show that made history for color, variety, and countless points of merit. Now the Big Show was trying to compete with Minsky's."

10. See my discussion of Kline's final act as Peter Pan's right-hand pixie, Tinker Bell, from 1961–64, in the introduction.

Epilogue

1. According to Kline's probate records, she constructed a "small unit," complete with plumbing fixtures, onto her garage during World War II, where she reportedly lived—in violation of local ordinances that zoned the area for single-family residences only: "That said decedent was an unusually small person, being known as 'Tinker Bell,' and did perform at Disneyland in Anaheim, California. That by reason of her size, the rooms attached to the garage were small, as [were] all of the plumbing fixtures in said small unit." "First and Final Account, Report, and Petition for Distribution, for Statutory Attorney's Fees, and Extraordinary Attorney's Fees, and Approval of Sale of Properties," p. 6, Tiny Kline Probate Records, Los Angeles County Court Records.

INDEX

JANET M. DAVIS is an associate professor of American studies and history at the University of Texas at Austin, where she is also chair of the Department of American Studies. She is the author of *The Circus Age: Culture and Society under the American Big Top*.

The University of Illinois Press
is a founding member of the
Association of American University Presses.

Composed in 9/13 ITC Stone Serif Medium
with Wide Latin and ITC Stone Sans display
by Jim Proefrock
at the University of Illinois Press
Designed by Kelly Gray
Manufactured by Sheridan Books, Inc.

University of Illinois Press
1325 South Oak Street
Champaign, IL 61820-6903
www.press.uillinois.edu